The Cudgel and the Caress

SUNY series in Contemporary Continental Philosophy

Dennis J. Schmidt, editor

The Cudgel and the Caress

Reflections on Cruelty and Tenderness

David Farrell Krell

Published by State University of New York Press, Albany

For information, contact State University of New York Press, Albany, NY
www.sunypress.edu

Library of Congress Cataloging-in-Publication Data

Names: Krell, David Farrell, author.
Title: The cudgel and the caress : reflections on cruelty and tenderness / David Farrell Krell.
Description: Albany : State University of New York Press, [2019] | Series: SUNY series in contemporary continental philosophy | Includes index.
Identifiers: LCCN 2018014242| ISBN 9781438472973 (hardcover) | ISBN 9781438472980 (perf.)
Subjects: LCSH: Cruelty—Philosophy. | Tenderness (Psychology)—Philosophy.
Classification: LCC BJ1535.C7 K74 2019 | DDC 179—dc23 LC record available at https://lccn.loc.gov/2018014242

10 9 8 7 6 5 4 3 2 1

This book—but only in its tender aspect—is for my brother

Jonathan F. Krell

Contents

Preface • ix

Key to the Principal Sources Cited • xiii

Introduction • xix

Part One Tenderness (*Zärtlichkeit*)

1. Tenderness and Tragedy • 3
2. Homer's *Iliad*, Hölderlin's *Briseiad* • 29
3. Tender Antigone—Forever Younger • 51
4. Tender Schlegel, Irascible Hegel • 73
5. Pulling Strings Wins No Wisdom • 101
6. A Woman Without Qualities? • 135

Part Two Cruelty (*Grausamkeit*)

7. Caress of Gestation, Cudgel of Birth • 177
8. The Nervous System of a Specter • 205
9. Freedom, Imputability, Cruelty • 243
10. Cruelty, Power, Art, Tenderness • 263

Index • 299

Preface

The Cudgel and the Caress consists of two parts, the first on the theme of tenderness (the German word *Zärtlichkeit*), the second on the theme of cruelty (*Grausamkeit*). After its ten chapters were finished, at least in first draft form, the problem became how they should be ordered. Should the discussion of cruelty come first, so that tenderness could then serve as a balm? Friends who looked at these chapters suggested that my ordering of them here be reversed, and it was a good suggestion—after all, in the title the cudgel of cruelty comes first. Yet I decided to retain the chronology of the chapters as they appear here, which is the order in which they were conceived and written. For the very first chapter, on tragedy, has to do with the *disappearance* of tenderness as the key to the cruelties depicted in tragedy. That chapter also begins with a kind of confession—involving the ease with which one can *fail* to write about tenderness, which is no doubt related to vulnerability and hence prone to avoidance, escape, and even reactive cruelty. To compensate for the cudgel that follows upon the caress, the final chapter of the book tries to find its way back to tenderness by way of an account of artistic creativity.

The style of almost all the chapters is less formal than rigorous readers may expect and demand. That comes from the fact that many of them were first formulated as lectures, not as scholarly articles. I have reworked all of them and tried to clarify my arguments and note all my sources, but I was loath to emend the informality, which I hope does not offend. There is something about the themes of tenderness and cruelty that resists formal scholarly presentation. And the royal or papal *we* has never appealed to me.

Chapter 1 was initially an address to faculty and students at the University of Manitoba in March 2005, while I was a visiting lecturer there. The piece appeared in a different form under the title "Tenderness: Aristotle, Hölderlin, Freud, Lacan, Irigaray," in *Mosaic: A Journal for the*

Interdisciplinary Study of Literature. I had the pleasure of being interviewed by Professor Dawne McCance, at that time the editor of *Mosaic*. The interview, part of her "Crossings" series of interviews, and the address, together with a generous introduction by Dawne McCance, appear in vol. 39, no. 1 of the journal (March 2006): v–vi, 1–43. This was the first of many visits to Manitoba. I owe more than I can express to Professor McCance, who also read parts of the present book and offered helpful suggestions, and also to her colleagues and her students for their encouragement and their thought-provoking challenges over the years.

Chapter 2, in its earliest form, was a lecture, "Zum Begriff der Zärtlichkeit bei Hölderlin und Freud," delivered at the Universität Freiburg-im-Breisgau on November 3, 2008. I never published it, perhaps because I am not a Graecist and cannot write on Homer with authority; yet even if my Homer is closer to Hölderlin's Homer than any classical philologist would tolerate, I still believe in the tenderness of those cudgel-wielding Greeks.

Chapter 3 grew out of my encounter with Jacques Lacan's interpretation of Sophocles's *Antigone* in Lacan's seminar *The Ethics of Psychoanalysis*. Chapter 11 of my *Tragic Absolute* took up that interpretation, emphasizing what Lacan calls the *éclat* of Antigone. David Jones, the editor of *The Journal of Comparative and Continental Philosophy*, asked me to elaborate on that chapter, and the result was "Forever Younger: A Reading of Sophocles' *Antigone*," published in the inaugural issue of the journal in 2009, 55–75. I have altered and expanded the article here. My thanks to David Jones for his invitation and for his generous support over the years.

Chapter 4 has a long history. I first read Hegel on Friedrich Schlegel's novel *Lucinde* in the early 1980s. Hegel was so upset by the novel that I simply had to read it. To my surprise, it was the "spiritual" quality of Schlegel's novel that impressed me, because it involved a very different kind of "spirit" than Hegel's. I first published an article on Hegel and Schlegel on the invitation of Drucilla Cornell. It appeared under the ironic title "Lucinde's Shame: Hegel, Sensuous Woman, and the Law," in *Hegel and Legal Theory*, ed. Drucilla Cornell, Michel Rosenfeld, and David Gray Carlson (New York and London: Routledge, 1991), 287–300. It was then revised and reprinted under the same title in *Feminist Readings of Hegel*, ed. Patricia Jagentowicz Mills (University Park: Pennsylvania State University Press, 1995), 89–107. My thanks to Drucilla Cornell and Patricia Jagentowicz Mills for their kind reception of the piece. It has changed quite a bit here in its new version, however.

Chapter 5 was first presented at the *Mosaic* conference "Freud—after Derrida," at the University of Manitoba in October 2010. "Pulling Strings Wins No Wisdom" was a plenary address at the conference and was then published in *Mosaic* 44:3 (September 2011): 15–28. My thanks, again, to Dawne McCance for the invitation and for the kind reception of the piece, which I confess has great personal significance for me, perhaps because of the Greek word for wisdom, Σοφία.

Chapter 6 appears here for the first time. It was the final piece to be completed for the volume. Yet my reading of Robert Musil goes back to the mid-1970s when a student of mine at the University of Freiburg—Michael Walter, now one of Germany's most renowned translators of English-language literary texts—pressed into my hands *Der Mann ohne Eigenschaften* with the words "*Dies ist unser Joyce.*" I have been reading Musil ever since. His extraordinary novel, never completed, comes up twice in my own book: first here in chapter 6, where I argue that the story of Ulrich and Agathe is one of the most remarkable accounts of tenderness in all of literature, then in chapter 9, where a very different story—that of the psychopathic serial killer, Moosbrugger—is recounted. If I am no Graecist, then neither am I a Germanist, so that these excursions of mine into Musil's world manifest nothing like masterful scholarship. But they do reveal my fascination with what I take to be the best of twentieth-century fiction in the German language.

Chapter 7, on Otto Rank's *Das Trauma der Geburt* (1924), also appears here for the first time. It grew out of my study of Sándor Ferenczi's *Thalassa: A Theory of Genitality*, published that same year. Ferenczi and Rank were close associates during that time, working on what they called "active therapy," and both were interested in the biological and physiological bases of psychic life. For Rank, the cruelty of the birth trauma truncates the tenderness of intrauterine existence.

Chapter 8 first took the form of a double review article on Derrida's remarkable seminar on the death penalty. Under the title "From Cruelty to *Grausamkeit*: Derrida's Death Penalty Seminar," it appeared in *Research in Phenomenology* in vol. 47 (2017): 263–96. I have revised and expanded it for the present book.

Chapter 9 originally appeared in somewhat different form in *Frei sein, frei handeln*, ed. D. D'Angelo, S. Gourdaine, T. Keiling, and N. Mirkovic (Freiburg: Verlag Karl Alber, 2013), 126–43. My gratitude to all my students at the University of Freiburg over the years.

Chapter 10 was the subject of a workshop presented at Brown University in March 2016. It has not been published before. My thanks to Professor Gerhard Richter and to all my colleagues at Brown, where, even if no Germanist, I am proud to be Brauer Visiting Professor of German Studies.

My thanks to Alexander Bilda, Julia Ireland, Andrew Kenyon, Dawne McCance, Denny Schmidt, and Michael Walter, along with the entire editorial and production staff at SUNY Press.

D. F. K.
Strobelhütte, St. Ulrich

Key to the Principal Sources Cited

Works by Jacques Derrida

BS 1, 2 *Séminaire: La bête et le souverain, Volume I (2001–2002).* Edited by Michel Lisse, Marie-Louise Mallet, and Genette Michaud. Paris: Galilée, 2008. Translated by Geoffrey Bennington as *The Beast and the Sovereign*, Volume I. Chicago: University of Chicago Press, 2009. Cited by volume and page of the French edition. And *Séminaire: La bête et le souverain, Volume II (2002–2003).* Edited by Michel Lisse, Marie-Louise Mallet, and Genette Michaud. Paris: Galilée, 2010. Translated by Geoffrey Bennington as *The Beast and the Sovereign*, Volume II. Chicago: University of Chicago Press, 2011.

CP *La Carte postale de Socrate à Freud et au-delà*. Paris: Aubier-Flammarion, 1980. Translated by Alan Bass as *The Post Card from Socrates to Freud and Beyond*. Chicago: University of Chicago Press, 1987.

DE *De l'esprit: Heidegger et la question.* Paris: Galilée, 1987. Translated by Geoffrey Bennington and Rachel Bowlby as *Of Spirit: Heidegger and the Question.* Chicago: University of Chicago Press, 1989.

DG *De la grammatologie.* Paris: Minuit, 1967. Translated by Gayatri Chakravorty Spivak as *Of Grammatology.* Baltimore: Johns Hopkins University Press, 1976.

EA *États d'âme de la psychanalyse: Adresse aux États Généraux de la Psychanalyse.* Paris: Galilée, 2000. Translated by Peggy Kamuf as "Psychoanalysis Searches the States of Its Soul: The Impossible Beyond of a Sovereign Cruelty," in Peggy Kamuf, ed., *Without Alibi.* Stanford, CA: Stanford University Press, 2002, 238–80.

ED *Écriture et la différence*. Paris: Seuil, 1967. Translated by Alan Bass as *Writing and Difference*. Chicago: University of Chicago Press, 1978.

G 1–4 The four "Geschlecht" papers: (1) and (2) are published in *Psyché*, while (4) is in *Politiques de l'amitié*, with English translations as follows: (1) by Ruben Berezdivin in *Research in Phenomenology* XIII (1983): 65–83; by Ruben Berezdivin and Elizabeth Rottenberg in *Psyche 2: Inventions of the Other*, ed. Peggy Kamuf and Elizabeth Rottenberg. Stanford, CA: Stanford University Press, 2008, 7–26; (2) translated by John P. Leavey Jr. in *Deconstruction and Philosophy: The Texts of Jacques Derrida*, edited by John Sallis. Chicago: University of Chicago Press, 1987, 161–96; by John P. Leavey Jr. and Elizabeth Rottenberg in *Psyche 2*, cited above. The third "Geschlecht" has recently been published by Éditions du Seuil (Paris, 2018), edited by Geoffrey Bennington, Katie Chenoweth, and Rodrigo Therezo. The fourth, "L'Oreille de Heidegger: Philopolémologie (*Geschlecht* IV)" appears in *Politiques de l'amitié*. An English translation by John P. Leavey Jr. appears in *Commemorations: Reading Heidegger*, edited by John Sallis. Chicago: University of Chicago Press, 1993.

Gl *Glas*. Paris: Galilée, 1974. Translated by John P. Leavey Jr. and Richard Rand. Lincoln: University of Nebraska Press, 1986.

MA *Mal d'archive: Une impression freudienne*. Paris: Galilée, 1995. Translated by Eric Prenowitz as *Archive Fever*. Chicago: University of Chicago Press, 1996.

PM 1, 2 *Séminaire: La peine de mort*, 2 vols. Paris: Galilée, vol. I, 1999–2000 (published in 2012); vol. II, 2000–01 (published in 2015). English translation by Peggy Kamuf and Elizabeth Rottenberg under the title *The Death Penalty*, published by the University of Chicago Press in 2014 and 2017. Because the Chicago edition cites the French pagination in its margins, I will not cite the English pages in the body of my text, but only the French.

RP *Résistances de la psychanalyse*. Paris: Galilée, 1996. Translated by Peggy Kamuf, Pascale-Anne Brault, and Michael Naas as *Resistances of Psychoanalysis*. Stanford, CA: Stanford University Press, 1996.

Works by Sigmund Freud

GW Sigmund Freud, *Gesammelte Werke*, 17 vols. Edited by Anna Freud et al. London: Imago, 1952.

StA *Studienausgabe*, 12 vols. Edited by Alexander Mitscherlich, Angela Richards, and James Strachey. Frankfurt am Main: S. Fischer, 1982. This edition reproduces the editorial notes of the English Standard Edition.

Works by Hegel

HB *Briefe von und an Hegel*. 4 vols. Edited by Johannes Hoffmeister. Hamburg: F. Meiner, 1952.

HW G. W. F. Hegel, *Werke in zwanzig Bänden, Theorie Werkausgabe*. Edited by Eva Moldenhauer and Karl Markus Michel. Frankfurt am Main: Suhrkamp, 1970.

PG *Phänomenologie des Geistes*. Edited by Johannes Hoffmeister. Hamburg: F. Meiner, "Philosophische Bibliothek," 1952.

JS G. W. F. Hegel, *Jenaer Systementwürfe III*. Edited by Rolf-Peter Horstmann. Hamburg: F. Meiner, 1976. In the paperback edition of 1987, this volume is no. 333 of the "Philosophische Bibliothek."

Works by Heidegger

BW *Basic Writings from* Being and Time *(1927) to* The Task of Thinking *(1964)*. Second ed. San Francisco: HarperCollins, 1993.

EGT *Early Greek Thinking*. 2nd ed. San Francisco: Harper and Row, 1984. Now out of print, the volume is available online at: http://cdn.preterhuman.net/texts/history/Heidegger%20%20Early%20Greek%20Thinking.pdf .

EM *Einführung in die Metaphysik*. Tübingen: M. Niemeyer, 1953.

H *Holzwege*. Frankfurt am Main: V. Klostermann, 1950.

N I–II *Nietzsche*, 2 vols. Pfullingen: G. Neske, 1961.

Ni 1–4 *Nietzsche*, in four volumes. Second edition. San Francisco: HarperCollins, 1991.

SG *Der Satz vom Grund*. Pfullingen: G. Neske Verlag, 1957.

SZ *Sein und Zeit*, 12th ed. Tübingen: M. Niemeyer, 1972.

27 *Einleitung in die Philosophie*, Gesamtausgabe volume 27. Freiburg lecture course, Winter Semester, 1928–29. Frankfurt am Main: V. Kostermann, 2001.

29/30 *Die Grundbegriffe der Metaphysik: Welt—Endlichkeit—Einsamkeit*, Gesamtausgabe volume 29/30. Freiburg lecture course, Winter Semester, 1929–30. Frankfurt am Main: V. Klostermann, 1983. English translation by William McNeill and Nick Walker, *The Fundamental Concepts of Metaphysics: World, Finitude, Solitude*. Bloomington: Indiana University Press, 1995.

53 *Hölderlins Hymne Der Ister*, Martin Heidegger Gesamtausgabe vol. 53. Edited by Walter Biemel. Frankfurt am Main: V. Klostermann, 1984. English translation by Will McNeill and Julia Ireland, *Hölderlin's Hymn, The Ister*. Bloomington: Indiana University Press, 2017.

65 *Beiträge zur Philosophie (Vom Ereignis)*. Gesamtausgabe volume 65. From the years 1936–38. Frankfurt am Main: V. Klostermann, 1989. English translation by Daniela Vallega-Neu and Richard Rojcevich, *Contributions to Philosophy: Of the Event*. Bloomington: Indiana University Press, 2012.

Works by Friedrich Hölderlin

DSR *Friedrich Hölderlin Sämtliche Werke*. 20 vols. Edited by D. E. Sattler. Basel and Frankfurt: Stroemfeld and Roter Stern, 1979; Darmstadt: Luchterhand, 1984.

CHV *Friedrich Hölderlin Sämtliche Werke und Briefe.* 3 vols. Edited by Michael Knaupp. Munich: Carl Hanser Verlag, 1992.

DKV *Friedrich Hölderlin Sämtliche Werke und Briefe in drei Bänden.* Edited by Jochen Schmidt. Frankfurt am Main: Deutscher Klassiker Verlag, 1994.

DSL Friedrich Hölderlin, *Sämtliche Werke, Briefe und Dokument in zeitlicher Folge,* 12 vols. Edited by D. F. Sattler. Munich: Luchterhand, 2004.

Works by Schelling

SW F. W. J. Schelling, *Sämmtliche Werke.* Edited by Karl Schelling. Stuttgart and Augsburg: J. G. Cotta'scher Verlag, 1859.

WA *Die Weltalter Fragmente: In den Urfassungen von 1811 und 1813.* Edited by Manfred Schröter. Nachlaßband to the Münchner Jubiläumsdruck. Munich: Biederstein Verlag und Leibniz Verlag, 1946. The 1815 version of *Die Weltalter* appears in vol. I/8 of the *Sämmtliche Werke,* cited above.

Works by Other Authors

A Aristotle, *De arte poetica liber.* Oxford Classical Text. Edited by Rudolf Kassel. Oxford: Oxford University Press, 1965. English translation, *Aristotle's Poetics,* by Richard Janko. Indianapolis: Hackett, 1987. See also the translation by Ingram Bywater in Richard McKeon, ed. *The Basic Works of Aristotle.* New York: Random House, 1966), 1455–87. French translation by Michel Magnien. *Poétique.* Paris: Livre de Poche, n.d. German translation by Olof Gigon, *Poetik.* Stuttgart: P. Reclam, 1961.

AC Augustine, *Confessions,* 2 vols. Translated by W. Watts. Loeb Classical Library. Cambridge: Harvard University Press, 1977 [1912]. Cited by book and chapter.

BG Jacob and Wilhelm Grimm, *Deutsches Wörterbuch.* "Das digitale Grimm." Zweitausendeins, 2004.

HP Hermann Paul, *Deutsches Wörterbuch.* 6th edition by Werner Betz. Tübingen: Max Niemeyer Verlag, 1966.

JB Jacob Bernays, *Grundzüge der verlorenen Abhandlung des Aristoteles über die Wirkung der Tragödie.* Edited by Karlfried Gründer. Hildesheim and New York: Georg Olms Verlag, 1970 [originally published in 1857].

JL Jacques Lacan, *Le Séminaire, livre VII: L'éthique de la psychanalyse, 1959–1960*, edited by Jacques-Alain Miller. Paris: du Seuil, 1986; in English translation, *The Seminar of Jacques Lacan, Book VII: The Ethics of Psychoanalysis, 1959–1960*, translated by Dennis Potter. New York and London: W. W. Norton, 1992.

KrV Immanuel Kant, *Kritik der reinen Vernunft.* Edited by Raymund Schmidt. "Philosophische Bibliothek." Hamburg: Felix Meiner Verlag, 1956.

LI Luce Irigaray, *L'oubli de l'air chez Martin Heidegger.* Paris: Minuit, 1983. Translated by Mary Beth Mader as *The Forgetting of Air in Martin Heidegger.* Austin: University of Texas Press, 1999.

LP J. Laplanche and J.-B. Pontalis, *Das Vokabular der Psychoanalyse.* 2 vols. Translated by Emma Moersch. Frankfurt am Main: Suhrkamp, 1972.

OR Otto Rank, *Das Trauma der Geburt und seine Bedeutung für die Psychoanalyse.* Giessen, Germany: Psychosozial-Verlag, 2007, originally published in 1924.

RC Roberto Calasso, *Le nozze di Cadmo e Armonia.* Milan: Adelphi, 1988. Translated by Tim Parks as The *Marriage of Cadmus and Harmony.* New York: Alfred A. Knopf, 1993.

RG Robert Graves, *The Greek Myths.* 2 vols. Baltimore: Penguin, 1955.

S Sophocles, *Sophokles Dramen: Griechisch und Deutsch.* Edited by Bernhard Zimmermann, translated by Wilhelm Willige and Karl Bayer. 4th ed. Düsseldorf: Artemis and Winkler, 2003.

TA Krell, *The Tragic Absolute: German Idealism and the Languishing of God.* Bloomington and London: Indiana University Press, 2005.

Note: When repeated references are made to the same text in any given chapter, so that the source is clear, I do not always cite the code.

Introduction

Aristotle tells us that the key to the plots of the great Greek tragedies is that in those places and situations where tenderness belongs—for example, in families—it often goes missing. Tragic cruelty is the result. In more modern times, Friedrich Hölderlin was particularly sensitive to the absence of tenderness (*Zärtlichkeit*) in his culture, and he was acutely aware of the tragic consequences of that absence. A century later, the founders and major figures of psychoanalysis—for example, Freud and Lacan, Melanie Klein, Theodor Reik, and Otto Rank—were likewise convinced that the stream of tenderness either flows or fails to flow in the most decisive human relationships, that is, in the Eros of love relationships and in the Thanatos of cruelly destructive relationships. The present book investigates Greek tragedy and Greek epic poetry through the eyes of Hölderlin and other moderns—principally Freud, Nietzsche, and Derrida—who are sensitive to the theme of tenderness. It also goes to encounter Robert Musil's *Man Without Qualities*, which is equally astonishing for its account of the tender relationship of "Ulrich" and "Agathe" and its portrayal of the psychopathic serial killer "Moosbrugger."

After studying Otto Rank's *Birth Trauma*, which reflects on the tenderness of gestation in the womb and the cruel necessity of birth, the book then turns to an examination of cruelty (*Grausamkeit*) in general. It focuses on Derrida's challenge to contemporary psychoanalysis and his analysis (and indictment) of the death penalty. Derrida sees the transition in modernity from cruelty as blood flow—for example, in Dr. Guillotin's "humanitarian" invention—to cruelty of a more "psychological" nature. The cudgel often takes the form of a mere word, a word that Hölderlin calls "factically murderous," *tödtendfaktisch*, or a mere gesture, perhaps a lethal injection. Herewith a brief outline of the book's ten chapters.

Somewhere along its way, chapter 1 calls itself a "tender rant," and this is not far from the truth. It is unkind to the churches and to much that has informed our Western culture, but for the sake of nothing more outrageous than "tenderness." The chapter begins with Aristotle's *Poetics.* It argues that for Aristotle the essence of a tragic "household" is the absence of φιλία, which is family feeling, kinship, friendship, and love. The skilled tragedian goes in search of those households where tenderness has vanished; the horrors that take place in them, the cudgelings and counter-cudgelings, arise from the absence of tenderness. The chapter then turns to Friedrich Hölderlin (1770–1843), who in an early essay searches for the essence of community. He finds it in what he calls "the more tender relations," *die zärtlicheren Verhältnisse,* without telling us exactly which relations he means. (An excursus on the German words *zart, zärtlich,* and *Zärtlichkeit* tries to uncover the meaning of this word group, which is somewhere between the English words "tender" and "delicate.") In any case, Hölderlin's insistence on the importance of tenderness is vital to my chapter and to the entire book. Finally, the chapter turns to Freud's essays on "lovelife," which I write as one word, imitating the German *Liebesleben.* The guiding thread of Freud's "Three Contributions to a Theory of Lovelife" is the difficulty of uniting the two "streams" of tenderness and erotic excitement that a viable lovelife needs—sensual thrills and chills combined with feelings of profound tenderness. One of the most surprising aspects of Freud's theories, and one that tends to subvert the famous Oedipus Complex, is his idea that children—boys included—often feel the intense need to express tenderness toward the father, no matter how competitive or conflicted their relationship has been. My "tender rant," which has a very wide range, from Aristotle through Luce Irigaray, closes with the utopian thought that our own time—lurching to the right and gripping the cudgel ever more desperately—is in need of a new mythology of tenderness, whereby the word *mythology* is not meant as a derogation.

Chapter 2 takes us back to one of the oldest documents in our literature—Homer's *Iliad.* It asks whether even on the battlefield beneath the walls of Troy something like tenderness can be espied, and it answers, yes, precisely in the figure of the wrathful Achilles. On the basis of several texts by Hölderlin, it argues that *Zärtlichkeit* characterizes the great Achaean warrior with regard to several other personages in the epic: Priam, who begs for the release of his son's mangled body, and receives it; Patroclus, whose death brings Achilles at long last out of his tent and out of his sulk; and Briseïs, the "prize" who is taken from him by Agamemnon, thus precipitating Achilles's wrath and the epic *Iliad* as a whole. Even though one cannot deny the power of κῦδος ("glory" or "fame") in the Mycenaean Age, Hölderlin may be right to see in Achilles's volatile character a dominant strand of tenderness.

Nor is such tenderness missing from the Classical Age of Athens, the age of Sophocles's *Antigone*. Chapter 3 reads the play in an admittedly unfamiliar way. Usually the figure of Antigone is celebrated very much in the way that Hegel celebrates her, namely, as a staunch representative of the Penates, the family gods, a woman who challenges patriarchy by insisting on the burial of her brother Polyneices and who then goes bravely to her death defending the law of the family. For the first third of the play such a reading is tenable, but not for what happens after the choral song in dubious praise of Eros is sung. For from that point on, clearly, Antigone grows younger and more tender; by the time she stumbles toward her tomb she is a mere child, and once in the tomb she is almost a fetus, one that will be stillborn. Jacques Lacan is not off the mark when he says that Antigone is the perfect image of the destruction-and-death drives turned against the self. Her entire Eros aims at Death, and achieves it. However, as the old men of Thebes who form the chorus see and say, she is in the end a child, tender and vulnerable. She is, after all, the child of her paternal grandmother and her eldest brother, one of those children who, used and abused by the gods, should not have been. Sophocles's *Antigone*, in other words, is a tragedy, not a manifesto.

The figure of Antigone emerges again in chapter 4, which takes us from antiquity to modernity. She emerges as the only woman Hegel can accept without reservations, that is, a girl who dies before reaching maturity and before hearing the marriage song. Hegel contrasts her with a woman he fears and despises, the eponymous heroine of Friedrich Schlegel's *Lucinde*. Yet Hegel hates the author of the novel even more than the woman it is about. Friedrich Schlegel stands for all the things Hegel feels are wrong with his times: the novel pretends to adopt "the form of reflection," but it is all sophistry, and its sophistry is that of a lascivious male who seduces a mere maid and so destroys her honor. For whereas a man has other fields in which his honor is at stake, the woman, if she does not die at puberty, has only marriage and the family as her rescue.

And yet. There is something in the sensuality of the lovers—Lucinde and Julius—that threatens Hegel's philosophy of spirit. One might even be tempted to say that it is precisely the tenderness of their caresses that troubles him, as though their illicit love (for they scorn the idea of marriage) threatens not only family law and civil society but also the very system of rational philosophy. The illicit lovers are obviously spirited in their lovemaking, and Schlegel's writing too is spirited: the lovers give themselves over to one another, and the writer who celebrates them surrenders himself utterly to his text. Hegel has to worry about the implications of these surrenders for the spirit on which his entire system depends. For there is a hint in his *Phenomenology of Spirit* that the phenomenologist too has to surrender to the phenomena in order to come to know them; the phenomenologist must give himself or herself over to the very "sake" of thinking, and such *Hingebung* is more than reminiscent of what lovers do—even the most shameless and illicit of lovers—when they give themselves over to one another. Schlegel seems to know about this. Hegel has to hate him.

Whereas chapter 1 discusses the Freud of lovelife, tenderness, and sensuality, chapter 5 highlights the Freud of mourning. Central to the chapter is Derrida's account in *The Postcard*, following Freud's own account in chapter 2 of *Beyond the Pleasure Principle*, of the game invented by Freud's grandson, the son of his daughter Sophie. It is a game that has the serious purpose of controlling the mother's presences and absences. It is as though the infant imagines that the mother is a toy tied to a string: pull the string and the mother, Sophie, will return. The chapter is called "Pulling Strings Wins No Wisdom," however, for the reason that at some point the game fails to work. Since mothers are mortal, they pass. It would be a wisdom, a Σοφία, probably a very great wisdom, to learn that no one and no thing can control or master the comings and goings of human beings, even and especially of those tender ones we love and need. Freud and Derrida alike attain that wisdom, but it is hard-won, because it is cruel.

Chapter 6 is a study of Robert Musil's *Der Mann ohne Eigenschaften*, "The Man Without Qualities," published (in part) in the early 1930s. The chapter focuses on Agathe, the sister of this indeterminate man. Whereas Musil's name for the man without qualities changed several times during the years he was writing the novel, which he never finished, his name for the sister remained constant: Agathe, the feminine form of the Greek word for "the Good," Ἀγαθή. Yet the sister too is hard to define in terms of qualities. She sometimes acts like a criminal; she sometimes drives to distraction the people who are trying to help her; and sometimes she feels like killing herself. She and her brother Ulrich are in search of tenderness, however, and Musil begins to use the word *Zärtlichkeit* more and more as he writes about the two of them. The siblings invent the expression "the other state" or "the other condition," *der andere Zustand*, to designate a relation to the world that would be *zärtlich*, tender. But not simply a relation *to* the world. At one point they actually say that the world *reveals itself* as tender; they speak of "the suddenly unveiled tenderness of the world that touches without cease all our senses and that all our senses touch." The claim is not psychological but ontological, or at least phenomenological. Yet in the end, after two thousand pages have passed (my chapter is not as long as that), Musil does not know what to do with Ulrich and Agathe; better, they cannot tell him what they can do or must do, and Musil died before he could resolve the complications of the plot. Nevertheless, once one has seen the Good, even in a woman without qualities, it is impossible to forget her.

Part Two of the book is devoted to the theme of cruelty. If life is cruel, as one so often hears, when does that cruelty begin? At birth, replies Otto Rank. Chapter 7 reads Rank's *Birth Trauma*, which traces all forms of anxiety and neurosis back to the cruel experience of birth. Rank is thinking not only of the crisis involved in the transition from aquatic existence to a life in the air, a life of breathing, and of the pressure on the skull as one makes one's arduous way, nor only of the comparatively rough handling one receives on the other end of birth. What makes birth particularly cruel is that it truncates our tender existence in the womb. Rank is fascinated by the infinite number of instances in art, literature, religion, and psychology in which intrauterine existence is celebrated as Paradise—the Paradise we all have lost. True, were we to remain in the womb, we might eventually drown or suffocate. Yet back then we were well equipped to survive there, nourishment was at hand, the lights were dimmed, and it seemed we could swim and somersault and frolic endlessly. The psychoanalysts are agreed that it was better than sex. Or at least that sex is an asymptotic effort to return to Paradise.

Who can be surprised that the anxieties that arise as soon as we are born often turn into aggression and cruelty of one sort or another, either toward ourselves if we are well raised or against others if we are raised in the absence of tenderness? In extreme cases of aggression and cruelty, cases of criminality, it occasionally happens—at least in countries that are somewhat backward in their development—that these cases result in condemnation to death by execution. It is surprising to find a philosopher troubling himself about the death penalty, but in the penultimate seminar of his life, this is exactly what happened to Jacques Derrida. He found himself troubled by the history of blood flow—for, as it turns out, the word *cruelty* comes from the Latin word *cruor*, "I am bleeding."

Chapter 8 is a close reading of the two published volumes of the transcript from Derrida's penultimate seminar in Paris during the years 1999–2001. This "death penalty seminar," along with the last seminar, "The Beast and the Sovereign," are remarkable philosophical events, and now remarkable texts. If it seems surprising that Derrida should take such a detailed look at the death penalty, practiced no longer in Europe but still energetically pursued both in the United States and in the nations that the United States regards as its mortal enemies, the surprise diminishes when we think of Derrida's preoccupations during the final decades of his life. Among them, the theme of sovereignty is paramount, and the right to execute malefactors or to grant them pardon is the principal privilege of the sovereign head of state. Add to this Derrida's involvement with Heidegger's analysis of being-unto-death in *Being and Time*, an involvement that stretches over all the decades of Derrida's writing career, and the death penalty seminar makes sense. Derrida claims that death by execution would have to have—even though it does not have—central importance for Heidegger's analysis. He begins to wonder whether the cruelty of the death penalty is precisely what is *proper to* humankind—what Heidegger calls the *Eigentlichkeit* or "authenticity" of Dasein. For philosophers have universally supported the death penalty, always taking the side of conservative theologians, whereas many of our greatest writers—Victor Hugo, Percy Bysshe Shelley, and Albert Camus are exemplary in this respect—have vigorously opposed it. Among the philosophers, Derrida pits Nietzsche against Kant, who regards the "law of the talion" and hence capital punishment to be equivalent to the categorical imperative. Nietzsche challenges Kant by asking whether the supposed equivalence of guilt (crime) and inflicted pain (punishment) is in any sense credible, or whether its vaunted rationality "reeks of cruelty."

However, Derrida sees a development taking place in which the death penalty may finally come to an end. That development he traces in what he calls "a history of blood." Does that development mean that cruelty is coming to an end? Or does it mean that a new word for cruelty has to be found? Derrida suggests the German word *Grausamkeit*, which means that which causes a shudder of horror to pass through us. It would denote a less bloody and more "psychological" sense of cruelty. Psychoanalysis therefore becomes another central focus of the death penalty seminar, as Derrida searches for a new notion not only of *cruelty* but also of the *unconscious*. And, one must add, a new notion of *conscious thought*, inasmuch as the *calculative thinking* that seeks suitable punishments for sundry crimes invariably participates in mindless cruelty.

Chapter 9 then takes a closer look at Kant and especially at Kant's idea of freedom. Freedom is essential in Kant's view. Were there no freedom, no one could be held accountable. The need to punish wrongdoing comes first in Kant's system of morality. But this means that the usual view of Kant's ostensible call for respect of the human being as end rather than means—respect for the human being's dignity and worth—is untenable. If the human being is midway between angel and beast, gravity causes it to slip toward the latter. Thus, imputability and accountability (*Zurechnungsfähigkeit, Verantwortung*) become principal concerns for Kant. One sees this not only in his *Metaphysik der Sitten*, which is Derrida's point of reference during the seminar, but also in his *Kritik der reinen Vernunft*, to which this chapter turns. Another principal source for the chapter is Robert Musil's *Mann ohne Eigenschaften*, this time not for its tale of Ulrich and Agathe but for its astonishing portrayal of the trial of Moosbrugger, a serial killer who has been condemned to death. The arguments of the jurists who insist on Moosbrugger's execution, even though everyone can see that he is completely mad, are principally Kantian in origin. The question soon becomes whether those arguments are as mad as the phantasms that rule and wreck Moosbrugger's mind.

The book ends by reporting on Derrida's address in July 2000 to the Estates General of Psychoanalysis, published as *States of the Soul of Psychoanalysis*. In part, the address continues to pose the question of cruelty as *Grausamkeit*, that is, a more "refined" or more "psychological" form of cruelty. Yet Derrida's principal interest is to move beyond such cruelty—if such a "beyond" is at all possible. What makes it seem unlikely, if not impossible, is that the principle of sovereignty and the power that sovereignty embodies perpetuate cruelty. Power especially comes into play with Freud's concept of *Bemächtigung*, a word that has *Macht* at its center. For "empowering" and "overpowering" appear to be at work in *every* "principle" of psychoanalysis. The "beyond" that Derrida hopes for would challenge not only sovereignty but the entire structure of "principles." For principles always have a "prince" or a nameless "potentate" behind them who is ready to enforce them with astonishing cruelty.

My own question to Derrida—better, my conversation with him—involves the possibility that what Nietzsche and Heidegger call "will to power as *art*" can show the way to such a beyond—a beyond of both cruelty and principles. For it seems that the creative power of art cultivates a kind of tenderness on the part of the artist toward his or her "objects" or "themes." Masterful artistry cultivates not mastery but receptivity, and receptivity goes gently with tenderness. At least, that possibility is the hope of the present investigation.

Part One

Tenderness

(*Zärtlichkeit*)

Chapter One

Tenderness and Tragedy

Where they love, they do not desire, and where they desire, they cannot love.

—Sigmund Freud

THIS FIRST CHAPTER (and perhaps the entire book) will be about a recent failure of mine, the failure, that is, of an earlier essay of mine to address its topic. I discovered the failure after I had "finished" the essay. I came across a journal entry of mine written in Santorini about a paper I intended to write on the subject of tenderness, *Zärtlichkeit,* a favorite word of the great German poet and thinker Hölderlin. Also a common word in Freud's texts. I will commit the sin of quoting myself, that is, of citing the journal entry that refers to the intended paper, the failure. Why this narcissistic beginning, even if the narcissism is punishing? Because I want to trace the reasons for the failure, which have to do with the at least temporary defeat of tenderness. Tenderness perhaps requires more courage than most of us can muster most of the time. A truism, I know, yet one that appears to be true. I wonder whether I can write a more forthright chapter now?

The journal entry goes back to the afternoon of May 29, 2004, a significant date for me, and it reads: "A thought about my paper for the ___ Society: to relate Empedocles' book *Purifications* to Hölderlin's *Zärtlichkeit,* 'tenderness.'" The journal entry goes on to show that I was also thinking of Luce Irigaray's phrase *la seule tendresse,* "the only tenderness," which in her Heidegger book she attributes to the feminine (LI 108–109). The journal note continues after several lines, making a transition that is still mysterious to me, "The overthrow of Saint Augustine; or, rather, the inversion of his wretched life, from his ultimate toothlessness and tuberculosis to the fathering of his son Adeodatus." Recall that Augustine is converted to Christianity only after his mother Monica insists that his concubine of thirteen years, the nameless mother of his illegitimate son, be shipped back to Africa. Augustine is promptly baptized and as soon loses his teeth; his lungs go bad; he and his mother are happy at last. The journal note continues:

> Not a feminism, if feminism is the production of a race of women with the voice of Stone Phillips. Not a feminism that adorns itself with the ludicrous worst of masculinity and considers itself empowered thereby. Instead of all this prating, the abashedness of tenderness. Models? Nikolas and Lefteris, Evangelitsa and the doves, and Jack the dog, whose chin is on my lap at suppertime, his eyes searching mine for a trace of canine tenderness.

Let me start at the end. Jack was the scruffy dog at the pension where I reside on Santorini (the Pension Carlos in Akrotiri, near the excavation of the ancient Cycladic city). Jack would arrive at my supper table every evening without fail and place his chin—delicately, lightly—on my left thigh. His big brown eyes would roll from left to right and back again, begging for a morsel, as eloquently as any hero out of Dickens: "Please, sir, may I have some more?" I would either encourage the beggar, because he is so tender, or I would cry, "Jack, *exo*!" whereupon he would quit the dining room, his tail between his legs and nothing in his tummy. At the door Jack would pause and look back to see if I really meant it. Sometimes I didn't. Sometimes I succumbed to tenderness.

Evangelitsa and the doves? She keeps them behind the pension. She handles them not gently but fairly roughly; she is so brisk and direct with her unsentimental hands. Yet they seem to love it. They shiver and ruffle and coo.

Finally, the reference to Nikolas and Lefteris, the first of my three references, is the decisive one, even though it has to do with two old men, two Greek patriarchs, where the feminine seems to have been banished or excluded by both nature and culture from the start. Here I will paraphrase my journal, since the entry is too long. Evangelitsa, the owner of Jack the dog and all the ruffled doves, also had a father, Nikolas, who was ninety years old at the time of this particular visit. Nikolas had a younger brother, Lefteris, who was a mere eighty-two. One afternoon I drove with Evangelitsa and her father to visit Lefteris, who was bedridden after surgery for bone cancer in his legs. At the risk of trying your patience, I quote a brief excerpt from my journal's record of that visit:

> The two brothers—Evangelitsa's father and her uncle—are eight years apart. Both are half deaf, so that they shout at one another and have to guess at about half of what the other is telling. They

> laughed heartily that whole afternoon. Evangelitsa's father seemed to regain decades otherwise flown. His eyes grew clearer every minute we were there and by the time we left they were the sparkling eyes of a boy. The gestures of the hand, the shouting, the laughter—so many signs of the most tender life. Like my friend E., I have been thinking a lot about Hölderlin's *Zärtlichkeit,* "tenderness," always in conjunction with Irigaray's *la seule tendresse.* It would be a good paper to give some day—to a friendly audience. What would lend it strong masculine presence and conviction would be the tale of these two brothers, each with the same dark eyes, silver hair, strong shoulders and arms, and massive hands. The complete abnegation of sentimentality. Nothing maudlin about these two. The refusal by Nikolas of any proffered help when walking or clambering into a car or a boat, throwing his cane ahead of him into it in noisy defiance.
>
> When it was time to go, the two brothers kissed on the mouth, kissed for a long time. . . . A ninety and an eighty-two year old man. As we were leaving the house, climbing up the steep path alongside the house toward the car, Nikolas took his cane and banged raucously on the shutters of his shut-in brother's bedroom. Lefteris shouted a final good-bye, and we set off for home.

The kiss on the mouth between two brothers—two tough old patriarchs you would not mess with even at age ninety and hobbled or eighty-two and bedridden—stopped my breath. It reminded me of another scene, an unspeakably tender scene, I witnessed on a night train during my first visit to Spain in 1968. I was squeezed into an uncomfortable, stuffy compartment with six young Spanish soldiers in starched khaki uniforms. They were facing one another, three by three, sitting well forward on the unforgiving wooden benches, each with his head on the opposite mate's shoulder, one head to the left, one to the right, their arms slung over one another's backs. They were all sound asleep. I gazed at the faces I could see. They were my age, perhaps a year or two younger. They were finding comfort on one another's bodies. And they were guys. From Macholandia.

Homophobia? I don't know the meaning of the word, he insisted, his hazel eyes blinking. And yet I am astounded by these expressions of tenderness elsewhere in the world, readily accepted and entirely undemonstrative except to the parties involved, yet denied me by my culture. Well, then, tenderness. *Zärtlichkeit.* What is it? *La seule tendresse,* says Irigaray, the only one. Does "she" alone have it? If so, how does she impart it to the young Spaniards, or to the wizened patriarchs, or at long last to me?

It seemed important to know these things, and so I wrote a paper—too long, twenty-eight pages—that discussed five points in hopes of getting to the theme of tenderness. Having rediscovered my journal entries after the paper was written, and fearing the worst, I did a word search for *tenderness* in my paper and found two entries, one quite negative, the other in a postscript, just at the point where the paper ran out of breath. The first entry touched on that moment in Sophocles's *Electra* when the hard-boiled Clytaimestra pauses in her life of murder in order to express a tender sentiment. Her son Orestes, whom she and Aigisthos have banished, fearing that he might avenge his father's murder, is now reported dead. Clytaimestra should be relieved: she and her lover are now in the clear, since Electra will only whine. Yet Clytaimestra does not celebrate her son's death. She mourns. Though he may be her mortal enemy, she is powerless with grief in the face of this reported death. As though apologizing for her inconsistent behavior, she tells the chorus, "To bear a child is something overwhelming" (S, *Electra* l. 770). The word she uses is δεινόν: overwhelming, monstrous, uncanny. As though the uncanny nature of sex, pregnancy, and birth, which are matters for what the Scots call "canny wives," were the source of tenderness! The second reference in my paper, the more positive one, came from Hannah Arendt, a hard-headed thinker with whom we do not normally associate tenderness. As a young woman—very young—she refers to a philosophical life that would be dedicated to longing and languor, and she speaks of "a palpating tenderness toward the things of the world."[1] I recall in the old woman whom I knew, old and yet still young in the final two years of her life, a sort of gruff tenderness, a camouflaged yet unmistakable tenderness, one of greatest gifts to my life.

Yet my paper did not reflect on these things. It was a scholarly paper, very scholarly, with several wonderful turns of phrase, believe me, concerning Empedocles of Acragas, the problem of catharsis in Greek tragedy, and Hölderlin's play *The Death of Empedocles*. I did not throw the paper away. In fact, I read it shamelessly before the unwitting members of the society that had kindly invited me. Yet I wonder if I can retrieve here and now the original inspiration for the project—this matter of tenderness? There will be some bookishness to the present chapter as well—I cannot suppress my schooling altogether. But this time let me remember what it is all for, what it is all about.

---

1 Hannah Arendt and Martin Heidegger, *Briefe 1925 bis 1975 und andere Zeugnisse*. 3d ed. Ed. Ursula Ludz (Frankfurt am Main: V. Klostermann, 2002), 21.

La seule tendresse. Is tenderness invariably hers, hers exclusively? It is not as though Irigaray wants to exclude men from the font of tenderness. Far from it! She wants them to bathe in it to the point where they are saturated, transformed. She is not afraid that they will lose their masculine flair, their drive, their competitiveness and athleticism, their will, all the wildflowers of testosterone. She merely wants to place these things in the service of life rather than death. Tenderness is the key to such service. Freud, as we will soon hear, says that modernity shatters on the reef of the contradiction between sensual excitement and nurturing tenderness. However much we fear and despise the father of psychoanalysis—or this obstreperous uncle, as Hélène Cixous more tenderly calls him, since by now he is a part of the family—modern and post-modern women and men continue to labor away at this recalcitrant problem, the difficult integration of the "two streams" of genital love, to wit, tenderness and sensuality. We usually collapse into defeatism and duality: two madonnas, one for home and church, the other for stage and screen and surreption; and two guys, one who is "sweet," and the other who looks and acts like Johnny Depp in *Don Juan DeMarco.* Of course, each year a dozen critics point out how hopelessly Victorian and outdated this supposed conflict of tenderness and sensuality is, while each year illustrated gossip magazines add a thousand names to their subscription lists with articles titled "Why He Can't Be Tender" and "So Where Did All the Pizzazz Go?" and a hundred hack screenwriters in Hollywood propose yet another sitcom on the novel idea of the boy-who-has-everything failing to sustain a relationship with the girl-who-has-everything. Freud, not famous for his smile, cannot help but grin at these critics who want to consign the conflict between tenderness and sensuality to the Victorian dustbin. He mutters, through a puff of cigar smoke, almost demurely, "You can make an appointment at the receptionist's desk."

Tenderness *with* sensuality is the surreptitious dream, and yet tenderness so often suffers defeat during sensuous adventures. *La seule tendresse*—where is it? What hangs on our finding it? Much of everything, I suspect. At least, we know the price of *not* finding it.

Aristotle knew about tenderness. In his *Poetics*, with all the skills of the philosophic sleuth, he traces the essence of an excellent tragedy. He treats tragedy as a household, one that requires effective household management. Ironically, or sleuthfully, he notes that the tragedies themselves have to do with households, specifically, those rare and special households in which dreadful things have occurred. The families that lend themselves to tragic mimesis are those that have done dreadful things to themselves. True, the families are heroic, one level below the gods; indeed, the gods themselves are often embroiled in tragedy. No matter how heroic and quasi-divine the tragic households may be, however, tragic action has to capture our attention in the way a corpse does, a corpse or a repulsive animal, a horrid bug, a mesmerizing serpent, a ghoul. What is the secret of this revulsion? Aristotle notes that when enemies quarrel no one pays any mind; they are doing what enemies do. Yet when quarrels irrupt in the household, when the enraged father grips his son or the son raises his hand against the father or mother, when the daughter plots with her brother to do the mother in, when husband and wife no longer cleave to one another but cleave one another—this, Aristotle cries, is what we are looking for. Eureka! The desired disaster is a repulsive crime against tenderness.

What we are looking for in a tragic plot or situation is what Aristotle in his ethical writings condemns as the most egregious crimes. These crimes transpire when the love or tenderness—Aristotle calls it φιλία, a word that suggests friendship and even kinship, family feeling—have gone missing from the house. Perhaps the most horrifying cases are those in which φιλία vanishes but then returns as a pure inversion or perversion of itself: David Lynch's "Bob" or "Diane," erstwhile tenderness looming as an ogre. This is what we are looking for, says Aristotle, when we enter the household of tragedy; here the ethos of tenderness has degenerated into something nefarious, something malicious.

If Aristotle is right, tenderness is of the essence, and that essence is of the family. Cassandra uses the word φίλος when, in a trance, she sees Thyestes serving up to his brother Atreus a meal of Atreus's children, his own nephews. Cassandra is beside herself, *out*side herself, held spellbound in an ecstasy that transports her to past times and ancient evils, evils that continue to haunt and inhabit the house. A Trojan princess and priestess—indeed, a prophetess[2]—abducted by Agamemnon and brought to the palace at Argos, Cassandra can smell the blood in the walls, the blood of past and future crimes, Agamemnon's and her own blood. In her broken Achaean, she tells of the children she can see. They have already been served up by one brother to another. These are brothers whose mouths should have kissed rather than eaten children. Herewith one of the most uncanny speeches in Aeschylus and in all tragedy:

2 See Kristina Mendicino, "Prophecy, Spoken Otherwise: In the Language of Aeschylus's Cassandra," in Mendicino, *Prophesies of Language: The Confusion of Tongues in German Romanticism* (New York: Fordham University Press, 2017), 94–117.

There! You see them? Sitting
In front of the house? So young!
Shapes that hover in dreams of a dream!
Young boys, murdered—am I right?—
By someone of their own blood, by kith and kin.
Hands grip meat, a home-cooked meal!
Their entrails now tripe, a most lamentable feast!
I can see them! Hands gripping meat!
Meat their father ate![3]

Her eyes and voice straining at the vision, her horror punctuated by mad wit, Cassandra captures the tragic mood perfectly. The children are murdered by kith and kin, a φίλος who ought to have been the embodiment of φιλία. When the avuncular becomes the murderous, horrid crimes are committed, and, eureka, this is what we are looking for. If we ask why the crimes of Atreus and Thyestes and Agamemnon are the ultimate horror, if we want to know why Aristotle too sees the lack of φιλία in the family as the seed of the worst evils, we need only recall the testimony of the woman who kills Cassandra. Clytaimestra proclaims, as we have already heard, δεινὸν τὸ τίκτειν ἐστίν, "To bear a child is something overwhelming" (Sophocles, *Electra*, l. 770). That is what the House of Atreus has come to know well: one does not eat τὸ δεινόν without suffering the most violent reaction. The last topic that Nikolas and Lefteris discussed on the day I visited them was a news report that had come over the radio that morning. A young man from Crete had butchered and cooked his mother, then called out to his father, "Oh, Papa, come and see how I have prepared Mama." The boy was under suspicion of being mentally ill, said the radio. The ancient Greeks would have shuddered and said that the boy's infatuating doom had gotten the better of him, and Aristotle would have added, "This is what we are looking for."

Yet what if we are more attuned to Main Street than to Mulholland Drive? What if we put aside the question of tragedy and tragic households and focus on the φιλία that doubtless often does go missing? Tragic households are quite rare, Aristotle emphasizes, and yet tenderness is getting harder and harder to find anywhere. This paradox derives from what I take to be the central enigma of Aristotle's *Poetics*. Even though excellent tragedies involve the smallest number

3 Aeschylos, *Agamemnon*, in *Tragödien*, 5th ed. Ed. Bernd Zimmermann, trans. Oskar Werner (Zürich: Artemis & Winkler, 1995), ll. 1217–22.

of houses, to which the poets return again and again in search of their stories, these tragedies speak in universals: tragedy is more serious and more philosophical than any scholarly inquiry, says Aristotle, because it shows us what might well be the case for all of us. Though the tragic houses are few, tragedy is of the universe. Jacob Bernays, whose analysis of catharsis has dominated the field since the mid-nineteenth century, says that tragedy manifests "the power of motion [that is, of dance] and song" at work "in the universe"; the spectators at a performance of tragedy, he says, are transported to a place from which they can witness "the frightening, sublime laws of the universe," or, again, "the rule of the universal law of the cosmos [*dem Walten des allgemeinen Weltgesetzes*]."[4] Preferring Main Street will not help: Mulholland Drive plays itself out in every house on Main Street where a girl dreams of being a movie star and of making her parents as proud of her as they were on the day she was elected Jitterbug Queen of her high school; she dreams of being loved, that is, of finding in the arms of some regal and voluptuous woman...finding what, exactly? If we cannot answer that question, Lynch tells us, we are going to witness universal misery, murder, and suicide, the recurrent snuffing of lives.

Clearly, I am failing again, evading again. It is absurd to want to reinvent the wheel of love. Even if φιλία seems a foreign word to us, its meanings are so commonplace that they are known to all under the skin if not on the tongue. I am therefore not at all certain that it will help to introduce another foreign word, *Zärtlichkeit,* which is a word of both Hölderlin and Freud. First, Hölderlin, where things become obscure, if only because of the brightness of his light.

•

Hölderlin's "Fragment of Philosophical Letters," sometimes called "On Religion," is precisely that, a fragment consisting of scattered pages from the year 1796 that the editors of his works assemble according to their best lights.[5] I will paraphrase these pages, which are often cryptic, with the sole intention of highlighting what Hölderlin calls the *tender*—or, as he commonly writes, using the

---

4 Jacob Bernays, *Grundzüge der verlorenen Abhandlung des Aristoteles über die Wirkung der Tragödie*, ed. Karlfried Gründer (Hildesheim, Germany: Georg Olms Verlag, 1970 [originally published in 1857]), 50. See my discussion in TA at 283–88.

5 I will read these pages in the form chosen by Friedrich Beißner and Jochen Schmidt in the latter's DKV (see 2:562–69 and 1254–56), although I accept D. E. Sattler's and Michael Knaupp's dating of the pages in CHV (2:51–57 and 3:387–89), DSR (14:21–39), and DSL (5:10–16), to wit, February/March 1796.

comparative form, the *more tender*—relations.[6] Perhaps surprisingly, he sees these more tender relations prevailing not in Christian culture but in classical Greek antiquity; not in Scripture but in myth, and precisely in the tragic myths.

An imagined interlocutor asks the author why when human beings rise above the level of mere subsistence and bare survival, achieving a higher level of life, they feel the need to form an idea or picture of their world and its destiny. For whenever human beings feel closely united to their world and their life, that is, whenever their life begins to cohere, they seek an idea or image of that life. Such an idea or image is not easy to find, inasmuch as the idea resists thought and the image is not available to sensuous intuition. Yet why do they so avidly seek a representation of their lives? Hölderlin replies, tentatively, that when communities rise above the level of mere fulfillment of basic needs they come to be mindful of something like their collective destiny. Such mindfulness or remembrance is above all an expression of *gratitude* toward life. As human beings develop an enhanced sensibility, they experience a deeper, more thoroughgoing cohesion with the element or sphere in which their life bestirs itself to act. Such cohesive action responds to challenges in the realms of both nature and culture. Finally, at the highest stage of cohesive action, the nexus of life—of all life—is gratefully remembered, at which point human beings achieve a certain repose and are at peace with the world. Grateful memory or mindfulness yields a kind of pleasure that transcends the satisfaction of their needs; an idea or image of their collective life—and of all life—takes shape.

Such transcendence is not guaranteed, of course: it will not supervene if human beings look too far ahead and are too restless, too indiscriminately willful; nor will it come about if they are too anxious, too inhibited and self-deprecating. Yet human beings can and do achieve this less definable yet more infinite contentment. At certain exceptional moments, their active life stands still. Whereas the animal sleeps after satisfying its needs, the human being, the grateful rememberer, repeats in spirit the arduous process that now gives

6 The Grimm Brothers cite several interesting comparatives, including Goethe's reference to "seeking what is higher, *zartere*," and Lohenstein's reference to a child "that is *zärter* than the children who came from Leda's egg." Yet the word does not seem to attract more comparative usages than any other adjective—at least from authors other than Hölderlin. One of the rare uses of "more tender relations" I have found in English appears in an obituary for Allan Melville, Herman's father: the obituary refers to Allan's business associates and then to "the nearer and more tender relations of domestic life." See Hershel Parker, *Herman Melville: A Biography*, 2 vols. (Baltimore: Johns Hopkins University Press, 1996), 1:62.

it peace. Such musing does not occur in pure thought, since thoughts deal with universal and necessary connections, that is, with the irremediable and indispensable laws of life. Rather, repetition in spirit accepts the risk of advancing beyond logic: it dares to think the more intense and more intimate cohesion of all life beyond all the strictures of law and duty. Sophocles's Antigone, for example, struggles to achieve a sense of cohesion, if the phrase "all life" may be said to include her dead brother. Whatever Aristotle may believe about the universality of tragedy, she resists the pure thought of universals, which are mirrored in Creon's decree that all enemies of the city—including her brother Polyneices—must remain unburied. She seeks a different kind of thinking, one that would respond to more archaic, higher or deeper concatenations, more tender imbrications.

Aristotle, in his *Nicomachean Ethics* (5:10; 1137b 10–20), interprets this problem of ethical universals and particulars in terms of an equity beyond legal justice. Legal justice deals with universals, whereas living and acting human beings deal with particular circumstances. Hölderlin too is searching for that Aristotelian ἐπιείκεια, not very well translated as "equity," which reaches higher or deeper than universality can toward a more subtle, more supple, and more inclusive cohesion.[7] Antigone's intense and intimate relation with her dead brother serves as a clue to the nature of this higher or deeper realm, albeit a troubling clue, inasmuch as Antigone's devotion has more to do with the lower realm, the underworld, than the higher. Is the repose she seeks for her brother in fact the cessation of life that she wishes for herself? *I am already dead,* Antigone likes to say, confounding living contentment with Nirvana. A famous psychoanalyst will one day say of her that she is the splendid embodiment of the unrestrained destruction-and-death drives.

According to Hölderlin, the higher, more intense, and more intimate cohesion of life cannot be found by following the guideline of duty, the Kantian moral/categorical imperative. Neither the duties of love and friendship, hospitality, and generosity toward one's enemies, nor maxims about how one should live, how one should treat one's elders or the members of the opposite sex, avail. Indeed, these "moral" precepts imprison the more tender and more infinite relations of life in a morality that one can only call "arrogant." Arrogant morality on the one hand and superficial etiquette and "good taste" on the other. The brittle concepts of both morality and etiquette take themselves to be enlightened,

7 On ἐπιείκεια see Kevin Thomas Miles, *Razing Ethical Stakes: Tragic Transgression in Aristotle's Equitable Action* (PhD Dissertation, DePaul University, 1998).

whereas they are benighted; they do not even approximate the wisdom of the ancients, for whom those tender relations (*jene zarten Verhältnisse*) were a *religious* affair. By *religious* Hölderlin means spiritual, and by *spirit* he means that memorious, grateful, and generous sphere in which tender relations with all of life flourish.

At least one page is missing from Hölderlin's manuscript here, and, as I mentioned, not even the order of the extant pages is established, so that it is impossible to speak of transitions. At all events, there is now talk of "divinity" or "godhead." Divinity cannot be invoked by some sort of profession of faith. Neither the so-called interior life nor the conglomerate of things around us suffices to demonstrate the sphere of spirit, that is, a sphere beyond the mechanistic world of Locke and Newton. If there is a spirit or a god active in the world, she or he must prevail in that memorious, grateful, and more lively relation to things that transcends sheer satisfaction of needs. Further, in these more animated, more vital, and more tender relationships, each individual has his or her own god, experienced in the sphere of activity that is specific to him or her. With Hölderlin, the priesthood of all believers becomes the infinite panoply of gods, and this—as the friend of his youth, Schelling, will also come to realize—is the truth of polytheism.

Nevertheless, there can be a communal sense of divinity. Indeed, there may be a divine sphere in which every human being can and does flourish. One of the central thoughts of Hölderlin's pages is the empathy that allows one human being to cross over into the sphere of another, or at least to see and feel how a given god has grown out of, and is at home in, that foreign sphere. Ultimately, says the young Hölderlin, it should not be so difficult for human beings to affirm the sundry forms of divinity that arise from all the particular spheres, unless of course their religious notions are held with excessive passion and with reckless, slavish insistence. In the latter case, spirit will always assume the shape of the tyrant or the lackey. In the former, more affirmative case, even a life that is severely limited ought to be able to come up with infinite notions of the godhead and to tolerate the disparate notions of others. As long as human beings are not irascible and bitter, as long as they are neither oppressed nor perched too high on their moral horse, and as long as they are not entirely caught up in some exhausting struggle, whether just or unjust, they ought to be able to *congregate* in religious matters, precisely as they do when pursuing other common interests. The limitations that adhere to every set of notions about the divine are thus overcome, says Hölderlin, meaning that human beings no longer run roughshod over alien notions and nations, but permit themselves to associate freely with every divergent view. There ought to be a harmonious whole of such notions, and a symphony of the sundry ways of life that produce them.

How neophyte, and how utopian, these ideas seem! Yet there is also in Hölderlin's pages the hint of the more hard-edged idea—albeit fragmented and fragmentary—that contrasting notions of divinity must challenge one another; indeed, such notions can become positive only when they are transgressed. This hint seems to anticipate one of the main ideas in the "Notes" on Sophocles that Hölderlin writes near the end of his active life, in 1803–04, namely, the idea that true spirituality flourishes only when a traditional god is met not with pious prattle and wheedling negotiation but with a word of blasphemy in one's mouth. The model religious relation for these later "Notes" is that of Lycurgus and Niobe, both of them cited in Sophocles's *Antigone*. Theirs is anything but the religion of a compliant, supine worshiper.

Lycurgus, like King Pentheus of Thebes, insults Dionysos and goes to war against him. But he is driven mad by the god of joy, whereupon he kills his own son, "pruning" his son's corpse as though it were a grape vine. The townspeople, horrified by Lycurgus's crime, condemn him to be quartered. Yet such a death, they say, was reserved for the yearly god-king in Babylon, so that Lycurgus, in spite of his crime against the god, seems to be himself divine. Lycurgus, godlike in his very madness, ends by leaping into the sea. Niobe, the haughty queen of Phrygia, insults Leto, the mother of Artemis and Apollo, by saying that Leto has only two children, one of them a man who looks like a woman and the other a woman who acts like a man. Niobe lives to see her many children slaughtered by the two archer gods she has insulted. Zeus takes pity on her, however, and transforms her into a snow-capped mountain; when the annual spring thaw comes, Niobe weeps endless tears of snowmelt for her children. Sophocles and Hölderlin might also have mentioned Ino, one of the daughters of Cadmus and Harmony. Driven mad by Hera, Ino boils the infant Dionysos in a cauldron. She then leaps to her death in the sea, holding in her arms the lifeless flesh of the god. It is precisely in this way, however, that Ino becomes Leukothea, "the radiant goddess," who rescues sailors in distress.

By the time Hölderlin is translating *Antigone*, the model religious relation is fraught: whereas Sophocles has Tiresias warn Creon that he is walking on the razor's edge of chance (l. 906: ἐπὶ ξυροῦ τύχης), Hölderlin translates this merely with the command, "Think, even now, in this delicate moment [l. 1053: *im zarten Augenblike*]." Tenderness is also fragility—the delicate situation of walking on the razor's edge. No doubt, Hölderlin is not prepared to go that far in his fragment on religion in early 1796. In the "hints toward a continuation" of the essay, he emphasizes the contrast between religious relations and intellectual, moral, and legal relations on the one hand, and physical, mechanical, historical relations on the other. Religious relations have to do with personality, autonomy, reciprocal limitation, and the coexistence of conflicting intellectual relations; they also have to do with an intense cohesion, in which the one is given over to the other, so that each is inseparable from the other, like elements in elective affinity. Religious notions are neither purely intellectual nor purely historical; rather, they are intellectual-historical, and that means *mythic.* In both the content and the narrative style in which we depict them, the more tender and more animated relations that are mirrored in religious representations are mythic.

When Carl Jung finds the archetypes of the collective unconscious to be the key to the modern soul, when Joseph Campbell sees the secret of human creativity reflected in the sundry masks of god, and when Gore Vidal declares that Roberto Calasso's *The Marriage of Cadmus and Harmony* should be read more religiously than the Bible, these thinkers and writers are all on a Hölderlinian course. A different sort of script and scripture is required for the more tender relations, one in which the stories both limit and expand upon one another. Spirit speaks tellingly through the lyric-mythic text, which balances universal significance with historical context and individual eccentricity; myth both limits and expands, is both powerfully assertive in its claims and infinitely tolerant of other competing and even conflicting claims. Myths are the folds of Apollo's cloak, says Roberto Calasso; every move of the god's shoulder and every wafting breeze can reshape them (RC 281). If one may at all hope for a communal life for humankind, it will materialize only where myth once again plays a central role in community life. The cohesion of life—of all life, Hölderlin emphasizes, from the most fragile plant to the most awesome deity—will be celebrated in myth.

At the instant when the fragment breaks off, Hölderlin is beginning to write about the new role of founders and priests in religion. One senses that he is about to repeat the words of "The Oldest Fragment toward a System in German Idealism," on which he worked with Schelling and Hegel during that very year, 1796. The "Oldest Program" ends as follows:

> Until we make the ideas aesthetic, i.e., mythological, they will have no interest for the *people*; and conversely, until the mythology is rational, the philosopher will perforce be ashamed of it. Thus the enlightened and unenlightened must at long last clasp hands;

> mythology must become philosophical, and the people rational, while philosophy must become mythological, in order to make the philosophers sensuous. Then eternal unity will prevail among us. No more the contemptuous glance, no more the blind quaking of the people before their sages and priests. Only then can we expect the *equal* formation of *all* forces, in particular persons as well as among all individuals. No longer will any force be suppressed; universal freedom and equality of spirits will prevail!—A higher spirit, sent from heaven, will have to found this new religion among us; it will be the very last and the grandest of the works of humanity.[8]

One can see why Greek tragedy plays such an important role in Hölderlin's thinking and poetizing, despite the optimism concerning mythology expressed in both the "Oldest Program" and the fragment on "Religion." The myths or plots of the tragedies invariably involve the more tender relations of humankind, those delicate relations in which φιλία ought to prevail but in which betrayal and bloody conflict ensue. The fact that tragedy itself has a religious and cultic origin suggests that complications in the more tender relations are somehow endemic in human experience. Hölderlin senses what Nietzsche, Benjamin, Bataille, and Girard will develop more fully a century or more later, to wit, the realization that the winds of violence and cruelty blow from Paradise. Are the more tender relations therefore bound for a fall? Will the caresses of tenderness inevitably succumb to a monstrous cudgeling? Theoreticians of aggression would be impatient with me for even posing such a naive question. Theoreticians of tenderness will often have to bow to them. By "theoreticians of tenderness" I mean above all the psychoanalysts.

•

Because Hölderlin has placed so much weight on the words *zart, zärtlich, Zärtlichkeit,* I hope I may be forgiven for a brief but bracing dip into the Brothers Grimm, whose *Deutsches Wörterbuch* offers us dozens of pages on these words. They are old words, probably as old as the human need for tenderness. Yet we need not go back so far—five or six centuries will do for the moment.

The primary sense of the word *zart* in Middle High German up to the present is that it is a "caressing" word, *eine Liebkosung,* an expression or a

---

8 I cite "The Oldest Program toward a System in German Idealism" from the translation that appears in chapter 1 of TA, at 25–26 and 37–40.

gesture of "endearment." The adjective *zart* means "dear, beloved, esteemed." The Indo-Germanic root *der-, dereta* means "honored or esteemed," and is perhaps the root of "adored." A Medieval passion play translates the Father's words at the baptism of his Son, "This is my beloved Son" as *Diez ist min zarter sone.* Religious references to Maria and her tender son are quite common. *Zart* also comes to mean beautiful, fine, or graceful, whether in a beautiful human being or a delicate flower. Oddly, or perhaps predictably, the word suggests delicacy if it is spoken of a woman, whereas when spoken of a man it appears to mean *stattlich,* tall and strong. (Precisely what the Father means to say about his Son, therefore, is not entirely clear.) The word, taken in a more active sense, comes to mean the kind of gentle behavior or handling that such a beloved, tender, or delicate object or person requires, a caressing and protecting. The implication—and it was there right from the start, in the oldest usages, in spite of robust young men—is that the object or person in question is delicate or fragile, perhaps even feeble, sickly, easily damaged or wounded. In the mouth of a preacher, *zart* can even mean overindulged, spoiled, accustomed to the good life, *delicatus, mollis,* effeminate, or even given over to lust. Various parts of the human body are often singled out as being *zart,* especially the ears, the mouth, the hands, or the breasts of a woman. Hans Sachs says of a particular woman that her ears were so *zart* that they could not hear the truth. Schiller speaks of "the *zarten* spider's web of a deed." From this the sense develops of something easy to break apart, to pulverize, or to chew and digest, as in a "tender" piece of meat or a "delicacy" of any culinary kind. Even a sound can be tender: in his book on Mozart, Otto Jahn declares that the oboe is *zarter* than the clarinet. As we might expect, there are countless references to children, tender youths not yet so robust and graceful maids, so that *zart* comes to be identified with all that is slight or small. Tipping again toward the preacher's negative, the word also very early on suggests sensibility and sensitivity, even hypersensitivity and fastidiousness. Particularly interesting for Hölderlin's sense of the word is Bettine von Arnim's remark that the relations between a prince and his people are often *zart,* something that Novalis confirms in his essay *Glauben und Liebe,* which takes the king's love for his queen consort to be the model for his relation to the people. Yet the second of Novalis's aphorisms says that objects that are *zart* are easily "mishandled."[9] Finally, one hopes very

9 Novalis (Friedrich von Hardenberg), *Werke, Tagebücher und Briefe*, 3 vols., ed. Hans-Joachim Mähl and Richard Samuel (Munich: Carl Hanser Verlag, 1987), 2:290.

much that Goethe is referring to his barber when he says, "I had never felt a *zarteres* knife on my cheek."

The word *zärtlich*, which is the basis for Hölderlin's uses of the word in the comparative, is a more recent form, often elided with other adjectives or participles in order to suggest a more delicate or tender version of the modifier. *Zärtlichdenkend* is "thinking tenderly" or "thinking tender thoughts"; Hölderlin himself writes of his *zärtlichbebend Herz*, "my tenderly quaking heart," a heart that is also *zärtlichpflegend*, "tenderly caring for" someone. Antigone is for Hölderlin the *zärtlichernste* heroine, "tenderly earnest," ever so young and delicate and yet so serious! The number of these combination words is quite astonishing; it is as though deeds and actions are often so harsh that they have need of a more tender application.

As for the noun *Zärtlichkeit*, which becomes common only in late Middle High German, it often refers to loveliness or charm, beauty or grace. The older, more negative senses of luxury, effeminacy, or excessive ease diminish in use, as do the senses of frailty and hypersensitivity. The sole remaining meaning by the eighteenth century, and that means by both Hölderlin's and Freud's lifetimes, is "that which evokes a feeling or expression of love or some lesser inclination." A poet has the nightingale "teaching her *Zärtlichkeit* to the glade." Goethe calls the moon "Sister of the first light, / Image of a *Zärtlichkeit* in mourning!" The word is often used to name family relations, especially those between parents and children or brothers and sisters. Just as often, however, it refers to lovers. Wieland writes, "He had her friendship, now he desired her *Zärtlichkeit*." Finally, the Brothers Grimm note that in the plural *Zärtlichkeiten* (now more likely to be translated as "caresses" than as "tendernesses") are sometimes desired as expressions of love and sometimes despised as unwanted liberties taken. The ambivalence of *Zärtlichkeiten* is something well known, however, to the psychoanalysts.

•

How strange to find in a dictionary of psychoanalytic concepts, alongside articles on all the technical jargon of psychoanalysis, a long article on "tenderness," precisely this same *Zärtlichkeit*! The good doctors, it seems, have to drop their stainless steel implements for a moment and palpate peaches—gingerly. It is an awkward moment for them, and I ought not to poke fun: their predicament is surely my own. Tenderness or *Zärtlichkeit*—for it is still Hölderlin's word that is being used—plays a key role in Freud's three *Contributions to the Psychology of Lovelife* (1910–1918). One does well to reread these three pieces ("On a Particular

Type of Object Choice in Males," 1910; "On the Most General Degradation of Lovelife," 1912; and "The Taboo of Virginity," 1918), and to read them with an eye to *Zärtlichkeit* (GW 8:69–91 and 12:159–80). What I say here will not gather all the references to "tenderness" together—there are too many of them.

How better to begin than with the definitions provided by Laplanche and Pontalis's *Vocabulary of Psychoanalysis* (LP 639–40)? They begin their article on tenderness by defining the opposition of tenderness to sensuality; these are the two "streams" that Freud says must converge if there is to be a river of genital love. Whereas sensuality finds its objects only after puberty, tenderness is there from the start in the child's dependence on its caretaker for nourishment and the restoration of comfort—the mother or nurse who extends the breast and changes, bathes, and soothes the infant. Even during puberty the stream of tenderness may continue to prevail, populated by representatives of the primary object choice (the caretaker-mother). The "properly sexual stream," the "sensual" stream, normally joins the stream of tenderness during adolescence. Only gradually can this more wild stream be tamed, and even then only if the object choices can be felt to be exemplars of the primary object choice. It is not too much to say that this gradual return to tenderness may be, and perhaps most often is, frustrated. To see why requires that we take a closer look at Freud's *Contributions to the Psychology of Lovelife*.[10]

Both the neurotic and the normal male, asserts Freud in the first of the three *Contributions*, choose the ones they love largely "on the basis of the infantile fixation on the tenderness of the mother" (GW 8:70). As the newborn's head may remain elongated weeks after the birth, due to the pressure of the birth canal, however, so too the grownup who seeks love is shaped by the mother—that bizarre parallel is Freud's own: we lurch through the world like J. D. Salinger's "Laughing Man," our elongated, grimacing faces desiring the mother and fearing the father, whom we hope to make "the damaged third," that is, the competitor who will be squeezed out. The term *Oedipus Complex*

10 An error in the German edition of Laplanche and Pontalis (639, ll. 6–7 from the bottom) is not without interest: after describing the stream of *Zärtlichkeit*, the text goes on to designate its *Gegensatz*—but it inadvertently repeats the word *zärtliche*, calling the "tender" stream "the properly sexual stream." Indeed, it seems problematic to assert that the sexual stream is the "opposite" of the tender stream. Most of the great river systems—one thinks of both the Rhine and the Danube—have a double source, but it is lovely to dream that the stream of tenderness continues to flow in sexual life. Freud's essay on "degradation" is about to shatter that dream, however.

appears as such for the first time in this essay (GW 8:73). Oddly, however, Freud soon speaks of a "parental complex," inasmuch as the child's feelings of tenderness may extend to the father as well as the mother. Freud cites the common fantasy of the child's *rescuing* the father, in order thus to repay him for the gift of life. He concludes with the astonishing statement, "All drives—the tender, the grateful, the lascivious, the spiteful, the self-aggrandizing—are satisfied by the single wish *to be one's own father*" (GW 8:75, Freud's emphasis). This total identification with the father, thought from *within* the Oedipus Complex or perhaps already *beyond* it, challenges the centrality of competition with and elimination of the paternal interloper. Freud concedes, albeit cautiously: "Occasionally, the fantasy of rescuing the father also contains a tender sense" (8:76). Perhaps more than "occasionally," we might object. That fantasy—the child's rescue of the father—expresses the desire to grant the mother a son who is just like the father who is just like the mother, which is to say, tender, *zärtlich*. No doubt, with the "parental complex" Freud is already thinking of the origins of religion—with all its stern fathers and suffering sons in search of the tender mother.

There is so much emphasis in psychoanalysis on the murder of the father by the sons—think of the "primal horde" of *Totem and Taboo*, so remarkably different from Hölderlin's vision of the cohesive community of life—that it seems advisable to pause here. Not much is said or written here or anywhere else, in either Freud or Lacan as far as I am aware, about these feelings of tenderness toward the father. Our writers of fiction—think of Kafka or Philip Roth or Paul Auster—always let such feelings shine through their work, but not our scientists of the soul. Surely, one of the most common frustrations in the life of a man or woman—though who can compile a statistic in this regard?—is the inability to express tenderness felt toward the father. Psychoanalysis has so primed us for battle, so honed the sacrificial blade, that we are undone theoretically, practically, and emotionally by the plea that the tender feelings be recognized for what they are. And, yes, what *are* they? When in 1925 Freud writes about the psychological consequences of the anatomical differences between the sexes, he stresses the bisexual, jointly active-passive character of the prehistory of the Oedipus Complex in the male (GW 14:21). "Tender identification with the father" will also turn out to be central to Freud's understanding (and critique) of religion, which from Augustine to President Schreber adopts what Freud calls a "feminine position" vis-is the father. Freud would observe that it is surely no accident that Hölderlin focuses on "the more tender relations" in an essay on religion. When in the thirty-third of the *New Introductory Lectures* (GW

15:125) Freud traces the role of tenderness in *female* development, he discovers that tender relations play an equally important role in a woman's life: a girl's tender pre-Oedipal connection with her mother is decisive, says Freud, for the future of femininity—regardless of all the intervening battles. In fact, however, when it comes to tenderness, men and women move in two opposed vectors or ecstases of temporality: while men look back to the past with nostalgia, dreaming of a return to the Golden Age of intrauterine existence or of the breast, women look ahead to *Zärtlichkeit* as to their authentic future. Tenderness is the existential desideratum of womankind and the having-been of the thrown male. In what present, one must wonder, could they ever meet?

Perhaps I am making too much of the role of tenderness in the downfall of the Oedipus Complex. Yet I am doing so for the sake of Hölderlin's *Zärtlichkeit* and for the project that Lacan calls *The Ethics of Psychoanalysis* and Irigaray *The Ethics of Sexual Difference.* On to Freud's central essay, then, for it is also central to my tender rant. The theory of the two streams of genital love, the tender and the sensual, finds its clearest expression in "On the Most General Degradation of Lovelife" (GW 8:79–80). The tender stream flows from the earliest childhood years, silting the banks of a life that survives only because of the nurture and care provided by maternal—and perhaps occasionally paternal—figures. As Freud emphasizes in "The Decline of the Oedipus Complex," sexual drives or erotic components, still inchoate and amorphous, are swept along in the tender stream throughout the period of latency (GW 13:399, 401). The ego too is shaped by the banks of this stream: recall the primal scene, not of the Wolfman case, but of the 1895 *Project Toward a Scientific Psychology*, for which the human being's survival depends on the primitive ego's ability to recognize in the lateral view of the breast the promise of the full moon and solar disc that has fed it, that is, the nipple and aureole in full-front view. Furthermore, Freud's 1914 "Narcissism" essay acknowledges in the primary narcissism of the primal object choice the essential role of tenderness. If the stream of tenderness dries up, the ego lies gasping on the strand. Moreover, in the 1925 anatomical differences essay, it is the *superego* that is developed through identification with the parents—the superego and all its "tender stirrings," *zärtliche Regungen* (GW 13:399). Thus, any theory of ego or superego, consciousness or conscience, indeed, any theory of the self, has to take the theme of tenderness with the utmost seriousness.

At puberty, the sexual goal of the erotic components of the tender stream announces itself. Or, to stay with the two-stream metaphor, the stream of sensuality must now flow into or out of the stream of tenderness. Staying with the metaphor is difficult, however, for even when we speak of sensuality and of explicit genital-sexual goals we are still talking about the larger stream of primordial tenderness. The banks of the stream are slippery, because tenderness characterizes the all-encompassing Okeanos, what Hölderlin calls the sea of memory. True, the stream of tenderness now eddies about parents and siblings in a new way, a deliciously forbidden way, as though tenderness were suddenly a name for libido as such. The incest prohibition requires that the stream rush on by, however, seeking extrafamilial objects for its flood. The new objects are still modeled on the primary one—for what paradigm could there be other than the parental? And if all goes well, "with the passage of time" such objects will draw to themselves the tenderness that was once identified with the mother (GW 8:80–81). Presumably, the extrafamilial objects will be perfect embodiments of both streams, or of the one great Ganges of tender sensuality: "The supreme degree of sensual infatuation will bring with it supreme psychic esteem" (GW 8:81), which is esteem for the source of all tenderness, the source of *la seule tendresse*.

At this juncture, however, Freud begins to recount all the things that can and usually do go wrong at the confluence of these two streams, the two streams that must be but one—the great Nile of libido, or perhaps the Mississippi of tenderness joined by the mighty Ohio of sensuality. Who will wish to follow him as he abandons the confluence and lights out for the marshlands of neurosis? Degradation of love life occurs when tenderness, bound up with feelings toward the nurturing mother and caring father, has to be sacrificed to a sensuality that needs a disgraced and belittled object for its satisfaction, an object that is strikingly different from the revered (and forbidden) nurturer. But is the prohibition of incest an adequate explanation of such a need? Or is some other form of repression involved here, a repression powerful enough to serve up the bitter brew of Eros and revulsion? Perhaps some form of misogyny plays a regrettable role here? Allow me, then, a brief, unhappy excursus on misogyny.

•

Is misogyny a mere symptom or the seed of the suppression of tenderness in our culture? Is it the mere result of the father's claim on the mother, who is the source of tenderness, or does it represent a still more potent prohibition? Is our culture, at least when viewed in terms of its principal religions, all about slurring Mary Magdalene in order to downplay the humanity of Jesus and thus to shore up the authority of Paul's and Constantine's church? In part, yes, no doubt, and fans of Dan Brown's *Da Vinci Code* can justly rage at a culture that for all its glitz and glamour remains militantly Puritan. But what is the relationship of our particular forms of misogyny to the overwhelming scarcity of tenderness in all the corners of our earth? Is misogyny but one strand of an apparently infinitely replicable misanthropy that is worldwide? And even in our own corner of the globe, why the attempted transfer of maternal tenderness to stories of fathers, sons, and paracletes, exclusive of womankind? Why the relegation of the mother to virginity, and virginity to pale blue chill? And why do other portions of the globe, other corners and cultures, often fail as dismally as we do? Perhaps I should stay in our own little corner, however, and remark further on one of the founders of our own perverse tradition.

The whole of Augustine's *Confessions* is an altar erected in memory of Monica, Augustine's nurturing mother. It should therefore be a book that is grateful to and gracious toward "the more tender relations." However, there is in the mother a trace of everything that is wrong with womankind since Eve. Indeed, Augustine calls his mother "a reliquary of Eve," *reliquarium Evae* (AC 5:8), and this presence of Eve in his otherwise saintly mother troubles the son. Her tears create the salt sea on which he sails to Rome and his conversion, but the ground beneath her is invariably swampy because of those same tears. She wants to hold on to him, does not want to let him go to Rome, so that he has to slip away in the night like a fugitive. Does she not know—she who has labored first to bear him and then, relentlessly, to convert him, she who sent his concubine, the mother of his son, back to Africa so that he could finally cleanse himself of "the birdlime of concupiscence" (AC 10:30)—does she of all people not recognize that he must be about his *father*'s business? The relic of Eve in the reliquary that is Monica is precisely her tenderness toward her son, her doting on him, her almost animal possessiveness with regard to her son. He calls it her *carnal* love of him, *illius carnale desiderium*, and he relates it directly to her having given birth to him (ibid.). Her carnal attachment to him from the time he passed through the birth canal, trailing the cord behind him, makes Augustine feel clammy, as though he needs a second cleansing. She is in the end a woman, a marshland, a morass. And she does have a drinking problem; the translators put it delicately when they say she is a "wine bibber" (9:8). Wine and tears and incessant mothering—all that liquidity! How disconcerting! How much better it would be if Monica were blue chill! To be fair, however, her predominant hue, in her son's estimation, is cobalt: Augustine praises his mother for the way she tolerated her husband's (Augustine's father's) abuse of her in bed, *toleravit cubilis iniurias* (9:9). How the son knows about this abuse is an arresting question, and Freud would have puzzled over it for some time, no doubt, inasmuch as birdlime sticks.

In contrast to all this, Schelling, the greatest of the German Idealists, in his Berlin lectures on the philosophy of mythology says that the femininity that can be both furious and tender is encrypted in the very names of the deity in all the great world religions. Yah-weh and Al-lah alike consist of male and female names and natures, designating not a monolithic male god but an initial pair of figures. Jehovah contains a suppressed reference to Melecheth Haschamaim, the Queen of Heaven, and Dionysos is forever united with Urania, who is pregnant with him. Herodotus says that for the Arabs, Dionysos/Urania is god, in the singular. Schelling writes, expanding on Herodotus, that if the Arabs call Dionysos Urotal and Urania Al-Ilat, then the first is Ulod-Allat, namely, the child Allah, and the second is his mother, the goddess (II/2:256). If he were alive today, of course, Schelling would have a price on his head because of this revelation. It is life-threatening to expose blue chill to the white heat of the desires and needs of fragile human beings.

Why tenderness, then, which always seems to revert to figures of the feminine, even when it arises in men? Why not try to squelch this need that is as insatiable and as dangerous as desire? Indeed, tenderness seems to cross the lines of Lacan's distinction between need and desire. It seems to have as much to do with the symbolic as the imaginary, and one might even wonder, granted its role in the survival of the subject and of the species, whether it is the essence of the real. The cooing of the mother, as though she herself were a dove, such cooing being a communication prior to all language, singing the desire of the other, the other as the (m)other who responds to this round lump of sweet skin and tender flesh—how can one possibly avoid the importance of tenderness for what Lacan would call "the whole structure" of his thought?

Well, then, tenderness, ineluctably and inevitably, whatever the ravages of misogyny. Tenderness loves what is most alive, to paraphrase Hölderlin, who is referring to Socrates's love of Acibiades. We must accept our inclination toward it, submit to it, entering willingly into its yoke. One of the most tender songs of Carl Orff's *Carmina burana*, sung by the soprano to minimal accompaniment, sings of this yoke as though in defiance of an august Augustinian tradition:

> In trutina mentis dubia,
> Fluctuant contraria,
> Lascivus amor et pudicitia.
> Sed eligo quod video:
> Collum ad iugum prebeo.
> Ad iugum tamen suave, suave transeo.

On the scales of my doubting heart,
Shifting this way and that,
Harness of love, hairshirt of shame.
But I choose what I can see:
I offer my neck to the yoke.
Into the yoke, then, tenderly, tenderly I go.

•

Let us return to Freud's prosaic "Degradation" essay, however, in order to conclude. *The most general degradation of lovelife* is a name for civilization as we know it, with all its discomfitures. Tenderness is relegated to whatever seems to have no erotic impact: puppydogtails and mother's day cards and love of country, even if the country excels in killing. In *Civilization and Its Discontents*, Freud says that *aggression* forms "the sediment [*Bodensatz*] of all tender and loving relationships," with perhaps one exception, namely, the love of a mother for her male child (GW 14:473). By 1929–30 in Freud's work, the tenderness of father-son relations seems a thing of the past. Yet in the 1936 letter to Romain Rolland ("A Disturbance of Memory on the Acropolis"), which admittedly does not use the word *Zärtlichkeit,* is it not possible to speculate that beyond all the guilt that is bound up with one's having surpassed one's father, indeed, beyond both the idealization of and contempt for the father, something like tenderness toward his life and his struggles is expressed? Freud and his brother have "come a long way" in order to stand in awe before the Parthenon, a building their father never saw. Yet the path there did not require the murder of their father—a father whom Freud reports to have been of a gentle disposition, like one of the sweeter characters out of Dickens.[11]

The divergence of the two streams of tenderness and sensual excitement is nothing new. It was best captured in Plato's *Symposium* with the speech of Pausanias, who distinguishes between a heavenly and an earthly Aphrodite. Heavenly Aphrodite is purely Uranian: she has no mother and no relation to the female, although this is an odd circumstance for Aphrodite. The split between the two streams or the two goddesses requires that the feminine vanish from the mother and that the mother vanish from terrestrial being. Tenderness and

---

11 See Ernest Jones, *The Life and Work of Sigmund Freud,* ed. Lionel Trilling and Steven Marcus (Harmondsworth, England: Pelican Books, 1964), 32.

nurturance proceed, as the maudlin Irishman at the pub loves to murmur, from "my sainted mother," which means from a woman who is always already disembodied and dead. Freud writes here as a prophet of our times and our world: "Where they love, they do not desire, and where they desire, they cannot love." *Wo sie lieben, begehren sie nicht, und wo sie begehren, können sie nicht lieben* (GW 8:82). These words, embroidered in pink and powder blue on white linen and framed in gilt, are nailed over the doorway to every bedroom in the Western world, and perhaps not only in the Western world. You will tell me that we have moved on, things are better now, and I will want to believe you. But Freud is so unkind. He speaks of our *wenig verfeinertes Liebesleben,* a lovelife that is relatively unrefined, inasmuch as the refinements stem from a tenderness that inclines toward what Freud otherwise calls "inversion" or "perversion" (GW 8:83). And we educated and refined ones, in spite of what we believe, are the worst off: the streams of tenderness and sensuality trickle in opposite directions through the desert of our lives, says Freud (GW 8:85). Our ethics and our aesthetics alike are dry-as-dust: parched as we are, we simply cannot give over, or give ourselves up, to tender love. Degradation and humiliation have spread to such a degree that Freud himself speculates—in those two devastating footnotes on organic repression at the beginning and at the end of chapter 4 of *Civilization and Its Discontents*—that our erect bodies, removed from the redolent earth and busy with all the vertical tasks our culture assigns us, cannot bend over either stream in order to imbibe. All we have to do to see the Death Valley of our lives is to stand up. Or to look down and see that we are born, as Augustine says, *inter urinas et faeces* (GW 8:90).

The role of tenderness in the third *Contribution,* "The Taboo of Virginity," is every bit as important, and it would allow me to say more about these matters from a feminine point of view—if such a thing were possible for me, beyond the necessity to listen to wise friends. In any case, we will have to return to this essay in the second part of the present book, inasmuch as Derrida will take us through a very punishing reading of blood flow and virginity—blood flow and a woman's revenge—in which not tenderness but cruelty is the theme.

Yet now that Augustine has brought us back to dirty diapers, it seems a good place to remember Hölderlin on religion and to bring this chapter to a close. Of course, this is only the beginning. Psychoanalysis has so much more to tell us about tenderness, both in Freud's texts and beyond. Consider the following passage from Gaston Bachelard. One might object to the term *dialectic* as Bachelard uses it here in order to elaborate on an idea of Carl Jung's, but his insistence on a *double* tenderness—rather than a sole tenderness—ought to give us pause. Indeed, it seems to conform to Freud's own most considered reflections on male and female:

> In the psychiatrists' clinics, in spite of all the anomalies, the man-woman dialectic remains bulwarked by traits in too sharp contrast. Under the two signs of the physiological sexual division, man seems to divide himself too brutally for anyone to initiate a psychology of tenderness, of the double tenderness, the tenderness of *animus* and the tenderness of *anima.* And that is why, in a desire not to fall victim to simplistic physiological designations, the psychologists of the depths have been led to speak of the *anima-animus* dialectic, a dialectic which permits greater nuance in psychological studies than the strict male-female opposition.[12]

Can we, through a new devotion to myth and story, as Hölderlin would urge, associate with one another in a spirit of greater tenderness? What are we to make of the recalcitrant fact that the two streams are really one, that *la seule tendresse* itself implies and implicates *une seule sensualité,* and in both men and women alike? Can there be a tenderness *with* sensuality that may prevail in civilization beyond all our disquiet? Will we be able to stop killing each other and ourselves?

One of the brightest lights of Freud's *Contributions,* it seems to me, is its exposition of the possibility of tenderness felt toward the father, the supposed source of prohibition and negativity. If the very name of negativity—Lacan's *nom [non!] du père,* the name and the *no!* of the father—can be gently challenged by the desire to rescue, to express gratitude, which Hölderlin says is the source of mindfulness and memory, is there not some hope that through gratitude we can find spirit in its fleshly element and under its mortal aspect? Meister Eckhart, in a passage remembered by Schelling, acknowledges that the desire to rescue requires that we let go of God. That is what Nietzsche means when he says in *Twilight of the Idols* that the only thing we have to learn is that there is no one out there to blame for our being what we are (KSW 6:96–97). Such releasement, Meister Eckhart's *Gelassenheit,* would mean, as Camus knew, not

---

12 Gaston Bachelard, *The Poetics of Reverie: Childhood, Language, and the Cosmos,* tr. Daniel Russell (Boston: Beacon Press, 1971 [Presses Universitaires de France, 1960]), 66. The passage was pointed out to me some years ago by Dr. Elizabeth Sikes, whom I thank for it.

that "everything is permitted," but that no violence receives official sanction. No fatwas, no preemptive strikes.

When we see in what atavisms we are still mired today all across the globe, but particularly in the United States, tender releasement seems impossibly remote. The empathy and association that ought to be fed precisely by the limitation of our individual notions—the conviviality that is Hölderlin's most fervent hope—all of this seems unreachable. The embittered world lurches to the right and rises on swells of aggression, waves that could make the excesses of the past century seem a prelude rather than a final act. Against all this, the only stream that promises to take us forward is the single stream of tender sensuality. And yet even our learned institutions dam(n) the stream, regard it as a cause for litigation, punishment, mindless aggression. That may be because we learned ones are the least prepared to revel in the stream that carries us along; we are so terrified of drowning that we opt for desiccation. That is why Irigaray's voice is so refreshing. When that voice speaks of *la seule tendresse*, of moisture and of the mucous membranes where tenderness is at home, one hears it even in the cry of the son or daughter who would rescue the father, or in the banging of that cane on the shutters of a brother's room, a brother one cannot bear to lose.

Fear of failure? What have *I* got to lose? I have nothing to lose but my authority and dignity, and what are authority and dignity in the face of the opportunity to become more tender, to practice a less defensive tenderness, perchance to change the world in the only way that ever did or ever will make a difference? For, even if tenderness exposes us to risk, the default of sensual, sensitive, and tender caresses guarantees the onset of tragedy.

Chapter Two

Homer's *Iliad*, Hölderlin's *Briseiad*

With your gentle heart and your gentle words.

—Homer, *Iliad*, 24:826

IS IT ENTIRELY MAD to look for tenderness beneath the walls of Troy, where warriors cudgel and kill one another? Everything points in the direction of madness. Surely, the warriors' focus on glory and the spoils of war, on the distribution of "prizes," excludes an emotion as fragile as tenderness? Sheila Murnaghan, in her comprehensive and insightful introduction to Stanley Lombardo's brilliant translation of Homer's *Iliad*, tells us about the overwhelming significance of κῦδος during the Mycenean Age, the tradition by which "glory" or "renown" is guaranteed principally by a fitting distribution of the "prizes" of war. The context is Agamemnon's bitterness over the loss of Chryseïs, the daughter of the Chryse, priest of Apollo. For when Agamemnon rudely rejects the father's plea that his daughter be returned to him, Chryse prays that his god, Sminthian Apollo, Apollo the Rat, shoot arrows of disease into the Greek camp. At first the pack animals die, then the heroes. The council meets and decides that Chryseïs must be returned to her father unharmed and accompanied by impressive gifts and sacrifices. Agamemnon thus forfeits his "prize," and, in order to defend his position as king and warrior-in-chief of the Achaeans, he declares that Achilles' "prize," Briseïs, must by way of compensation be handed over to him. This is the event that triggers the tale we know as the *Iliad*, which could therefore equally as well be titled the *Chryseiad*, or, in keeping with the importance of the wrath of Achilles for the epic, the *Briseiad*. Murnaghan comments:

> The desperate reactions of both heroes to the threat of losing a prize show how fully their sense of self is bound up in these external

> marks of honor. They know themselves in large part through their social status, which is created and expressed in public settings. Furthermore, as Sarpedon's speech makes clear [12:320–42], these prizes acquire added value from their supremely high price: the heroes' willingness to risk their lives every time they enter battle. The conflict between Achilles and Agamemnon also shows how hard it can be to apportion honor in a way that satisfies everyone. (xxiv)[1]

Is Briseïs, then, no more than a token in "the acceptable distribution of booty" (ibid.)? Briseïs—is she merely one of Achilles's prizes or is she *beloved* of Achilles? External mark of honor or heart's flame? Trophy wife—horrid expression, equal only to a former vice-presidential hopeful's "First Dude" and to a more recent but equally vulgar presidential instance—or intimate friend?

Chryseïs, Briseïs—it is perhaps the problem of Helen all over again. Murnaghan herself usually refers to the abduction of Helen by Paris precisely as that: Paris's "theft" of Helen. At a perhaps unguarded moment Murnaghan writes of Helen's "having long regretted her impulsive desertion of Menelaus for Paris" (ibid.), potentially rekindling the ancient war between the eulogists of Helen and her maledictors. Normally, of course, the blame for Helen's "impulse" is placed on Aphrodite, who repays an old debt to Paris by procuring for him the most beautiful woman in the world. Yet Helen is almost as old as Aphrodite herself, worshipped in Arcadia as the goddess of love, so that blaming Aphrodite, a common enough contrivance, does not really help. The truth is that we are not certain whom we should blame for extravagant beauty and its often untoward effects.

To put it in more formal terms: we may be certain that Love and Strife (ἔρως and ἔρις) are linked, and that the erotic and the combative are joined together, as the Empedoclean φιλία and νεῖκος are contained in a single sphere. Yet are we certain what ἔρως is, or about its other linkages? Are we also certain that tenderness—apart from Achilles's eventual acceptance of Priam's plea for the body of his son and Achilles's love of Patroclus—plays no role in Homer's

---

1 I cite Homer's *Iliad* by page number in the translation by Stanley Lombardo (Indianapolis: Hackett, 1997); sometimes I cite by song number and lines of verse, as above with 12:320–42. For the Greek text I have used the fifth Tusculum edition, *Ilias*, with a German translation by Hans Rupé (Munich: Heimeran Verlag, 1974).

Iliad, even if we dare to call it Homer's *Briseiad*, or in Achilles's life? Let us take a closer look.

It cannot be a question of confusing the Mycenean Age, symbolized by the rivalry between Agamemnon and Achilles, with the Romantic era of philosophy and literature in modern Europe. Whatever Hölderlin makes of Achilles, we may feel certain that it is not Homer's Achilles—even though Hölderlin has an affinity for the ancient Greeks that surpasses that of just about anyone. Nevertheless, the age of chivalry in modern Western Europe has passed, and the warrior ethic is in collapse long before the Age of Romanticism and Hölderlin. Cervantes's *Don Quixote* and Shakespeare's *Troilus and Cressida* are evidence enough of that. No doubt κῦδος, the Achaean warrior's glory and renown, has everything to do with the distribution of captives as prizes, and not with tender sentiments. Yet perhaps the high value of such prizes—especially if they be the offspring of priests and princes—involves something that *après coup* turns into tenderness or abides side-by-side with tenderness? We are understandably reluctant to admit such a thing. "Tenderness" sounds like treason and betrayal, both a public and a private sin—especially on the part of the victim—and it also sounds highly unlike both the warrior and the warrior's prey. And yet. If, as Murnaghan rightly says, Achilles "goes to great lengths to protest his loss of Briseïs," can we be certain that this has to do only with Briseïs's representing "the honor which is his only compensation for the likely loss of his life" (xxviii)? In the case of Agamemnon and Chryseïs, Murnaghan concedes that "Agamemnon refuses the ransom offered him by Chryses because it does not seem to him adequate to the value he places on Chryseïs, who is to him not just an exchangeable sign of honor but a woman he cares for" (xli). Yet if such "caring for" is true of Agamemnon, who is all about status and rank and recognition, and whose "caring for" his daughter Iphigeneia did not shield her from the sacrificial blade, it is surely equally or even more true of Achilles. Our last sight of Achilles at the end of the epic is of the hero—not yet dead, hence not yet immortal—asleep in his tent "with Briseïs at his side" (xlii). That vision, as Murnaghan eventually concedes, may involve more than Achilles's immortal glory as a prizewinner. It could be the victory, after so much bloodshed caused by Zeus's revenge on heroic humankind, of a more tender deity. Perhaps the Greeks were not entirely foolish to worship Aphrodite? Murnaghan, contrasting Homer's *Iliad* with other ancient epics, remarks on the "unremitting insistence on the constraints of mortal existence and the inescapability of death" for the Greeks (lviii). My only question, and it is a question, is whether even in the cruelest hostilities of *The Iliad*, when Death wields its cudgel, there is something like an ineluctable tenderness that shines through.[2]

Let us examine Hölderlin's Achilles first of all, Achilles with Briseïs, and then turn to Homer's *Iliad*. This may be a mere trick by which I hope to allow Hölderlin's tenderness to infiltrate the ancient text. Yet why do we fear so intensely this tender subversion?

The great poet Hölderlin writes a poem called "Achilles" in early spring 1799. This is about six months after the love of his life, if such a cliché may be uttered, Susette Gontard, who is no cliché, has been taken away from him. Not yet by death, which would strike her in three years' time, but by an aggrieved husband who reclaims his right of possession. Here is a rough rendering of Hölderlin's "Achilles":

> Splendid son of gods! when you lost the one you loved,
> You went to the ocean's rim, wept aloud into the flood,
> Lamenting, your heart plunging into the depths of the holy abyss,
> Into the stillness. There, far from the embattled ships,
> Far beneath the waves, in a peaceful grotto, azure Thetis
> Dwelled, she who protected you, goddess of the sea.
> Mother she was to the young man, this powerful goddess;
> In earlier days on the rocky coast of the island she suckled
> The boy lovingly, nourished him on the mighty song of the waves,
> Dipped him in the bath that lent him the strength of heroes.
> And the mother heard the youth's lament, ascended mournfully
> From the seabed like a puff of cloud that climbs the sky;

2 My counterposing *The Briseiad* with *The Iliad* may be related to Robert Graves's account of "The Wrath of Achilles," which is the poem, he argues, on which Homer bases his epic poem. The quarrels among the Achaean warriors, Graves contends, "are so unedifying, and all of the Greek leaders behave so murderously, deceitfully, and shamelessly, while the Trojans by contrast behave so well, that it is obvious on whose side the author's sympathy lay" (RG 2:311). Thus, the singer of "The Wrath of Achilles," and perhaps Homer himself, rather than being the author of an Achaean national anthem, is a "legatee of the Minoan court bards" (ibid.). As such, that author would be a devotee of the Great Mother of Asia. That would explain why the Olympian deities, newcomers as they are, and contemptible newcomers, as Xenophanes of Colophon never wearied of complaining, behave so outrageously. It might also explain why goddesses of love and tenderness may play a vital (though perhaps surreptitious) role in the epic.

With tender embrace she stilled the pains of her darling boy,
    And he heard the sweet nothings that meant she would help him.
Son of gods! would that I were like you, for then I could sing
    My secret suffering with confidence to one of the celestials.
I will not see that happen. I must bear humiliation, as though I belonged
    No more to her, though she's the one my tears remember,
You good gods! you who hear every human being who pleads with you.
    Ah! I have been loving you, holy light, intensely and so fervently,
Since the day I was born, and you, earth, with your fonts and forests;
    Father Aither, all too longingly and purely this heart of mine
Has felt you—oh, you who are beneficent, assuage my suffering,
    Lest the soul in me lose its tongue all too soon,

According to D. E. Sattler and Michael Knaupp (CHV 1:200, 3:108), the poem breaks off here, whereas a prose sketch from Hölderlin's hand contains several more lines. Friedrich Beißner and Jochen Schmidt (DKV 1:213) print these final lines as though Hölderlin himself had inserted them, but apparently it was Hölderlin's first important editor, Christof Theodor Schwab, who in 1846 completed the poem by versifying the final lines of the prose sketch:

That I may live and give you thanks, exalted powers of heaven,
    Thanking you all the fleeting day with fervent song,
For the good things that once were, joys of my vanished youth,
    And then in kindness take the lonely one to you.

The awkwardness of the final line, which is a part of the prose sketch, cannot be blamed on the poet—who stops writing the poem at the mere mention of his soul's loss of voice, *Daß die Seele mir nicht allzufrühe verstummt. . . .* The poet's struggle to maintain the piety of his youth, along with his lifelong struggle to make do without a mother who might embrace him and nurse him tenderly, murmuring sweet nothings, remains unresolved. At all events, the mourning that pervades the poem has to do with two women who are in various ways gone from Hölderlin's life, as Briseïs was gone from Achilles's life, but in other ways still all too present—his pious and parsimonious mother, Frau Gok, and his love, Susette Gontard. He had been separated from the latter after a terrible scene involving Susette's husband, the father of the boy Hölderlin had been tutoring at the Gontard household. As for his mother, Hölderlin had written her three months earlier a long and decisive letter (CHV 2:733–39), the letter we call his "confession," in which he makes it clear to her that he will never become the pastor she insists he become—indeed, his words against the "Pharisaic" church are harsh—and that he will devote his life to poetry. He was still waiting for a reply. Frau Gok was no Thetis.[3]

The image of Achilles receiving divine assistance from his mother, who promises to help him regain his beloved, is therefore doubly humiliating to Hölderlin, so that the elegy shifts to lamentation with the outcry, "Would that I were like you." Whereas Achilles's plaint is heard, the poet's will not be. And how could the pious Frau Gok help her son to rejoin an adulteress? The elegy is replete with words of maternal tenderness: azure Thetis dwells in a peaceful grotto, and she is acclaimed as his protectress (*die dich schützte*); the mighty goddess was a mother to him, lovingly suckling him (*liebend gesäugt*). She is full of mourning (*trauernd*) for her son, not only because of his loss but because of her own impending loss of him, and she rises from the sea in order to "still" his pain with a "tender embrace." The verb *Stillen* is of course the usual word for breastfeeding, so that the maternal aspect of the tender embrace is once again emphasized. She promises to help her son, promises "flatteringly," here translated as "with sweet nothings" (*schmeichelnd*). It is an odd word to use here: one usually flatters someone's vanity, not their distress. Yet if one's mother is a goddess, there may be a kind of condescension involved in her promising to help, and even the great Greek hero would have to be flattered by such a mother. However, the Old High German form from which the verb *schmeicheln* comes, *smeih*, means a loving embrace, once again *eine Liebkosung.* It is a very physical word, expressing not simply spoken words but actions, touches, such as those of a cat—*eine Schmeichelkatze*—between one's legs. Goethe uses the word in both this positive and the modern negative sense. Thetis's "sweet nothings" are therefore her embraces and pettings of her son. She thus serves as a striking contrast to the mother who never was one for embraces but also as a likeness of Susette Gontard, the mother of four who once wrote to Hölderlin that she wished her children had been his.

Yet there are reasons more internal to the *Iliad*, as Hölderlin reads it, to assert the presence of the tenderness that we normally would not associate with Achilles. Christa Wolff's *Cassandra* calls him "Achilles the beast," *Achilles*

---

3 In the collected correspondence, the "confession" to his mother comes nestled in between the third and fourth letters from Susette Gontard, a thorn between two roses. On the relationship between Hölderlin and Susette Gontard, see Douglas F. Kenney and Sabine Menner-Bettscheid, *The Recalcitrant Art: Diotima's Letters to Hölderlin and Related Missives* (Albany: State University of New York Press, 2000).

das Vieh, as an enemy princess might well do, but surely she is not alone in denigrating the greatest of the Achaean warriors—the most athletic, the most choleric, yes, but the most tender? Let me in defense of my thesis present two fragments of an epistolary essay on Achilles that Hölderlin intended to publish in his proposed journal, *Iduna* (DKV 2:510–11; CHV 2:64–65):

> I am happy that you spoke of Achilles. He is my favorite among the heroes, so strong and tender [*so stark und zart*], the most successful and the most transitory of all the blossoms of the heroic world. According to Homer, he was "born to live but a brief time," precisely because he was so beautiful. I might almost think that the ancient poet allows him to appear in action so rarely, allowing all the others to clash and shout while his hero sits in his tent, in order to profane him as little as possible in the chaos surrounding Troy. Homer had plenty of things to depict concerning Ulysses. Ulysses is a sack of copper pennies, which take a long time to count; one finishes counting much more quickly when it's gold.

The oxymoron or aprosdoketon *so stark und zart* says it all. For Hölderlin, Achilles wields the lyre as well as the cudgel. True, he weeps before his mother but he also taunts Hector, touches the tender bodies of Patroclus and Briseïs but also drags the corpse of Hector around the walls of Troy. He both honors the body and desecrates the body, both ravages the body and embraces the body.

Hölderlin tried his hand at a second "letter" on Achilles, this fragment much longer, so that I will cite only parts of it. This fragment too begins *in medias res*, a familiar trope of epistolary essays, which are always in response to a remark or a request that we surmise only as we read:

> But most of all I love and admire the poet of all poets on account of his Achilles. It is unique: the way he sees deeply into this character and with what love and *esprit* he sees, sustains, and elevates him. You will find a miracle of art in Achilles' character if you take the old lords, Agamemnon, Ulysses, and Nestor, with all their wisdom and foolishness, the loud-mouthed Diomedes, the blindly swinging Ajax, and hold them up against the ingenious, all-powerful, tenderly melancholic son of the gods, Achilles, this *enfant gaté* of nature; and also if you note the way the poet sets this youth who is full of leonine strength, *esprit*, and grace in the middle between pedantic wisdom on the one hand and brutality on the other. (CHV 2:64–65)

"Tenderly melancholic" is actually an inversion, for Hölderlin writes one of those remarkable elided words mentioned in chapter 1, *melancholischzärtlichen,* "tender with melancholy," or "melancholically tender." Hölderlin loves such combined words, especially when he comes to translate the names of the gods in his version of *Antigone,* where, for example, he renders Persephone as *zornigmitleidig,* "furiously compassionate." The names of gods can be rendered perhaps only oxymoronically. In any case, the youngest of Achaean heroes receives a more confluent epithet: as strong as a lion, as bright as Odysseus, though less wily, and above all tender, gentle to the point of melancholy. Like Goethe's moon.

The more interesting contrast, Hölderlin's letter continues, is with Hector. Hector possesses many of the qualities we ascribe to Achilles, yet he possesses them "out of a sense of duty and a finely-honed conscience" (CHV 2:65). By contrast, Achilles possesses his qualities "out of an abundant, beautiful nature," *aus reicher schöner Natur* (ibid.). It is the proximity of Achilles and Hector, proximity with a difference, that makes their conflict so tragic. Once again by way of contrast, Patroclus, who is above all friendly and loving, dwells peacefully with Achilles and serves as a complement and corrective to Achilles's often obstreperous nature.

Again Hölderlin remarks on the otherwise odd disappearance of Achilles from so much of the action of the *Iliad,* attributing it to the poet's reluctance to "profane" his hero. "The ideal dare not be presented in quotidian situations" (ibid.). Then follows what one can only describe as a Hölderlinian sentence, even though he is known for forcing his readers to turn the page in the course of a single sentence. Nevertheless, here is his further explanation of Achilles's absence from the "mayhem" beneath the walls of Troy: "And Homer could not really praise him in song more splendidly and tenderly [*nicht herrlicher und zärtlicher besingen*] than by allowing him to retreat (because the youth, who is himself infinite, feels himself to be infinitely insulted in his genial nature by Agamemnon, who is so proud of his rank), so that from that day forward every loss of the Greeks, when he is the single one in the army that they miss, because they sense his superiority over the entire crowd of lords and servants, and the rare moments when the poet allows him to appear before us are highlighted all the more by his absence" (ibid.). Achilles's appearances themselves "alternate" between terrible vengeance and "inexpressibly touching" lamentation; violence breaks out of him like a storm out of the sky. And yet, not long before his death, he achieves tender reconciliation with Priam. Hölderlin is presumably referring to the scene with Priam when, after a paragraph break, the final sentence of the fragment appears: "This last scene is heavenly—after all that has gone before" (ibid.). What has gone before, of course, is the desecration of Hector's corpse, his condemnation of Hector to what we will hear Lacan call "a second death." There is of course the possibility that by the "last scene" Hölderlin may be referring to the final glimpse we have of the hero, asleep at last beside Briseïs. In either case, it is a scene not of cruelty but of tenderness.

Roberto Calasso's *The Marriage of Cadmus and Harmony*, which while open to tenderness is never sentimental or maudlin, cites Hölderlin's second "Achilles" essay precisely at the moment it refers to the hero as "the *enfant gaté* of nature" (RC 126–27/105–106). Yet the spoiled child is destined to a brief life and a violent, painful death. "Instead of a god who would live longer than other gods, he became a man who would have a shorter life than other men" (ibid.). If, according to Calasso, "intensity" and "facility" are his two principal characteristics, there can be no doubt that Achilles—very much like the god Dionysos—has a special relation to the feminine:

> No hero was on more intimate terms with women than Achilles. At nine he was playing in Scyros as a girl among other girls. . . . Born of a sea goddess, brought up by two Naiads, Achilles' girl companions nicknamed him Pyrrha, the Blond, the tawny blonde. Thus he enjoyed a bliss never granted to any other male: that of being at once a girl and a seducer of girls. . . . Playing with them, Achilles could be distinguished only by the brusque way he would toss back his hair. (Ibid.)

Robert Graves tells us that at Achilleum on the Hellespont a temple dedicated to Achilles contained a statue of the hero "wearing a woman's ear-ring" (RG 2:317), as though to symbolize his intimacy with women. According to more than one recounting in antiquity, Agamemnon tricked his daughter Iphigenia into joining the calmed fleet at Aulis by promising her Achilles as her husband. That would make Agamemnon's theft of Briseïs the second offense against the gods and goddesses of tenderness, the first abuse involving the brutal deception and sacrifice of his own daughter, the second involving Achilles's "prize." These two abuses would make Achilles's redoubled fury against Agamemnon comprehensible.

It will not do to close a discussion of Hölderlin's fragment before noting that the character of Achilles has an impact on Hölderlin's reading of the entire *Iliad*, and therefore on a whole series of early essays in which the name of the hero does not appear as such. Indeed, in the fragment titled "A Word about the *Iliad*," there is not a word about the *Iliad* (CHV 2:66–67). There is instead a very general consideration of *character* and of the inevitable weaknesses that accompany various strengths of character. For example, we admire someone who is in harmony with his or her surroundings, someone who has learned to limit personal demands and live a "natural" life; what we may miss in them, however, is energy of feeling and *esprit*, whatever it is that enables the exceptional person to despise and rise above mediocrity. Someone else interests us because of their strength and persistence, a grandeur of character possessing courage and the willingness to sacrifice; yet they sometimes seem too tightly wound, too taut, too domineering, and hence one-sided, too much in conflict with their world. Another strikes us as a harmonious character, well-integrated and empathic, taking genuine interest in the world of others; yet his or her ability to adapt to all those other worlds suggests that this is someone who is good at seeing the trees but not the forest. It seems that our proclivities and our peculiarities determine us one way or another, so that it is too much to expect universal aptitude. Yet perhaps with a "genuine character" what happens is that the qualities we often miss in that type have merely receded into the background but are still present. Here the fragment breaks off, probably not because Hölderlin stopped writing, but due to some unforeseen accident—and Hölderlin's papers were subject to many accidents of fate.

One has the sense, although it is only a suspicion, that Achilles will be for Hölderlin the character who is not missing any of the qualities we most admire—those that we seem to miss are merely biding time in their tent, as it were, at some point bound to emerge. Hector we recognize as the man of grand character, willing to sacrifice himself, yet perhaps one-sided, in spite of the scenes with Andromache and their infant son. One could go on this way, trying to characterize—in the literal sense—all the heroes, Agamemnon, Menelaus, Odysseus, the two Ajaxes. Yet the important point is confirmed by a second essay fragment with the title "On the Various Ways to Poetize" (CHV 2:67–71). This larger fragment begins with the identical opening words of *Ein Wort über die Iliade*, confirming Hölderlin's focus on *character*. Epic is not preeminently a national tale—the word *Volk* does not appear in these essays—but an exposition of character, *exceptional* character. The exceptional character may, however, also be the *most natural*. It would be the kind of character that is capable of perceiving—and asserting—that all things consist of water, as the sage Thales perceived and said. The natural tone, in the case of the *Iliad*, is struck by old Phoenix, who tries to convince Achilles to rejoin his comrades by appealing to the child Achilles's affection for the old man, Phoenix himself. A merciless mind does not befit a mortal, he pleads, and even gods are known to have had a change of heart. The "naturalness" of epic demands that the poet *and* his characters avoid extremes. In the "character portrait" that is the *Iliad* (CHV 2:69), however, it is the main character that counts. And that would be Achilles.

One has the sense that Hölderlin is here engaged in a debate with Schiller, whose notion of Homeric art as "naive" and in that sense "natural" as opposed to "sentimental," perhaps causes him to overlook the fact that Achilles is clearly above and beyond the natural, if the natural is Phoenix or Agamemnon. Yes, Hölderlin has already contrasted Achilles with Hector by saying that Achilles is *by nature* what Hector is by *education* or *formation.* Yet here, by emphasizing "the individual," the character who achieves his own actuality, "through nature and formation a determinate and proper existence," *ein bestimmtes eignes Daseyn* (CHV 2:70), Hölderlin is clearly thinking of Achilles as a character that unites extremes. Indeed, says Hölderlin, Homer's main character "necessarily loses himself in extremes" (ibid.). "Had Homer not removed his volatile Achilles so tenderly and carefully from the noise of battle, we would scarcely be able to distinguish the son of gods from the element that surrounds him; the youth appears right before our eyes only when we find him quietly in his tent, finding his joy in lyre play, singing the victorious deeds of the men while Patroclus sits across from him waiting silently until the song comes to an end" (ibid.). Achilles as Orpheus.

Here the tenderness of Orphic Achilles is attributed directly to the poet who sings him. Achilles himself is *entzündbar,* highly flammable, and the natural tone of the epic can prevail only by hiding him—and enabling him to sing precisely in the way Homer sings. And as Achilles imitates Homer, so the other warriors, at the games in honor of Patroclus, imitate Achilles—they even become more like Achilles, "they all take on his hue," says Hölderlin (CHV 2:71). The final transformation is that of old Priam himself, who through his contact with Achilles "seems to grow younger" (ibid.). However, if the other Greek heroes in their mourning for Patroclus rise to the stature of Achilles, or at least tend toward an Achillean character, and if Priam himself is affected in the same way, this means that Homer has actually "transcended the natural tone" (ibid.). But how? And in what direction? In the direction of volatility, one must say, well beyond the natural tone: such *excess* is the destination of Hölderlin's entire poetology. From now on he will conceive of his heroes, whether Empedocles, Socrates, Oedipus, or Antigone, as excessively intense and singular, as an exceedingly rare combination of organizational skill and something more akin to a greater chaos, *das Aorgischere,* "the more aorgic." The more savage, perhaps, untamed and untamable; more volatile, more prone to extremes. Yet tenderness will sooner find a home in volatility than in staid organization.

From this point on in the essay, Hölderlin will be focused on the "alteration of tones" in poetry. Perhaps the alteration that best describes Achilles's victory over Hector and the catastrophe of Hector's desecration is captured in the second of the three possibilities for epic poetry: "Does not the natural catastrophe, when the initial heroic tone becomes its opposite, dissolve into the ideal?" (CHV 2:108). The ideal in this case would be the Achilles who relents, not in the face of Agamemnon, but before the supplicant Priam. It would be the Achilles who has learned singing from someone like Homer and tenderness from both Patroclus and a young woman we know only as "the Briseiade," the daughter of Briseus of Lyrnessus, a city not far from the Anatolian Mount Ida.

Perhaps the final word on Achilles and tenderness is Hölderlin's letter to Casimir Ulrich Böhlendorff, the second of his two famous letters, the one from November 1802 (CHV 2:920–22). Here Hölderlin tells his friend that southern France—the area around Bordeaux, from which he has only recently returned—has brought him closer to a sense of what the ancient Greeks were all about. He invokes "the athletic quality" of human beings who live in the south of Europe and are raised under the "overwhelming element" of the sun. The wisdom of the Greeks, he says, has everything to do with the vitality of their bodies; the highest form of understanding (*Verstand*) among them is rooted in a "force of reflection" (*Reflexionskraft*). That force in turn enables them to cope with the overwhelming power of "the fire of heaven." We northerners, he says, will gain a sense of the vitality of ancient Greek culture only "if we grasp the heroic body of the Greeks." He identifies the specific quality of that body as "tenderness": *sie ist Zärtlichkeit.*

•

Calchas the seer calls Agamemnon's Chryseïs, in Lombardo's translation, "the dancing-eyed girl" (4); Hans Rupé calls her *freudigblickende* (11), the one who is a joy to look at and who, in spite of her fate, herself looks joyful. Her epithet, ἑλικώπιδα κούρη (l. 98), is marvelous, because it reminds us of quick-glancing Aphrodite as well as the nymphs of Mount Helicon in Boeotia, where Mnemosyne and the Muses dwell. Lombardo's "dancing" is a wonderful rendering, since it saves the twirling, spinning sense of the helix. Both Chryseïs and Briseïs are called "fair-cheeked," and as the former is released to her father, who receives her "tenderly," the latter is kidnapped once again, taken this time from Achilles's tent by Agamemnon's emissaries. When she emerges from the tent, led by a reluctant though obedient Patroclus, her cheeks are "flushed," whether from anger or tears, and, Homer tells us, "She went unwillingly" (l. 348).

Achilles, in tears, then goes to his mother, who lives at the bottom of the sea. To Thetis he mentions only his dishonor, the loss of his prize:

> "Mother, since you bore me for a short life only,
> Olympian Zeus was supposed to grant me honor.
> Well, he hasn't given me any at all. Agamemnon
> Has taken away my prize and dishonored me." (Lombardo 11)

Thetis responds to her son with the tenderness of a mother who understands much more than she is told. He asks her to secure Zeus's intervention, and she agrees to do so. "And she left him there, angry and heartsick / At being forced to give up the silken-waisted girl" (ll. 428–29). Both angry, with a furious heart, χωόμενον κατὰ θυμὸν, and as heartsick and as importunate as a suppliant, λιπής, with glistening tears in his eyes. This double affliction is perhaps what is most appropriate to the extreme character of the raging and mournfully tender Achilles.

And what about that silken waist? More sober translations have her beautifully girdled or girded, εὐζώνοιο γυναικός, now as a woman, a woman well-girded. (Lombardo wraps or unwraps the silk around or from her waist perhaps because this "girding" of the loins, εὔζωνος, is in Greek so close to the verb for "to live well," εὐζωείω, and perhaps because, as with Aphrodite, it is difficult to distinguish what is donned from what is doffed.) It is equally difficult to say anything about Aphrodite's girdle. Even Hera borrows it, in Book XIV, when she plans to seduce (and reduce to sleep) her husband Zeus. "And with that she [Aphrodite] unbound from her breast / An ornate sash inlaid with magical charms. / Sex is in it, and Desire, and seductive / Sweet Talk, that fools even the wise" (271). It is easy to laugh at Aphrodite, as gods and mortals alike tend to do, especially when they are secretly overwhelmed by her power. Yet if Athena is able to assure Diomedes that Aphrodite is the only god a mortal may wound "with bronze" (87), perhaps that is because, as excitingly sensual and as full of magical charms as she is, Aphrodite is the most tender of deities. Vulnerable, as we say, reflecting perhaps the collective development of the gods during the centuries that separate the time when Homer is singing and the remote time of the sacking of Troy. Aphrodite would not yet be the pathetically suffering

Venus of Shakespeare's *Venus and Adonis*, centuries later, but tenderness—and hence the possible mischance of wounding—is built into her future.

For the longest time, as we know, Achilles lays idle in his tent, "Nursing his wrath because of the girl, / Fair-haired Briseïs... / Heartsick for her, and angry" (43). Once again, the double epithet serves to represent a split emotion—or perhaps it simply portrays a volatile character tending to extremes. When in Book IX the mission to Achilles tries to placate the enraged and mournful hero, it is clear that the other warriors fail to understand his bifurcated θυμός, the anger *and* the heartbreak. Hulking Ajax does not understand all this fuss about a girl: "The gods have replaced your heart / With flint and malice, because of one girl, / One single girl. . . . " (ll. 358–60; Lombardo 177). And so the mission to persuade Achilles to join the campaign fails.

The failure of the mission may also have to do with Agamemnon's assurance, backed up by Odysseus's redoubled assurances that Agamemnon is telling the truth (as though the wily Odysseus could know anything about the matter), that Achilles can have his prize back and that, as Agamemnon protests, "I never went to her bed and lay with her" (164). Achilles knows Agamemnon, as do those of us who hear the *Iliad* sung or who read it, and the skepticism is probably universal. Achilles retorts, "Every decent, sane man / Loves his woman and cares for her, as I did, / Loved her from my heart. It doesn't matter / That I won her with my spear" (169). Achilles's breast or heart, his θυμός, here makes room for something besides anger and the spear. He loves Briseïs ἐκ θυμοῦ φιλέει, with that friendship or feeling of kinship, φιλία, that is so important both to the Achaeans who live in the age of knights and the Greeks who live in the age of citizens. Much later in the epic, in Book XVIII, as Thetis tells Hephaistos the story of Patroclus's death, she reduces her son's double emotion to one, as perhaps a mother would, and it is the emotion of mourning or grief for a woman: "He was wasting his heart out of grief for her," she says (645): ὁ τῆς ἀχέων φρένας ἔφθιεν, mourning in his mind and heart. She uses the words for mourning, ἀχέων, in both heart and mind, φρένας, and consumption or withering away, φθίσις (l. 446). Briseïs is not one of Hephaistos's golden girls, his gorgeous robots, who have only now come on the scene. Gilt they may be, but it is neither the glittering gold of Aphrodite nor the true gold of Briseïs's tenderness and Achilles's tender character.

As for that earlier expression, to the effect that a good man loves his woman and cares for her, it renders well the following lines: . . . τὴν αὐτοῦ φιλέει καὶ κήδεται . . . ἐκ θυμοῦ φίλεον. Twice the word φιλία rises, the unmistakable word for love, never far from tenderness. The verb κήδεται is rich in meaning. Rupé translates it with *pflegen*, to take care of, cultivate, nurture, and see to someone's well-being. Recall that other combined word favored by Hölderlin, *zärtlichpflegend*, "tenderly caring for" someone. Yet the story contained in the word κήδεται is far more complicated and calls for another excursus.

•

Although an exact etymology is impossible, it seems that κῆδω, κήδεται is related to one of the Greek words for heart, τὸ κῆρ. It is perhaps merely a series of phonemic accidents, and accidents that would have occurred over eons of time, but anyone who has read Heidegger in English since the early 1960s responds to the sound of "care," *Sorge*. Heidegger explicitly relates the word *Sorge* to *cura*, especially in Augustine's vocabulary; but as far as I know Heidegger never mentions τὸ κῆρ in the context of *Sorge*, not even in *Was heißt Denken?* which at least in J. Glenn Gray's and Fred Wieck's wonderful English translation is all about taking-to-heart.[4] Perhaps they were influenced by Boris Pasternak's *Doctor Zhivago*, whose character was such that he took everything to heart. There is no established etymological link between κῆρ and *cura*, and the Germanic *kar* bears no known etymological relation to *cura*. It is to μελέτη and ἐπιμελεία that Heidegger directs our search for the ancient precursors of *Sorge*, "care," or what in the early 1920s he was calling *Bekümmerung*, "feeling or taking trouble." Yet it is κῆρ in its multiple genders and various senses that concerns us now. For κῆρ can be *Kummer*, "trouble, worry," as much as *Herz*, "heart." Indeed, ἡ κήρ, with the feminine article, is "doom," which is very big trouble.

In addition to words related to μελέτη, used in the familiar senses of "to concern oneself with, to take care of" (I 1:523; 6:492; O 1:305; 21:352; among many other references), there are the words κῆδω, κήδεται, apparently quite close in meaning to μελέτη (I 9:342), and κήδεα, τὸ κῆδος, sufferings or troubles

4 See part one of Heidegger, *Was heißt Denken?* (Tübingen: M. Niemeyer, 1954); translated by J. Glenn Gray and Fred D. Wieck as *What Is Called Thinking?* (New York: Harper & Row, 1968). Heidegger's phrase, *in-die-Acht-nehmen*, might be more literally translated as "to heed," or "to take into heed," but Wieck and Gray decided, wisely, to avoid the archaism, since no one heeds or hearkens much anymore.

(O 23:306).[5] The negative of the latter word appears to mean "without cares," *sanssouci*: whereas mortals are *bekümmert*, ἀχνυμένοις, the gods themselves are *sorglos*, ἀκηδέες (I 24:526). Yet on occasion the latter word means not "trouble-free" but failing to take trouble concerning something or failing to care for someone (O 17:319; see also O 20:130 and 24:187). It is almost as though being troubled is a prerequisite of taking care of or being concerned about someone. Yet how close are we here to κῆρ in any of its senses? How close are we to the heart, τὸ κῆρ, or to trouble and doom, ἡ κῆρ?

Of the many words that one may translate as "heart," ἦτορ, θυμός, κραδίη, φρήν, the word τὸ κῆρ is particularly notable. It too, like the word δαίμων, appears almost always at the end of a line of verse, which is not the case with any of the other heart-words. Some examples of τὸ κῆρ are the references to Hector's courageous heart (I 12:45; cf. O 21:247), Menelaos's loss of heart (compare Apollo's words to Poseidon at I 21:464–66, and Odysseus's words at O 10:497), Odysseus's heart brooding on the suitors' end (O 18:344), the Phaeacians' hearty reception of Odysseus, περὶ κῆρι (19:280, in mid-line, however), and, finally, Penelope's anxious heart, oppressed by cares (19:516–7: κῆρ...μελεδῶναι). However, to repeat, κῆρ is not only the heart and the concerns of the heart. It is also the oppressive care or trouble of mortality itself and "as such," if one may say so. One wonders if it is related to the ancient Sumerian word for the underworld, the abyss, and doom, *kur*, which at least *sounds* like the simple Latin word *cur*, "why?" or, again, the Latin *cura*, "trouble" or "care." At one point in the *Iliad*, ἡ κῆρ, "Doom," is addressed as a goddess or daimon, and portrayed as a formidable figure on Achilles's shield. Dominating one of the shield's two cities of mortals, the city at war, are Ἔρις, Strife, Κυδοιμός, Uproar, and ὀλοὴ Κήρ, "murderous Ker" (I 18:535).

I pause to note that the circumflex of κῆρ usually becomes an acute in the shift from "heart" to either "doom" or "lot," and that while the heart is neuter, doom is feminine in gender, as are all such words in Greek. The words therefore cannot be conflated, nor, linguists tell us, can they be convincingly linked etymologically: τὸ κῆρ appears to be a contraction of κέαρ, meaning a carpenter's axe, related to κεάζω, to pound or rub to pieces, as though our troubles cudgel us. Liddell-Scott lists "A" and "B" forms of the verb κηραίνω,

---

5 In what follows, the letter "I" refers to the *Iliad*, the letter "O" to the *Odyssey*. I cite the latter according to the fourth Tusculum edition, translated by Anton Weiher (Munich: Heimeran Verlag, 1974).

the "A" sense meaning to harm or destroy, the "B" sense to be sick at heart or anxious. Liddell-Scott does not speculate on an etymological connection between these two morphologically identical words, even if the semantic link seems compelling—how could one not be sick at heart or full of anxiety in the face of destructive power?[6]

The overwhelming sense one has when reading both Homeric poems is that ἡ κήρ and μοῖρα and perhaps even Ἄτη are identical, both as the collective fate of a city and as the allotment of individual destinies—which is to say, in the case of mortals, the dispensation of death. Zeus tosses two lots, δύο κῆρε, onto the scales, one representing the Trojans, the other the Achaeans, both spelling death, θανάτοιο (I 8:70). At the moment in question, the κήρ of the Achaeans causes the scale to sink to the earth, while the lot of the Trojans climbs to high heaven. Soon, however, the balance will shift. Achilles proclaims himself ready to receive his own κήρα now that Patroclus's and Hector's fates have been set in stone, inasmuch as even Herakles could not flee his κήρα when μοῖρα compelled him (I 18:115–19). Once again, Zeus tosses two lots onto the scales, those now of Hector and Achilles, with the anticipated outcome (cf. δύο κῆρε: I 22:365). By far the most common appearance of κήρ is as a pendant to θάνατος and a synonym of μοῖρα. After Thersites αἴσχιστος, the "Ugliest Man," has upbraided Agamemnon, Odysseus appeals to the prediction by Calchas the seer of eventual victory over Priam's Troy: "For we held it well in memory [ἐνὶ φρεσίν, often translated as "in our hearts"]; you can testify to it, all you whom the keres of death [κῆρες θανάτοιο] have not swept away" (I 2:301–302).

6 See Jane Ellen Harrison's long and detailed exposition, in chapter 5 of her *Prolegomena to the Study of Greek Religion* (Cleveland: World, Meridian Books, 1966), concerning the *keres* or sprites, those tiny winged creatures who generally mean mischief. Harrison makes no explicit reference to the *ker* of the heart. Yet she does argue that Eros himself is a form of *ker*, so that matters of the heart are not altogether excluded from her purview. She writes: "Eros is but a specialized form of the Ker; the Erotes are Keres of life, and like the Keres take the form of winged *Eidola*. In essence as in art-form, Keres and Erotes are near akin. The Keres, it has already been seen, are little winged bacilli, fructifying or death-bringing; but the Keres developed mainly on the dark side; they went downwards, deathwards; the Erotes, instinct with a new spirit, went upwards, lifewards" (631). Finally, on all these questions, see D. J. N. Lee, who argues that the principal meaning of κήρ is μοῖρα or "fate." Lee resists Liddell-Scott's later reading of the word as "goddess of doom," yet it is difficult to interpret "fate" in any other way than as death. See D. J. N. Lee, "Homeric κήρ and Others," *Glotta* 39 (1960–61), 191–207.

Parallel with the phrase πορφύρεος θάνατος καὶ μοῖρα κραταιή, "purple death and mighty destiny," or simply θάνατος καὶ μοῖρα, we find θάνατος καὶ κήρ (I 17:714; O 12:157; cf. O 18:155; 22:14; 24:127 and 414), or θάνατος καὶ κῆρες, in the plural (O 2:352; 5:387), or, less commonly, φόνος καὶ κήρ, "murder and annihilation" (I 3:6; O 17:82; this is clearly the "black ker" that Penelope wishes on Antinoos: O 17:500). The sense of κήρ as allotted destiny, shifting unpredictably between singular and plural, in this way so reminiscent of the μοῖραι, is simply this: "No one can elude death and the keres" (O 17:547; 19:558).

No one? No one except, surely, the immortals? However, can the gods themselves elude κῆρα, even Zeus Pater, who occasionally usurps the prerogative of Μοῖρα in order to manipulate lots? Or do the immortals inevitably join the mortals in both loving and mourning, that is to say, in what we might call "the more tender relations"? This was Hölderlin's lightning-bolt thought, the thought for which Apollo struck him in the back. And it may be that Heidegger's concluding section of the *Beiträge zur Philosophie,* invoking "the last god," is pursuing that Hölderlinian thought: as the last god vanishes, as furtively as Kirke or as subtly as Kalypso, there is in Heidegger's view a kind of signaling, a kind of greeting in going. The god comes to presence precisely as an absenting—at best a parting, at worst an already achieved and perfect concealment. The last god is eucalyptic.[7]

•

However, let us leave the gods in abeyance and return to the heart of Achilles. There can be little doubt that his heart nurses tender feelings toward Briseïs. After Patroclus's death, however, as Briseïs is about to be restored to Achilles, a very strange scene unfolds. Sheila Murnaghan notes the following concerning the death of Achilles's friend: "Patroclus's death awakens in Achilles a sense of connectedness to other people as he experiences anguish for the loss of his beloved friend and shame for his failure to protect him" (xxxiv). However, perhaps this sense of connectedness has arisen earlier and in another context, namely, precisely that of Briseïs. For Briseïs also has something surprising to do with Patroclus, something rather more complicated than we would otherwise attribute to Homer, whose poetry is said to be "naive," or at least in "the natural tone." Let me present Lombardo's rendering of the entire scene:

---

7 See Heidegger, *Beiträge zur Philosophie (Vom Ereignis),* Gesamtausgabe vol. 65 (Frankfurt am Main: V. Klostermann, 1989), part VII.

Briseïs stood there like golden Aphrodite.

But when she saw Patroclus' mangled body
She threw herself upon him and wailed
In a high, piercing voice, and with her nails
She tore her breast and soft neck and lovely face.
And this woman, so like a goddess, cried in anguish:

"My poor Patroclus. You were so dear to me.
When I left this hut you were alive,
And now I find you, the army's leader, dead
When I come back. So it is for me always,
Evil upon evil. I have seen my husband,
The man my father and mother gave me to,
Mangled with sharp bronze before my city,
And my three brothers, all from the same mother,
Brothers I loved—they all died that day.
But you wouldn't let me cry when Achilles
Killed my husband and destroyed Mynes' city,
Wouldn't let me cry. You told me you'd make me
Achilles' bride, told me you'd take me on a ship
To Phthia, for a wedding among the Myrmidons.
I will never stop grieving for you, forever sweet."

Thus Briseis, and the women mourned with her,
For Patroclus, yes, but each woman also
For her own private sorrows. (19:299–322; Lombardo 382–83)

The only words we hear from Briseïs throughout the entire epic are these tender words for Patroclus, "forever sweet," who comforts her after Achilles kills her husband. Patroclus, always kind, gentle, soothing, like a propitious Zeus Meilichios, forever tender, or like honey soothing an angina. Patroclus, whose name is the inversion of the name of Meleager's wife, Cleopatra (xxxiii), is gentle to womankind; this may be the secret of Achilles's love for him. Joyce writes of Bloom, the latter-day Ulysses, "Woman's woe with wonder pondering."[8] Is

8 James Joyce, *Ulysses* (London: Bodley Head, 1960), 507; cited from hence as U with page number. For Molly's words, cited below, see U 933.

Bloom as much the latter-day Patroclus or Achilles as the wily Odysseus, and is this not the secret of Molly's having chosen him? "Well as well him as another," she says at the end, feigning an indifference she does not feel. Does Achilles feel a tinge of jealousy to see Briseïs mourn Patroclus as she would a husband? "I will never stop grieving for you," she says. Apparently, Achilles is too consumed by his own mourning to feel jealousy, even though Briseïs also says, "So it is for me always, / Evil upon evil," as though Patroclus were indeed another dead husband. "The army's leader," she calls him, as though confusing him with either the brute she has been with until recently, Agamemnon, or Achilles, the army's greatest warrior. Even though Achilles is still alive, Briseïs keens and scratches her neck and face, as a wife might; she disfigures herself for Patroclus, not for the living hero who loves her. Achilles and Briseïs, united in their love of Patroclus? Is her tenderness, then, *la seule tendresse,* the link between the two warriors? And how much tenderness Achilles would have to possess toward Briseïs not to be troubled in the least by her devotion to Patroclus!

We do not see the two of them—Briseïs and Achilles—together again until the end of the epic. In the meantime, Apollo has lamented Achilles's desire for a second death, or an endless series of further deaths, for Hector. "For he defiles the dumb earth in his rage" (468). This is the very crime that the Creon of Sophocles's *Antigone* will commit against Polyneices's body. Tiresias says that Creon confuses the upper world with the nether: he sends a living girl to her tomb and will not grant a dead man his dust. "The Fates have given men an enduring heart," says Apollo, who like all the gods condemns Achilles's desecration of Hector's corpse and expects Achilles to curtail his wrath. Murnaghan calls the enduring heart "a harsh virtue," inasmuch as it requires human beings "to let go of the most precious attachments" (xxxix). Yet even the shaggiest of hearts may be touched by tenderness, precisely at the harshest moments. If we may say of the heart what Faulkner says of Dilsey, "She endured," perhaps that endurance depends on the tenderness that Dilsey can show all the Compson children, even Jason. Such tenderness rejects above all what Lacan calls "the second death," that is, the raging desire, arising from life-envy (*Lebensneid*), to desecrate the corpse, as though only a second death were good enough for the dead enemy (JL 287/237). Achilles finally relinquishes this desire when confronted with Priam's plea. Whether he could ever relinquish it in the confrontation with Agamemnon is another matter. Perhaps only after Clytaimestra and Aigisthos have done their work on Agamemnon, long after Achilles's death, would Achilles's hatred abate; with Agamemnon trapped in the net at his bath and under multiple wounds, ignominiously assassinated, yes, perhaps then something akin to chagrin, if not tenderness.

Thetis tries to soothe her son's mourning and his rage by means of an apt suggestion, not one that every mother is likely to come up with: "My son, how long will you let this grief / Eat at your heart, mindless of food and rest? / It would be good to make love to a woman" (471). She does not mention Briseïs by name. And, indeed, during the time of Achilles's mourning, Briseïs disappears. Or, at least, she lies hidden to the singer of the song. Only after Achilles's reception of Priam and his release of Hector's corpse do we see the two sleeping together—our last glimpse of the greatest Achaean hero, the glimpse that so impressed Simone Weil. "But Achilles slept inside his well-built hut, / And by his side lay lovely Briseïs." "Lovely" is perhaps not specific enough; καλλιπαρήος means that her cheeks were beautiful. If a woman has the gold of Aphrodite, a silken waist, cheeks all roses, and many secret mournful things that she carries in her breast, perhaps even a wrathful man will have to capitulate.

At that point the focus of the epic shifts to defeated Troy and the burial of Hector. The epic becomes in the end what its title promises: *Ilias*. The Trojan women, later to be a favorite topic among the Greek tragedians, who show a tender generosity we today cannot even approximate, dominate the close of Homer's epic. Perhaps Helen is now one of these Trojan women. At least, the last words we hear from her have nothing to do with her husband Menelaus, who has survived the long war but who is of no interest to her. Nor do they have to do with Paris; it is Hector she tries to seduce away from the battlefield. If Briseïs mourns Patroclus, Helen mourns Hector. After Andromache and Hecuba have spoken their laments, Helen, who like Briseïs stands there as a goddess of tenderness, speaks:

> "Oh, Hector, you were the dearest to me by far
> Of all my husband's brothers. Yes, Paris
> Is my husband, the godlike prince
> Who led me to Troy. I should have died first.
> This is now the twentieth year
> Since I went away and left my home,
> And I have never had an unkind word from you.
> If anyone in the house ever taunted me,
> Any of my husband's brothers or sisters,

> Or his mother—my father-in-law was kind always—
> You would draw them aside and calm them
> With your gentle heart and gentle words.
> And so I weep for you and for myself,
> And my heart is heavy, because there is no one left
> In all wide Troy who will pity me
> Or be my friend. Everyone shudders at me." (491)

Until now, Hector has not seemed the gentlest of folk, but just as Briseïs celebrates the best in Patroclus, so Helen brings out the best in Hector. And once again she is mourning and grieving for one who is *not* her husband. "Gentle heart and gentle words" (l. 773: ἀγανοφροσύνη, ἀγανοῖς) in each case belong to the brother, whether in-law or in effect.

Does this mean that Hölderlin is mistaken when he sees the other characters in the epic approximating the character of Achilles rather than that of Patroclus? Not necessarily. Especially not if Achilles is the warrior who weeps tenderly for both Patroclus and Briseïs—and perhaps also for Priam and for Priam's and Helen's Hector. For Achilles is the warrior whose very body, for all its athletic prowess, is tenderness—*sie ist Zärtlichkeit*.

Chapter Three

Tender Antigone—Forever Younger

ὦ παῖ παῖ, "O child! child!"

—Sophocles, *Antigone*

If tenderness can be found among the knightly Achaean warriors, may we not also seek it in the tragedies of classical Athens? For example, in Sophocles's *Antigone*? So many contemporary readings and productions of *Antigone* portray Antigone as a brilliant trial lawyer representing, as Hegel says, the ethicality of family law, or, if not that, then as an august priestess and spokeswoman of the underworld gods and goddesses. She would embody the archetype that informs Joan of Arc, Susan B. Anthony, and any other woman who can stand up to a man, an advocate who engages successfully—if only ironically—in dialectical strife with a patriarchal civil society. Antigone should therefore live and die as a dignified and very vertical figure, firmly planted on her own two feet. Never mind her odd family background.

The first several hundred lines of Sophocles's play lure us into thinking that Antigone can be portrayed this way. Yet everything that transpires in the play after Antigone's initial confrontation with Creon works against such a portrayal. For in Sophocles's play Antigone becomes ever younger and more tender—more delicate, more fragile, increasingly vulnerable, and ultimately childlike—as the scenes proceed. If she begins as a minion of the unwritten law, representing the underworld deities, she ends as a helpless infant, or even as a fetus suspended from a gauzy umbilical cord in a womb of stone. Her mother, in the end, is not Jocasta, who in any case is her paternal grandmother, but the mythical Niobe in tears for her children. (Zeus, taking pity on Niobe, has turned her into a mountain, but thanks to snowmelt Niobe still weeps for her slaughtered children, all of whom died so young because of their mother's carelessness.) It is as though the temporality of Sophocles's play were that of the

Golden Age, in which the earthborn humans emerge from their graves and grow younger with each passing day, advancing from maturity through adolescence to childhood, until they disappear as tiny seeds, consigned once again to the womb of the earth. Heroism in the Golden Age is not about maturation; rather, it is regression to a time of absolute dependency. Antigone's death—as a child, an infant—is as painful as those deaths recounted in Mahler's *Kindertotenlieder*.

It is futile to speculate about Antigone's age at the outset of Sophocles's drama. The inconsistencies among the three plays, *Antigone*, *Oedipus Tyrannos*, and *Oedipus at Colonos*, which in any case never constituted a trilogy, certainly do not help us. Yet it is not a question of birthdays; it is a matter of Antigone's going backward. Not forever young, as the song says, but forever younger.

If Creon is taken to be the tragic hero of the play, as he is by many, then we have to say that his ἁμαρτία or tragic flaw is hyperbolic: his political clichés, his evident paranoia, his jealousy felt toward his son, his anxiety in the face of both Ismene and Antigone, his masculist bravado—all this makes it impossible for us (and presumably for Athenian audiences) to think of him as being on equal footing with Oedipus. (In the most recent production of the play that I have seen, back in the days of the presidency of George W. Bush, a production based on Hölderlin's magnificent translation, Creon wore a white cowboy hat, and the audience laughed and laughed. Soon, no doubt, he will be portrayed as a sourpuss populist with very bad hair.) Creon is not a hero, then, but a caricature of the tyrant. This is perhaps the sense of Goethe's reply to Hegel: Creon does not represent civil law in dignified dialectical opposition to family law, but the failure of all law. Goethe to Eckermann on March 28, 1827:

> Creon does not by any means act on the basis of political virtue. Rather, he acts out of hatred toward the dead man. If Polyneices tried to reclaim his paternal legacy, from which he was violently barred, this was no unheard-of crime against the state, such that his death would not have sufficed. His innocent corpse meriting no further punishment.
>
> One should never invoke "the good of the state" when referring to an action that counteracts virtue in general. When Creon forbids Polyneices' burial, and when the decomposing body not only infests the air but also serves as the source of food for dogs and scavenging birds, which carry off morsels of the dead man and thereafter soil the altars, such an act, which insults both humanity and divinity, is not a political *virtue* but a political *crime*. Add to this the fact

> that everyone in the play opposes him. The elders of the state, who constitute the chorus, oppose him; the people in general oppose him; Tiresias opposes him; his own family opposes him. Yet he does not listen; he stubbornly blasphemes, on and on, until he has sealed the fates of all his family members and until, in the end, he himself is but a shade.[1]

If Antigone and not Creon is the hero of the play, as its title suggests, we nonetheless have to ask whether her qualities are directly opposed to Creon's. Is she devoid of jealousy? Is she free of paranoid traits? Does she think outside of cliché, whether political or masculist? Is she a paragon of virtue? That she is not the straightforward contrary of Creon is suggested by Bernhard Zimmermann's trenchant judgment concerning her tragic quality: "Antigone's tragic quality consists in her destroying, by means of her rigorous action, precisely what she claims to represent: the family."[2] Not that her family was not dysfunctional to begin with; we would hardly expect a girl who cannot tell her mother from her paternal grandmother to turn out to be a heroine. Well, then, who *is* Antigone? Whence her willfulness, her determination, her drive? What desire propels her? If it is her love for her brother, then which brother—for she has several? And if she is the victim of confusion in this regard, we have to ask: How do the gods, principally the goddesses of doom, Ἄτη and Κήρ, use and abuse her?

If we reject the formulaic Hegelian dialectic of family and civil society, we are nonetheless compelled to wonder whether and how social and political involvements are driven by family structures, strictures, and struggles. At the heart and hearth of the πόλις is the οἶκος, or household, as we saw in chapter 1. And the most uncanny person at the fireside, the most monstrous παρέστιος, will assuredly turn out to be the tragic hero or heroine.

For such a reading of Sophocles, the two most important sources form an odd couple indeed—if Hölderlin and Lacan can be said to form a couple at

1 Johann Peter Eckermann, *Gespräche mit Goethe in den letzten Jahren seines Lebens*, 3 vols. (Magdeburg: Heinrichshofen, 1848), 3:127; quoted by Bernhard Zimmermann, *Die griechische Tragödie* (Düsseldorf: Patmos Verlag, 2005), 73.

2 See Bernhard Zimmermann's Afterword to the plays of Sophocles, S 729. For Hölderlin's translation, see DKV 2:859–921. The lines of Hölderlin's translation do not quite match those of the text of Sophocles that we use today; yet readers will be able to locate them in DKV without much difficulty.

all.[3] In any case, the reading attempted here will search for the psychophysical energetics of social, political, and familial action, with Antigone as its guide. Such a search is vaguely threatening or even positively alarming: the suspicion obtrudes and seems inescapable that the psychophysical dynamics of any collective action are somehow "in the family way"—and that means somehow embarrassing or even sordid. At least, we have to be prepared for the circumstance that the idealizing tendency of our social and political commitments and engagements will be subverted by any investigation into the sources of the energy we devote to them. We love to think of Lenin as a reader of Marx and a dedicated Bolshevik, but we hate to think of him witnessing his older brother's execution by a Czarist firing squad. We do not really want to know what happened to Vladimir Ilyich Ulyanov on that day. Likewise, no evangelical Christian wants to be shown anything about his or her highly charged frenzy—it is enough for him or her to be convinced of the Pentecostal authenticity of Borat's inspired conversion and his orgasmic babble of tongues. In short, no one who is engaged to a cause of any kind wants to know about the sources of the energy invested in that cause, because such a source could only be demeaning. If the cause is heroic, the energies are human, all-too-human, never "better" than we are.

How does a "causist" read *Antigone*? Answer: quickly, and only up to line 470 of the 1,353 lines of the play, losing interest and courage after Antigone's confrontation with Creon. True, tragedy *is* heroic, and its heroes *are* idealized; they are, as Aristotle says, indeed "better" than we are. Yet it is important to see what happens to these idealized figures; also important to speculate on what drives them toward their destiny. Tragedy is neither documentary nor manifesto. Tragedy is, as Jacob Bernays has already informed us, a revelation through music, dance, and drama of the frightful laws of the universe, or at least of the universe of humankind.[4] It may well be that such a psychophysical energetics or dynamics is too Euripidean an exercise to be suitable for Sophoclean tragedy. Antigone is not a candidate for analysis, not even for Lacan. Yet her power as a tragic figure, her splendor, her *éclat* and her clout, as Lacan calls it, require that we read the entire Sophoclean play cleansed of our idealizing

3 See TA, esp. 10–11, 376, and 388–90. Chapters 8–11 of *The Tragic Absolute* are all about this odd couple, odd because Hölderlin and Lacan are so often in agreement, even though Lacan makes no reference to Hölderlin. For Lacan's interpretation of *Antigone*, see JL, chapters 19–21.

4 See JB 47, discussed in TA 286–88.

simplifications. At some point, no doubt, the energetic analysis will dissolve in the face of the figure herself. Antigone herself, if one can say such a thing, will have to suggest other modes of reading, as well as other modes of what Lacoue-Labarthe calls *theatrality*.[5] At some point, the question of Antigone's *desire* has to fade before the larger question of "the divine use" of her. It may well be that she is used not only by the goddesses of doom but also by the god of theater, Dionysos.

One further caveat. As one attempts to read *Antigone*, and even to translate its text, one finds oneself in Hölderlin's position, though without the corresponding talent. One is forced to be not so much a reader of the text as the *director* of the play's production, or at least the *dramaturge* for such a production. Needed is a director or dramaturge who feels compelled to talk with the actors deep into the night about the words Sophocles is asking them to say. In what tone or tones and with what gestures are these lines to be uttered? From what positions of desperation and seclusion? Dreaming what sorts of dreams? Under the pressure of what sorts of forebodings and nightmares? Driven by what pulsions? In what follows, it will be a matter of a few scattered remarks toward such a production, not a very thoroughgoing *Inszenierung* or even "staged reading" from beginning to end. Yet even a selective reading is nothing if it fails to contemplate the complexities involved in "blocking out" the scenes, respecting their "flow" and their "velocity," but also allowing the caesuras to take whatever time they demand, as Hölderlin insists one must. *That* would require something more than talent.

To begin with, the title, although it has been discussed endlessly in the literature. Here, just a few reminders: Ἀντὶ-, a preposition governing the genitive case and suggesting (1) over against, opposite, *en face*; (2) instead of, in place of; (3) in Homer, as good as, as much as, just like, in exchange for. In composite words, such as the name *Antigone*, the preposition may mean either "over against" or, more starkly, "against, in opposition to." It may indicate a mutual or reciprocal relation, that is, a relation of equality or correspondence, or a relation of substitution, this "instead of" that. And γονή? Derived from γένεσθαι, the word γονή means (1) offspring, children, fruits; (2) race, stock, family; (3) generation. It may refer to seed, to that which engenders, or to the organs of generation, especially the womb. It may refer to the act of generating, especially to the mother in childbirth, or to her infant; it may also refer to a

5 Philippe Lacoue-Labarthe, *Métaphrasis:* (Paris: Presses Universitaires de France, 1998), throughout. Discussed in TA at 275–79.

cure for sterility. Finally, it is a name, a Pythagorean name, for unity, indicating perhaps that one dot at the center of the tetractys that is not exposed to any of the three sides of the figure. And Ἀντιγόνη, with a shift of accent? Robert Graves says simply, "In place of a mother," although Carol Jacobs, by highlighting that scene in which Antigone returns to her brother's naked corpse once again and shrieks "like a mother-bird" at her ravaged nest, has shown how complex such a replacement can be.[6] Antigone: "instead of" or "as opposed to" a mother, she has only a paternal grandmother; granted the confusion of generations in her, she may be in opposition to all seed and every womb. What speaks against this last possibility is the fact that as she grows younger in the course of the play she mourns her silenced marriage song. Finally, instead of a father she has only brothers—although as she grows younger and more tender in the course of the play she comes to focus on her eldest brother, who is her father.

The very first words of the play, when Antigone sees her sister Ismene's face, form an apostrophe, "Oh, face of Ismene, you who shared with me the selfsame mother's womb (κοινὸν αὐτάδελφον)." Hölderlin translates the phrase as *Gemeinsamschwesterliches!* "Shared sisterhood!" After lamenting what Zeus and Oedipus have done to the two sisters, Antigone again stresses the womb that both sisters share with their dead and unburied brother, Polyneices. Such emphasis is meant to engage Ismene in collective action, but it also makes Antigone's imminent exclusion of her sister and her expressed hatred of her all the more ghastly. Polyneices is "yours as well as mine" (l. 6). Later, at lines 31–32, Antigone says, "You as well as I, you hear what I'm saying? and it is I who am saying it." And later still, at lines 45–46, "At all events, mine, and yours too, even if you'd rather not, our brother." Hölderlin translates, *Von dir und mir, mein' ich, auch wenn du nicht es willst, / Den Bruder.* Immediately before this, Antigone has issued the challenge to her sister, and in the oddest possible way. At lines 37–38 she says, "And soon you will show whether you are well-born or are the bad seed of noble parents." For Antigone to be speaking eugenically is nothing short of bizarre, given her and Ismene's twisted and knotted family ties; and to refer to the nobility of their progenitors, apart from the fact that they once ruled the city, seems dubious in the extreme. That Ismene should prove in Antigone's estimation to be "the evil that has sprung from the good" seems hyperbolically ironic—no matter what Ismene might or might not do. Yet Antigone is either too old or too young to pause over the irony and the anomaly of her accusations. She begins now to concentrate on the dead brother whom

---

6 Carol Jacobs, "Dusting Antigone," in *Modern Language Notes* 111 (1996), 889–917.

she loves—with a love that seems to embrace all the senses of φιλία. As though looking forward to the punishment that will follow upon her forbidden deed, and as though the deed were undertaken precisely for the sake of the punishment, she employs the word κείσομαι more than once: I will lay me down, I will lie, I will sleep, now I lay me down to sleep. Lines 73–76 read as follows:

> καλόν μοι τοῦτο ποιούσῃ θανεῖν.
> Beautiful, after such a deed, is death to me.
> φίλη μετ'αὐτοῦ κείσομαι, φίλου μέτα,
> Beloved of him, I'll lie with him, my beloved,
> ὅσια πανουργήσασ' (. . .)
> Having dared to commit so righteous a crime. . . .[7]
> ἐκεῖ γὰρ αἰεὶ κείσομαι.
> For there I will lie through all time.

As if these words were not cause enough for alarm, Antigone urges her sister not to remain silent about her crime but to shout it from the rooftops of the city. At which point Ismene offers us a characterization of Antigone that should never cease to astonish us: θερμὴν ἐπὶ ψυχροῖσι ἔχεις (l. 88), "You have a hot heart for cold things." The word ψυχρός refers to dead things, to the cold corpse, as opposed to warm-blooded creatures. Much later in the play (l. 650), when Creon warns his son that to go to bed with a bad woman is to invite "chilly embraces," he uses the same word, and he too of course is referring to Antigone. In fact, Creon's word confirms Ismene's judgment—one of the unkindest cuts of the play. *Warm für die Kalten leidet deine Seele,* writes Hölderlin: "Warmly for ones who are cold your soul suffers." A whole range of possible translations assails us in the case of this expression of Ismene's grief and chagrin, and her words to her sister ring out in many possible registers: *For a warm-blooded creature, a girl with a heart pumping hot blood, you are cold-blooded, cold-hearted. Your ardor burns for ice. Your heart beats for what has no pulse. My living sister, why are you dead-set on death?* It may be that Antigone is chastened somewhat by Ismene's grief. No doubt, Antigone denounces Ismene in the strongest possible terms: "When you speak this way you make me hate you, and rightly so does our dead brother loathe you as well" (ll. 93–94). Nevertheless, her words become more somber, more sober, as the scene draws to a close. "But let me now, through my own bad judgment, go to suffer what is monstrous," she says (l. 96). Antigone's self-confessed "bad

7 For Creon's use of the same word for Antigone's crime, πανουργία, see l. 300.

judgment," δυσβουλία, is very close to that ἀβουλία which at the very end of the play the chorus says is the source of the worst mistakes that a human being can make (l. 1242). "Let me go to suffer what is monstrous, uncanny," παθεῖν τὸ δεινόν, she says, to suffer what human beings as a whole are condemned to suffer; for this word, τὸ δεινόν, anticipates the famous choral ode that begins, "Many things are monstrous, but nothing more monstrous than human being." As though to expose this monstrosity, Antigone assures her sister that her death will be glorious, a "beautiful death," as she says. Yet in a sentence of ten words four of them are negatives: πείσομαι γὰρ οὐ τοσοῦτον οὐδὲν ὥστε μὴ οὐ καλῶς θανεῖν, leading us to translate, "Whatever it is that I won't fail to suffer, nothing will stop me from having a death that isn't beautiful" (ll. 96–97). All is *anti-*. The scene ends when Antigone's sister promises to love her as a *living* sister: "If it seems so to you, then do it. Yet know that even if your deed is mindless [ἄνους] you are rightly loved by your loved ones." Leaving us only to ponder what it means to love, and to love rightly, to be "a proper friend to your friends." Is Antigone rightly loved by her living sister? Is Antigone right to love their dead brother in the way she does? Would it not be important to be clear about these two loves between siblings, both on the earth's surface, but one a love of the living, the other a love of what is lifeless?

"Even the worst sort of moron will not be in love with death," growls Creon (l. 220). He has yet to confront Antigone. There are wonders in the world, among them the wonders (τὰ δεινά) that occur at the site of Polyneices's corpse, buried under dust that does not seem to have been scraped from the earth's surface; the chorus thinks that this first symbolic burial may be the work of the gods. Creon thereupon warns the messenger-guard to be on the lookout. Should he fail to discover the criminal, the guard will die not one but at least two deaths. "Hades but once will not satisfy me where you are concerned: I'll hang you up alive" (l. 308). Creon is never satisfied with one death for his enemies; he needs a second death for them, a death of pointless torture and desecration. Like Achilles raging over Hector's corpse, Creon rejects the sole or singular death of his enemies, their "one Hades." For Lacan, this phantasm of a "second death," which he finds expressed later in both Sade and the Christian Hell, captures Creon's desire. In our own dismal time, the desire for the torture and desecration of bodies has become a national institution: to compel the other to abide on the cusp of death, to cause him or her to die over and over again, to hear the blessed phrase from one's victim, "Let me die now," and then to refuse the request. This twisted Eros that plays with Hades is perhaps the central theme of the Sophoclean tragedy *Antigone*. Perhaps Creon and Antigone share precisely this refusal of the one Hades: "Not for me this single death, this one death once and for all." To be sure, they share it on quite different terms, Creon desiring it for the others, Antigone for herself.

And yet. Will not a single Hades, *one* death, satisfy her? If not, what would be the additional death she envisages for herself in lying down beside her dead brother, Polyneices? Could it be that she desires a second death, one that would allow her also to lie with her *eldest* brother? To multiply and exponentialize her grandmother's crime? Much in the world is monstrous, but nothing more monstrous than the human being.

Πολλὰ τὰ δεινὰ. Hölderlin translates, *Ungeheuer ist viel,* "Much is monstrous." Heidegger: "Much is uncanny, unhomelike, but the most uncanny, *das Unheimlichste,* is the human being."[8] What is most unhomelike in the case of Antigone is her clairvoyant being-toward-death; it is this being *toward* and *unto* the end that makes her death, according to Heidegger, beautiful. In this, Heidegger and Lacan are in perfect agreement. Furthermore, Hölderlin, Heidegger, and Lacan are all in agreement when it comes to a reading of the contested lines 360–61 and 370. We need not go over the philological debate here (see TA, 374–76), but merely listen to the various versions of these key statements of the second choral ode. The putative optimism of the Sophoclean text as currently edited says of the human being that he or she "is quite resourceful; he or she goes to face nothing in the future without resource. Death alone . . . " Heidegger, considerably less optimistic, has:

> Everywhere under way, striding forth, he's going nowhere, he comes to
> nothing.
> That single thrust upon him, death, he cannot escape, even if
> In the face of dire illness he has had the skill to evade. (EM 113)

---

8 See the Heidegger Gesamtausgabe 53:127ff.; see also EM 112–26. One might also say that Hölderlin, Heidegger, and Lacan are also in agreement with Melville, for whom "wonder" and "woe" are the defining words for humanity. In chapter 107 of *Moby-Dick* Ishmael tells the reader: "Seat thyself sultanically among the moons of Saturn, and take high abstracted man alone; and he seems a wonder, a grandeur, and a woe." In chapter 110 Ishmael asserts: "For whatever is truly wondrous and fearful in man, never yet was put into words or books." Except perhaps by Sophocles, one might reply.

Hölderlin has—if one may try to render his translation in English:

> . . . All-experienced,
> Inexperienced. He comes to nothing.
> That future place, the place of the dead, it alone
> He knows not how to flee,
> And flight from unstoppable epidemics,
> How to outwit them? (DKV 2:873–74)

Lacan, less disposed to translate poetically, says simply that the human being "advances toward nothing [οὐδὲν] that is likely to happen [τὸ μέλλον]." In short, the reputedly skillful, resourceful human being is ἄπορος, out of place and therefore *toujours couillonné,* forever buggered, always screwed, completely fucked. (That is the way analysts talk; they have no shame.) To be sure, the choral ode does praise the skills of humankind. Line 366 speaks of man as "possessing technical skills that exceed every hope." The word ἐλπίδες, "hopes," reminds us of a passage in pseudo-Aeschylus's *Prometheus Bound,* l. 252, which invokes τυφλὰς . . . ἐλπίδες, "blind hopes." The chorus of Oceanides is asking about Prometheus's gifts to humankind, searching for the betrayal that has so offended Zeus; for the theft of fire is not Prometheus's worst offense:

> CHORUS: Didn't your gift-giving deed go much farther?
>
> PROMETHEUS: I caused human beings not to foresee their lot.
>
> CHORUS: What medicine or poison did you devise to achieve that?
>
> PROMETHEUS: Hopes, blind hopes, I planted in their hearts.
>
> CHORUS: This gift you gave to mortals was the one that helped them most.

Sophocles embraces this Promethean lesson of his forebear: human beings are uncannily skillful, beyond anyone's hopes and dreams; yet in one decisive respect they are blind, and they *have to be* blind. It as though all their skills depended on the blind hopes they entertain—above all, the hope that they will live forever. The messenger-guard, reporting to Creon a second time now, explains that he and his motley band really had "no hopes" of catching the perpetrator. They waited, παρ' ἐλπίδας, *unverhofft,* as Hölderlin says, "without hopes." And we recall the striking reference to hope in the second stasimon, or third choral song: even though "in the life of mortals nothing runs for very long outside of doom," hopes abound—ἐλπίς πολύπλαγκτος, hopes as plentiful as plankton in the sea (ll. 614–16). With all the technical skills buttressed and buffered by such blindness, a human being can rise to the top of the pile, can be the king or queen of the hill, the leader of a city. Yet a second paradox, modeled on that of the πάντaπορος ἄπορος, now shatters the vision. Whoever occupies the heights of the city is also expelled from the city, ὑψίπολις ἄπολις. The toast of the town will soon enough be toasted by the town. All collective idealizations are hollowed out by tempestuous drives, drives that gather head early on in the uncanny family. And these words apply as much to Antigone as they do to Creon.

Pages have flitted by, however, and nothing more has been said about Antigone, the tragic heroine, becoming younger and more tender. Yet at the end of the first stasimon, or second choral ode, which I have been considering here, we hear some "throwaway lines" that suggest something of Antigone's impending youth. Lines 376–83, spoken by the chorus, are no longer part of the ode as such, or so it seems. At the end of their meditation on human uncanniness and monstrosity, the old Theban men see Antigone approaching, under arrest and in custody. She seems to them an apparition from the underworld realm of spirits, τὸ δαιμόνιον, but their amazement surrenders to the realization that this is indeed "the child Antigone," παῖδ' Ἀντιγόνη. Doubtless, to a chorus of old Theban men every woman under forty must seem a child, and will be called one. It is therefore far more significant when, later in the play (l. 693), young Haimon himself calls his fiancée τὴν παῖδα, "the child," as though he himself were a cradle robber. Yet the old men elaborate on the meaning of Antigone as a child, forever young, and perhaps ever younger, as the fatality of her birth becomes powerful in her life: "O unlucky child of an unlucky father, Oedipus" (ll. 380–81). Antigone is wretched because she is born of the wretched. And from this point on in the play, once this recognition of her catastrophic birth announces itself, Antigone's path will be downhill; she will dwindle as she moves—haltingly, with the first uncertain steps of an infant—in the direction of her tomb. This decline or descent is not regression in any typical psychological sense. Rather, her growing younger is something written in her stars as a kind of cosmic destiny. Which brings us to Plato's *Statesman* (268d 5–274e 2) and the myth of the Golden Age, where everything runs in reverse. The myth has been mentioned earlier, but now it is time to take a closer look.

•

The Stranger emphasizes that his tale is for children, that it is a funny story, a kind of game or treat for the kids, although he admits that children are always rapt in utter seriousness to tales that are told to them. They are also absorbed entirely in their own games, as the words for "children" and their "play"—παῖδες, παιδιά—suggest. The Stranger explains that the era in which Kronos rules, the Golden Age, is that of "earthborn" humans. In the Golden Age, to repeat, infants do not emerge from the bodies of their mothers. Rather, cadavers rise out of the earth and gradually become young again. Time goes backward until the humans, having become children, then infants, finally disappear like tiny seeds, σπέρματα, in the earth. How can we not think of child Antigone in her tomb?

Going backward is the closest approximation to eternal motion that mortal bodies, σώματα, can have, explains the Stranger, at least if their forward motion has gone as far as it can go. Yet the very form or profile of the human body, the σωματοειδές (oxymoron of all oxymorons!) stems from a still earlier era, back before the Golden Age. The Stranger will not call it the epoch of Chaos, but one does think of it in Hesiodic terms. If we remain with the Golden Age for a moment, however, we should note the phrase that characterizes the enhanced youth of the earthborns: they become οἷον νεώτερον καὶ ἁπαλώτερον, "as it were, younger and more tender" with each passing day (270e 1). "More tender"? The word ἁπαλός means soft to the touch, delicate, tender; it is predicated of children and young animals, and, as with the German word *zart,* of certain parts of the mature human body. The word exists in many combined forms in Greek. In the Golden Age, maturation does not mean hardening; sclerosis is not the final stage of life but a mere beginning. The Stranger reminds us also that during this era there are no wars and no meat-eating. Instead, the earthborn human beings hold rational discourse with the animals, and that explains why during the Golden Age humans have superior knowledge, ἐπιστήμη. Because humans are born of the earth, there are no wives and no children; no sex takes place; one is almost driven to the conclusion (the Stranger remains discreet) that the human body must have looked different, must have had fewer ragged edges. No phallus, no testes, no womb, no lips—unless these were present as vestigial organs, but vestiges of what, we must ask, if we are thinking back to the beginning of the beginning. Instead of all that, perhaps, something like a cave, a hollow in the ground where a body could go to seed.

After the age of Kronos comes the era of Zeus. This is the age of unaided humankind, of the human being as the prosthetic technical giant. It is an age of waxing oblivion and increasing chaos. These are the times when the old inherited disharmonies that mar human life as we know it come to the fore. The Stranger uses the remarkable phrase, τῆς παλαιᾶς ἀναρμοστίας πάθος, "the feeling [or the experience] that arises from the ancient disharmonies."

Hölderlin, a careful reader of Plato, seems to be recalling this phrase from the *Statesman* myth when he ends his *Rhine* hymn with a similar expression. After evoking the image of a "feverish" humanity that fills the day with its own noise, he refers to the night:

> Bei Nacht, wenn alles gemischt
> Ist ordnungslos und wiederkehrt
> Uralte Verwirrung. (CHV 1:348)

> At night, when everything is jumbled
> Without order and what recurs is
> Primeval confusion.

One of the most puzzling aspects of the Stranger's story, however, is that he blames the human body for these disharmonies, the body that was formed prior to the Golden Age. Those ancient disharmonies must therefore be older than the known ages of the world. If one asserts that Antigone is going backward, it cannot be that she abides in the Age of Kronos, the Golden Age. She certainly does not lead a carefree life, shepherded by a god. She does not talk with the animals and so gain wisdom, even if she shrieks like a mother-bird. No, she is heading back toward the womb of the earth in order to disappear forever. Perhaps the child points in passing to the ancient disharmonies that continue to disturb our oblivious present. The very tenderness of her body—which, as in the case of Achilles, is what makes her heroic—indicates that Antigone is returning to the oldest epoch, that of nature or pure upsurgence, φύσις, when the form or idea of the body, the oxymoronic σωματοειδές, first took shape.

One really ought to pause over that oxymoron, *the* oxymoron of all metaphysics and morals: σωματοειδές. If there could be a form of the human body, then the Platonistic condemnation of the body (including the Stranger's expressed scorn for it) would become altogether inexplicable. Ideas are grasped by the mind, not by the bodily senses, says the metaphysician. That horribly troublesome body with its deceptive and seductive senses, adds the moralist. One might just as well say that there could be ideas or forms for hair, excrement, and dirt.... Or is it simply youth and inexperience that cause us to gape uncomprehendingly at such a possibility? If so, we have been gaping for millennia, ever since the day old Parmenides spoke with young Socrates (Plato, *Parmenides*, 130c-e).

The Stranger refers to this primordial era when he speaks of the formation of the body "in the earlier epoch," τὸ σωματοειδὲς... τὸ τῆς πάλαι ποτὲ φύσεως

(273b 4–5). He associates that epoch with brute necessity, ἀνάγκη, very much in the way that Timaeus will; for it is here that the trouble with matter, the trouble *of* matter, began. Even in the present age, where man gets on unaided as best he can, our ancient disharmonies send us hurtling back beyond the Golden Age to this primeval and necessitous time of the body. Antigone's living yet dwindling body—no marriage song, no sex, no children for her—is the simulacrum of a Golden Age gone awry. Antigone comes to her body only very slowly in Sophocles's play, and only on the downward path of a funeral march. Hölderlin, in his *Anmerkungen* to *Antigone*, says that in the end she stands for a bygone time, a time that is bygones for the body. Creon, the eternal loser, prevails as the time of future disharmonies. These dissonances of the future go on and on, repeating throughout Hesperian history the cacophony of all the ancient disharmonies. Among the items that are mislaid in all that human hubbub is tenderness.[9]

•

Let us return to Sophocles's play, at the point where Creon interrogates Antigone concerning her deed. Antigone's reply to Creon at the time of her arrest

---

9 See now the remarkable commentary on *Statesman* by Michael Naas, *Plato and the Invention of Life* (New York: Fordham University Press, 2018), along with his chapter on *Statesman* in David Jones, ed., *A Philosophy of Creative Solitudes* (London: Bloomsbury, 2019), forthcoming. My own meager contribution to Naas's thorough reading of Plato in terms of Derrida's *lifedeath* would pursue the following five steps. First, the entire myth of the two ages, those of Kronos and Zeus, is recounted because the Stranger sees that he must start out "on a different path, one that has another beginning," ἐξ ἄλλης ἀρχῆς (268d 5). Second, that new start and other beginning must be older than the ages of Zeus and Kronos; it would have to be something like the age of Hesiodic Chaos and of the Platonic χώρα as discussed in *Timaeus*. Third, this was the age when the very idea of the body and of all bodies, the σωματοειδές, was generated by the father and conceived by χώρα; it is, as the Stranger says, an age "of old," prior to the age of Kronos, τὸ τῆς πάλαι . . . φύσεως (273b 4–5). Schleiermacher translates this as *das körperliche . . . von ihrer vorigen Beschaffenheit*, "the corporeal . . . from [the time of] its earlier constitution." Fourth, all of today's disasters stem from our "experience of the old disharmonies," those that arose well before the ages of Zeus and Kronos. They stem from what one might call the Age of Lifedeath. Fifth, the Stranger remarks that no one as yet ventured to discuss the "experience undergone," the πάθος, that lies at the origin of the entire myth, πᾶσι τούτοις αἴτιον (269c 1). I would not be surprised if Michael Naas is the first to make this venture into the Platonic Age of Lifedeath; it would make us all grow younger again.—But to return now to Antigone.

(ll. 450–70) can be neatly divided into two sections. If the first half (ll. 450–60) is all about Δίκη and Antigone's just cause, the second half is all about her desire to die. She appropriates Creon's word, κέρδος, "profit, gain," to describe her death as her advantage, sinecure, and perquisite. In balance with this life, this death, as it were. She repeats the word at line 464, as she weighs her life's sufferings and misfortunes (κακοῖς) against the repose of death, where she will rejoin all her brothers. She insults Creon to this end, which is her own end: "If now my deed seems to you moronic, perhaps the moron is the one who accuses me" (ll. 469–70). Hölderlin translates, "If to you I am a fool for having done this deed, perhaps I owed a bit of foolishness to a fool." The chorus of old Theban men comment, "In the child one sees the truculent traces of a truculent father." Truculent, raw, rough-edged—thus Antigone at the outset, working to achieve her end.

Antigone assures Creon that she was born to love, not to hate, but only twenty lines later, when Ismene tries to join her in her fate, Antigone snarls, "I do not love a friend who loves in word only" (ll. 523, 543). Antigone's cruelty toward her living sister is made more remarkable by the fact that Ismene too has been accused virulently by Creon: Ismene, he says, is a succubus lowering in his house, λήθουσά μ' ἐξέπινες, "secretly sucking me dry" (l. 532). When Ismene pleads with Antigone, "What life can be dear to me if you leave me?" Antigone replies, "Ask Creon. He's the one you care for!" Her first two words, Κρέοντ' ἐρώτα, cause us considerable confusion—as they confused Hölderlin. The verb ἐρωτάω, "to ask," is easily confused with ἐράω, "to love." Citizens in the top rows of the ancient Theater of Dionysos must have wondered—did she just tell her sister to make love to Creon? Some well-meaning souls may wish to interpret Antigone's cruelty toward Ismene as a clever ruse designed to protect Ismene through dissociation. Yet it seems far more likely that Antigone's truculence is real, and it marks her principal affinity with Creon: both confuse the realms of the living and the dead, Creon by trying to kill a dead man, Antigone by loving the dead sibling and scorning the living one. "You chose to live, I to die," she says to Ismene (l. 555). And when Ismene tries to seduce her sister back into life, Antigone replies, "My soul died a long time ago [πάλαι / τέθνηκεν], to be of service to the dead" (ll. 560–61).

Antigone's belief in the nobility of her service is precisely what the second stasimon or third choral song challenges. Here we find four references to ἄτη, the infatuation and doom to which mortals are heir. And perhaps not only mortals, inasmuch as infatuation is surely a word for Zeus. As for mortals, the chorus says, "To believe that the ignoble is noble—this is what the god does to a mind that he wants to lead to doom [πρὸς ἄταν]; only for the briefest moment does such a mind act beyond the reach of doom [πράσσει δ' ὀλίγιστον χρόνον ἐκτὸς ἄτας] (ll. 622–25). To esteem a dead brother and to want to see him properly buried—this is surely noble; but to scorn a living sister and to invite one's own death, as though to lie with the beloved sibling in death? The peculiar Eros of the play needs commentary, and the chorus provides it. The third stasimon, or fourth choral ode, introduces a major turning point in the play, one that might be called a "shadow caesura." It comes immediately after the midpoint of the play, in which Haimon confronts his father. The choral song begins (ll. 781–90):

> Eros, unconquered in battle;
> Eros, you who seize your prey,
> Who spend your nights settled
> On the tender cheeks of a young girl,
> You storm across the sea and
> Strike the farmer's house;
> And not a single immortal can outrun you;
> Nor are those ephemeral human beings,
> Once seized, sane.

The chorus continues (ll. 791–94): "You, Eros, are the one who caused the just to be unjust, luring their minds to evil; you kindled the strife [νεῖκος] between these men who are blood relations." In short, Creon is infatuated with Antigone, and perhaps with her sister as well, the succubus. His struggle with Haimon is more pathetic than it at first seems, having at least as much to do with the οἶκος as with the πόλις. Although the father has ridiculed his son as "weaker than woman" and "maid-servant to a woman" (ll. 746, 756), there is some erotic confusion and competition at work there. The choral ode now says (ll. 795–800):

> The winner, shining in her gaze,
> Is desire [ἵμερος], promising the bed
> Of a young girl, her power well beyond human
> Decree; without a struggle she plays
> Her game, Aphrodite divine.

Hölderlin translates these astonishing lines in an astonishing way, granting Aphrodite her perhaps obvious meaning, "Divine Beauty," and portraying love-making as "magnificent understandings" or "grand alliances," the kind that have occurred since time immemorial:

Und nie zu Schanden wird es,
Das Mächtigbittende,
Am Augenlide der hochzeitlichen
Jungfrau, im Anbeginne dem Werden großer
Verständigungen gesellet. Unkriegerisch spielt nämlich
Die göttliche Schönheit mit. (DKV 2:890)

And never will it lose advantage,
That mighty pleading
On the eyelids of the young
Bride-to-be, in the beginning of what come to be
Grand alliances. Without going to war she plays
With us, this divine beauty.

The chorus cannot hide its tears as the ode ends and again the elders of Thebes see Antigone, but this time "coming to the end of her journey," heading toward "the marriage bed that will bed us all," τὸν παγκοίταν … θάλαμον (ll. 804–805). For that which will "bed us all" is παγκοίτας Ἅιδας, "the all-bedding Hades" (ll. 810–11). Hölderlin translates these shocking phrases modestly but compellingly as "the all-silencing" bed and "the all-silencing" Hades. By this time in the play, the chorus of old men itself seems to be caught up in the confusion of the living and the dead. It is as though while Antigone grows younger, her face aglow with a gaze as old as time, her pulsion toward death infatuates the entire city. Or perhaps the very beauty of Antigone has helped the old men to become more perspicuous. They now see, as perhaps we too have to see, that as Antigone becomes younger and more tender before their very eyes she is actually rushing to the end, telescoping all the years of her frustrated future life into this "delicate moment," which is the razor's edge on which she walks to her tomb. They cannot tell whether she is an infant or a crone. They tell her that she lives by her own law; she is αὐτονόμος, and is therefore like the gods, ἰσοθέοις (ll. 821, 837). She replies that she is at home with neither the living nor the dead, μέτοικος οὐ ζῶον, οὐ θανοῦσιν (l.852). In a sense, this lack of a secure dwelling makes her a hero—a kind of δαίμων, hovering between the spheres of mortality and immortality. Her autonomy and her friendlessness—for she is friendless (ἄφιλος) and has no relationships one might call "more tender" (οὐδεὶς φίλων)—make her the prototypical Sophoclean hero (ll. 876, 882). Autonomous, friendless, like Persephone (for that is surely what the old men mean when they say she is like a god) she goes as one living to the dead, ζῶς ἐς θανόντων (l. 920).

Precisely at the moment when the chorus announces her divine antecedents—they do not mention Persephone in fact but Danaë, Lycurgus, and Cleopatra of the Northwind—the old men stress her childlike character: ὦ παῖ παῖ, they cry (l. 948). Divinity, whether in the form of Divine Beauty or Dionysos, shines from the eyes and on the cheeks of the mortal who is forever younger. Such is the power of fate itself, which is uncanny, even monstrous, and never more so than when the young die: ἀλλ' ἁ μοιριδία τις / δύναμις δεινά (ll. 951–52). *Aber des Schiksaals ist furchtbar die Kraft,* translates Hölderlin: "Yet the force of destiny is frightful." Μοῖρα is decidedly more powerful than Zeus, who falls in love with ever-younger mortal women and men over and over again. And even if they are imprisoned in a cell, as Danaë is, she is the one—either she or Aphrodite, who radiates from her—who at least for a time rules over the father of time and the earth. Hölderlin translates:

Sie zählete dem Vater der Zeit
Die Stundenschläge, die goldnen. (DKV 2:896)

She counted off for the father of time
The strokes of the hours, the golden strokes.

If Hölderlin here intentionally "mistranslates" the golden seed of Zeus, Ζηνὸς . . . γονὰς, as "the strokes of the hours," that is precisely because he understands Zeus to be the father of time and the earth, the father whose stream of seed is the flux of time. The name *Antigone* now means "in place of the seed of god," or rather, in keeping with Hölderlin's daring rendering, "in place of the strokes of the hours." Antigone runs counter to *time* as we know it. In the *Anmerkungen,* Hölderlin will say, quite simply, that Antigone is *Antitheos,* acting "against the god," acting against the father of time and the earth (DKV 2:917). Her future is all history.

Much of what transpires and is said in the drama between the third and fourth stasima (the hymn to Eros and the stories of Danaë, Lycurgus, and Cleopatra) is itself in quasi-choral, highly rhythmic form. The play itself becomes a kind of processional, funeral march, or dirge. Even Antigone's long soliloquy, which follows the remarkable strophes of the chorus that proclaim her isomorphic with god, even this long lament has a musical quality about it. At its culmination stands that bizarre "logic" that so disturbed Goethe: husbands and children can be replaced, but once a mother and father are dead one can never engender another brother (ll. 905–907). Nor another sister, one would have wanted to remind Antigone. But perhaps by this time, so late in the game, she is too young to be reminded. She says she would never break the law for a mere husband, a moldering corpse of a husband, and this assertion makes her seem very young indeed. In these final lines of her life (ll. 863–71), she thinks of the doom of her (grand)mother Jocasta, who each time she went to bed embraced the man to whom she had given birth, Antigone's own fraternal father; she thinks of her brother Polyneices, fallen in a treacherous marriage—for it was Polyneices's wife, Aegeia of Argos, who urged him to attack Thebes. Yet what more treacherous marriage can there have been than that of Oedipus and Jocasta? The "brother" who has so disastrously "fallen" may therefore be either Polyneices or Oedipus, it is difficult to say. For a young unmarried woman like Antigone, walking toward the end of her young life, it may be utterly impossible to say. All she can say is that, husbandless, she will join her brother—one always assumes that she means Polyneices, but by this time the matter is unclear—in death. Her lament is not without a complaint against that brother, whether he be Polyneices or Oedipus: "And I, I who was simply there, / By your dying you drag me down as well," which is a rendering of Hölderlin's translation of lines 869–71. "I who was simply there." Yet what could be more complex than Antigone's *Da-Sein*?

Concerning Creon's end we need not say a great deal, inasmuch as Tiresias has said it all. Creon's goal throughout the play has been to kill a man who is already dead, "to kill the dead man once again" (l. 1030). Hölderlin translates, *Welche Kraft ist das, / Zu tödten Tote?* "What sort of force is that, / To kill the dead?" That is precisely Lacan's question to Creon, the question of "the second death." Yet Lacan finds Antigone herself "between two deaths," whether these be the deaths of her father and her brother(s) or the deaths of her own life, which is a life, she says, neither of the living nor the dead. Or it may be that her two deaths are her own and that of Haimon, who will join her in death. No moldering husband, he.

The messenger who comes to tell Eurydice, the chorus, and all of us about the deaths of Haimon and Antigone speaks of luck or chance, τύχη. Indeed, he uses the word four times in lines 1158–59. Luck, chance, or hazard "forever raises up those whose luck is good and brings to fall those whose luck is bad," he says. Cause and effect are conflated in this one fateful word. Hölderlin's translation is astonishing—and impossible to render in English: *Undenklichs hebt, undenklichs stürzet nämlich / Allzeit den Glücklichen und den Unglücklichen.* "That which does not submit to thought, that which resists thought, that which thought cannot subjugate"—that is τύχη. Neither Creon's nor Eurydice's thought could suppress or divert what was coming; neither Haimon's nor Antigone's thought could resist or evade the funereal procession of events.

The messenger then adds something that seems obvious to everyone: a human being who has lost all of his or her pleasures, ἡδοναί, seems to be no longer alive; he or she seems rather to be "an ensouled corpse," ἔμψυχον ... νεκρόν (ll. 1165–67). What is not so obvious is that the definition of human being for two millennia of Christian philosophy, that is, for the entire history of metaphysics and morals, is perilously close to this one; indeed, when one thinks of Descartes's fresh cadavers, with their springs and levers still agile and their pineal glands not yet melted, the definition fits perfectly. How odd to think that the barely living Creon—for at the end he says that he is less than nothing—defines much of Hesperian humanity; barely living he may be, but incredibly long-lasting, as enduring as those ancient disharmonies. This too is confirmed by Hölderlin's *Anmerkungen*, which say that the future belongs to the hapless, hopeless Creon, the past to Antigone (DKV 2:920–21). For even if he stumbles onward as future history, she has collapsed against her defunct brothers like an exhausted runner—her race is run.

As luck would have it, the messenger leads Creon first to Polyneices's corpse. By the time they burn what remains of it and bury the ashes beneath a mound of "our homeland's earth," Antigone has hanged herself by her linen clout. The messenger, anticipating what his tale is about to reveal, calls her cave "the stony marriage bed of Hades" (ll. 1203–05). Haimon, perhaps kneeling on the floor of the cave, embraces her corpse—perhaps about the knees. She hangs there as her mother and paternal grandmother before her had hung. Creon hears his son's cries of grief and enters the tomb. Haimon spits in his father's face, tries to stab him, fails, then falls on his own sword. Although Sophocles does not explicitly say so, Haimon must have enough life left in him to sever the clout and release Antigone's body, lowering it carefully to the floor. Or perhaps the messenger has done this; he does not say. In any case, the two corpses now cover one another in an act, or still-life, of love: "The dead lies with the dead," κεῖται δὲ νεκρὸς περὶ νεκρῷ (l. 1240). Sophocles's messenger also tells us that a spray of bright blood from Haimon's mouth spatters her white cheek, the cheek where Eros should have passed his nights. It is not hymeneal blood, but perhaps the blood of birth that marks her tiny corpse. She could not have grown any younger.

Lines 1283, 1301, and 1315 emphasize that Eurydice, upon hearing the news of her second son's death, kills herself by the sword, not by hanging. Like son, like mother. Antigone, though a virgin, has hanged herself, as though she were a married woman. Like daughter, like (grand)mother. Finally, lines 1325–27 lead us back to Oedipus, "Swell-foot," by way of the feet. "Lead my feet away from here," cries Creon (l. 1324). The chorus, searching for something to say, tells him that there may be some profit in bad luck, inasmuch as "what is best is to have evil underfoot as briefly as possible" (l. 1327). Which is a little bit like saying *never to have been born is best.* Indeed, many of Antigone's own utterances during the play also seem to conform to the wisdom of Silenos, and Antigone herself seems to be in hot pursuit of what is "second best" for humankind. Creon too has by now been reduced in size, age, and wisdom to almost nothing: "Lead me by my feet away, I am no longer in being, I am no more than a nothing," τὸν οὐκ ὄντα μᾶλλον ἢ μηδένα (l. 1325). Hölderlin translates, *Mich, der nun nichts mehr Anders ist, als Niemand,* "I who am now no longer anything other than no one." Which becomes the name of the avatar of the Hesperian future, the future of the West.

Some final thoughts about tender Antigone, forever younger. She is an ageless, unending challenge for every reader of the tragedy, her "use" by the gods a mystery to her and to us, a mystery that remains unsolved. And the "gods" themselves? Hölderlin writes of the need to translate the names of all the gods for the modern ear, and his translations of these names are among the most mysterious of all his renderings. Perhaps the strangest translations are those of mother and daughter, Demeter (or Deo) and Persephone. The latter he calls "furiously compassionate—a light," the former "the impenetrable." Perhaps he means to remind us of the earth near Polyneices's corpse, which shows no signs of scraping, no signs of human intervention. At all events, the final choral ode of *Antigone* invokes Dionysos, the god of theater, as πολυώνυμε, "many-named." Hölderlin has "Creator of names," *Nahmenschöpfer.* The old men of Thebes are praying to their home god, Dionysos, grandson of Cadmus and Harmony, the son of their daughter Semele, praying that the god of joy may come to Antigone's rescue. The god of the maenads, of the raving women—could he be the god who uses Antigone? Would he not have to be the one, if, as Heraclitus says, "Hades" and "Dionysos" say the same?

For it seems as though Antigone is the latest victim of King Pentheus, if Creon is the latest incarnation of the tyrant of Thebes. If Antigone *is* a maenad follower of Dionysos—though surely she was once too old to be such, and now she is far too young—she is an odd maenad, one with a death-obsessed spirit that we, rightly or wrongly, do not associate with the women worshipers. The confusion of the living and the dead of which Creon is guilty is a crime against the living god, the god of liquid life. Yet what of Antigone's own confusion of the living and the dead? Can Dionysos have returned to Thebes to punish her as though she were one of his aunts, one of the women who scorned and mocked their sister Semele—or in this case Ismene?

If Dionysos and Hades are the same, then the confusion of the living and the dead is older than both Antigone and Creon. Although Antigone as typically portrayed would be likely to scorn the worship of Dionysos, perhaps her growing younger and more tender as the play proceeds reflects her having learned—too late, which is the way tragic heroes always learn—to worship life instead of death. Perhaps we have to entertain the very odd notion that Antigone, as she takes her first awkward steps toward her tomb, learns the worship of the new god. *Antigone maenadica*? A dissonance, to be sure. Yet no more dissonant than all those ancient disharmonies to which mortals are heir. Perhaps all those disharmonies stem from the startling contrast between the rigorous corpse and tender, living flesh, especially the flesh of the young; or they may stem from the incomprehensibility of a human being's being *toward* or *unto* death—the preposition *zum* being the most enigmatic word in Heidegger's famous phrases, *Sein zum Tode* and *Sein zum Ende*, taken up by Lacan at the very end of *The Ethics of Psychoanalysis*. The unbearable contradiction between the chill of the cadaver and the heat of the heart is at least one axis about which all tragedy turns. Empedocles believed that mortal thought is borne by the flow of blood through and about the heart, such that all thinking is pericardial. A woman who has a hot heart for cold things would embody this unbearable contradiction of mortality most unbearably. Her only chance would be to grow so young that she moves back beyond the Golden Age to the Age of Φύσις, the age of the neophyte body, the age of her own *birth*. If the human body, with all its chaotic energies and pulsions, is the source of all those ancient disharmonies, that may be because the gods themselves cannot get over their infatuation with and use of those tender, beautiful mortals. Hölderlin's famous "Rhine" hymn expresses the thought incomparably well:

> Yet they have enough of their own
> Immortality, the gods, and if they need
> One thing, these celestial ones,
> It would be heroes and humans
> And all that's mortal. For if
> The most blessed feel nothing of themselves,
> It must be, if to say such a thing
> Is allowed, that in the names of the gods
> Another takes their part and feels for them;
> They need him. (DKV 1:331)

In the present instance, of course, they need *her*. And their use of her will reduce her to the child that she is—infinitely tender, forever younger.

Chapter Four

Tender Schlegel, Irascible Hegel

> Ethicality turned somewhat pale and her eyes welled with tears. "But only yesterday I was so virtuous . . . . It's all I can do to deal with my own reproofs; why must I hear still more of them from you?"
>
> —Friedrich Schlegel, *Lucinde*

AS WE MOVE AWAY from the world of antiquity and enter the modern world of the Romantics, the world of Hölderlin and his contemporaries, we might expect an inquiry into tenderness to have an easier time of it. Yet if Freud is right when he defines modernity in terms of the widespread *failure* of tenderness, especially when it comes to modern lovelife, we may also expect something of a struggle between the cudgel and the caress. For every Romantic who champions the caress we will find a Knight of the Pure Spirit, and no knight rides unarmed. The present chapter focuses on one of the many sorties for and against *Zärtlichkeit* in the era of German Romanticism and Idealism.

Despite widespread belief to the contrary, Hegel does not rhyme with Schlegel. Not ever. Hegel is contemptuous of so many of his contemporaries, but he hates no one as much as he hates Schlegel, Friedrich. The brother, August Wilhelm, is not so bad. But Friedrich! He incorporates well-nigh everything Hegel abominates. In his foreword to Friedrich Wilhelm Hinrichs's *Philosophy of Religion* (HW 11:61; cf. 18:81), Hegel identifies Friedrich Schlegel as a paragon of every fault of the times: the accidental and fortuitous quality of subjective feeling and opinion, which is bound up with the particular "formation of reflection" that dominates Hegel's times (HW 7:311, 383), corrupts Schlegel's spirit to the point where it cannot know the truth—an incapacity the ancients called *sophistry*. Sophistry shares with philosophy the "formation of reflection," yet it does so in a merely spurious and empty way. And because it rejects the truths of Revelation, Schlegel's sophistry has no other ground to stand on than its own bottomless vanity. Schlegel's is a "worldly wisdom," for he is expert in the temporal, the transient, the contingent, and the untrue; he elevates vanity and mere fripperies of feeling to the Absolute. No wonder Schlegel is able to produce such a scurrilous novel as *Lucinde* (1799). No wonder he later converts to Catholicism. *Madonna mia.*

A letter Hegel wrote in October 1824 reveals that the heraldic eagle of German philosophy never crossed Schlegel's path until that date, and even then it did not come to a genuine meeting between the two men. That is perhaps fortunate. Schlegel's conversion to Catholicism and his support of the defunct House of Habsburg against Napoleon no doubt disgusted Hegel (HB 1:283, 2:165; HW 7:284). Yet it is doubtless Schlegel's liaison with Dorothea Veit—taken by virtually every early reader of *Lucinde* to be the heroine-in-real-life of that scandalous work—that most disturbs him. When Schlegel seduces good Dr. Veit's wife, he duplicates the crime committed by Hegel's former friend Schelling against Schlegel's own brother, August Wilhelm: just as Schelling inveigles himself with Caroline Schlegel, so Schlegel insinuates himself with Dorothea Veit, thus profaning the sacredness of both marriage and fraternal fidelity. Indeed, Friedrich Schlegel becomes something of a fratricide, committing the very crime against another that has been perpetrated against his own fraternal flesh. Reason enough to stir Hegel's ire.

Yet what is it about Schlegel's flippancy and vanity that so infuriates Hegel? What is it about *Lucinde* that gets under Hegel's spiritual skin? Has Schlegel in some way, perhaps unwittingly, encroached on Hegel's territory, invading the land of spirit? Yet how could a work of tender and unbridled sensuality, and a mere novel at that, manage to trespass onto the property of exalted spirit, there to purloin the closely guarded property of the concept?

•

Doubtless, Hegel wants spirit *alive.* Spirit alive is not only rational, not only thinking and willing spirit, not only the spirit of logic, but also spirit sentient, sensible, and sensuous. The present chapter is therefore about sentience, sensibility, and sensuality, so essential to tender life and yet so difficult to get under rational control, so mobile and prolific. A tradition as old as that of "spirit" identifies sentience and the sensuous with various figures of woman—as though spirit alive were at least in part *of woman,* whatever that strange genitive may mean. Hegel's philosophical system confronts the following predicament: if woman were purged from the system of spirit, spirit would die; remaining within the system, however, woman condemns spirit and its system to a fate worse than death.

In the handwritten notes and the Addendum to §164 of Hegel's *Philosophy of Right* we find two explicit references to Friedrich Schlegel's novel *Lucinde*, first published in 1799.[1] Lucinde is the second of three major figures of woman dominating the first part of the first division of "Ethicality" (§§142–360), treating the family (§§158–81) and marriage (§§161–69). The first figure is *Venus vaga* (mentioned in the handwritten notes to §161), the wandering, vagrant, or vagabond Venus, whom the Greeks called Pandemian, or "Common," "Vulgar" Aphrodite; the third is of course the heroine of Sophocles's *Antigone* in her adversarial guise (§166). Hegel's dialectical account of marriage and the family reacts intensely to these three figures of woman, negatively to the first two, enthusiastically to the third: the goddess of sensual love and beauty is hastily abandoned for the infinitely free personality of the Romantic beloved, the free personality ostensibly symbolized by and portrayed in Schlegel's *Lucinde*, while the figure of Lucinde—infinitely free but totally out of control—is in turn abjured for Antigone, at which point the law of woman surrenders to the law of the state. Antigone does not grow younger and more tender, in Hegel's view; she matures as the law of the family, and then, in her tomb of stone, she succumbs to the bedrock of civil society.

I do not have the leisure to survey the entire process of the three figures. Allow me to focus on the middle figure, Lucinde, and to ask what it is about her that so attracts and unnerves Hegel. For whenever Lucinde is invoked in his text, Hegel's irritability, irascibility, and even anxiety or sense of jeopardy wax strong. What has the system of philosophy to fear from her? Nothing—if we trust Hegel's account of her pitiable position, forever on the brink of shame and ruin, even if she is but a fiction, a persona in a novel. Everything—if she represents the irrational underside of nature, the nature that will not submit to the concept, the nature that is monstrous; *everything* once again if Philippe

1 G. W. F. Hegel, *Grundlinien der Philosophie des Rechts,* in HW 7:317. I will cite Hegel's *Rechtsphilosophie* principally by section number in the body of my text. Friedrich Schlegel's *Lucinde: Ein Roman* was first published in 1799 by Heinrich Froelich in Berlin. I have used the text edited by Wolfgang Hecht, Friedrich Schlegel, *Werke in zwei Bänden* (Berlin and Weimar: Aufbau-Verlag, 1980), 2:5–99. After my work was done I discovered the fine English translation of *Lucinde and the Fragments* by Peter Firchow (Minneapolis: University of Minnesota Press, 1971), containing Schlegel's novel, the Athenaeum Fragments, and other writings. I cite the German edition of Lucinde simply by page number in the body of my text. As for English translations of Hegel's *Philosophy of Right,* they omit Hegel's handwritten notes, which are essential to my topic; I shall therefore refer to the German edition throughout.

Lacoue-Labarthe is right to see in her poetry, literature, and the aesthetic as such, the troublesome parts of the system, the subordinated and dejected materials that inevitably return to haunt the speculative.[2]

I will take up Lacoue-Labarthe's thesis in some detail later in the chapter. Taking my cue from him already now, however, I want to ask about those troublesome parts of literature and life. I will examine some of the predicates that cling to Lucinde in Hegel's text, comparing them to passages in Friedrich Schlegel's *Lucinde*; I will then examine quite briefly Hegel's Jena lectures on the *pudenda*, the "shameful parts"; and I will close with some speculations concerning sensuous woman—if one can write such a phrase in the singular, as though she were one—and the law of tenderness, which appears to be in conflict with the law of the state. But first a word, merely by way of introduction, about Friedrich Schlegel's scandalous novel, the fiction that so offends the heraldic eagle of philosophy.

Throughout Jacques Derrida's *Glas* much is made of the fact that when the French pronounce the name *Hegel* it comes out sounding like their word for *eagle*.[3] And there is some truth in saying that Hegel himself identified with the heraldic Prussian eagle, the high-flying, sharp-taloned bird of philosophy, at least when philosophy flies by day. By contrast, Friedrich Schlegel, in his impudent "Prologue" to *Lucinde*, citing the examples of Petrarch, Boccaccio, and Cervantes, identifies himself with the *swan*: whereas the eagle expends its energies lording it over the lowly crow, says Schlegel, the swan dreams only of how it can ingratiate itself with a beautiful woman, how it can "cling to the bosom of Leda without doing any harm" (6).

It is not easy to describe this self-proclaimed "smiling, touching" book of Schlegel's, though it is easy to imagine a sober reader's indignation over it. A brief novel of about one hundred pages, Schlegel's *Lucinde* ("Part One" is all Schlegel ever completed) consists of thirteen unnumbered sections. Some of the more insolent section titles communicate the peculiar humor of the book's

---

2 Philippe Lacoue-Labarthe, "L'imprésentable," in *Poetique* no. 21 (1975), 53–95.

3 *Hégel, aigle.* Perhaps in English we could say *Heagle.* See Derrida, G 7a, 22a (insert), 46a, 65a, 68b (insert),106a, 117a, 138b (insert), 206–207a (insert), 217–18b (insert), 234a (insert); in the English translation by John P. Leavey, Jr. and Richard Rand (Lincoln: University of Nebraska Press, 1986), see 1a, 15a (insert), 37a, 54–55a, 57b (insert), 91a, 102a, 120b (insert), 184a (insert), 194b (insert), 209a (insert). I am grateful to John Leavey for these references; see his remarkable Glossary to *Glassary* (Lincoln: University of Nebraska Press, 1986), 213.

"smiling" visage: "Dithyrambic Fantasy Concerning the Loveliest Situation," "Allegory of Impudence," "Idyll of Idleness," "Fidelity and Frolic," "Apprenticeship to Manliness," "Metamorphoses," "Languor and Repose," "Baubles of Fantasy," and in the midst of all this, "A Reflection." In these ironic and overdetermined "arabesques," as Schlegel liked to call them, the novelist elaborates a theory of love, marriage, and the status of women that can only be called revolutionary for its time. The two leading characters, Lucinde and Julius, embrace one another with as much religiosity as sensual abandon; what others would regard as obscenity they celebrate as their system; voluptuosity is not only their virtuosity but also their virtue; their carnival of carnal love and lust builds cathedrals, and when they weary of cathedrals, they laugh and tear them down like children at play. In fact they often seem to regress to childhood, playing at innocence, aping one another, she playing the man, he the woman. They let their feelings and their fantasies flow unchecked. In their sensuous passivity, a passivity they seem to cultivate actively, Lucinde and Julius alike scorn the heroic and opt for the sentimental. They disdain Prometheus and worship Hyacinth.

Lucinde is an artist, a painter. She is a mature woman, and in giving herself over to the younger Julius, she sometimes seems to be adopting an orphan, and he sometimes seems to be falling back into his mother's arms. She mixes her colors well, swirling the sacred blues of motherhood into the roses and reds of profane and passionate love. All her works and all their works together consist of baubles, bangles, and bright shiny rosary beads: they act like happy beasts, with the express intention of transforming humanity into divinity. Hegel has no choice: he has to take an interest in this, for the spirited lovers claim to be the agents of spirit as such—agents of a spirit born out of wedlock and proud of it. Julius and Lucinde are the bastard son and bastard daughter of spirit—children that spirit may be forced to acknowledge but can never recognize as legitimate.

For Hegel, by way of contrast, love-and-marriage in real life, not in novels, is entirely a matter of proper sequence, succession, and consequence. It is essentially a matter of reversing the *natural* chronology or sequence of events by grace of a spiritual anachronism. If nature brings together a particular "this" (who happens to be a male) with a second particular "this" (who happens to be a female), as it must do if the species is to perpetuate itself, and if natural passion causes all the "chords" of one self-consciousness "to reverberate only in this other one, only in the possession of this *one contingent* person," then spirit will have to elevate the merely accidental conjunction of these persons by reversing the order of dependence established in the natural course of events (HW 7:313). Meeting and mating will not *lead to* marriage; mating at least will be *consequent upon* marriage and *subsequent to* it. Love and marriage will go together like a horse and carriage only if the carriage is placed before the horse. Schlegel would of course observe that such a vehicle is not going anywhere, but Hegel remains adamant. For him the proper order, the order of spirit, will be: marriage and (only then) love. Only in this way will the particularity and contingency of passionate sensibility be elevated to the universality of bonded spiritual love. Only in this way will the high necessity of the spiritual progression to family, civil society, and the state prevail. Only in this way will love slough off its natural integument and rise on the divine afflatus of spirit proper.

Yet the stakes are hardly the same for the two "thises" destined to be elevated by the spiritual anachronism of matrimony. Hegel sees that the stakes are set high, infinitely high, for a woman, inasmuch as her honor (*Ehre*) is won solely on the field of marriage (*Ehe*). Honor and matrimony are in fact one for woman, and could be written as *Eh(r)e*. All else is ignominy, if not evil. That becomes clear in the otherwise elliptical notes that Hegel jots into his own copy of the *Grundlinien*.

Let us examine extracts from two sets of these notes, those to §162 and §164. First, those from §162, which begins with a question that is speedily answered: "What does the man want, what does the girl [*Mädchen*] want? The girl wants a man; the man wants a woman [*eine Frau*]" (HW 7:312). The slippage between *Mädchen* and *Frau*, in contrast to the dependable repetition of *Mann*, indicates that in the natural course of events some essential dissymmetry is at work. The exchange of desires seems fair enough at first. And yet the difference in the stakes is already clear. Twice the word *Mann* (man, husband) asserts itself, serving as both the subject and the object of desire: the girl wants a man (or *husband*), whereas the man, confronting a girl, wants a *woman*. As the subject of desire, the girl is apparently equal to herself (although even here the self-sufficiency is illusory), whereas as an *object* of desire she will have to be transmogrified from girl to woman.[4] How will this happen? Hegel

---

4 I am of course using the phrase that serves as the title of Judith P. Butler's by now classic study, *Subjects of Desire: Hegelian Reflections in Twentieth-Century France* (New York: Columbia University Press, 1987). Butler concentrates on Hegel's *Phenomenology of Spirit,* especially chapter 4, on the "ontology of desire" and on lordship and bondage, all of which I shall have to leave out of account here. See Krell, "Pitch: Genitality/ Excrementality from Hegel to Crazy Jane," in *boundary 2*, special issue "On Feminine Writing,"12:2 (Winter 1984), 113–41, which takes its point of departure from a passage in Hegel's remarks on "Observational Reason" in the *Phenomenology*, a passage that has to do with *Pissen*.

continues, if only by indirection: "She loves him. Why? Because he is to become her husband" (HW 7:312). It is still the same word, *Mann,* that serves for male, man, and husband alike. But to continue: "He is to make her into a woman [*Frau*]. She is to receive from him as the man [or husband] her dignity, value, joy, and happiness as a *wife* [Ehefrau], insofar as she becomes woman [*Frau*]. *Love*—she recognizes the basis of her interest in the man; this is preeminently *the girl's sensibility*" (ibid.).

At least two kinds of appropriation are going on here. We are by now accustomed to one of them—appropriation of the names *girl, woman,* and *wife* as tokens of masculine desire, pawns on the chessboard at which a man appears to playing all by himself. Yet the second appropriation, albeit every bit as traditional, is far more difficult to descry and less calculable in its effects: the first stage of ethicality as a whole, namely, the stage of *love* as the nonmediated substantiality of spirit, the *family* as a unit of sensibility (§158), is in effect being relegated or surrendered to the girl. Without (the girl's) sensibility, Hegel himself stresses, the life of spirit would be dry and brittle (Addendum to §33); indeed, without sensibility in the Kantian sense, the processes of *intelligence* and *cognition* would not have their start.[5] However, to repeat, sensibility and receptivity are delivered over to and appropriated by a young girl—neither a goddess nor a mortal woman, but a mere maid, as one used to say. Antigone, perhaps, at least if we think of the Antigone in the play that bears her name, and not the Antigone of *Oedipus at Colonos,* who ought to be younger than *Antigone*'s Antigone, but who seems much older. *Antigone*'s Antigone, we recall, is a girl who is under arrest. And, because she will die as a *Mädchen* rather than as the *Frau* of the king's own son, she is and remains a case of either arrested development or movement in reverse, growing ever younger. But does that mean that Hegel is on the side of Creon, the king and patriarch?

On the one hand, Hegel holds no truck with patriarchy, which makes slaves of its children and even arranges their marriages, as though love were a matter of contract (as it apparently was for Kant the bachelor). On that same hand, Hegel does not wish to reproduce the Romish-monkish mistake of vilifying

---

5 See G. W. F. Hegel, *Enzyklopädie der philosophischen Wissenschaften 1830,* eds. Friedhelm Nicolin and Otto Pöggeler (Hamburg: F. Meiner, "Philosophische Bibliothek," no. 33, 1969), §§ 399–402, and 445–47. I have discussed sensibility and intelligence in the context of "interiorizing remembrance," *Erinnerung,* in chapter 5 of Krell, *On the Verge: Of Memory, Reminiscence, and Writing* (Bloomington: Indiana University Press, 1990).

natural vitality; he does not wish to mortify sensuality as negative in itself. On the other hand, sensibility and sensitivity are for Hegel all too clearly "of" woman, perhaps even "of" the girl. The problem is that in the transition from tender girlhood to sensuous womanhood sensitivity and sensibility can readily become what a novelist like Schlegel unabashedly calls "the sensibility of the flesh" (26). Sentience, sensibility, sensitivity, and sensuality will thus—all of it—have to be but a passing moment for Hegel and for spirit, if not for Lucinde and Julius, who will therefore have to be discarded. It is no accident that all the predicates of sensibility, otherwise the life's blood of spirit and an essential component of the system, assemble in one place in *The Philosophy of Right*: these predicates—naturalness, contingency, accident, particularity, inclination, drive, and desire—loom at and as the origins of evil (§139).

The second set of handwritten notes (those to §164) takes up the seducer's familiar sophism, Prove-That-You-Love-Me-Darling, and the high stakes for an Oh-Please-Don't-Make-Me-Prove-It maid. Of course, the notes become compelling only in the context of §164 viewed as a whole. Herewith, then, a brief résumé.

Only when solemnization of the lovers' union through matrimony takes place in the presence of the family and community as witnesses does natural love receive its spiritual bond. Hegel emphasizes the importance of the "antecedence" of the ceremony, this antecedence alone reversing the natural sequence of events in such a way that "the sensuous moment pertaining to natural vitality is posited in its ethical relationship as a consequence and mere accident" (HW 7:315). The repetition of "mere accident" is troubling here: one might have hoped that marriage would make the consequent natural vitality essential. Yet dialectic cannot perform miracles. When the cart is placed before the horse, not only does the vehicle falter, but something irreversible happens to the horse. Perhaps this is Schlegel's insight, one that would have to cause Hegel considerable discomfort insofar as it reveals something that dialectic cannot preserve but only cancel, not lift up and "relieve" but simply squelch. And that something would be nature. Some Romantic moderns (for Schlegel is certainly not alone, and Friedrich Schleiermacher, from whom we will soon hear, is not his only ally) take solemnization—funereal word!—itself to be accidental and superfluous, an extrinsic formality, a civil instance that uncivilly interrupts the intimacy of the lovers' union. The witnesses may be weeping sentimental tears, but the tears flow from eagle eyes that are there to see to it that "natural vitality" yields to ironclad obligation. Schlegel calls the liturgy of solemnization "vain words, without a blessing in them" (75). Romantic moderns, when they themselves constitute the loving couple, do not accept that the formal ceremony is "the antecedent condition of their mutual and total abandon" (HW 7:316). (The word rendered here by "abandon," or sometimes "surrender," is *Hingebung,* literally a giving-over of oneself to another, and it will soon return to haunt the spiritual bond.) These Romantic moderns even believe that love is divided or sullied by such ceremonial or ceremonious intrusion. "Divided" tries to translate the word *veruneinige,* "to disunite." Georg Lasson reads it, however, as *verunreinige,* with a second *r,* and that would mean "to pollute," as though the source of pollution could be the altar or the civil registry rather than the natural order of events. Even Friedrich Schlegel, presumably, would not dare go so far!

Modern, Romantic love is no doubt superior to the "Platonic love" of popular conceit, in Hegel's view, for it is closely tied to the essential individualism of modernity and of Protestant Christianity as such. That would be the attraction of Lucinde, if not of Schlegel's *Lucinde.* Nevertheless, Romantic love often engages in the "pretense" of being purer than purity itself (§164 "Remark"). It denies the ethicality of love, rejects "the more elevated inhibition and suppression of the mere physical drive," an inhibition and suppression that occur naturally through "shame" and spiritually through the inculcation of "chastity" and "decency" (HW 7:316). Why natural shame is insufficient and needs the supplement of inculcated "decency" would be an arresting question, as would the question as to why "natural vitality" needs the supplement of spiritual oversight. In any case, Hegel insists that the natural and sensuous moment be subordinated or demoted (§163); else all is insolence, impudence, and even impudicity—for we are already talking about Lucinde and her paramour Julius. Insolence or impudence is the very allegory played out so shamelessly by the author of *Lucinde,* an author possessed of intellect and wit but blind to the speculative nature of love and marriage—which is acknowledged, on the contrary, by the legislation of all Christian peoples.

Let us now take a closer look at Schlegel's novel, asking about the *categories* and even the *logic* that might explain Hegel's hatred of it. For a hatred as furious as Hegel's has many facets and deserves to be studied philosophically. In the "Prologue" to the novel, as I have noted, Schlegel identifies himself as the swan who preens his feathers and thinks only of applying himself to Leda's lap; the other birdlike guise of Zeus, namely, the eagle, with which Hegel is more likely to identify himself, Schlegel obviously spurns (6). Hegel's scorn therefore has something defensive about it right from the start. *Lucinde* is an accusation against everything the heraldic eagle stands for. In his very first letter to Lucinde, Julius admits that he is "not especially attuned" to the analysis of *concepts,* so that he readily and admittedly confuses spirit with "voluptuosity" and "sensuous blessedness" (9); he is indeed a lover of "romantic confusion . . . of a wondrous mish-mash," and not of the clarity of the concept (10). He claims the right to pursue "stimulating confusion" and to experience "the most beautiful chaos of sublime harmonies" (11–12). Yet when such confusion spreads, the harmonies clash in such a way that a bemused Schlegel feels he can identify sexual embrace with religion: "We embraced with as much abandonment as religion" (10). Surely, Hegel would say, enough is enough. When Julius boasts that "the extremes of unbridled lust and serene intimation cohabit in me" (13), and when he writes explicitly of "the religion of love" that he and Lucinde adopt as their confession (15), he is mocking Christianity, and enough is too much. Yet Julius never has enough: "I didn't merely enjoy; rather, I felt and enjoyed my enjoyment" (ibid.). The reflexivity by which Schlegel loves making love mimics universality, but Schlegel's "formation of reflection" fails him precisely here, where sophistry rules. "Let me confess that I love not only you," he writes to Lucinde, "but also womanliness itself. I don't merely love it, I adore it, because I adore humanity and because womanliness is the blossom at the summit of the plant, its natural beauty and formation" (29). Any woman with a brain in her head would hear in this suspect universality the telltale sound of cracked crystal: Schlegel does not ring true.

Schlegel's hero calls his worship of womankind "the oldest, most childlike, simplest religion," and there he is certainly right in Hegel's view. Julius even begs to be ordained into the priesthood of this idolatry, and in the end the blackguard priest confesses to Lucinde, "Really, one ought to love all women in jest" (40). The thinly veiled contempt for both womankind and Christian faith extends in fact to all of bourgeois society. Schlegel writes:

> Out there, a man loves only the species when he loves a woman; the woman loves only the degree of his natural qualities and his bourgeois existence; both love their children because they made them and now they own them. Out there, fidelity is something one has earned, and a virtue; in addition out there is where you will always find jealousy. For they feel uncommonly correct about this, it goes without saying, the belief that there are many others out there who are just like them, and since they are all human, one is worth about as much as another, and taken all together, they are not worth much at all. (41)

It comes as no surprise to Hegel that the religion that "adores" womankind is also bound to cost a man his manhood, so that he surrenders his dignity along with his sex: "Among all the things we do," says the besotted Julius, "the cleverest and loveliest is when we switch roles and with childlike pleasure challenge one another to see which of us can ape the other more convincingly, whether you are better at the protective vehemence of the man or I am better at the seductive surrender of the woman. . . . I see here a wonderfully sensuous and significant allegory of the completion of male and female in a humanity that is whole and entire" (16). Seductive surrender, indeed, murmurs Hegel's ghost. *Aping* the other, indeed.

Once the family is despised, the children as well as the parents, Hegel suspects that nothing can prevent Schlegel from dallying with paidophilia. Schlegel's Julius observes the two-year-old Wilhelmine planting a kiss on her dolly and writes as follows:

> Of course! It lies deep in human nature that it wants to eat everything it loves and puts every novel thing that appears to it directly into its mouth, in order, if possible, to reduce it to its constituent parts. The healthy craving for knowledge desires to seize its object entirely, to penetrate to its inmost core and chew it up. By contrast, touching merely remains isolated at the outer surface, and every conceptualizing proffers incomplete and only mediate knowledge. . . . And now, behold! This lovable Wilhelmine not rarely finds inexpressible enjoyment in lying on her back, gesticulating with her little legs high in the air, unconcerned with her skirts and the judgment of the world. . . . If Wilhelmine does that, what may I not do, since, by God, I'm a man, and I don't have to be more delicate than the most delicate female creature? (18–19)

If clarity of concept is not Schlegel's strength, since he only wants to eat it, neither is a serious engagement with the history of spirit. The only thing that calls for "precision" and for a "compact" recounting, in Schlegel's view, is "the history of our foolishness" or "lightheadedness" (11). Julius's infatuation, his dizziness over a woman, is the only thing that strikes him as "so ceaselessly progressive and so inflexibly systematic" (ibid.), whereby the word *systematisch* should scorch Schlegel's tongue or vaporize his pen. As for this woman, Julius sings the praises of her *Geist* over and over again, but we know he means her breasts and hips and other items. "How firm and independent they are!" he exclaims, "How smooth and fine!" (37).

Thinking himself a poet and a writer, Julius proclaims that the secret of his success in literature is leisure and inactivity. It shows. Hegel would ask: Was ever a book so repetitious and so heavy-handed in its forced levity? Julius believes that *Gelassenheit und Sanftmut*, releasement and gentleness, will suffice;

he takes the "tender and sweetly formed spirit" of India as his model (33). He clearly has not read Hegel on the depravities of Indian religion and culture. Who can be surprised, then, when Schlegel's hero says that "the supreme and most perfected form of life is nothing other than a *pure vegetating*" (34: *ein* reines Vegetieren)?[6]

It is not Schlegel's use of the words *zart, Zartheit, Zärtlichkeit* that ruffles the eagle's feathers, even if one or other of these words appears repeatedly on every page of *Lucinde*, the book as a whole being what Schlegel himself calls *ein zärtliches Furioso.* What troubles the eagle is that in Schlegel's novel tenderness is consistently confused with sensual excitement—as though Julius were determined to solve Freud's problem *de bonne heure.* And such sensual excitement, Hegel would agree, is essentially "of" woman. Perhaps Schlegel has seduced Hegel by suggesting that in the "tender hearts" of all women, as Julius says, "the holy fire of divine voluptuosity lies deeply sealed" (25). And yet Hegel senses that from time to time Lucinde has had enough of Julius: "Your tenderness is flowing today like a cloudburst," she says (37). She is also right to feel jealousy when confronting a man who says to her face that a lover should love all women only in jest. The joke will always be on her, of course. In *Lucinde* too, predictably, the result of all the high jinx is pregnancy (75). Hegel knew it all along, and in fact he predicted it. Schlegel says of his hero, "A stream of importunities, flatteries, and sophistries flowed from his lips" (47). At that moment, as "the bud of her beautiful mouth opens with tender longing" and as Lucinde "gives herself over to him utterly," Schlegel himself, having forgotten his heroine's maternal uxoriousness, describes her "tender virginal body and the fruit of her young breasts" (ibid.). Lucinde is merely another Lisette, the young professional woman whom Julius earlier on in his life has also made pregnant—and then has abandoned to her fate, which is suicide. Had the novel been called *Lisette* it would not have sold so well: the story would have been too true-to-life.

When Julius learns of Lucinde's pregnancy, he prates ecstatically for several pages about his future "son." After several more pages, it occurs to him that the baby might be a girl. This is about the same time he refers to Lucinde's "immaculate conception," and to her status as the Madonna (79). Presumably he is happy to have played the role of the Paraclete. *Madonna mia.*

---

6 Some, of course, would find this a good thing. See Elaine P. Miller, *The Vegetative Soul: From Philosophy of Nature to Subjectivity in the Feminine* (Albany: State University of New York Press, 2002). I ask the reader not to take this lighthearted reference to Miller's book as a slight: it is a brilliant and wonderfully readable book.

•

Schlegel has no sense of dialectic, Hegel would say; he never moves from thesis and contradiction to a third determinate object. Hegel may therefore expect—and perhaps has every reason to hope—that Schlegel would never be able to perceive something like the failure of dialectic to preserve natural vitality in the advance to marriage. Surely, Schlegel is too simple to perceive such a thing. If something is green Schlegel calls it red, if it is red, he calls it green, and then he gapes at his readers to see if they find him witty rather than merely colorblind. He thinks by opposition only, he inverts merely for the sake of inversion, taking that to be wit, and he wants to be witty in order to shock the burghers. He is so busy epataying the bourgeois that he has no time to think seriously. For him, the "Idea" has a lap, and his only desire is to fall into it (13). If Hegel, in his *Philosophy of History*, celebrates the cunning of reason, Schlegel celebrates the cunning of nature. Presumably both Lisette and Lucinde are the recipients of the effects of such cunning "natural vitality." Schlegel jests about determination and indeterminacy, identifying the first with the male, the second with the female, but he ends his "Reflection" with the following words: "The reflection, penetrating deeply into the matter of individuality, took such an individual direction that it soon began to cease and to forget itself" (89). So much for the "formation of reflection" in the case of Schlegel.

One last aspect of Hegel's ire needs to be mentioned, even though it seems to involve merely formal matters. Once Goethe had published *Wilhelm Meisters Lehrjahre,* every third-rate poetaster thought he could pile all his unpublishable manuscripts together, whether short prose tale, drama, dialogue, fable, or fantasy, and publish the whole mess as a novel. It is one thing, however, when the author of *Faust* and of *The East-West Divan* does it, another when a weak wit tries to do the same. Schlegel's choice of titles for the various sections of *Lucinde*, as we have seen, tells the tale: it is all about insolence, fantasy, and *Tändeleien*, which one might translate as tinsel or baubles; Schlegel himself understands it as the absurd noises a mother makes over her infant to evoke laughter. And when Schlegel counterposes to his own vaunted "youthfulness of soul" to the "the vicious cunning of the precocious understanding," *die Arglist des Altklugen* (98), Hegel knows who is meant, and he knows how to defend himself.

However, it will be more difficult for Hegel to defend his system against the charges brought against it by Philippe Lacoue-Labarthe, which I may introduce here, having only now spoken of "formal matters." Lacoue-Labarthe discusses in some detail Hegel's references to *Lucinde* in *The Philosophy of Right*, as I have been doing here, but he focuses principally on the *Lectures on Aesthetics* rather than Hegel's *Philosophy of Right.* Lacoue-Labarthe's thesis concerns the uneasy presence of poetry (and of art and literature generally) in Hegel's system of speculative philosophy. He challenges Hegel's moral accusation against Schlegel's *Lucinde*, an artwork that in Hegel's view establishes the epoch not of Romantic art proper but of moral turpitude and dissipation. Even though, as Hegel concedes, Schlegel's novel does mark an epoch in the history of art and literature, it is nonetheless to Schiller's more edifying poesy that Hegel constantly reverts. Unlike Schiller, Friedrich Schlegel proves to be (as we heard Creon saying of his son Haimon) "weaker than woman." Yet behind the contempt in which Hegel holds Schlegel, Lacoue-Labarthe senses a certain anxiety—indeed, an anxiety concerning the fate of the whole speculative system. Whereas Schiller's work ostensibly can be reduced to the concept, posing no threat to logic, Schlegel's cannot. Yet not because Schlegel's work is scurrilous, as Hegel maintains, but because literature cannot be tamed, not even the literature of Schiller. *Lucinde* is, says Lacoue-Labarthe, "unpresentable"; it is *l'imprésentable* as such, one might say. The thesis cuts in two ways: on the one hand, it seems as though Hegel is simply guilty of a moral prejudice—as Nietzsche would say, *the* moral prejudice posing as an aesthetics, a metaphysics, or a philosophy of law; on the other hand, as Lacoue-Labarthe would insist, Hegel is as mistaken in the case of Schiller as he is in the case of Schlegel, inasmuch as no figure of literature is reducible to the concept. Hegel is then guilty not of a moral prejudice but of a category mistake; he misunderstands the genres, fails to see literature for what it *is*, which is what it *performs* beyond presentation. The incapacity of the system to integrate literature is therefore not a moral failure, one might say, but an *absolute* failure. As a figure of literature, Lucinde herself, whatever she is, cannot be reduced to what anyone might say "of" her, whether that anyone be Schlegel or Hegel. Because the figures of fiction are irreducible and unpresentable, and perhaps because the figures of fiction are men and women *without qualities*, the names Schlegel and Hegel will never rhyme.[7]

---

7 Hegel's references to Friedrich Schlegel in his *Lectures on Aesthetics* and in other works would have to occupy a separate study—not to mention the names Schiller and Goethe. In a nutshell, the references to Schlegel relate Schlegel's moral lassitude to his poor poetry, bad prose, and contemptible pathos. See HW 13:93–95, 348, 383, 404–405, and 513; 14:116, 180, and 305; and 15:497. In the context of *The Philosophy of Right,* see especially Part Three of Lacoue-Labarthe's fine essay, "Impudicity: The Veil and the Figure," 64–75. The clearest and most succinct statement of his thesis appears in Part Four, "The Subornation of Aphrodite: Poesy and Philosophy," 78, second full paragraph, and in the concluding paragraphs of 85–86. My thanks to Rodolphe Gasché, who, decades ago now, first introduced me to Lacoue-Labarthe's "L'imprésentable."

•

Perhaps now we are in a position to work our way through the handwritten notes to the "Remark" of §164, and to cite verbatim that section's Addendum. Sophistry, the seducer's art, as Schlegel all but admits (recall that "stream of importunities, flatteries, and sophisms"), demands sensuous abandon as proof of love *before* marriage, whereas a truly spiritual love believes without demanding proofs, and spiritual consciousness has irrefragable faith. The girl, when victimized by sophistry, surrenders her honor. Not so the man. For the man still has another field for his ethical efficacy, for example, the corporations of the state (§255, "Remark"). Not so the girl. For her, ethicality resides essentially in the relation of marriage. Here there is no parity. On the part of the man, sensuous abandon is no proof of love and no threat to honor. Love, Hegel notes laconically, can make demands that are different from those of marriage. For love is the substantial unity of spirit in sensibility (§158) but also "the most monstrous contradiction, one which the intellect cannot resolve" (Addendum to §158). With love, all is one and undivided, both sensuous and ethical. However, as we have already heard, only the supplement of solemnization in the presence of representatives of the family and the larger community, the public exchange of spoken words and stipulated promises, establishes the relation in such a way that sensuous abandon is not its cause but a consequence. Ironically, it is a consequence that is essentially inconsequential for marriage. For in marriage sensuality soon evanesces to the humdrum, so that connubial equanimity is not disturbed by passion (Addenda to §§163–64.) In agreeing to the marriage, concludes Hegel cryptically, "the girl concedes this too" (HW 7:317).

This last phrase is unclear. What does the girl concede? Does she concede that sensuous abandon will now follow? Or does she concede that sensuality itself will become merely a supplement, indeed a bothersome and superfluous appendage to the ethical bond, one that happily will soon disappear? What does the girl concede in marriage? We do not know, even if Hegel's remarks on the role of the housewife (Addendum to §167) certainly give us some indication of the concessions involved on her part. What we do know is that at the end of these handwritten notes appears the underlined word *Lucinde*. The juxtaposition of the title of Schlegel's novel with these notes on a victimized girl is nothing short of bizarre, inasmuch as Lucinde is no "girl" in search of a "husband"; she has no intention of becoming a "spouse" and a "housewife." But let me now cite and discuss the Addendum to §164 in its entirety:

> *Addendum*. That the ceremony which sets the seal on the marriage is superfluous, a mere formality that can be set aside inasmuch as love is what is substantial, and that love even loses some of its value through this solemnization—this has been argued by Friedrich von Schlegel in *Lucinde* and by an anonymous supporter in a series of letters.[8] Here sensuous abandon [*sinnliche Hingebung*] is represented as though it were demanded as a proof of the freedom and intense ardor of love, an argumentation not foreign to seducers. Furthermore, one must note concerning the relation of man and woman that the girl surrenders her honor in sensuous abandon, which is not the case with the man, who has yet another field for his ethical activity than the family. The girl is defined essentially only in the relation of marriage; what is called for is that love receive the form of marriage and that the sundry moments of love assume their truly rational relationship to one another. (HW 7:317–18)

As we have seen, the truly rational relationship enjoined by Hegel is the inversion, not to say perversion, of the natural order or sequence, whereby sensuous abandon either follows upon matrimony (rather than inducing it) or dies a sudden or a gradual death. Let us now examine more closely the scene of sensibility. The girl's honor is at risk; she is being asked to surrender herself, to give herself over to utter abandon and erotic transport, possibly to sheer degradation and enslavement. (It is surely no accident that Freud will elaborate on this most common form of degradation in lovelife in a strikingly similar way, even though marriage will prove to be not the solution but part of the problem.)

---

8 That anonymous supporter was Schlegel's "roommate," or host, Friedrich Schleiermacher, whose *Vertraute Briefe über* [Intimate Letters on] *Friedrich Schlegels 'Lucinde'* was first published in 1800. I have used the edition by Karl Gutzkow (Hamburg: Hoffmann und Campe, 1835). No doubt Schleiermacher is an ally of Schlegel's: "And now we have this work, which stands there like a vision from a future world—God alone knows how far in the future!" (2). And: "Love must be resurrected, a new life must unify and ensoul its fragmented members, so that it can prevail joyously and freely in the hearts of mankind and in all its works, driving out the lifeless shadows of once-vaunted virtues" (9). How difficult such an alliance is for Schleiermacher becomes clear in the sixth letter, "To Eduard," in which the divine advocate tries rather desperately to condemn Wieland's erotic writings while blessing Schlegel's. See especially 94. Yet Hegel's difficulties are far more severe.

On the scene of sensibility, in Hegel's view, the man's honor will not be at risk in this transaction, inasmuch as he performs his ethical activity not only in marriage and the family but also in civil society and the state. Honor, abandon, and activity: let us focus on these three aspects of the scene of sensibility.

Honor is ubiquitous in Hegel's *Philosophy of Right.* This is surprising, since it belongs more to the bygone era of chivalry, the Age of Heroes and Patriarchs (§71, handwritten notes), or even the Age of Oriental Potentates (§§348–49, 355) than to the modern world. Yet even for the modern girl, the meaning of honor is exhausted in her resisting sensuous abandon prior to marriage. (That claim is true of course—if it is ever true—only if we forget for the moment that Antigone too is a girl, one who pays her brother "the ultimate honor" [§118, handwritten notes], confronting the state with the stubbornness of a Cassandra.) For a man, honor is more a matter of involvement in the corporations of the state, or of his class and status in civil society (§§244, 253, 255), than of the family. Even a criminal has his honor (§132), namely, the honor that consists in reaping punishment for his deeds (see the "Remarks" to §§100 and 120). Honor is also a matter of right, thought, and the concept itself, inasmuch as in a philosophical system all these principles and concepts of right must "come to honor" (see §§140a, 140e, 211 Addendum, and 189 Addendum).

One matter of honor to which Hegel attaches great importance is that of "spiritual production," for example, in the authorship of books (§69, "Remark"). Such honor is threatened by overt plagiarism and covert pilfering. Yet no legal code can protect an author from such pilferage, just as no act of law can protect neophytes from the sophistry of seducers. Yet how well does honor function without the express stipulations of the law? Given the fact that we no longer hear about plagiarism in the learned world, says Hegel, one must assume that honor has thoroughly "suppressed" such dishonor. Either that, or we have come to accept that adding a tiny windfall of one's own to someone else's work, a touch-up here, a touch-up there, suffices for originality. Ah, yes, the precarious honor of all spiritual production, of every fragile flower of spirit! Some two hundred pages before he mentions Schlegel's *Lucinde*, Hegel complains bitterly about the fact that "the most wretched novel can have a higher [financial] value than the most thoroughly researched book" (handwritten notes to the "Remark" of §64). That *Lucinde* might well outsell *The Philosophy of Right*—cruelest irony, irony of ironies!

With regard to irony, the Romantic quality par excellence, allow me to note that in his review of Karl Wilhelm Ferdinand Solger's *Posthumous Writings and Letters* (HW 11:215, 234, 255), Hegel refers to the "most audacious and luxuriant period of irony" in German letters, mentioning by name *Lucinde* and Schlegel's *Athenaeum Fragments.* Hegel endorses Solger's view that Schlegel's notion of irony is "one-sided" and "dogmatic." Schlegel will not condescend to make arguments and give reasons and grounds for his ironic proclamations; his high perch on "divine impudence" is therefore in reality altogether "Satanic," "diabolical" impudence. Claiming to straddle the peak of philosophic wisdom, Schlegel never penetrates the valleys of science. When in 1816 Schlegel offers a course on "transcendental philosophy" at the University of Jena, Hegel says, he runs out of things to say after only six weeks, thus defrauding his listeners (HB 2:98; HW 4:420–21.) Although devilishly clever and no doubt well-read, Schlegel remains utterly uninitiated in "the reason that thinks." Schlegelian irony is Fichtean subjectivism without the saving grace of Fichte's practical, ethical philosophy: that is the gist of Hegel's judgment on Schlegel in the *Lectures on the History of Philosophy* (HW 20:415–17). In the Solger review (HW 11:256–57), Hegel refers his readers to his own discussion of irony in §140 of *The Philosophy of Right,* which treats of evil as it appears in modern philosophy itself. (See also the Addendum to §140; HW 7:284–86.) As significant as the polemic no doubt is for Hegel's critique of Romanticism as a whole, let the following observation suffice: whereas Plato's Socrates ironizes the pretensions of the sophists, he never ironizes the Ideas themselves—whereas this is precisely what Schlegel does (HW 18:460–61). Finally, since irony is the subject here, allow me to note that K. W. F. Solger's own views on tragic irony and tragic downgoing may well strike us as far more radical than Hegel's, and as pointing forward to Nietzsche. Precisely for that reason, they resist reduction and summarization.

But to return to *The Philosophy of Right*, taking up now the theme of *abandon* or *Hingebung.* As we have seen, sensuous abandon (*Hingebung*) is essentially the girl's capitulation to the man, in order to attain womanhood through the man or husband she desires. In the "Remark" to §164 Hegel speaks of abandon as mutual; in §168 he emphasizes that "*unconstrained abandon*" proceeds from the infinitely proper personality of the two sexes bonded or bound to one another in marriage, although never in incest (HW 7:321–22). (Always the afterthought of incest, which poses the gravest danger to civil society. . . .) In another context, Hegel speaks (only once, as far as I know, and we will have to return to it below) of sensuous abandon as resulting from the activity of the *man*; otherwise, such devotion, surrender, and sensual transport or ecstasy are markedly feminine, or female, or—in a sense that, to repeat, is very difficult to determine—"of" woman. In this respect Hegel does seem to rhyme with Schlegel. For Lucinde gives herself, there seems to be no doubt about that. Where

Hegel departs from Schlegel is in his insistence that a man must try to prevent her from giving up her frangible honor too soon. Such prevention is no doubt a burden and a nuisance for the man. She is inclined by nature to give herself wholly, yet her donation condemns a conscientious thinking man to guilt and chagrin. One hears it in Hegel's wry, doleful phrase, "an argumentation not foreign to seducers." The Voice of Experience. The Voice of Hegel.[9]

She gives herself actively, with no thought to herself, and often with no thought to anything, not even to her honor. For the love of spirit, who can stop her? "As easy stop the sea" (U 351). It is much more than a mere nuisance. She actively gives herself somewhere on that shifting scene of sentient sensibility and sensuality, somewhere between Act I, Girlhood, and Act II, Womanhood.

In Schlegel's novel too sensuous abandon is of woman, but of woman inextricably entangled in a man's desire. "I begged you," remembers Julius, "to abandon yourself utterly for once to furious passion, and I implored you to be insatiable" (10; cf. 28, 47, and 58). In his "Dithyrambic Fantasy Concerning the Loveliest Situation," which culminates in a childlike ringaroundarosy of male-female roles, his (now Lucinde's) role is "the protective vehemence of the man," while her (now Julius's) role is "the inviting abandon of woman, the charming, seductive surrender that draws the other toward itself" (16). *Hingebung* is the ultimate oxymoron: a giving-over that ineluctably draws the other toward oneself and takes the other in, a surrender that is gloriously victorious, an abandonment that joins the other tightly to oneself. Julius accounts it an allegory of the consummation of human species and he concludes impudently: "A lot lies in this—and what lies there certainly will not rise as quickly as I do when I lie under you" (16). An impudent translation, no doubt, of the more ambiguous German: *wenn ich Dir unterliege*, "whenever I am defeated by you, am inferior to you." Sensuous abandon is Julius's happy defeat, his glorious infirmity, his situated and saturated inferiority. He gives himself over to her giving-over.

Hegel would agree at least with this: Julius's "foolhardy enthusiasm," "divine to the point of vulgarity," his identification of freedom and impudicity, can prevail only "at the cost of manliness itself" (17). And so the tables are turned. He is taken. "She was not a little surprised, although she sensed it all

---

9 I will carefully avoid any reference to Hegel's biography here. Yet allow me to refer the interested reader to a work of fiction: see Krell, *Son of Spirit: A Novel* (Albany: State University of New York Press, 1997). Perhaps this work of fictional biography helps to clarify some of Hegel's problems with Lucinde, both the book and the figure.

along, that after the surrender he would be more loving and more faithful than before. . . . They were altogether devoted and one, and yet each was altogether himself, or herself, more than they had ever been" (66–67). However, there is one more reference to sensuous abandon, in another text of Hegel's, to which I will now turn.

Activity: doing deeds, or doing the deed. Or, as Hegel calls it in §166, engaging "the mighty and the activating." No doubt Hegel is thinking preeminently of the man's *Tätigkeit* in business and politics, along with the far more restricted *Tätigkeit* of the woman in the home. (Why he does not consider the *Tätigkeit* of the artist—in this case, of Lucinde the painter—is an arresting question.) Yet one could certainly argue that the gender division that is clearly visible in all such assigned *Tätigkeit* has at least something to do with sensual *Hingebung* and with the respective roles of man and woman in sexual reproduction. Whereas nature often has to submit to spirit—for example, in terms of the logic that nature often fails to obey—it is clear that when it comes to activity something like nature, or what Hegel takes nature to be, dictates a certain hierarchical distribution of roles.

In Hegel's 1805–06 lectures at Jena on human genitality and the mating process, "activity" is attributed to the "bifurcated part," the self-differentiating part that belongs exclusively to the male: it is not the testicle, which although twofold is "closed in," like the ovary of the female, "which does not emerge into its opposite, does not become for-itself, does not become an active brain" (JS 160–61).[10] Hegel does not specify this bifurcated, self-differentiating, diaphoric male organ that moves across space toward its opposite, although he cites its passive homologue in the female: "And the clitoris is inactive feeling in general; in contrast to it, we have in the male active feeling, the upswelling heart" (ibid.). "Thus," Hegel can conclude, or believes he can conclude, although we will have to return to all this in a moment, "the man is the active one, by the fact that his activity possesses this distinction" (ibid.).

Active feeling, the upswelling heart, is of course the penis in something like diastole. Whose heart? And where is it located? The handwritten notes to §165 invoke "the hearts of men." Oddly, the metaphoric or metonymic hearts of men—so powerful and all-activating—fall under the spell of another power. Among the exceedingly rare words of *poetry* that appear in *The Philosophy*

---

10 I have discussed these materials at greater length in "Pitch," cited above, and at even greater length in chapter 10 of Krell, *Contagion: Sexuality, Disease, and Death in German Idealism and Romanticism* (Bloomington: Indiana University Press, 1998).

of Right are some verses extracted from that great epic poem of honor and chivalry, *El Cid*:

> The mystery is—the power of
> Women over the hearts of us men.
> This mystery hides in them,
> Deeply concealed; the Lord God,
> I believe, cannot plumb such depths. (Now you've gone too far!)
> When on that Great Day
> The sins of all are brought to light,
> God will look into women's hearts:
> *Either he will find them all*
> Culpable, or all equally innocent,
> So interwoven is their heart. (HW 7:318)

The hearts of us men, the upswelling hearts of us men, are defenseless when subjected to the power of the tightly interwoven heart of womankind. Like Julius under Lucinde, the male heart submits to the power of the singular and single heart of woman, a heart so close to God that He cannot see it (no matter how bravely Hegel's marginal exclamation tries to restore orthodoxy). The undifferentiated and undifferentiating heart of woman, as tightly woven as a wreath of rush, is closer in its undeveloped unity to the spirit of origins and the origins of spirit than My Lord Cid will ever be. For, as long as sensibility prevails, all individuality surrenders and abandons itself, giving itself over to *her*. Thus, for all the talk about *activity*, the man—when he is not engaged in those activities that constitute his *honor*—finds himself tossed back to sensuous *abandon*. She gives, but she also takes. She receives, harbors, and conceives. Indeed, she conceives in a way that seems to absorb the concept itself:

> Conception is the contraction of the whole individual into simple self-surrendering unity; contraction into the representation of the individual; semen [or, the seed: *der Samen*] the simple physical representation—altogether one point, like the name, and the whole self.— Conception nothing else than the becoming-one of these abstract representations. (JS 174)

The simple physical representation, the simple seed of semen, Simple Semen, contracting in self-abandoning unity, now becomes the unit that serves as the congenital mark of woman, the fertilized egg in the womb; contracting in spasmodic waves, the foaming waves of Aphrodite, the shuddering waves of *Venus vaga*, she gives, she takes, she harbors, and she conceives. She conceives the creature and the name, if not the concept. Let us see if the hearts of us men can escape the implication that if spirit is alive, (s)he is in some vital sense *of woman*, and that to conceive the creature is to do the work precisely of the concept. Can our male hearts escape the ties that bind, the ties that bond, in life, love, and logic? Can an essentially phallocentric and phallocratic system spill over into something gynocentric and gynocratic? Can it do anything other than that?

•

Derrida's *Glas* is very much interested in working out an answer to these questions. In his remarkable account of Hegel's "Holy Family," that is, the scene in which spirit and its concept are formed in the family and remain within the family, even though the family is ostensibly merely one passing moment for spirit, Derrida pays particular heed to Hegel's account of woman. Derrida's account appears about a third of the way through his treatment of the "remains" of absolute knowing in Hegel's phenomenology and philosophy of spirit (G 126–35/110–17). It follows his treatment of Hegel's early theological text on the "spirit of Christianity," the first part of which deals with the spirit of *Judaism*, and leads to his detailed treatment of Hegel's early text on "natural law," his mature *Philosophy of Right*, and the figure of Antigone in the *Phenomenology of Spirit*.

Derrida begins by noting the importance for Hegel of sexual union (copulation) as the sublation that cancels the particularity of the two sexes and raises men and women to the level of species-identity proper. To be sure, it raises them in a merely bestial way, that is, in a way that humanity shares with certain animals and even some plants. In both sexual difference and the specific difference between humanity and other life-forms Derrida sees Hegel's desire to establish a parallel between the opposites man/woman and human/beast. It is a desire that mirrors a fundamental yet undiscussed *hierarchy* in Hegel's dialectic. For example, it is not merely a matter of one element prevailing in male genitality, another in female genitality. For the passive, "indifferent" part that defines the essence of the female for Hegel, in opposition to the "active difference" that defines the male, mirrors the hierarchy by which spirit prevails over matter generally—activity over passivity, light over darkness, transparency over opacity. If the male embodies difference in the phallus and paired testicles, then in some sense he embodies difference *as such*, and hence *is* the sexual difference as such. If the indifferent part (the uterus) in woman lowers itself in man and becomes a mere gland (the prostate), then the male's hovering testicle, which is only a pace behind the erect penis, has as its counterpart the female ovary, which "remains enveloped." The development, the unfolding of the inside to a free and autonomous outside, is hindered in the female parts, which, enveloped rather than developed, "remain" indifferent and lag far behind those of the male. The ovary does not activate itself, does not rise to meet its opposite; neither the uterus nor the ovary "step out" into the world of opposition. Nowhere in the female genitalia is there an "active brain"; everywhere we find instead a fundamental lethargy and torpor, receptive and passive. Even the clitoris, which has an active-sounding name (the German word *der Kitzler,* masculine in gender, means "the tickler"), does not share the action of its morphological paradigm in the male: it is "inactive feeling in general."

"In general?" asks Derrida. Who or what pronounces this "in general"? What hierarchy, derived from where, and applied by whom? Every answer to questions like these betrays the fact that Hegel's onto-theo-teleo-logy—in a word, his *system*—"articulates the most traditional phallocentrism" (G 130/113). The male possesses "active feeling." His "upswelling heart," despite the euphemism, travels like a winged metaphor through space (autonomously? at will? dependably? predictably? on schedule?), thanks to the fact that it retains the blood that flows into it and does not expend it in a debilitating menstruation. The turgescent, tumescent "heart" of the *glans* guides the active brain and its contents to its passive opposite and its fulfillment.

Yet what about that object of its fulfillment, over there, so pitiably passive but so undeniably alluring, which does not need to budge in order to move? Sounds like the Prime Mover. Derrida helps us to see the strange reversal that awaits all spiritualist hierarchies, the reversal by which phallocentrism establishes willy-nilly a feminism:

> The man's superiority costs him an inner division. In passively receiving, woman remains one (close) by herself [*une auprès d'elle-même,* which is the very earmark of *spirit,* which as Hegel says is *ganz bei sich*—D.F.K.]; she works less but lets herself be worked (over) less by negativity. "The receiving [*Das Empfangen:* this is also the conceiving of the child—J.D.] of the uterus, as simple behavior, is accordingly in the male divided in two (*entzweit*), into the productive brain and the external heart (*in das produzierende Gehirn und das äußerliche Herz*). The man, then, through this difference, is the active (*Der Mann ist also durch diesen Unterschied das Tätige*); but the woman is the receptacle (*das Empfangende*), because she remains in her undeveloped unity (*weil sie in ihrer unentwickelten Einheit bleibt*)."

> *Remaining* enveloped in undifferentiated unity, the woman keeps herself nearer to the origin. The man is secondary, as the difference that causes his passing into opposition. Paradoxical consequences of all phallocentrism: the hardworking and determining male sex enjoys mastery only in losing it, in subjugating itself to the feminine slave. The phallocentric hierarchy is a feminism; it submits dialectically to Femininity and Truth, both writ large, making man the *subject* of woman.[11]

In genitality as everywhere else, woman remains the cryptic figure of the family, eluding conceptuality as the very one who conceives, as the very concept of conception.

The opposition of active organs and passive receptivity brings us back one more time to sensuous abandon, surrender, and erotic devotion. In the margin of the Jena lectures, just above the paragraph on conception, at the point where woman is designated as the one who conceives, Hegel enters a marginal note about the breast: "Digestion turned to the outside—woman, milk of the breast." Next to this, as marginalia to marginalia, Hegel writes: "The metaphorical surrender [or abandon, or giving-over, *Hingeben*] of heart and soul to the woman." As one confronts the necessity to translate the phrase *metaphorisches Hingeben des Herzens und Seele an das Weib*, one puzzles long and hard. It should be the *woman* who gives her heart and soul. The marginal note should read: *an dem Weibe, am Weibe, beim Weibe*, in the dative case. Yet Hegel's accusative clearly points the finger: *he* gives, the man gives, *to her*, his heart and soul; *to her*, his upswelling heart and his active brain. Or, without the commas: he gives to her (his) heart and soul, gives to her (his) upswelling heart and active brain, giving them over to (her) conceiving—as though none of these things were any longer "his," as though in the history of spirit they were "his" for only a fleeting moment. And all it takes to bring about this catastrophic destitution is a brief glimpse of "digestion turned to the outside."

---

11 G 130/113. The slight discrepancies in the wording of the quotations from Hegel results from the fact that Derrida used the only edition of the *Jenenser Realphilosophie* that was available until 1976, namely, that of Johannes Hoffmeister for the "Philosophische Bibliothek," no. 67, published by Felix Meiner in 1931. Even though it remains beyond the scope of this chapter, one ought to complement Derrida's analysis by the remarkable pages of Luce Irigaray, "The Eternal Irony of the Community," in *Speculum de l'autre femme* (Paris: Minuit, 1974), 214–26; trans. Gillian C. Gill as *Speculum of the Other Woman* (Ithaca: Cornell University Press, 1985).

Let me therefore not abandon the margin too quickly, but linger on the breast. For it too, according to Julius, is engorged and magnificently swollen, though not with blood. Lucinde's body, bathed in the glimmer of twilight, is luxuriant, uxorious (67), and the very vision of her goads his love to fury. These are not the breasts of a girl, Schlegel's Julius tells us; this is not a maidenly body trembling on the brink of maturity, a tremulous body stammering its O-Please-Don't-Make-Me-Prove-It. Her swelling outlines, which he is mad to touch, tell him and us once again—even if we are as yet untouched by the extraordinary force and heat of her embrace—that Lucinde is not a girl at all. Lucinde is a woman. Julius has already told us that some time ago she has borne a son who in the meantime has died (65). Mourning marks her past and something of her present. Because she is an accomplished painter, her eye, hand, and brain are markedly active. As is her heart, no doubt, which gives itself over tenderly to the objects and subjects of her art. She too is a human being who produces spiritually, like those who write books on spirit or deliver lectures in the university. She thus bears an uncanny resemblance to Hegel. Except perhaps for those swellings—although even in those swellings she is not *altogether* different from Hegel or from other male members of her species. Julius, watching waves of ebon hair flow over the snowfields of those white breasts murmurs, "Magnificent woman! Masterly woman! Lordly woman!" *Herrliche Frau!* (66).

Lucinde—a helpless girl ripe for the blandishments of seduction? Friedrich Schleiermacher never took her as that. When his young interlocutor, "Karoline," advocating "the honor of maidens," complains that Julius should never have left his younger and more innocent beloved (Lisette, who in Karoline's view is no professional at all) for Lucinde, Schleiermacher's epistolary hero replies that "a kiss from a woman who has already seen love face-to-face is undeniably more significant and more decisive than a maiden's very best approximation" (*Intimate Letters*, 87). The Voice of Experience is now the voice of Schleiermacher, telling what he sees behind all the veils that are woven into his name. In the face of Hegel's juxtaposition of the seduction story and Schlegel's *Lucinde*, one must ask: Can Hegel have *read* Friedrich Schlegel's novel?[12]

---

12 My former colleague Stephen Houlgate poses this question quite seriously: we have no definitive evidence that Hegel actually *read* the novel; he may be reacting merely to the brouhaha that surrounded its publication. In which case, of course, the avatar of spirit is condemning something of which he is ignorant, something concerning which he remains in the indifference of an undivided unity, but without reception, without conception, without the name.

Of course he read it. That is why the third figure, the figure of a stalwart Antigone, has to be conjured once again. An adolescent girl who accompanies her honor into the tomb, joining her brother and lover in death. The law of the state seals her tomb with a granite boulder. In the same way, Antigone's lips are sealed: no further impudence against the substantial spirit of the state. She will contract into simple unity one last time. In the nick of time: no swelling profile, no uxoriousness. For Lucinde's is the law that unsettles every law and deranges all positing and presenting. Lucinde undercuts religion with sensuous transport; Julius, as we have heard, adores her (10, 15, 29, 71, 81). She undercuts matrimony with what he calls "the elevated lightheadedness of our marriage" (14, 63, 75–76). Homely ethicality pales before her (23), and all wisdom is baffled by her (28). She is a spirited woman. And she absorbs his activity utterly, thus undercutting society, law, and the state:

> You feel everything entirely and infinitely, you know nothing about things' being separated off, your essence is one and indivisible. That is why you are so serious and so joyful; that is why you take everything to heart and are so careless of it; and that is why you also love me wholly, leaving no part of me to the state, to posterity, or to my men friends. Everything belongs to you. . . . You pass through all the stages of humanity with me, from the most liberated sensuality to the most spirited spirituality, and only in you did I see true pride and true womanly humility. (14)

What is this "most spirited spirituality," *die geistigste Geistigkeit*? The redoubling of the word, driving it to the superlative, is in Hegel's view the proper death of spirit. That is why Hegel must stop her, for the sake of Julius and all men of the state. In order that the *work* of spirit be advanced. In order, for example, that the possibility of *war* be assured. For what results from Lucinde's and Julius's sensual play? As we noted earlier, they begin to ape one another, she acting as though she were the man, he mincing and mewing like the woman or child he is becoming (16). Schlegel himself is aware of the danger: all this frivolity may come at the cost of masculinity itself (17). "Or am I wrong," he asks, "when I look for . . . tenderness and delicacy [*Zartheit und Zierlichkeit*] in thought and in word primarily in the female sex?" (19). "By God!" we have already heard him exclaim, "Am I not a man, so that I don't have to be more tender than the most tender female creature?" (ibid.). Seal Lucinde's lips, then, and seal her fate, as though she were Antigone. For in the dark caverns of her multichambered heart, her singular heart, there is an unstoppable diastole, an upswelling and an engorgement of the lips with blood and the breast with milk. And Lucinde's words, Lucinde's tears and laughter, Lucinde's give and take, Lucinde's *pudeur* supplemented not by chastity but by sensuous abandon. The law of woman will be heralded not by Antigone, the interred adolescent who becomes child, infant, and fetus in her death, and not as the law of the ancient *gods*, as Hegel has it; hers is the law of the goddess, *Venus vaga*, Lucinde's glory, the contracting waves of subterranean power, "eternal law of which no one knows from what dawn it appeared."[13]

Has Hegel successfully sealed off and fully interiorized the law of woman? Can he now step over the threshold of the family home and go out into the state and civil society? Has he forgotten nothing? In the Preface to the *Phenomenology of Spirit*, Hegel depicts the moment at which extraneous preoccupation with results, conclusions, and generalities *ends* and thinking *begins* not as remembering but as self-forgetting. Like Lucinde giving herself over to Julius's mouth and ardor, or Julius's surrendering himself to Lucinde's snowscape and tropics, the phenomenologist does not hesitate to give himself or herself over to the "matter," to the "sake" of thinking—*die Sache*, which is feminine in gender: "to linger with the matter in question and to forget himself in her, . . . abandoning himself to her," "*in ihr* [*in der Sache*] *zu verweilen und sich in ihr zu vergessen, . . . sich ihr* [*hingeben*]" (PG 11).

13 Sophocles' *Antigone*, ll. 456–57, cited by Hegel in both the *Phenomenology of Spirit* and the *Philosophy of Right* (see the Remark to §166 and PG 311).

Chapter Five

Pulling Strings Wins No Wisdom

Sophia sei mein Schuzgeist. ("*Sophia* [Wisdom], be my protective spirit.")

—Novalis (Friedrich von Hardenberg) to Sophie von Kühn, 1795

Blown away by a gust of wind. Nothing to say.

—Freud to Ferenczi, 29 January 1920

IN THE AUTUMN OF 1990, Derrida lectured on the Romantic poet and thinker Novalis. Novalis often wrote in fragments, trusting that his aphorisms would capture a sense of the whole, attain the absolute in the most compact possible form, and recover wisdom without remnant or residue. Novalis's fiancée, Sophie von Kühn, who boldly bore the very name of wisdom, Σωφία, was to have been Novalis's tutelary guardian in this effort: he gave her a ring engraved with the plea, *Sophia sey mein Schuzgeist,* "Sophie, Wisdom, be my protective spirit." But Sophie died of tuberculosis at age fifteen. Novalis built an altar to her, believing that if he could focus and worship her with absolute intensity she would reappear. He clung to the hope that he could transform everything that exists into Sophie, or Sophie into everything else. He hoped that if he loved her ardently enough he could pull some strings and recuperate everything.

Derrida clearly loved this tender, spectral love of Novalis's, and he loved the idea that a philosophical fragment could capture all of wisdom without remnant or residue. He loved them—but he did not believe them. Over and over again in his lecture Derrida affirmed that fragmentary writing can recover much, indeed virtually everything, everything, but then he would look up from his text and say over and over again, "*le tout, tout—sauf Sophie.*" One can recuperate everything, absolutely everything—except Sophie. And because women named Sophie often have the nickname "Soph," it was as though Derrida were saying *sauf sauf.* In German and in French a philosopher is a *philosoph(e),* a lover of Soph, but now, irremediably, without Soph. We listeners laughed the first time Derrida uttered this *sauf Soph*, although he himself was not smiling; we laughed because it seemed to involve one of those phonemic leftovers or remnants we had learned to love (or fear) in *Glas.* Yet when he repeated it almost compulsively at each twist and turn of the lecture, the laughter died away. After that there was mostly silence.

La Carte postale pretends to begin with "*Spéculer sur 'Freud,'* " as if the first 273 pages, under the title "*Envois,*" did not themselves constitute a book-length story, the story of a one-sided clandestine correspondence written out on postcards in a script that no nosy postman could ever decipher; postcards from lover to beloved, begging her (for the beloved is a she, even if she is the writer's own voice, *la voix,* or another voice, *une autre voix*) to burn it all, the whole sheaf of postcards, and to burn him too, burn him and eat his ashes baked into a brioche served with the afternoon tea. "To Speculate—on 'Freud' " itself begins abstrusely, like every text of Derrida's. It pledges to focus on Freud's *Beyond the Pleasure Principle*, from the years 1919–20, and on the oxymoron "lifedeath," *la vie la mort.* More precisely, it promises to examine a certain remnant or residue of psychoanalysis to be found on the scene of writing, indeed, to explicate the process by which every feast celebrated at the table of theoretical or scientific systems yields inassimilable leftovers, the process Derrida calls *restance.* Knowing that we will be quick to remember the right-hand column of *Glas*, with Jean Genet's literary scraps and scrapes making trouble for Hegel's system, Derrida denies that in the case of Freud's *Beyond* the process of *restance* can be identified straightforwardly as "the fictional" or "literary," as "fable" or as "myth" making trouble for science. For Freud himself does not shy from telling stories. Indeed, Derrida affirms that the theme of lifedeath appears and disappears in Freud's *Beyond* by virtue of its author's "telling lots of stories, making up lots of stories, making them up or causing them to be recounted" (280).[1]

The French *histoire,* like the German *Geschichte,* lies tantalizingly between "story" and "history," between the stuff we make up for our analyst or confessor

---

1 Alan Bass's excellent translation of *La Carte postale* was not available to me at the time and place this piece was written; hence my translations often diverge from his. I cite Freud from *Gesammelte Werke*, as earlier in the book; yet from time to time I cite the Standard Edition in its German form, which I refer to as StA, followed by volume and page number in the body of my text.

so that she will have a nice day and the stuff she will decode as the genuine *happening* of our life history, better, of our life-and-death story. That story often has to do with quite tender matters, some of them cruel, all of them delicate. Derrida is most interested in what will be left over after the psychoanalytic encoding or decoding of such tender or cruel experiences, although not because deconstruction wants to devour the scraps that fall from the table of analysis. Derrida is intrigued by the table talk itself, especially when such talk, telling tales or spinning yarns, disconcerts both analysis and deconstruction; it is almost as though every learned strategy sooner or later falls silent before the humblest *raconteur*. The teller of tales or spinner of yarns need not be as intense as Blanchot or as intricate as Melville, but can be as simple as a Hemingway sentence or an opening incantation by Marguerite Duras. Both psychoanalysis and deconstruction love these tales, which spread a patina of affect across the surfaces of things.[2]

For the moment, one particular story fascinates Derrida, but it is one of the most famous in the literature of psychoanalysis: Freud recounts it in chapter 2 of *Beyond the Pleasure Principle*, first published in 1920. The story begins after one of the most bizarre caesurae in the psychoanalytic literature. For Freud begins the chapter with a haunting description of traumatic neurosis, war neurosis, what we today call PTSD, "post-traumatic stress disorder." He is fascinated by the *repetition* of the traumatic event in the dreams of these sufferers who would love to forget but who, like hysterics, suffer above all from their "reminiscences." Anxiety, fear, and fright or terror (*Schreck*) form the conceptual framework of this gloomy chapter—until, after a double paragraph break, Freud decides to change the subject. Let us talk about child's play instead, he suggests—child's play, to see how pleasure is achieved there, if pleasure it may be called, so that we may then advance beyond pleasure in the direction of destruction and death. Freud writes: "Without intending to grasp the totality of these phenomena [involved in child's play], I took advantage of an opportunity I had to shed light on the first self-invented game of a boy aged eighteen months" (GW 13:11). Later, Freud will say that it does not really matter whether or not the boy made the game up himself, or whether it was somehow suggested to him—by whom? one wonders. And how Freud can know that it

---

2 I have learned a great deal from what Nicholas Royle has to say about the subject of Freud's uncanny relation to literature. See his remarkable book, *The Uncanny* (Manchester, England: Manchester University Press, 2003), throughout, but especially chapters 3 and 5.

is the child's *first* self-invented game is a mystery. "It was more than a fleeting observation," he continues, "for I lived under the same roof with the child and its parents for several weeks, and it took a rather long time before I was able to surmise the meaning of the child's enigmatic and constantly repeated activity" (GW 13:11–12).

The story is already full of narrative magic. What is Freud doing under that roof? These are either very close friends or family. Freud does not say. Normally, one would not draw upon family or friends, Hölderlin's "more tender relations," for material in a psychoanalytic study, although, on the other hand, family matters—such as the death of one's father—play a covert but crucial role in the development of this science and its literature. Yet what mother would allow Sigmund Freud to observe her baby? The story continues: "The child was by no means precocious in its intellectual development: at eighteen months it had only a few recognizable words at its disposal, along with a number of sounds that had meaning and could be understood by those around it" (GW 13:12). Again, what mother would allow Freud to observe her not-so-precocious child? But to continue, for the little dummy has some compensating qualities inasmuch as "it had good rapport with its parents and with their sole servant girl, and it received praise on account of its 'decent' character" (ibid.).

The German word for *decent,* appearing in quotation marks, is *anständig*: proper, seemly, respectable, decent—precisely what we look for in an eighteen-month-old. If the quotation marks indicate that the word comes from the mouth of the parents, we suddenly wonder less why Freud was permitted to observe the child. Freud now tells us why the child was "decent." "It did not disturb its parents during the night, and it obeyed conscientiously [*gewissenhaft*] whenever it was forbidden to touch certain objects or to enter certain rooms; above all else, it never cried when its mother would leave for hours at a time, even though it clung tenderly to this mother [*es dieser Mutter zärtlich anhing*], who not only nurtured the child herself but also cared for it and saw to all its needs without the help of anyone else" (ibid.).

Did someone say "decent"? This baby is a paragon of reason and probity: to cling tenderly to a perfect mother who sees to all its needs, and then to let her go without tears, without theatrics, to release her to and share her with the waiting world—this child has the wisdom that Socrates achieved in his late fifties. Yet one wonders already at this early point in the story whether we have really left the war-wounded, the traumatized, behind. For every "decent" lad or lass of even the most tender age conceals a wound or two—what does psychoanalysis teach us if not that? Allow me to insert a different story at this point, surely a more typical story, one told from the point of the view of a mother who, because she has to go to work, arranges daycare for her baby—but then has to face "the first separation." That was the title chosen by the mother who sent the account to me:

> I am going to try to remember—but then how could I forget? Lya. The first separation.
>
> She knew, I don't know how, that this time I was going to leave her. Let me fill you in on the background. It was early morning, winter, pitch black. I was walking with Lya in my arms toward the door of the caretaker, who reminded me of the sorceress in "Sleeping Beauty": long black hair, thin lips, bitter, with eyes that didn't want to meet yours, never a smile. . . . My Lya, from this moment on what lies in store for you?
>
> I give you over to her, I offer you up. She takes you. Your whole body stiffens.
>
> You look at me. You know I am going to leave and that something terrible is going to happen. Inscribed on your visage, pure terror.
>
> Your face is all mouth, a gaping abyss that releases a heartrending scream, a scream without end. All mouth, expressing horror. And your eyes. A look so intense, so harrowing, a look of terror and of powerlessness.
>
> From now on I will not be able to smile.
>
> Once again it is your eyes that I see, darker than death, darker than all things dark. I read in your eyes the absolute fright, the fright of abandonment.
>
> Upon this image the door closes.
>
> Back down the hall. I am running. I have betrayed you.

If I told you that little Lya was as beautiful as the morning sun and her mother as beautiful as the evening moon looming over mountaintops mournful and splendid at the full you would believe me, there would be no reason not to believe me, whereas if I told you that the mother's name was Sophie you would be convinced that I was making it all up, spinning yarns. And if I told you that there were brilliant philosophers who even late in life could not cross the threshold of an academic institution without a rising of the gorge, a sense of foreboding, and even a reflux of tears, so lacerating was that severance from the mother on schoolday mornings, you would be incredulous.[3]

So let me return to the less harrowing story of a little boy who is more stalwart than any child we know and most mothers and philosophers to boot. Freud now enters a demur or a doubt about the boy, and the plot, as they say, coagulates:

> This well-behaved child had the occasionally disturbing habit of tossing every small object it could get its hands on into a far-off corner of the room or underneath a bed, and so on, so that it was often no easy task to gather up all its toys. It tossed these things with an expression of interest and satisfaction, along with a long, drawn-out *o-o-o-o,* which, as the mother and this observer agreed, was not an interjection but the word *gone.* I finally saw that this was a game and that the child was using all its playthings precisely in order to play "all gone" with them. (Ibid.)

What mother or father has not played "all gone" with an infant when its fruit cup or porridge bowl is empty? But that a child should play "all gone" with its own toys, beyond merely tossing them for the pleasure of watching them fly and observing the grownups fetching them like Fido—this commands our attention.

One of the toys is a wooden spool or bobbin, perhaps from a spinning wheel, a spool to which a string is attached. A new element in the game occurs when the child holds the end of the string while tossing the spool up into its vacated crib. The sides of the crib are draped with a curtain, so that the spool disappears from the child's sight, whereupon, *o-o-o-o,* "All gone." Gone but not forgotten. Absent, yet, as Heidegger says in "The Anaximander Fragment," *present* in the form of absence (H 319–20; EGT 34–35). Our little ontologist holds in his clenched fist the string attached to what Heidegger calls ἀλήθεια, "unconcealment." Baby then pulls the spool out of the bed into *present* presence and greets it with a joyous cry, *a*, presumably meaning *Da!* "Here!" This *Da*

---

3 Michael Naas, after reading a first draft of this paper, played me a recorded interview with Jacques Derrida by Amy Kaufman, conducted, I presume, at about the time of the *Derrida* film. In the interview Derrida talks about the trauma of his *école maternelle* years, a trauma that never abated. Little wonder that Derrida loved the lachrymose philosophers—Augustine, Rousseau, Novalis, Nietzsche—who are always exiled from home, or feeling as though their home were abandoning them, even when they are heading home, in any and every case always under tears.

is of course the *Da-* of *Da-sein*, the openness to being itself, beyond all mere preoccupation with beings. The unprecocious child has mastered the ontological difference. From hence it knows what metaphysics has forgotten for two millennia, to wit, that truth is φύσις, upsurgence into unconcealment and return, eventual and ineluctable, to concealment. The infant has been musing upon the tragic choruses of Sophocles.

Freud's theme, however, is not the ontological difference, although he is always close to tragic thinking, as he is, for example, at the end of chapter 2 of the *Beyond*. "Pleasure" and "pain" are Freud's themes, and they would cause Heidegger to put a fair question to Freud, a question Heidegger touches on whenever in *Being and Time* he thinks about "attunement" or "mood" and the general sense of "how one finds oneself to be," *Stimmung* and *Befindlichkeit*. Heidegger's question would be whether upsurgence into unconcealment is the precondition of pleasure and pain alike. Just as pointedly, however, Freud's themes would incite him to ask Heidegger in turn whether openness to being itself occurs under the aegis of the pleasure principle. Or the "reality" principle. Or perhaps under some darker principle that may not in fact be a principle. Every infant who plays hide-and-seek with its mother or father expresses the joy of ἀλήθεια, has fun with φύσις, enjoys the thrill of arrival in unconcealment. Instead of sagely nodding its head like a grad student, the infant squeals with delight. Yet does not the squeal betray something like anxiety, an anxiety that—for the moment—is held in abeyance? Held on a leash or a string?

What I am treating here so lightly, namely, the conjunction of Freudian and Heideggerian thought, Derrida treats as the weightiest of matters. For example, in *La Carte postale* (376–84), he shows that the notion of *Eigentlichkeit*, "appropriateness" or "authenticity," is the axis not only of Heidegger's fundamental ontology of Dasein but also of Freud's idea of the death drive, which by some unknown scheme or ruse guides us to the death that is "proper" to us. Such propriety—in the thought of both grandfathers—has everything to do with *mortality* as the fundamental human condition and is therefore the weightiest of weighty matters. Weighty and yet uncertain in its effects. When Freud wonders whether the notion of an *immanent* death, a death that is *proper to* an organism, a death one would therefore have to *wait for*, is in fact a source of comfort—for would it not be worse to think that mere contingency and extrinsic accident rule in life?—Derrida turns Freud's doubt against Heidegger. Is "readiness for anxiety" or "resolute openedness" toward one's own mortality a daunting task, or is it a source of comfort and hence pleasure? Derrida writes:

> And what if the authenticity that is proper to Dasein as *Sein zum Tode* ["being toward death"], what if its *Eigentlichkeit* ["appropriateness," "authenticity"] were only the lure of a proximity, of the presence-to-self (*Da*) of the proper, even if in a form that would no longer be that of the subject, of consciousness, of the person, of man, of living substance? And what if precisely the *poem*, the poetic itself, were this death that is immanent in and proper to life? A grand narrative poem, the only story, the one that is recounted always, the one that one tells oneself, the poetics of the proper as reconciliation, consolation, serenity? (386).

Yet what sort of pleasure does such *proximity* grant? What consolation does the *grand narrative* or *poem* offer? And is the pleasure pure, the consolation perfect? These are Freud's questions to his own story, and his answer is that the infant's pleasure lies in the "cultural achievement" of an at least temporary renunciation of the satisfaction of its own drives, allowing the mother, the purveyor of such satisfaction, to be at least for a time "all gone." This particular infant is able to find a palliative or some recompense—*Es entschädigte sich* for the mother's repeated disappearances, was able to find some compensatory satisfaction in its mise-en-scène (*selbst in Szene setzen*) of a game played with the objects available to it. A cultural and a *poetic* achievement, one must say: the invention of prosopopoeia, and perhaps of metonymy and metaphor as well. The child has been reading Novalis.

As we suspected all along, however, Freud is making his way back to traumatic neurosis and even to the war-wounded. Abandonment by the mother is no pleasure. How then make a game of it? What is the secret of this poetic repetition-with-a-difference of absence and presence? The pleasure ought to lie of course in the reappearance of plaything or mother. Freud enters a footnote into his account, referring to an incident that "fully confirms" this supposition:

> One day when the mother was absent for several hours she was greeted by the baby upon her return with this: *Bebi o-o-o-o!* Incomprehensible at first. Yet it soon became clear that during its long period of solitude it had found a means of making itself disappear. It had discovered its image in a full-length mirror that reached almost to the floor; the child squatted so that its mirror-image was "all gone." (GW 13:13n. 1)

Now we have to fear that this unprecocious infant has been reading Lacan as well, but this is evidently not so. Had he been reading Lacan he would, on seeing his own image in the mirror, then seeing it disappear, simply have fallen to pieces. Yet not only does he preserve a sense of self in the presence *and absence* of his image, he also achieves the complex apperception-through-analogy that enables him to understand that as things go with baby so they go with mother. He has discovered intersubjectivity. He has been reading Husserl. The infant has therefore earned the right to garner whatever pleasure he can.

At the end of this footnote an editor of the Standard Edition (StA 3:225n. 1) informs us of two things, one we already surmise, but another that surprises us. The first revelation is that the infant is one of Freud's grandchildren (we are not told which one, nor whether its father or mother is Freud's child); the second revelation, really a reminder, is that this mirror scene has already been reported in the fifth edition (1919) of *The Interpretation of Dreams*. The context there is the strange disjunction in dreamlife between the modified content of a dream and the original affect that the dream awakens. In dreams we may be blasé about the most threatening situations but then terrified over nothing. Freud explains the disjunction in terms of the dream's latent meaning, to which the affect remains attached no matter how much the dream work has displaced the content. Freud enters into the 1919 edition of *Die Traumdeutung* the following footnote:

> If I am not mistaken, the first dream of my twenty-month-old grandson that was reported to me demonstrates that the dreamwork was able to transform the dream material into a wish-fulfillment, whereas the affect belonging to the dream persisted unchanged even in the state of sleep. In the night before the day when his father was to be sent to the front, the child, sobbing desperately, called out: Papa, Papa—bebi. That can only mean: Papa and Baby should remain together, whereas the tears acknowledge the imminent departure. The child was at that time perfectly able to express the concept of separation. "Gone" (expressed by a peculiarly emphatic, long, drawn-out o o o h) had been one of its first words, and for several months prior to this first dream it had produced the game of "all gone" with all its playthings, which referred back to the child's early successful self-overcoming in allowing its mother to depart [*die frühgelungene Selbstüberwindung, die Mutter fortgehen zu lassen*]. (GW 2/3:463–64n. 1; StA 2:444–45n. 1)

The infant is acknowledged and recognized as a grandson already in 1919. Perhaps there is simply no need for Freud to remind readers of the consanguinity in 1920. Yet we still do not know whether the father—who now faces grave danger—or the mother is Freud's progeny. There are other things that are difficult to know. The baby's "first dream"—can even a mother know such a thing? and is the disjunction between the sobs and "Papa, Papa—baby" at all clear? Household pets know when we are about to take a trip, but what does a twenty-month-old infant know about the battlefield? Perhaps it has been alerted by its mother's tears or by the father's disquiet—Freud's story does not tell us. Yet it does give us the wonderful Nietzschean word *Selbstüberwindung*, "self-overcoming," that key word of *Thus Spoke Zarathustra*, which is now added to the infant's already considerable library. *Triebverzicht*, the forswearing or renunciation of drive, namely, of the drive for pleasure, is self-overcoming. Nietzschean or Zarathustran "self-overcoming" does not play a role in the final pages of *La Carte postale*, which nevertheless do focus on the thinker of *will to power*. Such self-overcoming is perhaps the bridge that connects the thoughts of will to power and eternal return—which is the thought of repetition and difference. Yet Derrida leaves it to us to build that bridge. As we will see in Part Two of the present book, this never-completed move to the thinker of will to power—the move from Freud back to Nietzsche—is typical of every one of Derrida's encounters with psychoanalysis, right up to the end.

Yet the story of the pleasure principle is now being complicated by the need to overcome oneself, to learn renunciation, to assuage the sense of abandonment, to be compelled (perhaps by the reality principle) to simulate—by means of every object at hand, as though each object is "transitional," and as though successful transition itself has already been mastered—control over the mother's repeated absences and the father's imminent departure for war. In short, the pleasure principle is being complicated by another inchoate principle that will prove to be harsher than reality. Freud sometimes calls it *Bemächtigung*, an assertion of power over or a "hold" on things, an *emprise*; sometimes, in a less blithe mood, Freud associates *Bemächtigung* with the "destruction-and-death drives." But to return now to the *Beyond*.

Almost laconically Freud notes that the child was observed to play repeatedly the "all gone" part of the game without the happy end of the *da!* part, even though the pleasure principle ought to have induced it to play the return, to reiterate the *Da-* of *Da-sein* just as often. Gone tomorrow, perhaps, but *here* today! The child, however, is playing something else. It is giving itself an active role in the passively experienced infidelity of the mother. Perhaps, to repeat, there is a drive we have to call the *Bemächtigungstrieb,* the compulsion to attain power over what in reality disempowers us? Freud might well fear this hostage to the Adlerians, but he is compelled to wonder.[4] Or, on the darker side, perhaps there is a drive to seek revenge on all objects as a result of the mother's perfidy, "the satisfying of an impulse toward revenge against the mother, an impulse that in our life is suppressed" (GW 13:14). Freud even invents some baby talk to express this revenge, although the rhetoric shows us a baby that has added years to its repeatedly menaced life: " 'Sure, go away, I don't need you; I'll send you away myself.' " The adolescent rhetoric, with its forward-looking *Nachträglichkeit,* betrays some further twists and turns of the story, which now makes the infant seem less "decent" than its progenitors believed:

> The same child that I observed at its first game, played at eighteen months, a year later had the habit of tossing aside a toy it was displeased with and saying, "Go to the wa(r)!" They had told it at that time that the absent father had gone to war; the child did not miss the father at all, but gave every indication that it did not want to be disturbed in its exclusive possession of the mother. (Ibid.)

And so the tale shifts, from the sobs of a bereft infant who in the night cries for its father to the snarl of an upstart Oedipus. Sophocles has been teaching the infant something else about the mortal condition, and perfidy, it seems, does not pertain to the mother alone.

However, before we attain too much readerly satisfaction over the Complex that made Freud as famous as Sophocles, and before we become too breezy about this speculative jaunt beyond the pleasure principle to the destruction-and-death drives, Freud enters an addendum to a later edition of the *Beyond*, presented in both the *Gesammelte Werke* and the *Studienausgabe* as a footnote, and we had better read it: "When the child was five-and-three-quarters years old, the mother died. Now that she was actually 'all gone' (*o-o-o*), the boy showed not a trace of mourning for her. To be sure, in the

4 The word *Bemächtigung* will occupy Derrida's attention in "Spéculer—sur 'Freud' " from beginning (with the infant's drive to gain control over, or to empower himself in the face of, his mother's absences) to end (when Derrida identifies *Bemächtigung* as the very "transcendental predicate" of all drives as such). It will not be Adler, however, to whom Derrida refers, but the thinker of will to power mentioned a moment ago, Nietzsche. See *La Carte postale,* 430–37. And see chapters 8 and 10, below.

meantime a second child had been born, a child that had awakened in him the fiercest jealousy." End of note.[5]

If the father of the child was Freud's son, Freud abandons him at the battlefront; if the mother was his daughter, o-o-o, what a frigid footnote for a father to enter into the ledger of his science. Freud shows as little grief here as his grandson does, the grandson who is five-and-three-quarters years old, precisely reckoned, a "boy" now, a "he" and a "him." And his mother "all gone," forever. Not a trace of mourning—at least not here. To be sure, in the case of the child sibling rivalry is in play, producing a jealousy caustic enough to cause the child to growl, "Sure, go away, I don't need you, I'll send you away myself." When the curse of banishment and death actually works, however, when mere words of ours prove to be "factically murderous," as Hölderlin says of the words spoken by a Greek tragic hero, o-o-o, we are all Misfits, and "it is no pleasure in life."

We now arrive at the juncture at which Derrida begins to tell *his* story. I will take it up after one or two final remarks about the remainder of chapter 2 of the *Beyond* and some of the theoretical problems attending it.

Repeated enactment of a beloved and needed person's disappearance by tossing away objects instead of that person is, according to Freud, a common childhood ritual. Even Goethe engaged in it. Freud's article, "A Childhood Memory from *Dichtung und Wahrheit*," written three years before *Beyond the Pleasure Principle* (GW 12:15–24), informs us of Goethe's breaking his little play dishes, then, egged on by his neighbors, all the family dishes too. The reason? Goethe says he was bored with the dishes. Freud counters by speculating that Goethe wished to celebrate the birth of a little sister in the special way that older siblings often have. Yet Freud's question concerning this ritual is uncommon; indeed, it is highly speculative. Freud wonders whether in order to come to terms with and seek control over an event that challenges and even traumatizes the psychic apparatus *repetition* is enough, and whether repetition operates as "primary," which means quite independently of the pleasure principle (GW 13:15). Out of reiterated pain, pleasure? Or is it something *beyond* pleasure? But *repetition* in what sense? as reminiscence? as replay in imagination? with an emotional charge as potent as that which accompanied the original

---

5 The footnoted addendum must have been added to the third edition (1923) of the *Beyond*, if not later, although the editors of neither the *Gesammelte Werke* nor the *Studienausgabe* tell us anything about it (see GW 3:14n. 1; StA 3:215–16). Is the chilly nature of the note explained by the time that has elapsed since the mother's death?

event? What is it that flows from reiterated pain? Is it the *unpleasure* that Kant associates with the sublime? At all events, can one say that such rebarbative, displeasing pleasure truly conforms to the pleasure principle? Is there not too much spleen in it? If so, what principle undergirds it, what pulsion drives it? And why should the repetition compulsion need or use *objects* to throw away and sometimes smash? These are the questions that spur Freud's initial postulation of something like the "destruction-and-death drives."

If the word *pulsion* seems strange, it nonetheless captures the sense of "drive," *Trieb,* as such. Once we understand the importance of binding (*Bindung*) in primary process, inasmuch as excessive flows of pulsional quantity within the organism threaten to traumatize it and therefore must be "bound," and once we understand that such binding works not only on the side of life and pleasure but also on the side of death, insofar as perfect constancy of quantity flow = zero excitation = death, once we understand these things, we are prepared for Freud's massive uncertainty (expressed in chapters 6 and 7 of the *Beyond*) concerning his own "speculation" as well as Derrida's most stubborn and unyielding reading of speculative undecidability in *La Carte postale* (413–21). As we will see, however, many recalcitrant questions will delay our understanding of "these things."

At the very end of this second chapter Freud refers to Greek tragedy. "Imitation of an action that is serious," says Aristotle. Freud translates μίμησις, however, not as "imitation" but as *repetition.* In truth, that is what a director demands of his or her actors each day or night of a performance: you will suffer what you are called upon to suffer here and now for the first time—once again and always for the very first time. This is not the drive to imitate, which Aristotle agrees is pleasurable: this is the drive to *suffer repeatedly.* The "elevated enjoyment" of the theatergoer who attends a tragedy may cause us to think that the pleasure principle can accommodate suffering, can even use it to refine and intensify to the point of discharge the emotions of the spectator, at first fear, then compassion. Yet such an *aesthetics* of tragedy is of doubtful value to Freud, as it was to Nietzsche before him and to Heidegger and Max Kommerell after him. For what is the point of suffering repeatedly the instances of suffering when there is no one there who sees, no one there in the desert of the self abandoned to itself? Surely, some second principle is at hand, or, if not at hand, then moving its slow thighs?

Derrida says he will say just a few things in passing about the *fort/da* game, but I calculate some forty-five book pages in "To Speculate—on 'Freud' " that devote themselves to it, and I know the position that the bastard—and I mean him, Derrida—will put me in, the position of having to do injustice to his own text; that's where he always wants his readers to be, right there with him, unable to do justice to any text, misery loves company. Quickly, therefore, these few indicators of moments where and when Derrida expands or complicates the story, joins in the game, and teaches us about friction in the play that transpires on the scene of writing.

One cannot write these words without thinking of Derrida's "Freud and the Scene of Writing," which is such an astonishingly programmatic piece (ED 293–340). Every theme of the "*Spéculer*" essay is anticipated in it, including the recondite theme of lifedeath. Indeed, in the closing pages of the "Scene," Derrida is quite explicit about the relation of writing to mortality and the trace to an unrecoverable absence of origin. If Freud is a writer, and he is, it remains true that "writing is unthinkable without repression" (ED 334). And if Freud claims the privilege of being the master producer of psychoanalytic texts, the sovereign writer, Derrida replies: "The 'subject' of writing does not exist, if one understands by that some sovereign solitude of the writer. The subject of writing is a *system* of relations among the various layers: of the magic writing pad, of the psychic, of society, of the world. In the interior of this scene, the punctual simplicity of the classical subject cannot be found" (ED 335). At the heart of the scene of writing are trace and supplementarity, both of these as marks of the finitude of our being-in-the-world, of "the history and the play of the world" (ED 337). I will return to this "Scene" at the end of the chapter.

If Derrida is relentlessly tough on Freud, especially on Freud's vaunted "avoidance" of all "philosophical speculation," and if his deconstructive readings of Freud and Lacan seem to lack the generosity that the second moment of the double reading always shows to Husserl, Heidegger, and others, it may be the very proximity to Freud that irritates. The Bohemian Jew and the Algerian Jew, each needing to defend a hard-won science against the most inane miscomprehensions and polemics, each knowing how difficult and yet how necessary confession or circumfession is for their work, each hating intellectual mediocrity yet painfully aware of the deceptiveness of all intellectual legerdemain, each respecting the need to paint in chiaroscuro in order to avoid obscurantism, each loving precision and yet realizing that "hovering attention," *schwebende Aufmerksamkeit,* as Freud calls it, perhaps alluding to Novalis, better describes the work of both psychoanalysis and deconstruction than "science" or even "discipline"; each skeptical of sublimation, yet each investing more libido into study than the rest of us have for all of life; each knowing that words and images also have the status of symptoms, yet each knowing that no diagnosis ever gets to the bottom of them; each devoted to what is called *love,* but Derrida confessing himself the purest of bastards and Freud admitting that whereas everyone around him proves to be noble his own self-revelations show him to be a singular villain.[6] To Oskar Pfister the villainous Freud writes that if the analyst possesses no trace of criminality then he's not really doing his job. And whereas each listens attentively to the sounds of Eros, each knows that the drive to destruction and death is "working noiselessly," *geräuschlos arbeitend* (GW 14:84).

One word more, if I may, about that "criminality." Freud finds evident joy in writing to that "man of God," Pastor Pfister, the following lines:

> What I mean is that psychoanalysis suffers from the original sin of—virtue. It is the work of an all-too-decent human being, who thus also believes that he is duty-bound to observe discretion. . . . Yet discretion cannot be conjoined with psychoanalysis, properly conceived; one has to become a rogue, an outlaw, one has to surrender everything, betray oneself, act like an artist who buys his paints with his wife's household money and burns the furniture to keep his model warm. Without such a touch of criminality nothing will ever be really achieved [*Ohne ein solches Stück Verbrechertum gibt es keine richtige Leistung*].[7]

End of confessions, though not of concessions.

•

Freud has great *legs.* At least in France, where his *legacy* was inherited by Jacques Lacan—although the inheritance is contested most powerfully, if I am right, by Jacques Derrida. Derrida begins his second chapter, "*Legs de Freud,*" by describing his own effort as a "rerouting of" or a "diversion from" the École

---

6 This and the following remark on "criminality" are cited by Ilse Grubrich-Simitis in her introduction to Sigmund Freud, *Selbstdarstellung* (Frankfurt am Main: Fischer Taschenbuch Verlag, 1971), 21, 18.

7 Sigmund Freud and Oskar Pfister, *Briefe 1909–1939,* ed. Ernst L. Freud and Heinrich Meng (Frankfurt am Main: S. Fischer, 1963), 36.

Freudienne—if not a hijacking or abduction of it, even a misappropriation or embezzlement of its funds. All this in the one word *détournement*.[8]

Insofar as *Beyond the Pleasure Principle* is for Lacan the cardinal text, Derrida's encroachment on it can only be an abduction of Lacan. We have to think of Lacan's concept of "morcelization" when little Ernst (for that is the infant's name) uses *his* mirror phase to duplicate joyously his mother's absence with the disappearance of his own image. However, Derrida's emphasis falls not on the ego's fragmentation in the face of a specular wholeness but on the *other* who comes and goes in and out of a life, especially the *(m)other* whose permanent presence remains forever a phantasm. (The mother's name in the case at hand is Sophie, and she is Freud's "Sunday's Child," his "favorite"; in his letters Freud sometimes refers to her by her nickname, "Soph.") To be sure, the death drive is the cardinal concept for Lacan, inasmuch as even the most wretched patient must be taught to move beyond the pleasure principle in order to confront destruction and death. No matter how miserable the patient may feel, he or she must learn that the death of Dasein is in each case one's ownmost, inalienable, unsurpassable, certain and as certain eminently indeterminate—perhaps even overdetermined—possibility of existence. This certainly speaks to Derrida, even if for him Heidegger's being-toward-death is thoroughly aporetic.

In the first section of chapter 2 of "To Speculate," entitled "The 'Same Roof' of Autobiography," Derrida alludes to a remark in Freud's "*Selbstdarstellung*," a remark Freud drops without much notice or fuss. We heard it a moment ago. Freud remarks that the death drive is always at work "noiselessly," *geräuschlos*. Whereas love is loud, destruction is taciturn. Derrida writes of it precisely as "not speaking, inscribing itself in silence" (314). No wonder the opening chapters of Freud's *Beyond* fail to establish the palpable existence of any principle other than pleasure: if there *are* other pulsions, they say nothing, exhibiting themselves by hiding themselves, that is, by desisting from all self-showing and by "hollowing out" the pleasure principle from the inside (317).

---

8 Of the many texts by Derrida on Lacan, see especially "For the Love of Lacan," which is the second part of Derrida, *Résistances de la psychanalyse* (cited here as RP). Lacan's is the chiasm of a "philosophical reconstitution" of psychoanalysis and of what is "deconstructible" in it. Because of the primacy of the signifier in Lacan's system, Lacan is both "closest to" deconstruction and "the most deconstructible" (73–74). Naturally, Lacan's emphasis on Heidegger's *Sein zum Tode* makes him all the more significant for Derrida (85).

Freud's account of the infant's bobbin or spool on a string is "neither a story nor a history nor a myth nor a fiction," says Derrida, "nor the system of a theoretical demonstration" (319). It is rather a fragment of a painting that depicts a scene of domestic life, a piece of pointillist canvas, perhaps, in which the points are all elliptical and held in suspension. It is the most discussed Freudian scene, at least of those in the *Beyond*, and yet Derrida finds its *silences* most compelling. Freud paints himself into the picture as well, so that the canvas is part autobiography—with all the heterogeneities to which autobiography is heir—and part scientific observation, both "under the same roof." It is a picture of hearth and home, of the οἶκος, of a familiar familial site, but also, although Freud barely alludes to this, the site Derrida calls "domestic-funerary" (321), as though tragedy were close by. Freud does not tell us—at least not in the *Beyond*—that he is the grandfather of the boy whose name is Ernst, and he does not tell us that the mother of Ernst, Sophie, is his own daughter. Silence descends over these two autobiographical details. Freud is the scientific "observer," but he is also nonetheless father and grandfather to the two main personae of the story. (Throughout the *Envois* that precede "To Speculate" in *The Post Card*, Derrida refers to Freud and Heidegger as "our two grandfathers," as though psychoanalysis, ontology, and deconstruction were all under the same roof, perhaps all playing the same desperate *fort/da* game.) It is a canvas one might title "Grampa Comes to Visit," with Freud exercising the recognized right of the older generation to "descend upon" the younger—an odd expression when you think about it. Granddad descends upon his favorite daughter in order to have the pleasure of her company, the company of a daughter who is a mother, but also the pleasure of identifying in mystifying ways with his grandson, who is Sophie's firstborn, the one who for a brief time delights in the exclusive possession of his mother.

Derrida, like all French philosophers before him, does not disclose all his sources—the biographies and the collections of letters—but he knows a lot about this family vacation and its aftermath; he injects what he knows into the story, not to embarrass or expose Freud or to reduce psychoanalysis to the peculiarities of Freud's person or his family, but to ask about the silences and silencings at work in this particular scene of writing. At work, one must say, *geräuschlos*. Derrida's reading is "interested," as he admits, and it proceeds by "sifting through" material that is available to him which would not have been available to the earliest readers of the *Beyond*.

Ernst is the oldest of Freud's grandchildren. His game with the spool or bobbin, while pleasureful, is serious play—*ernst* in German means serious or earnest, as in the importance of being earnest, which Derrida does not fail to cite (322). The Freudian genealogy passes through Freud's daughter, and the mother of Ernst, Sophie, is by Freud's own admission his best beloved. Ernst is not Freud's favorite grandson, however, perhaps because he is not so clever; his younger brother "Heinele," who is the cleverest boy Freud will ever have encountered, is in fact Freud's heir apparent. Are such details important? one may ask with some impatience. Surely they are incidental to the point to be made—somewhat like the frame one selects for a painting? Derrida admits that these details are marginal, even parergonal (324), and yet the truth in painting can often be found not at the center of a canvas but on its periphery. Seurat loved to paint a pointillist passe-partout around the edges of his canvases, and sometimes he even framed them himself and then pointilized the wooden frame, as though he hoped that painting *and* frame would be exhibited in a pixilated gallery filled with people wearing polka dots, so that his entire art world would consist of "hides and hints and misses in prints."[9] Derrida believes that texts are like this, and that the scene of writing—while entirely silent—never establishes borders and never remains within anyone else's declared borders. A text, to alter the image, is a cell without a cell wall, as much exposure as exposition. In a word, these details of biography and autobiography are remnants, leftovers constituting a mere residue or patina with regard to what wants to be said—they are perhaps like chunks of phoneme stuck in the throat or on the page. They do not *tell* us anything, and we but barely sense that they are at work beneath or within what comes to the fore. Derrida refers to *le reste qui travaille en silence la scène,* the remnant that works the scene in silence (324). Here it is the earnest scene of Ernst coming to terms with his mother's absence and the serious scene of Freud's writing about the earnest scene of Sophie's death a few years after their having been under the same roof. As Derrida was wont to say of the 1930s and 1940s in Germany, the years 1919–20 too were "not just any years" in Freud's life.

At what point, asks Derrida, does Freud's self-analysis cease, in order to transform itself into a worldwide institution? What sort of repetition is it, when insights into one's own dreams and drives found a science and a therapy designed to be repeated over much—though not all—of the world? Derrida

9 James Joyce, *Finnegans Wake* (New York: The Viking Press, 1971 [1939], 20.

assures us that his own text has no thesis, but if it has an argument it would be this: "The value of abyssal repetition in Freud's writing stands in a relation of structural *mimesis* to the relation between the pleasure principle and 'its' death drive. The latter, to say it again, is not in opposition to the former but hollows it out with testamentary writing 'abyssally,' originarily, at the origin of origin" (325). The legacy of psychoanalysis as a world institution is thus not mastery or successful *Bemächtigung*. Its inheritors are condemned by this noiseless excavating action at the core of the pleasure principle to a certain "mutism," and even to a "precocious death" (326). It is that chilly, chilling footnote or addendum on the death of Sophie that has been drawing Derrida on, or hollowing him out—he who had no daughters—all this time.

"There is a mute daughter," Derrida writes at the outset of the second section of his second chapter, clearly disturbed by the way Sophie is made to conform to her father's judgments and desires, as though she were a puppet on a string, or a bobbin. Or a character in a narrative that is impossible to characterize. A number of other biographical details disturb Derrida. Above all, the fact that Ernst does not cry when his mother abandons him, the mother who nurtured the baby herself. (An indiscreet aside concerning that nurturing: the German says *genährt*, "nurtured," not "breastfed," although it is certainly not odd to read this "nurturing," *genährt*, as *gestillt*, "nursed, suckled," which is how Derrida reads it, inasmuch as he (or perhaps a translator) adduces to Freud's text the words *au sein*, nurtured "at the breast," whereas Freud himself is more discreet or more reticent.) And does not Freud too—or the narrator of the tale—seem a bit perplexed and even irritated about this lack of tears in Ernst? Derrida thinks so. Is there not something of an "accusation" raised by the grandfather against unprecocious little Ernst, who, seriously, is too dumb to know when tears are called for? Lya knew better.

Freud *or the narrator*, I just now wrote, as though the text were fiction, in which narrator and author never coincide. Yet Derrida himself deploys a different image of the scene of writing in the present instance, an image now not of painting but of the theater:

> The grandfather, the father of the daughter and of the mother, actively selects the traits of the description. I see him, pressed for time and disquieted, like a dramaturge or director who also has to play a role in the piece. *He's got to hurry*, blocking-off the scene, getting it all under control, before dashing off to get into costume so he can play

> his role. What suggests this is his trenchant authoritarianism, the decisions he does not pause to explain, speeches that are cut, questions to which he will not respond. (329)

Derrida is also struck by the hard work in little Ernst's play, dispersing and regathering not only his toys but his mother and himself, especially when he is at the mirror. With only a slight bow to Lacan, not mentioned here, Derrida calls Ernst himself a "collective," a "combinatory of ensembles" (331). Furthermore, Sophie too forms a collective with the observer-grandfather-father, identifying for Freud the sense of the phonemes *o* and *a* in *fort* and *da* as the names of the game. As for Derrida himself, a careful student of Saussure, he is aware of all the unspoken and unwritten hypotheses that Freud (and Sophie?) assume(s) in his (their?) interpretation of Ernst's game. Derrida does not take the time to unfold them all, but he counters Freud's declaration that the infant's game is "complete" in its *o* and *a*, its omega and alpha, by saying that the necessary *repetition* of the scene shows it to be a scene of supplementation, which means that it *never* achieves completeness. The (m)other is never reined in or drawn back to perfect presence. In this respect, alpha and omega—or, rather, alpha and *omicron,* not omega—share the incompleteness of every scene of writing, no matter how authoritarian the director and dramaturge.[10]

Derrida invokes his notion of *obséquence,* a theme in *Glas* but also in his second Nietzsche book, *Otobiographies,* in and as the scene of writing. In the latter book Derrida traces the bizarre "logic of the living woman," that is, of the mother who in some way survives the son even when she dies before him. Nietzsche, you will recall, propounds the following riddle of his existence, or of his provenance, in *Ecce Homo*: "As my father I am already dead, as my mother I live on and grow old" (KSW 6:264). Yet such *survivance* is threatened and even doomed from the start: recall Derrida's often-expressed fear that when a mother, foundering in senility or adrift in Alzheimer's, no longer remembers

10 Samuel Weber argues that the play and interplay of *fort/da* tend to blur the distinction between the imaginary and the symbolic in Lacan's psychology, blur it to the point where the symbolic no longer rescues us from a narcissistic imaginary. Weber asks, "Whether or not mastery of the renunciation of drive, and above all, mastery of the loss of the *mother,* is made possible and is produced by the appropriation of a *mother tongue*? And whether or not this second 'mother' allows herself to be retained just as little as the first?" See Samuel Weber, *Freud-Legende: Drei Studien zum psychoanalytischen Denken* (Olten und Freiburg-im-Breisgau: Walter Verlag, 1979), 125.

her child's name, the child has indeed lost that name forever. If we imbibe our identity with her milk, nurtured *au sein,* are not the generations forever out of sequence, and is not our identity always at forfeit? Does not one generation "descend upon" the other, the older upon the younger, such that Antigone's situation is not as unique as one might think? Now, to be sure, no one understands the logic of obsequence, which hovers somewhere between the *sequence* of generations and the *obsequy* that the dead generation writes for the living, and no one apart from Derrida, Wordsworth, and Plato's *Statesman* will believe in it. Does the logic of the living woman suffer no refutation, however, if in fact she dies? if in fact she dies when her oldest child is, say, five-and-three-quarters years old? Derrida does not write anything more about this, but he allows the uncanny logic of the living woman to work on us in silence.

Derrida does remark on Freud's puzzlement as to why Ernst fails to draw the spool-on-a-string along behind him as if it were a wagon or a car or a train. Derrida wonders why Freud, who has had bad experiences on trains, wonders about this. Derrida cites Freud's "train phobia," but he does not mention the most striking and uncanny event in Freud's ferrocarrilian experience. In "The Uncanny," Freud reports an unsettling night in a sleeping car, when an ugly old man burst into his compartment. After the initial shock and indignation, Freud was astonished to see that it was not the outer door but the door to the bathroom that had swung open. This door had a full-length mirror, just like little Ernst's mirror back in Hamburg. The horrid old man bursting onto the scene, and who aroused in Freud something akin to disgust, was his own reflection in the mirror (GW 12:262–63n. 1).

Why does Freud, in his *Beyond*, insist on the train, or on Ernst's drawing the spool behind him "in train," as it were? In Derrida's view, Freud wants little Ernst to play Orpheus, leading Eurydice back from the underworld; or perhaps he wants him to be like an analysand, who draws the analyst along behind him by means of his yarn. For the analyst is behind the couch, and the patient has to sacrifice vision for hearing (337). But no, Ernst tosses his bobbin up into the curtained crib. Freud says little about the tiny bed itself, or about the way the mother and daughter are drawn from absence to presence by means of it. Derrida, by contrast, loves the hymeneal veil of this bed, loves the diaphanous border of presence and absence. He is tempted to say that the curtain or veil is itself Sophie in the guise of Eurydice, but he says he will not risk saying this, and one is doubly grateful. He *will* risk pointing out a strange throwaway remark by Freud, to the effect that it does not really matter whether little Ernst invented the *fort/da* game—which could be a game of either mastery over or vengeance upon the mother who is Freud's daughter—or whether he picked it up from someone else. Derrida does not say that Ernst picked up the game of mastery or vengeance from the scientific observer, his grandfather; yet on the scene of writing it is difficult to exclude such an eventuality from the realm of unconscious possibilities. For why else would the repulsive interloper throw the throwaway remark, not away, but into his text?

Of course, Derrida loves the *fil,* the thread or string held in the tiny fist of the *fils.* Pull the string and Ernst masters absence, recovers Sophie, the mother and the daughter. Or so it seems. Derrida sees little Ernst's problem this way: mastery and the pleasure principle are one and the same, and the recalcitrance of what refuses to return is not *opposed to* the pleasure principle; rather, Derrida repeats, what lies beyond this principle is not some dialectical opposite but a more mysterious power that *hollows out* the pleasure principle and *undermines* all principles. The destruction-and-death drives will not be forms of mastery but something quite foreign to mastery, if by that we mean our ability to attain power. Even unprecocious little Ernst will have noticed that it is necessary to repeat the game, that the *re-* of reappearance has disappearance as its pendant, so that no single playing of the game will ever guarantee Sophie's presence. Nor does the game of idealized identification, played in front of the mirror, making baby go and come back just like mommy, alter the necessity of repetition. If the dream is the royal road to an unconscious dominated by the pleasure principle, compulsive repetition is the eroding rainfall that eats away at the roadbed of all our dreams.

It is *mastery* as such that is the issue in the *Bemächtigungstrieb* mentioned earlier. At the heart of the latter word stands the word *Macht,* power, as in "will to power." Derrida thinks it as *emprise*, "hold," which is the standard French translation of the word. Every drive, whether of life or death, Eros or destruction, is driven (tautology intended) by the drive to seize and hold—which is to say that lifedeath is dominated, as Nietzsche will have seen, by power, or by will-to-power. And yet at the very end of Derrida's meditation, once the "transcendental predicate" of power, "postal power," has been established for both the pleasure principle and the death drive, the latter retains its haunting quality—as though the domain of power, that is, of every drive and every principle, lies irrefragably *beyond* the pleasure principle, beyond *any* principle, beyond every "hold." As Derrida puts it later, in *Mal d'archive*: "The death drive is not a principle. It threatens the very reign of principles as such, every archontic primacy, every desire for an archive," so that Freud, who is only "coolly benevolent" toward his own speculation, always full of doubts, will have been right to doubt.[11]

The final part of Derrida's second chapter bears the title, *La séance continue.* We recognize it as a quotation, and we look for it (in vain) in Mallarmé, the subject of Derrida's "Double Séance" in *Dissémination.* Yet "the séance continues" is in this case spoken closer to home—to Freud's home. Derrida always loved to telescope his remarks near the *chute* or end of a text. Allow me to do the same, reducing Derrida's own complex séance to a spare chronology of events. These events are not mentioned in Freud's *Beyond*, not all of them, in any case. They are not speculations but more like specters haunting the scene of writing. Derrida writes, elliptically, cryptically, "The death drive is *there*, in the pleasure principle, which involves a *fort:da*" (344). A *fort* [colon] *da*, as though to say that the pleasure principle conceals an "all gone" that is always silently at work right there where pleasure ought to be.

21 January 1920. Sophie, aged twenty-six and pregnant with her third child, dies of pneumonia after a week of illness. "Blown away by a gust of wind.

---

11 See Derrida, *Mal d'archive* (MA 27). For Freud's *kühles Wohlwollen* toward his speculation, see GW 13:65; for Derrida's allowing the death drive to haunt even the transcendental realm, the realm of power and *emprise,* see *La Carte postale,* esp. 432–37.) As we will see in Part Two of the present book, the theme of *Bemächtigung* becomes increasingly important to Derrida after 1980: in *Résistances* and *États d'âme de la psychanalyse: Adresse aux États Généraux de la Psychanalyse*, the concept is of central importance. (In EA see esp. 14, 35, and 47.) Here too it is a question of the power that all mastery presupposes—the *Macht* of *Bemächtigung.* Let me at this juncture not miss the opportunity to cite the final chapter ("Why the Death Drive?") of Jean Laplanche's *Life and Death in Psychoanalysis,* tr. Jeffrey Mehlman (Baltimore: Johns Hopkins, 1976), 103–24: a step-by-step comparison of the two strategies of reading the *Beyond*, Derrida's and Laplanche's, would certainly be worthwhile, yet far too difficult for me to attempt here. Perhaps the most fruitful exchange between the two thinkers would occur on the basis of Laplanche's demonstration (113–16) that the "constancy principle" and the "tendency toward zero-excitation," which are equated by Freud, cannot by any means be conflated—and that in fact the former has to do with the "exigency of life," *die Not des Lebens*, and therefore with Eros, not with the death drive and the Nirvana principle. The result is what Laplanche calls "the proliferating or fissioning in relation to origins" (112) in Freud's speculation, a fissioning that Derrida has always referred to as "the nonorigin of origins." That fissioning goes so far that Freud himself, in his open letter to Einstein, *Why War?* refers—perhaps tongue in cheek—to his "mythological theory of drives" (GW 16:22–23; EA 46).

Nothing to say," writes Freud to Ferenczi.[12] Freud received news of her alarming condition only two days before her death, while he was attending the funeral of one of his most respected young associates and benefactors, Anton von Freund. The pan-European influenza epidemic (the "Spanish flu") that snatched away young Sophie also snuffed the lives of architect Otto Wagner and painter Gustav Klimt. The years 1919–20, when reflections on destruction and death ought to have been subsiding, were a harvest season for death. They were the years not only of *Beyond the Pleasure Principle* but also of "The Uncanny," published in the fall of 1919. That same year spawned Maurice Ravel's *La Valse*, which, while reminiscent of Viennese grace and charm, is full of demons and doppelgänger; as conductor François-Xavier Roth once remarked, "You cannot dance to this waltz." Sophie's death must have sparked in Freud a recollection of E. T. A. Hoffmann's Coppelius/Coppola, and above all of Professor Spalanzani—good father? bad father?—who desired to produce a daughter who would last, a daughter who would dance the night away with her young man. Derrida, near the end of *Mal d'archive*, muses upon that daughter of Freud's (the context tells us that it is Anna, but we may equally think of Sophie) who, like Jensen's Gradiva, has vanished so thoroughly that she may have never been alive, may never have been *Zoé*, "but merely a phantasm or a specter, a Gradiva *rediviva*" (MA 148).

27 January 1920. Less than a week after Sophie's death, a day before the cremation, Freud writes to Oskar Pfister: "She who was in the blossom of health and who led an active and full life, an excellent mother and a tender wife, was snatched away in four or five days as if she had never been."[13]

Freud reports that he and his wife are unable to attend the funeral because of train problems—the unavailability of trains having been a critical difficulty in postwar Germany and Austria. Not even trains for the emergency transport of (living) children are available. He then remarks that Sophie's husband will

---

12 On Sophie's death, see among other sources Sigmund Freud–Sándor Ferenczi, *Briefwechsel*, ed. Ernst Falzeder, Eva Brabant et al. (Vienna: Böhlau Verlag, 2003), III/1:49n. 2. For Sophie's being snatched away by the wind, see (III/1:50).

13 See letter 50 in Sigmund Freud and Oskar Pfister, *Briefe 1909–1939*, 77–78, cited by Derrida in *La Carte postale* at 350–51. This letter also appears in Sigmund Freud, *Briefe 1873–1939*, 344–45. My thanks to Samuel Weber for suggesting the translation of Freud's *hinweggerrafft* as "snatched away": it is as though Sophie had been seized and snatched away like Persephone by Hades or Eurydice by snakebite, both of them victims of terrible violence. (The homology of *raffen* and *rapere*, despite what the etymological dictionaries tell us, is too painful to be ignored.) The fact that there is no one to prosecute or blame, nowhere to carry the lament, does not diminish but intensifies the pain for both Freud and Derrida.

have to pay dearly for the seven years of bliss he has enjoyed with her. Near the end of the letter Freud adds, "I am working as hard as I can [on the *Beyond*] and I am grateful for the distraction. The loss of a child seems to be an instance of grave narcissistic chagrin [*eine schwere, narzißtische Kränkung*]; what one calls mourning will presumably come only later" (ibid.).

If Freud's remark to Pfister concerning Sophie's widower Max Halberstadt seems harsh, and it does, Freud's correspondence with his son-in-law over the years of his marriage with Sophie demonstrates genuine affection. No doubt, Sophie's father has some difficulty in releasing her to her adult life. In an early letter to Max, dated July 24, 1912, Freud quips—and the quip would have caught Derrida's eye had he seen it, although I presume he did not, "It is a very curious thing when such a little daughter suddenly turns out to be a loving wife." Yet releasing her to her death was excruciatingly difficult. The following letter to Max, dated 25 January 1920, which Derrida also does not cite, reflects Freud's affection and desperation, and it merits quoting at length:

> My dear Max . . . it seems to me that I have never written a more superfluous letter. You know how great our pain is, and we know what sort of pain you must be in. I'll make no effort to console you, precisely as you can do nothing to console us. Perhaps you think that I don't know what it means to lose a beloved wife and the mother of one's children, inasmuch as I have been spared that agony. You are right. But, in turn, the bitter chagrin [*Kränkung*], so late in life and so close to death of surviving a young, blossoming child, has to be equally alien and incomprehensible to you. I don't have to tell you either that this disaster changes nothing about my feelings for you; you will remain our son as long as you want to be—this follows from our relationship heretofore and is self-evident. So, why am I writing you? I believe it is simply because we are prevented from being together now, because in this wretched time of our imprisonment we cannot travel to one another, so that I cannot tell you in person the things I've said to my mother and to my brothers and sisters, namely, that it is a senseless and brutal act of destiny that has robbed us of our Sophie, something in the face of which we cannot sue for justice, something we cannot even brood over; all we can do is bend our heads like the miserable, helpless human beings we are, exposed to this stroke by which the higher powers have blasted us. Enough. She was happy as long as she was living with you, and, in spite of the difficult times, in the seven years that were granted to your brief marriage, her happiness was thanks to you.[14]

14 Sigmund Freud, *Briefe 1873–1939*, 343.

29 January 1920. Freud writes to Sándor Ferenczi, "My wife is quite crushed. I am thinking: *la* séance *continue.* But it was a bit much for one week."[15]

4 February 1920. In another letter to Ferenczi, Freud writes, "Deep inside I sense the feeling of a profound narcissistic chagrin with which I will not be able to come to terms [*das Gefühl einer tiefen, nicht verwindbaren narzißtischen Kränkung*]."[16] Four days later, in a letter to Ernest Jones, he calls Sophie's death "a loss not to be forgotten."[17] The earlier letter to Ferenczi, which holds out the hope that scientific work can dull the pain of such a loss, is also worth quoting at length:

> Don't be concerned about me. I'm still the same, only a bit more tired. This death, as painful as it is, doesn't change the way I look at life. For years now I've been preparing myself for the loss of my sons,

---

15 Freud-Ferenczi, *Briefwechsel*, III/1:50. The editors add the following note to the French phrase: "An allusion to a custom in the theater, which says that when an actor dies the play must continue without interruption." In short, whatever the catastrophe, "the show must go on."

16 Freud-Ferenczi, *Briefwechsel*, III/1:51. The word *Kränkung* is translated into French as *offense*, and this makes sense: to be *gekränkt* in German is to be bitterly offended. The usual English translation as *hurt* does not go far enough in the direction of insult and offense. I have opted for the word *chagrin*.

17 Derrida's text has "a loss that must be forgotten," *une perte qu'il faut oublier*, which is precisely the reverse of what appears in *The Complete Correspondence of Sigmund Freud and Ernest Jones, 1908–1929*, ed. R. Andrew Paskauskas (Cambridge: Harvard University Press, 1993), 368, letter no. 266. No light is shed on this problem in the German supplement to the letters, *Briefwechsel Sigmund Freud–Ernest Jones 1908–1939*, ed. Ingeborg Meyer-Palmedo (Frankfurt am Main: S. Fischer, 1993), 24–25. I have not seen the French edition of the letters that Derrida is using, but I imagine that it is a question of a mistake in translation. In any case, I want to take this occasion to make a strong complaint with regard to the published volumes of Freud's correspondence: one has to lament the wretched dispersion of Freud's letters (particularly the German originals) among countless volumes and numerous editors and publishers. It is nothing less than shocking to see that one of last great letter writers of Europe has not yet had his letters gathered in a collected edition, much less a well-edited and annotated *Studienausgabe*. What are all those worldwide psychoanalytic societies for, one must ask, if they cannot spare the time and the cash to insist on and carry out a historical-critical collected edition, along with an annotated *Studienausgabe*, of Freud's letters? Such an edition, one hopes, would at least get all the negatives right. My thanks to Paul Turner, of DePaul University, and Alexander Bilda, of the University of Freiburg, who helped me across two continents to chase down the fugitive volumes of Freud's correspondence.

> and now it is my daughter who is dead. Because I am a man who is utterly without faith, there is no one I can blame, and I know there is no place to which I can carry my lament. The "eternally invariable hour of duty" [Schiller, *Die Piccolomini*, 1:4] and "the sweet habit of existence" [Goethe, *Egmont*, 5:4] will see to the rest, so that everything goes on as usual. Deep inside I sense the feeling of a profound narcissistic affliction with which I will not be able to come to terms. My wife and Annie are, in a more human way, quite shattered.[18]

These desperate thoughts, less than two weeks after Sophie's death. Two months later, on March 15, 1920, Freud confesses to Ferenczi: "The pressure we feel since Sophie's death has not abated."[19] Three years later, when Ferenczi informs him of the death (in childbirth) of a young colleague, Freud replies, "The death of a young woman and mother is yet one more repulsive detail [*noch ein garstiges Detail*] of this world in decline."[20]

27 May 1920. Four months after Sophie's death, to Max Eitington: "I am currently correcting and completing the *Beyond*—of the pleasure principle, that is—and once again I find myself in a creative phase. *Fractus si illabatur orbis, impavidum ferient minae* [Horace, *Carmine*, III 3: 'If the sky above him caves in, he will observe with equanimity the debris descending over him.'] It's all a question of mood, as long as it holds out."[21]

Allow me to interrupt the chronology with a blunt remark. If Derrida finds one thing about Freud unacceptable and even unforgivable it is his account in *Mourning and Melancholia* of the work of successful mourning as the narcissistic withdrawal of libidinal investment from the defunct and reinvestment in a new object. Derrida counters that mourning itself, which is both impossible and ineluctable, does not submit to such work, much less attain power and achieve success. No *Bemächtigung* succeeds in mastering grief. Nor does mourning yield to play, as though in a child's game. Here it is true to say that pulling strings wins no wisdom. No return *of* Sophie, no return *on* Sophie. There are no capital gains in cases of profound mourning. Winner take nothing.

---

18 Cited at Derrida, 351; see the Freud-Ferenczi *Briefwechsel*, III/1:51. This letter also appears in Sigmund Freud, *Briefe 1873–1939*, at 346.

19 Freud-Ferenczi *Briefwechsel*, III/1:58, not cited by Derrida.

20 Ibid., III/1:152, not cited by Derrida.

21 Cited at Derrida, 351. See Sigmund Freud–Max Eitington, *Briefwechsel 1906–1939*, 2 vols., ed. Michael Schröter (Tübingen: edition diskord, 2004), 2:207.

Derrida's reply to the common wisdom that we have to move on, have to get over it, is that paralysis is preferable and in any case inevitable. The step that would move us beyond is in French *un pas*, a pace, but one that offers *no* moving beyond, *pas du tout*. Freud's written responses to Sophie's death show that he realizes this fully.

18 July 1920. Reacting to the negative response of many of his disciples to the concept of the death drives—with some of these disciples even wishing to exclude the *Beyond* from Freud's collected works, convinced as they are that the concept of the death drives arises purely from Freud's melancholia after the deaths of Anton von Freund and Sophie—Freud writes to Max Eitington: "The *Beyond* is finally finished. You will be able to confirm that it was already half-completed during the time when Sophie was still alive and in full bloom."[22]

18 December 1923. Some four years after Sophie's death, Freud writes to a biographer, Fritz Wittels, a more candid yet equally insistent note: "I would certainly have insisted on the connection to be made between the death of a daughter and the concepts of the *Beyond* . . . in every analytical study involving someone else. *Beyond* was written in 1919, at a time when my daughter was young and in full bloom. Her death occurred in 1920. In September of 1919, I sent the manuscript of this part of the book [presumably, chapter 2] to friends in Berlin, to have their opinion of it, so that the only part that was missing was that on the mortality and immortality of protozoa. *Probability does not always signify the truth of a matter*."[23]

---

22 Cited at Derrida, 349. See the Freud-Eitington *Briefwechsel*, 2:213. See also the helpful editorial note 2 on that page of the correspondence, which confirms Freud's desire to separate his notion of the death drive from the personal catastrophe of Sophie's death.

23 Derrida cites this letter at 349–50, yet the letter as printed in Freud's *Briefe 1873–1939*, edited by Ernst and Lucie Freud, does not contain this passage. See 363–64, which shows no ellipsis points indicating an excision. No doubt the passage belongs to the "list of corrections" that Freud appends to his letter, which the German edition, alas, does not include. Fritz Wittels, an early biographer (and critic) of Freud, had argued that the death drive—apart from being putatively a discovery of Wilhelm Stekel rather than of Freud himself—loomed in Freud's thinking "while he was under the pressure of the death of a blossoming daughter," indeed, that Freud's negation of life in the *Beyond* is a cry "at the graveside of his daughter." See Fritz Wittels, *Sigmund Freud: Der Mann, die Lehre, die Schule* (Leipzig: E. P. Tal Verlag, 1924), 231.

". . . [I]n every analytical study involving someone else." But not the master himself. And yet. Derrida reports (although without naming his source, and I have been unable to confirm or disconfirm the report) that in his latter years Freud wore a bracelet containing an image of Sophie, as though the bracelet were a string gripped in a little boy's or a father's fist (353). Her death confounds the generations and is thus a prime case of *obséquence*—in this case involving not a mother but a daughter, albeit a daughter who is a mother.

During the year 1923, Freud's cancer of the mouth discloses to him his fate. His great fear, expressed already in 1918, is that he might die ahead of his mother, and that someone would have to break the news to her, news of the "monstrous" fact that children can and sometimes do die before their parents, sometimes even before their grandparents. Freud is convalescing from his first oral surgery at the same time that Sophie's second son, "Heinele," the infant who was the object of his brother Ernst's fierce jealousy and Freud's own delight, is recovering from a tonsillectomy. "Heinele" is "a splendid little fellow," "the brightest child for his age" that Freud has ever seen, but also a labile boy, "nothing but eyes, hair, and bones," and, further weakened by the surgery, he dies of miliary tuberculosis on June 19, 1923. Nothing will enable Freud to get over this loss: when the boy dies, Freud refers to him not as one of several grandchildren but as "my child," *mein Kind*, as though he and Sophie have had a child together. They say it is the one and only time Freud is seen to weep.[24]

2 November 1925. Freud confesses to Marie Bonaparte that after Heinele's death he cannot find any hold (355); in a letter to Felix Deutsch he speaks of a "comprehensive indifference concerning the trivialities of existence" (356), noting that this is a sign of the work of mourning in him (he does not say melancholia), and adding, incidentally, that one of the trivialities of existence is all his science (ibid.).

Lionel Trilling's account of these deaths and of Freud's reaction to them also tempers to some extent Derrida's objections to *Mourning and Melancholia*. It is as though Freud's theory in that work has less to do with his own life than one would have imagined. Trilling writes:

---

24 See, among other sources, the Freud-Ferenczi *Briefwechsel*, III/1:151, 161, 166n. 1, 244; Sigmund Freud, *Briefe 1873–1939*, 361–62. To Binswanger Freud writes, "He ['Heinele'] represented all the children and grandchildren for me, and since his death I don't like the grandchildren anymore, nor do I take any more joy in life. That is the secret of my indifference in the face of the menace to my own life—and people call it courage." Sigmund Freud and Ludwig Binswanger, *Briefwechsel 1908–1938*, ed. Gerhard Fichtner (Frankfurt am Main: S. Fischer, 1992), 208.

> A few days later [after the death of Anton von Freund] Freud received the news of the death, at twenty-six, of his beautiful daughter Sophie, whom he called his "Sunday child." In 1923 Sophie's son Heinz ["Heinele"] died at the age of four. Freud had a special love for this little grandson—he said that Heinz stood to him for all the children and grandchildren—and his death was a terrible blow. He experienced each death as the loss of a part of himself. He said that Anton von Freund's death was an important factor in his ageing. Of Sophie's death he said that it was a "deep narcissistic hurt that is not to be healed." He believed that the death of little Heinz marked the end of his affectional life.[25]

And yet Freud's response to Sophie's death may not be as remote from Freudian theory as the thesis of *Mourning and Melancholia* might suggest. At about the same time he was working on that text, Freud wrote the following in "Our Relation to Death," the second part of his *Timely Meditations on War and Death*:

> This conventional cultural posture with respect to death [namely, our tender regard and respect for the deceased] has as its supplement the complete collapse [*Zusammenbruch*] that occurs when death strikes one of the persons who stand quite close to us, a parent or spouse, a sibling, a child, a dear friend. With such as these we bury our hopes, our claims, our enjoyments; we do not allow ourselves to be consoled and we refuse to replace the one we have lost. We behave as though we were a member of the Asra people, *who, when someone they love dies, die along with them.* (GW 10:343)

The Asra are an Arab people cited in works by Heine and Stendhal, a people for whom the distinction between introjection and incorporation in the mourning process is not an option. As for Derrida, the title of the French collection of his necrologies for deceased friends and colleagues says it all: *Chaque fois unique—la fin du monde.* Yet is this not precisely Freud's reaction to the deaths of Sophie and "Heinele"?

One final detail, expressing a belated solidarity between the grandfather and the unprecocious survivor named Ernst. Freud himself was not yet one year old when an interloper by the name of Julius—no relation to Lucinde's

---

25 See Lionel Trilling, Introduction to Ernest Jones, *The Life and Work of Sigmund Freud*, 18–19.

paramour, though equally as tender—was born into the Jakob Freud family. Sigmund, the first-born son, proved to be furiously jealous now that he was no longer in exclusive possession of their mother. He wished the interloper gone, and Julius promptly died. O-o-o, those factically murderous words uttered in silence and yet heard by the obedient cudgeling Fates. In a letter to Fliess dated October 3, 1897, Freud confesses that ever since Julius's death the "seed of self-accusation" is sown for all time in the field of his life.[26]

To conclude. The scene of writing is labyrinthine, a bit like life. Ariadne ravels a string behind her for Theseus to grasp so that he might save himself, but the yarn may get tangled at each corner of the labyrinth. That's the way with yarns. For Derrida, it is never a matter of psychoanalyzing Freud, although it sometimes looks like that; in the end it is a matter of respecting, above all of Freud's ideas, the idea of "overdetermination," and of pursuing the overdetermination of all ideas and events and, yes, texts, in the direction of a silently working "undecidability." Freud, in his wonderful letter to Else Voigtländer, in which he declares the equal importance of "character" and "contingency" for psychoanalysis, citing the words δαίμων καὶ τύχη from Goethe's *Urworte: Orphisch*, declares the importance of overdetermination (as opposed to oppositional thinking) for his science: "We are more disposed to overdetermination and less disposed to opposites than other observers are."[27]

Freud, after Derrida, will have been an exemplary grandfather, not only to Heinele and Ernst, but also to Derrida. Derrida's tutelary spirit or δαίμων is none other than τύχη or chance itself—overdetermination to the point of undecidability. Not in order to be captious or obscurantist, but to be as alert as one can be on the uncannily silent scene of writing. Like little Ernst, the writer pulls all the strings, spins and twines all the yarns, and what happens? Does the mother return? Recall these words from the catechetical episode of *Ulysses*, "Ithaca" (U 816–17):

> The irreparability of the past: once at a performance of Albert Hengler's circus in the Rotunda, Rutland square, Dublin, an intuitive particoloured clown in quest of paternity had penetrated from the ring to a place in the auditorium where Bloom, solitary, was seated and had publicly declared to an exhilarated audience that he

26 Sigmund Freud, *Aus den Anfängen der Psychoanalyse*, ed. Ernst Kris (London: Imago Publishing Co., 1950), 233.

27 Sigmund Freud, *Briefe 1873–1939*, 300.

> (Bloom) was his (the clown's) papa. The imprevidibility of the future: once in the summer of 1898 he (Bloom) had marked a florin (2s.) with three notches on the milled edge and tendered it in payment of an account due to and received by J. and T. Davy, family grocers, 1 Charlemont Mall, Grand Canal, for circulation on the waters of civic finance, for possible, circuitous or direct, return.
>
> Was the clown Bloom's son?
>
> No.
>
> Had Bloom's coin returned?
>
> Never.

Like little Ernst squatting before the mirror and so "disappearing," the masterful writer keeps a low profile and seems to disappear from his or her spectral writing, only to pop up from time to time. And what happens? Does the mother then return? Sometimes yes, sometimes no, but at some irreversible moment nevermore. Recall these words about the trace of writing from the very end of "Freud and the Scene of Writing":

> The trace is self-effacement, effacement of its proper presence; it is constituted by the menace or the anxiety of its irremediable disappearance, the disappearance of its disappearance. An ineffaceable trace is not a trace, it's a full presence, an immobile and incorruptible substance, a son of God [*un fils de Dieu*], a sign of parousia and not a sowing of seed, that is, a mortal germ.
>
> This effacement is death itself. . . . (ED 339)

All gone: here you are. O-o-o. Wisdom, Sophie, in the door out the door, if you try to pull some strings you discover there are no strings attached, she's not a bobbin or a spool she's a tutelary spirit she's the moon looming over mountaintops mournful and splendid at the full and she's here to say that when you love a thing or a person and you want to get a hold on them firmly and write about them she's in the door out the door leaving it all in your hands—leaving it all up to you, all of it, everything, absolutely everything in your clenched fist and under your control, *le tout, tout—sauf*. . . .

•

My text ends here, with the ellipsis of *sauf*. . . . And yet. Yehotal Shapira, of the Hebrew University, after she heard my paper, informed me that—to her ear at least—the word *soph*, the Hebrew פּ נ ס, reading right to left *samech nun fe* (unless my eyes deceive me) means "the end." The end, or more fully, "the end of the road, finish, conclusion, termination, quietus, ruin." Shapira—and I thank her for her kind intervention, along with Joel Shapiro, who helped me with the transcription of her letters—speculated that Derrida may well have heard in the phrase *sauf Soph* "the end," which is to say, redoubled end and ruin.

Michael Naas then reminded me of a story recounted in Benoit Peeters's biography of Derrida.[28] Peeters tells us that Derrida used to drive his young niece and nephew (the children of his sister Janine, who had arrived from war-torn Algeria in May 1962) into Paris, where he would park their 2 CV in the courtyard of the École Normale, to see quickly to some academic business. He would ask the children to wait in the car, explaining that he had to go and feed Sophie the Whale, *Sophie la Baleine,* who was so fussy that she permitted only him to approach her with his tins of sardines. Years later his niece reflected that *Sophie la Baleine* may have had something to do with philosophy.

28 See Benoit Peeters, *Derrida* (Paris: Flammarion, 2010), 155–56.

Chapter Six

A Woman Without Qualities?

What we are missing today are not human beings of action [*Tatmenschen*]; what we are missing are actions that are human [*Menschentaten*].

—Robert Musil, *Der Mann ohne Eigenschaften*

ROBERT MUSIL'S *Der Mann ohne Eigenschaften* ("The Man Without Qualities," "Attributes," "Properties," or any given "Particularities")[1] is not a novel about tenderness. It is the story of events in Austria in 1913–14, some of which lead to absolutely nothing, delightfully nothing, and others that lead to World War I. Yet it is also the story of a brother and a sister who, rejoined after many years of living entirely separate lives, wonder whether they might be, or might become, Siamese twins. In the final pages of the published novel—and that means after a thousand pages have been written and rewritten, inasmuch as Musil is never able to bring his novel to an ending and a finality—the words *zart, Zartheit, zärtlich, Zärtlichkeit* recur with increasing frequency, especially when the brother (Ulrich) and the sister (Agathe) take center stage. In fact, the narrator of the novel, in all things omniscient and yet normally either mildly ironic or altogether reticent, takes the extraordinary step of warning the reader about what might occur in the chapters to come:

1 Maurice Blanchot prefers "the most natural translation" of *Eigenschaften* into French, which happens to carry over well into English and is also "closest to the German," namely, *The Man Without Particularities*. See chapter 4 of Maurice Blanchot, *Le livre à venir* (Paris: Gallimard, 1959), 165–84, here 169. Cited from hence in the body of my text as LA with page number. I am grateful to Kasra Saghafi for the reference to Blanchot.

> However, anyone who has not as yet recognized traces of what transpired between these siblings should set this report aside. For an adventure will be described there that the reader will never be able to approve of: a journey to the edge of the possible, which would pass on by the dangers of the impossible and unnatural, indeed of the repulsive; yet perhaps not forever would it pass them by; a "limit situation," as Ulrich later called it, of restricted and particular validity, reminiscent of the freedom with which mathematics sometimes makes use of the absurd in order to arrive at the truth. He and Agathe wound up on a path that has much to do with the affairs of those who are in God's grip, and yet they walked it without piety, without believing in God or the soul, indeed without even believing in the beyond or the once-again; they came upon that path as human beings of this world, and as such they walked that path: and precisely that is what merits our attention [*und gerade das war das Beachtenswerte*]. (761) [2]

How are we to characterize the path on which brother and sister walk in the grip of some sort of god? Musil will call it *der andere Zustand*, "the other state" or "the other condition." Before we get there, however, even if Musil's narrator is right and we should shudder to get there, a certain amount of retelling is in order, since Musil—the Austrian Joyce, if Joyce is the Irish Musil, and the Austrian Proust, if one can talk this way at all, which of course one cannot—is not yet read widely enough in the worlds of Joyce and Proust. A complete account of tenderness in the novel would have to take into account Ulrich's passion for the Major's wife, for Leona, Bonadea, Diotima, Clarisse, and Gerda Fischel, and then go on to recount in detail all thirty-eight chapters of Part Three of the novel and a thousand pages of literary remains. Here we will proceed more modestly, beginning with a brief listing of the principal *dramatis personae*.

---

2 I cite Robert Musil, *Der Mann ohne Eigenschaften*, in the two-volume edition by Adolf Frisé (Reinbek bei Hamburg: Rowohlt Verlag, 1978), 761. Volume One contains the first three parts—the sole published parts—of the novel, Volume Two the *Nachlass*, parts of which were set in type but then withdrawn for further emendation. Musil worked on these chapters, designed to continue Part Three, "Into the Millennial Kingdom (The Criminals)," until his death on April 15, 1942. The pages of the two volumes are numbered continuously, so that I will cite this edition merely by page number in my text.

Ulrich—a man without qualities, at least according to an estranged friend of his youth, but nonetheless a well-educated and talented mathematician and a budding moralist. "He should have become a philosopher," notes Musil in one of his plans for the novel, suggesting that Ulrich should have done precisely what Musil did. Like Musil, whose doctorate in philosophy focused on both contemporary science and issues in moral philosophy, Ulrich is a proponent of both precision and soul, *Genauigkeit und Seele,* even if the passage cited above seems to have banished every traditional sense of the word *soul.* It is Ulrich who spins and weaves most of the threads in the tapestry of Musil's epic. These threads have to do with the impending collapse of European civilization and the unsuccessful search for principles or guidelines for what used to be called "the good life." Maurice Blanchot's description of Ulrich is apt: "If he lives at all, it is in a world of possibilities and no longer of events, a world where nothing happens that could be *recounted.* Strange situation for the hero of a novel, stranger still for the writer" (LA 171). Musil's Ulrich thus represents "the double version of modern man," capable of both mathematical exactitude and the most nebulous theoretical speculation, both disciplined in his search for sense and utterly susceptible to what makes no sense at all (LA 175). Above all, what Ulrich senses about his world is the default of tenderness, *Zärtlichkeit,* in the lives of men and women in early-twentieth-century Vienna. Freud, for both Ulrich and Musil, is, like apple strudel, *à la mode*—however secretly feared and openly despised he may be—and yet in their view psychoanalysis is itself symptomatic of the default of tenderness, not a possible remedy.

Agathe—Ulrich's younger sister, plays no role at all in the first two of the three parts of Musil's story, the first part published in 1930–31, the second in 1932–33. Her arrival sets the novel off in an entirely new direction. Five years younger than Ulrich and absent from his life after their early childhood years together, Agathe will surprise him by arousing feelings of tenderness in him that neither he nor Musil's readers thought he could have. How she arouses them remains something of a mystery, inasmuch as Agathe is arguably—apart from her wit, courage, beauty, and good heart—a woman without qualities.

Walter—that estranged friend of Ulrich's youth, dreams of being an artist and a musician. Those dreams are crumbling under the pressures of a normal job and a not-so-normal wife. His sole consolation is, in Musil's words, the "swampy marshlands" of Wagner's music.

Clarisse—the not-so-normal wife—cannot deny her growing disgust with the failed artist she has married and the growing attraction that Walter's friend Ulrich exercises on her. The other two men in her life are Nietzsche, whose collected works Ulrich has given her as a wedding present (he may have no qualities but he certainly knows how to give quality books), and Moosbrugger, a convicted and confessed (more or less confessed, inasmuch as Moosbrugger is clearly psychotic) serial killer. Moosbrugger's crimes are, to say the least, crimes against tenderness. Yet Clarisse is certain she can rescue him, and she solicits Ulrich's help in plotting Moosbrugger's escape from the psychiatric ward.

"Bonadea," the good goddess—is Ulrich's name for the woman who becomes his lover. Or, more precisely, his sex partner. For even though the tip of her breast is a poppy petal, Bonadea can never become a matter of love for Ulrich. And yet the good goddess works a bit of tenderness into the otherwise steely man without qualities. Otherwise, the quality of mercy is exceedingly strained in Musil's hero, the quality of tenderness almost entirely absent until Agathe's arrival. It may even be that Ulrich's love for Agathe softens his hard-heartedness toward the good goddess.

"Diotima," not to call her by her real name, Ermelinde Tuzzi—is Ulrich's beautiful aristocratic cousin, idealistic and idealizing in both politics and love. Her salon becomes the site of discussions, endless discussions, surrounding the "Parallel Campaign" (*Parallelaktion*) to celebrate during the year 1918 Kaiser Franz Joseph's eighty-eighth birthday and the seventieth anniversary of his reign. These discussions form the comic core of Musil's epic, which is often mock epic, as the violent stormwinds of war gather head and the salon-goers blather endlessly on about nothing. The blithe indifference of almost all the characters to a Europe-wide conflict that seems inevitable and therefore almost welcome to them is by turns hysterically funny and altogether chilling. Indeed, the *Königliches-Kaiserliches Reich*, the Royal-Imperial Monarchy of Austria-Hungary (called *das k. und k. Reich*, and thus *Kakania* for short, an appellation clearly derived from *kaka*), appears to be as mad and as murderous as Moosbrugger. One careful reader of Musil notes that the *Parallelaktion* seems to be "an assembly of catatonics," with each character held spellbound by his or her particular *idée fixe*, all of them unwittingly murderous Moosbruggers; the very year that they envisage for their celebration of their Kaiser and King Franz Joseph, the year 1918, is of course the death year of the Habsburg monarchy.[3]

As for Moosbrugger himself, an important subplot in the novel is the debate among the jurists—Ulrich's father being the leading jurist of his time—who seek to justify by a hair-raising logic and by patent sophistry the mad

3 Wilfried Berghahn, *Robert Musil mit Selbstzeugnissen und Bilddokumenten* (Reinbek bei Hamburg: Rowohlt, 1963), 95, 99.

Moosbrugger's execution. As we will see in Part Two of the present book, the madhatter logic of the death penalty informs not only Kant's and Schelling's lofty lucubrations on the "intelligible character" and the "intelligible deed" but also the criminal codes of both past and present days, at least in those countries that are still barbaric enough to demand and practice capital punishment. It is the selfsame logic that urges catatonic Kakania on its homicidal rush into war.

General Stumm von Bordwehr is perhaps the tenderest general that never went to war. Delightfully incompetent as a soldier, he is assigned to the *Parallelaktion* by his superiors in order to lend a military presence to the civilian effort to celebrate the Kaiser's birthday and anniversary. Stumm's job is to absorb but also reconnoiter whatever he can of the "civilian spirit." His bafflement over the nonsensical discussions in Diotima's salon reflects the bafflement of Ulrich—and the reader.

A host of other characters, the supporting cast, as it were, includes Graf Leinsdorf, the aristocratic sponsor of the Parallel Campaign, Paul Arnheim, a German industrialist and seemingly high-minded author (modeled on the historical Walter Rathenau), Professor Meingast, a dubious philosopher-windbag (modeled on Ludwig Klages),[4] who becomes the prophet worshiped by Clarisse and Walter and one of the *bêtes noires* of the man without qualities. (Arnheim is the other one.) Finally, one has to mention the Fischel household, the father (Leo) a Jewish banker whom Ulrich admires, the mother a hen-pecking and anti-Semitic Christian who is impatient with her husband's waxing paranoia, their daughter Gerda, in love with Ulrich but in terror of her body, and Gerda's suitor, Hans Sepp, an anti-Semitic Pan-German who, had he lived for another two decades would surely—although Musil does not say so—have relocated to Munich or Berlin and become an officer in the SS. Another important subplot of the novel is the way in which a second European suicide attempt is destined to follow upon the first.

These characters and their frenzied efforts to determine how or how not to celebrate the Austro-Hungarian emperor's birthday and jubilee, I will here leave behind, in order to concentrate on Ulrich's search for tenderness and a love worthy of the name. The first candidate we meet is Leona, a singer in a

---

4 No doubt "windbag" is too harsh and too one-sided a description, especially when aimed at Klages rather than Meingast. My colleague Don Kelly Coble, whom I cite at length in chapter 9, below, tells me of the positive influence of Ludwig Klages's 1922 *Vom kosmogonischen Eros* on Musil's idea of "the other state" or "other condition."

cabaret, "tall, slender, uxorious, and excitingly lifeless [*aufreizend leblos*]" (21). She has a face reminiscent of bygone romantic days and she sings the sentimental songs of yesteryear; she has (in spite of her slender waist) an enormous appetite for sweets and for all well-prepared savory dishes; she is incredibly slow to react, laughing suddenly at jokes told her days earlier; she incurs impressive expenses that her gentlemen friends must cover. Although she sings for her supper, she takes offense at the fact that Ulrich wants to entertain her and feed her at his home rather than at the fine restaurants for which Vienna is famous. Their relationship is brief.

After a mugging, a battered Ulrich is rescued and cared for by a lovely and generous woman he comes to call "Bonadea," the good goddess. Here, tenderness has its first genuine chance. First in terms of the narrative, albeit not in Ulrich's life. For we later learn of his first adult love, if a twenty-year-old is an adult, during Ulrich's tour of duty as a soldier—to wit, the major's wife. This dangerous liaison is passionate yet never consummated. Very soon it becomes a long-distance relationship, not because the major banishes Ulrich but because Ulrich himself begs for reassignment. The major's wife is reported to have been an artist and a virtuoso pianist, and Ulrich falls in love with "the concept of her" (123). The concept lacks empirical filling, however, and is "blindingly empty, as only very great concepts are" (ibid.). The lovesick lieutenant does not desire to possess her; his love is, rather, "a gentle self-unveiling of the world," *ein sanftes Sichentschleiern der Welt* (ibid.). Each of the two is therefore secretly relieved when the young lieutenant departs on extended leave, far, far away. Every evening Ulrich writes love letters that he never sends. The letters are subdued nocturnes, *nachtstille Briefe* (124), played in the night under stars. Many years later Ulrich says to his sister Agathe, "As soon as I felt I was safe from her actual embraces, I howled for her like a dog at the moon" (764). But to return to the good goddess, who has rescued the battered hero and accompanies him now to his home.

Already in the cab Ulrich senses "something maternally sensual next to him, a tender cloud of altruistic idealism" (28). He talks to his rescuer about sports as a new theology for the times; she believes he may have a concussion. The final paragraph of the chapter that introduces Bonadea reads as follows: "Two weeks later Bonadea had been his lover for the past fourteen days" (30).

Ulrich calls her Bonadea in honor of the Roman goddess of chastity, whose temple becomes the site for what others would call sexual license. Bonadea is the wife of a well-known magistrate. She is the "tender mother" of two sons. She is not driven by lust, declares the narrator; she is merely "sensual," *sinnlich* through and through (42). Throughout her life men have used and abused her tender vulnerability. "For the more tender feelings of male abandon [*Hingabe*—shades of Hegel!] are approximately the same as the purring of a jaguar over a piece of meat" (ibid.). The authorial intrusion or narrative aside makes the reader wonder whether this search for tenderness in Musil's novel is a sign of one's own concussion—but, taking courage, we press on. Bonadea oscillates between fits of consuming passion and dire remorse, her only constant being the tender feeling (*zartfühlend*) of a nurse attending a sickbed (43). Depressed by her marriage to the renowned judge, manic in her affairs with men who need her care, Bonadea can ease the contradictions of her life only by lowering "a veil of moist tenderness over her eyes" (ibid.).

These repeated references to the good goddess's maternal tenderness—Musil writes of her "tender maternal midriff" (126)—should give us pause. For Bonadea combines tenderness and the active, passionate sexuality that Freud calls erotic excitement. This means that both of the "streams" that are essential to lovelife flow through her terrain, so that (for Freud at least, if not for Ulrich) she is the ideal partner, the good goddess indeed, both maternally tender and wickedly alluring. Musil's narrator calls her a nymphomaniac, however, even if that word is being replaced in today's vocabularies by the words *normal* and *healthy,* and even if, by way of contrast, deterrent dosages of Prozac are being regularly prescribed against such health. As for nymphomania, the experts tell us that it is doubtless present in one out of several thousand females and absent from the fantasies of one out of a million males. At all events, Ulrich is not satisfied with or by Bonadea, and learning why this is so will tell us as much about him as about her. Furthermore, if the goddess is "good," *bona,* we will remember that the Greek equivalent of *bona* is ἀγαθή, "Agathe." Bonadea is as close to Ulrich's sister as he can get, at least in the earlier parts of the novel.

When Bonadea arrives at Ulrich's house one day unannounced (126), she berates him for neglecting her. She scolds, weeps, and kisses him. Because of her importunities, he is *zu Zärtlichkeiten verführt,* "seduced to expressions of tenderness," one might say. Yet we recall that the German word, when used in the plural, means "advances," "fondlings," and in the case of Ulrich and his goddess something much more advanced than fondlings. In one of the popular dictionaries of contemporary German, the very first example of the word *Zärtlichkeit* in the plural is "I didn't care much for his *Zärtlichkeiten.*" In the case of Bonadea the possessive pronoun would have to be *her.* Ulrich, the mathematician and scientist, along with the brooding moralist, describes the interruption of his work by this unannounced visitation as a sudden flight "through a cloud of lunacy," *eine Wolke des Irrsinns* (115); during a later visit, after many months of separation, Bonadea herself feels that the four walls of her consciousness have been wallpapered by madness (259). "Whoever could describe it would be a great artist," she says to herself, but then she emends the thought: "No, he would be a pornographer!" (ibid.). Clearly, Bonadea's is not the very puritanical and even prudish madness of Moosbrugger, who kills because out there on the streets young women insist on molesting him.

Just as Clarisse is drawn to the charismatic figure of the condemned killer, so too Bonadea hopes to use Ulrich's sympathy for the condemned wretch to win her lover back. During his conversation with her Ulrich admits that Moosbrugger "challenges our uttermost tenderness," precisely because he is convicted of violent crimes against women. And now the state will violently hang him (262). His diminished accountability or imputability, which is not diminished but decimated, will not diminish his sentencing. Such ruined accountability applies not only to Moosbrugger, however: Bonadea, while listening to Ulrich on the subject, adjusts her stocking and lets a shoe drop from her foot, so that "from her leg a bouquet of diminished accountability ascended to his nose" (263). Ulrich continues to expatiate on the state, which he predicts will be too stupid not to execute Moosbrugger, as Bonadea takes his hand:

> Bonadea unfolded his fingers and spread his hand over her breast. The accompanying look would have melted a heart of stone. During the next few seconds Ulrich felt as though he could feel two hearts beating in his own breast, the way all the clocks in a watchmaker's shop chime in wild cacophony. Commanding all his force of will, he restored order to the breast and said softly, "No, Bonadea." (264)

In order to assuage her injured pride, Ulrich continues to talk about Moosbrugger's diminished accountability, although minutes of awkward silence obtrude. They both wish he did not have to talk this way and talk so much. Bonadea hates the fact that Ulrich always serves up thoughts instead of feelings, a characteristic that will later disturb Agathe as well. Yet she senses the weakness in him, the diffidence of a boy who is overchallenged and who needs his mother. "For the longest time now she felt a tenderness toward him, a tenderness without bounds or limits" (265). She is mindful of her jealousy, anger, and frustration, but she also remembers the moments of silent sympathy. The result is a kind of *Benommenheit,* a numbness or dullness of wit that settles over the two of them. Suddenly Bonadea feels, or believes she feels, or says that she believes she feels, a flea somewhere on her person. She begs Ulrich to help her search for the miscreant, even if the flea is known "to prefer the same regions that a lover prefers" (266). Not a trace of a flea is found, however, and Musil ends the chapter this way:

> "I don't know what that was!" said Bonadea. Ulrich smiled in an unexpectedly friendly way.
>
> Whereupon Bonadea, like a little girl who has behaved badly, began to weep. (Ibid.)

The title of an earlier chapter involving Ulrich and Bonadea asks the question, "Who would you say is right?" No humane reader of either my or Musil's text could forgive either me or him or the narrator or Ulrich for the rapid reduction of Bonadea from lover to mother to little girl. It is safe to say that every reader grows as impatient with Ulrich's endless talk as Bonadea does. Such talk gives us the pleasure of Ulrich's brilliance but the pain of his obstinate chill. Indeed, even after Bonadea steps aside and cedes her place to Ulrich's beloved sister, Ulrich will continue to submerge his feelings in a pool of sententious thoughts and words. And yet. Ever since Alcibiades sought to seduce Socrates, the impossible position of the one who is loved but who loves too little or not at all has been recognized, if only reluctantly. One of the last scenes in which Ulrich and Bonadea meet will help us, not to decide who is right, but to see how tenderness may work for both sides.

Bonadea decides to "crash" one of Diotima's "Parallel Campaign" salon meetings, knowing that Ulrich will be there. Ulrich is called out of the meeting room by the servant who has answered the door; the servant takes the two to Diotima's bedroom, since it is the only room where the two can speak in private. Bonadea believes, mistakenly, that Diotima is her rival, so that the bedroom is for her the lowermost circle of her own private hell. She walks to a window and leans into it in order not to have to see her rival's things; her forehead and the tips of her breasts touch the cold pane. "Tenderness and tears moisten her eyes" (580). She then turns to Ulrich and utters the remarkable words, "Ulrich! You aren't nasty! You just pretend to be. You invent as many difficulties as you can so that they will keep you from being good" (ibid.). These words, writes Musil, are not spoken out of some moralizing desire for self-justification; "rather, here the beauty of this body itself was declaring its right to the gentle worthiness of love" (ibid.). Ulrich feels "a soft insecurity on his skin"; he takes Bonadea in his arms. He wants to tell her how pointless it is to take up Moosbrugger's case, especially with the feckless members of Diotima's salon, but instead he says something very strange. "It is as though I dreamt that the tip of your breast is like a poppy petal. Could I believe on that account that it really is one?" (ibid.). Musil titles the chapter, "The tip of your breast is like a poppy petal." Each of the two meditates on this strange question. Ulrich seems to think that for every human being every other human being is a series of similes. Bonadea thinks, and says, "Come, let's go" (ibid.). Ulrich replies that he cannot slip out of the meeting, and Bonadea retorts, "Why can you never do the obvious thing to do?" (581). Ulrich reflects. Perhaps he really did dream that her breast was like a poppy petal? He thinks and thinks, for an entire page. Bonadea says, simply, "In dreams you don't think, you live out some sort of story" (582).

> He pressed her hand. Suddenly she had tears in her eyes again. Very slowly they ran down her cheeks, and the skin of her cheeks, bathed in the salt, released the indescribable fragrance of love. Ulrich breathed it in and felt the great languor, the longing for this slippery-slimy something, for giving-over and forgetting. Yet he pulled himself together and led her tenderly to the door. (Ibid.)

The earlier fragrance of leg, foot, and shoe is now the saline fragrance of love. Salty it may be, but it is always a matter of the nose, this tenderness. A nose up against the soft haptics of poppy petal. Digestion turned to the outside? By this time Bonadea's jealousy has subsided, as has her feeling that things have come to an end between them. She puts on her hat, kisses Ulrich, thinking that she would rather make a cross of protective benediction on his forehead, as one does with children. She lowers her veil, kisses him through the veil, and slips out the door. When, four hundred and thirty-two pages later, Bonadea attends another salon session, this time by invitation, Ulrich feels as he greets her "something weightless on him, something like a shadow or a warm breeze" (1014). Musil writes, in the simplest sentence of his long and infinitely complex book, "The world is beautiful when we take it as it is" (ibid.).

Yet do we—we who either lack or possess qualities of one kind or another—learn to take the world as it is? The question sounds like the title of Derrida's final interview, "Learning to live, finally." Ulrich learns very little and only very slowly from Bonadea, perhaps because she shares so little of his strangely bookish world. Yet Ulrich does not learn at all from his cousin Diotima, named after Plato's priestess of love, who is ready to reform both the political world and the practices of sexual intimacy, and reform them by the book—the book(s) by Freud, for example. Diotima occupies the same bookish world that Ulrich occupies, the world of high ideals and lofty thoughts, albeit without having undergone the mathematical and the Nietzschean purges, which means that the cousins occupy two entirely different worlds. If we are to learn, with Ulrich, about tenderness, it will have to be from Agathe, who enters the story in Part Three, "Into the Millennial Kingdom (The Criminals)."

•

Their father has died, and so Agathe comes home. Brother and sister find themselves fascinated with one another right from the start, and their fascination will gradually close its shutters on the rest of the world. Together they will become "millennialists," after those enthusiasts on the eve of the eleventh century who awaited apocalypse and the Second Coming; they will try to enter the as yet undiscovered "millennial kingdom" of love, *das Tausendjährige Reich*, a term that in the meantime, even before Musil's death, becomes degraded to the point where he would have had to alter it. Even so, to repeat, both he and his characters are looking back to the early Middle Ages and not to the disastrous future of their own century. In what follows I will examine a handful of chapters from Book II, Part Three of *Der Mann ohne Eigenschaften*, "Into the Millennial Kingdom (The Criminals)," after a few preliminaries.

Why "criminals"? For several reasons, the two principal ones being (1) that Ulrich and Agathe will challenge the prohibition of incest, and (2) that Agathe will forge her father's will in order to exclude both herself and her despised husband from all inheritance. There is constant talk between brother and sister about the possibility of their becoming "Siamese twins," as close as two human beings can become. One of the earliest traces of this desire in Ulrich is a memory from their childhood. They are close as children, yet they are separated early on after their mother's death and, losing touch entirely, they do not see one another again for any length of time until their father's funeral. However, Ulrich now remembers having seen his little sister dressed for a party, and he recalls being overwhelmed by the desire "to be a girl" (690). In a late sketch toward the completion of the novel, Musil alludes again to Ulrich's memory of the beautiful sister, that is, of a beauty that makes him "long to be her" (1311). The narrator wryly speculates that it may have been the harmless tale of a vampire who wants to suck the existence of a beautiful other into himself, but then corrects himself: "Yet this little man did not want to draw the little girl into himself; he wanted to be entirely in her position, and his wanting it occurred with that blinding tenderness [*mit jener blendenden Zärtlichkeit*] that belongs only to the early experiences of our race [*die nur den Früherlebnissen des Geschlechts zu eigen ist*]" (690). "Race" could of course mean "sex" or any of those things Derrida has written about so insightfully in his four "Geschlecht" articles.[5] In any case, throughout the novel Ulrich sees Agathe as a more finely wrought version of himself; the word *Glanz*, "radiance," often accompanies her appearances in the novel, as though she were an "aura."[6]

Finely wrought she may be, but Agathe is capable of deeds that cause her brother to shudder. At their father's funeral, she removes the father's valuable medals from his coat, replacing them with cheap copies; as though by way of compensation, she removes a garter from her thigh and places it in an inner pocket of the dead man's coat. Her father, who has been distant from both children from the start, forced her to marry the husband she now despises; it could be that her action is an expression of bizarre tenderness toward a man who was never tender toward her; or it could be the most flagrant of desecrations, an act of sardonic revenge, to play *Sonnez-la-cloche* with the dead progenitor. Ulrich is flabbergasted: "the barbaric notion of giving the frosty dead man a garter that was still warm from the leg of his daughter took his breath away and created in his brain all sorts of disorder" (707). Agathe's later forgery of the will is continuous with this desecration of the father's remains, both of which Ulrich can neither countenance nor stop.

Who is this beautiful young woman, so quiet and apparently unassuming and yet so outrageously daring? She is not very interested in "emancipation," nor in motherhood. All that can be said about her is that she is a human being who does not allow herself to be fooled, *der sich nichts vormachen läßt*, and that she never fails to notice the attempts of males to fool her (728). During a mysterious childhood illness, she enjoys the failed efforts of the learned doctors to discover what the trouble is. At seventeen, she falls in love with a young man and marries him; at nineteen, due to her husband's sudden illness and death, she is a widow. Her father soon convinces her to marry again, and she bows to

---

5 For an account of these pieces, including the recently published third "Geschlecht," see Krell, *Phantoms of the Other: Four Generations of Derrida's Geschlecht* (Albany: State University of New York Press, 2015). The materials from Derrida's 1984–85 seminar, "The Phantom of the Other," have now been published as *Geschlecht III*, edited by Geoffrey Bennington, Katie Chenowith, and Rodrigo Therezo (Paris: Éditions du Seuil, 2018), with a preface by Rodrigo Therezo. He and Katie Chenoweth are slated to translate the volume into English for the University of Chicago Press.

6 Wilfried Berghahn notes that Robert Musil would have grown up with an older sister had she not died at eleven months. Musil often thought that, had she lived, they would have been close. Her meaning for Musil's life, says Berghahn, is that "one must think the world otherwise than as it appears, inasmuch as it could just as well have been quite different." See Wilfried Berghahn, *Robert Musil*, 25.

his wishes. Now she is surprised by the nausea that grips her when she thinks of her husband, Professor Hagauer, and she decides during the train voyage to her father's funeral never to return. She will live with her brother.

She is not yet out of her twenties, but already she senses the passing of time. "Her body told her that in only a few years it would begin to lose its beauty" (732). In a later chapter, the twenty-first, "Throw Everything You Have into the Fire, Down to Your Shoes," she subjects her body to a detailed examination in the mirror, looking at it "without vanity," as though held "spellbound by the landscape of her self":

> She arrived at her hair, which was still like lustrous satin; she opened the collar of her mirror image and slipped her dress down to her shoulders; finally, she undressed that image entirely and examined it closely down to the rosy coverings of the nails where, on hands and feet, the body comes to an end and scarcely belongs to itself. Everything was as still and as clear as daylight when the day is reaching its zenith: on the ascendant, pure, precise, and permeated by the becoming that is forenoon, expressing itself as it does in a young person or young animal in the identical and indescribable way in which a ball has not yet reached its apogee but is only slightly below it. "Maybe the ball is passing through its high point at this moment," thought Agathe. The thought terrified her. But then there might still be some time left: she was only twenty-seven years old. Her body, uninfluenced by sports instructors and masseurs, unaffected by pregnancy and motherhood, had been shaped by nothing other than its own growth. Had one been able to relocate it to one of those vast and lonely landscapes where tall mountain peaks face the sky, she would have been borne on the broad and infertile crests of the heights like a pagan goddess. In such a natural landscape the midday exudes no vapors of light and heat; it seems merely to climb to its highest point and then linger awhile, passing unnoticeably into the hovering and descending beauty of the afternoon. Out of the mirror came the somewhat uncanny feeling of the indeterminate hour. (852–53)

The examination ends, succumbing now to the play of imagination. She is still standing before the mirror:

> Agathe grew curious about herself, as though she were seeing herself really for the first time. This was possibly the way the men she had

> gotten involved with could have seen her, and she herself had had no idea. This feeling was not altogether pleasant. But in some strange movement of fantasy she thought she could hear, behind all the memories of the things she had experienced, and before she had time to call these memories to review, the long and desperately passionate love cry of the donkey, a cry that had always excited her: it sounds so infinitely foolish and ugly, but precisely for that reason there is perhaps no other heroism of love that is as hopelessly sweet as his. She shrugged her shoulders over her life and turned her attention purposefully to her image once again, to see if she could find a place where her appearance was already making concessions to age. Those small places around the eyes and ears that are the earliest to change, looking at first as though something had slept on them, or the curved line beneath the inner side of the breasts, which so easily loses its clarity: it would have satisfied her, promised her peace of mind, if she had noticed a change there, but there was none to be perceived, and the beauty of her body hovered well-nigh uncannily in the depths of the mirror. (854)

After such passages as these it comes as a shock to learn that for some time now Agathe has kept close to her person a metal capsule containing a lethal poison, for use at the kairotic moment, as it were. She often has a feeling—her uncanny image in the mirror evokes it here—that can be expressed in the words, "I am a little bit dead" (855). The early death by illness of her first husband, and now the passing of her father, may be calling forth that feeling; yet the cause is more likely to be the feeling of health and the assurance that the mirror has only now given her. For it is a feeling that she often has "in moments like this one, when she became quite conscious of the symmetry and health of her young body, of this tensed beauty that is as groundless in its mysterious cohesion as it is in the dissolution of its elements in death" (ibid.). Her mood then shifts from "happy security" to one of "worry, astonishment, and silence," the sort of mood that might arise "when one leaves a room full of people and steps out into a night under shimmering stars" (ibid.).

Whereas her brother is occupied with the problem Heidegger describes in *Sein und Zeit* as the crisis of foundations in mathematics, a crisis occurring in the debate between the intuitionists and the formalists (SZ 9; MoE 865), Agathe embodies the existential characteristic Heidegger calls *Bewegtheit,* "animatedness" or, better, "movedness." Human beings, even if they are the movers and shakers of thought, are preeminently beings that are *moved*—for example, by moods, by dispositions, and by the way they "find themselves to be" in the world, their *Befindlichkeit.* Agathe is an exemplar of what Musil calls "affective thinking" (affective as opposed to effective), and it is Agathe's closeness to "the nothing," *dem Nichts,* that grants her an exceptional relation to this sort of (obscure) thinking. For in every human being, whether overtly or covertly,

> alongside the logical thinking that has its stringent and simple sense of order, one that mirrors the order of our relations to the outside world, an affective thinking asserts itself, a thinking whose logic, if one may use that term at all, corresponds with the peculiarities of feelings, passions, and moods, such that the laws of these two kinds of thinking relate to one another somewhat in the way a lumber yard, where stacks of wood cut at right angles stand ready to be shipped, relates to the darkly twisting laws of the forest, where things grow and winds rush. (857)

Ironically, it is precisely through her conversations with her brother that Agathe gains enough confidence to realize that she is not simply an illogical creature but an avatar of the other sort of thinking, which is a thinking more appropriate to "the other state," *den anderen Zustand,* which both siblings desire. Early on in their conversations, Ulrich describes it as the state or condition into which the heart slips unawares, entering into "those utopian regions that are found somewhere or nowhere between an infinite tenderness and an infinite loneliness" (753). If there is a difference between the two siblings, however, and there is, it would be this: Ulrich feels more constrained to find words to describe that state of infinite *Zärtlichkeit,* words that never quite satisfy him, however, and that therefore must give way to further words, whereas Agathe is more disposed to let the things themselves come to her unbidden, seeking as she does to "be at one with supreme meaning by way of the slightest movement of the spirit," *ein Einssein der höchsten Bedeutung mit der geringsten Bewegung des Geistes* (860). A slowly augmenting impatience with her beloved brother becomes palpable in Part Three of the novel, so that neither the reader nor, apparently, the narrator knows how the siblings will ever find their way to the millennial kingdom. Agathe feels certain that it will not be by way of words. It will instead be the result of some sort of deed. What she now remembers is an old saying, which doubtless is a saying of words, but what the words say is, "Throw everything you have into the fire, down to your shoes. When you possess nothing more, do not even think of your shroud, and throw yourself naked into the fire!" (863). She cannot help but wonder, "Would Ulrich really throw everything into the fire?" (864). To repeat, what Ulrich constantly tries to do is define conceptually *den anderen Zustand*, as in the following sketch for the novel from the mid-1920s, where Ulrich begins to sound like Bishop Berkeley, for whom being and perception coalesce:

> "The state in which one perceives it [that is, the other state] has been given many names: a state of love, goodness, renunciation of the world, contemplation, beholding, rapture, inward-turning, quiescence of will, intuition, unification with God—all of them names that express an unclear accord, designating an experience that is described with equal amounts of passion and imprecision. Crazy farmer's wives became familiar with it, as did professors of theology, Catholics, Jews, and atheists, people of our own time and people from earlier millennia: and they have described it in a remarkably identical way, so that these descriptions have remained strangely without development; the grandest spirit has not told us anything more about it than the pettiest, and it seems as though you and I have no more to learn from the millennia than what we already knew:
>
> What does that signify?" (1643)

Chapter 25 of Part Three of *The Man Without Qualities* is called "The Siamese Twins." Here Ulrich and Agathe articulate—late one night—their desire to be more than siblings, to be twins, *identical* twins, and beyond that, twins joined at the torso.[7] Ulrich begins by confessing that he has never entertained anything like "a tender relationship" with himself (899). He speculates that such tenderness is felt only in early childhood, and that it disappears at puberty. He elaborates a metaphor: "For at that point a meadow of tenderness, in which one has been playing up till then, is mowed down in order to harvest fodder for a particular drive" (901). "So that the cow can give milk!" replies Agathe with a knowing smile. Ulrich continues, elaborating

7 I interrupt to note that I first wrote about this chapter in the Preface to *Lunar Voices* some twenty-five years ago. I draw upon that sketch in the following paragraphs. See Krell, *Lunar Voices: Of Tragedy, Poetry, Fiction, and Thought* (Chicago: University of Chicago Press, 1995), xii–xv and xix–xx. It seems, then, that I have been trying to write this chapter for twenty-five years—another one of those failures I mentioned in chapter 1. Perhaps it will elude me even now (November 2, 2017).

the metaphor that (as we have seen in the preceding chapter) is substantially the same as Freud's two "streams," or the two tributaries of the stream called *Zärtlichkeit*. "There comes a moment when our lives lose practically all their tenderness, which joins forces with one sole exercise, which is then supercharged: doesn't it strike you, as it does me, that a horrible drought dominates the entire world, while, on one single spot, the rain pours down ceaselessly?" (ibid.). Agathe replies that she loved her babydolls with a greater intensity of tenderness than she has loved any man in her life. After several moments have passed, she asks Ulrich whether he remembers Plato's old story (a story she simplifies a bit, for she invokes only "the children of the moon") about the bifurcation of the "originally whole human being" into two halves, man and woman. She is immediately embarrassed by her own question: of course he knows it, everybody knows it.

" 'And now the unhappy halves pull all sorts of silly stunts in order to get back into one another again: that story is told in all the manuals of higher education, although the story doesn't say why they fail' " (903–4). Ulrich knows why. So many halves are in circulation that the true fit will most likely never be found. And when these wandering halves do go for their other half they not only err but compound their silliness: together they engender a "third half" as a monument to their mistake. While Agathe has been reading *Symposium*, Ulrich has been reading Hegel, learning the lesson of our species' wicked infinity: " 'Humanity "halves itself" physiologically on and on, and the essential union stands motionless like the moon outside the bedroom window' " (904).

That moon is the celestial key that opens the entire story of tenderness between lovers, whether they be children of the sun, the earth, or the moon, presumably because only the children of the moon procreate "third halves." Sexual preferences are one thing, the moon another. In a moment we will examine an early text of Musil's called "Lunar Rapture." But to return for an instant to Hegel's—and Ulrich's—bad infinity. Agathe resists her brother's leap to a sadder but wiser spirit; she keeps her eye on the moon, even though she is on the bed and her eyes are closed.

> "You'd think that brothers and sisters must have already traveled halfway there!" observed Agathe in a voice that had gone hoarse.
>
> "Twins, maybe."
>
> "Are we not twins?" (Ibid.)

Ulrich thinks now of Pygmalion, perhaps the most one-sided of twins, but then of Hermaphrodite and of Isis and Osiris. He thinks of all the figures that would delight the Jungians and all other creative mythographers, whom he now ventriloquizes: " 'This craving for a double [*Doppelgänger*] of the opposite sex [*im anderen Geschlecht*] is primeval. It wants the love of a creature that is entirely the same as we are but also has to be different from us, a magical figure that is us but that also remains a magical figure' " (905). Soon Ulrich is on to the inevitable dream and delusion of "the *fluidum* of love" that the alchemist vainly seeks in his retort. Yet Agathe's retort is less skeptical than her brother's: " 'That is the way it has been for thousands of years now: is it any easier to understand when one explains it in terms of two delusions?' " (ibid.). Ulrich is silent. Much later in their exchange, as their words become intermittent, even sparse, and as the silences seem to infiltrate their bodies, Ulrich says: " 'I'd rather have to say that a "being-in-the-very-midst [*ein <Mitten-inne-Sein>*]," which is a state of undisturbed "intensity" of life [*<Innigkeit> des Lebens*] is probably something one cannot command when one's senses are rational' " (908). That is probably as close as he comes to defining *den anderen Zustand,* the "other" state. " 'One would have to be a pair of Siamese twins,' Agathe rejoined. 'Well, then, Siamese twins!' her brother repeated" (ibid.).

Yet as their companionship develops, becoming increasingly exclusive of the world, Agathe grows impatient with these conversations. She begins to wonder whether her brother's fascination is flagging, suffocating under the weight of his discourses, discourses to which she never feels equal. Ulrich, for his part, does not seem to share her intensity of feeling and desire; or, if he does feel it, he is efficient at suppressing those feelings and desires. Thus, a difference between the two begins to gape: "Because she was not so fanatical a person as her brother was, she felt what she felt. When she was tender, she was tender, not with scintillating thoughts or moral illumination, even though she loved these things about him even as she shied away from them" (942). However, it never comes to an open discussion of the difference. "She simply felt that he was avoiding a decision, and that he ought not to. And so the two of them concealed themselves within a jocular happiness without depth and gravity. Agathe grew sadder from day to day, even though she laughed as often as her brother did" (945). When her husband writes her an aggressive letter, demanding his rights, Agathe is perturbed by Ulrich's seeming indifference. She interrupts their conversation, leaving the house precipitously so that her brother will not see her tears. Her sole explanation of her despair is that Ulrich "should have done something other than talk" (961). A feeling of utter superfluousness overwhelms her, and she senses that if she can keep walking until evening she will be able to take her life. As it turns out, a stranger distracts her from her purpose: it is the moralizing Professor Lindner, with whom Agathe will have many conversations—different sorts of conversations than those with her brother, for Professor Lindner will try to make a conscientious Christian out of her.

Other characters and subplots of the novel interrupt the moment of crisis for Ulrich and Agathe. General Stumm von Bordwehr joins Ulrich and Clarisse in their effort to seek the release of the condemned Moosbrugger; their hair-raising visit to a psychiatric ward is something from which no reader will ever recover; and, on the normal side of total madness, the "Parallel Campaign" churns out its grandiose patriotic nonsense. All of this is consistent with Musil's plans for the novel: the catastrophic slide into war will bring it all to an end, just as Thomas Mann brings Hans Castorp down from *The Magic Mountain* to die on the battlefield.

Yet Musil is unsatisfied. He will try to resolve the dilemma of his Siamese twins who are in fact not yet joined at the hip—resolve it rather than simply kill them off. But how to resolve their dilemma?

•

Volume Two of the Frisé edition of *Der Mann ohne Eigenschaften* contains more than a thousand pages of unpublished chapters, plans, and notes from Musil's literary remains. I will focus on those sketches that attempt to elaborate a happier fate for Ulrich and Agathe than skepticism and suicide. In 1937–38, Musil had twenty chapters set in print, chapters that were to continue but not end Part Three of his novel, but to his publisher Ernst Rowohlt's consternation he withdrew them from publication. Up to his death on April 15, 1942, Musil worked on six chapters as variants to what he had withdrawn. One particularly remarkable chapter, "Breaths of a Summer's Day," he sketched out fully in five different versions. If I may say so, these chapters are not at all "tentative"; you and I, I believe, would have been delighted to sign off on each of them. Yet Musil remained unsatisfied. And a good portion of his dissatisfaction had to do with the problem of Ulrich and Agathe.

Let me begin, however, by saying something about the very last fragment in Volume Two. It comes from the year 1933 (April 16, to be exact), and it is paradigmatic of the most radical resolution of Musil's problem. Interestingly, the sketch, "Lunar Rapture," *Mondrausch*, deals not with Ulrich and Agathe but with two unnamed characters.[8] They have married, "against their intention" (2032), whatever that might mean, and like most newlyweds they generally avoid invitations or socializing of any kind. Yet they have been invited to a dinner party and, having accepted, they are now getting dressed to go out. The young woman is bending over a raised leg and foot with the full attention that donning a stocking requires. Her husband, suddenly struck by her "lovely corporality," comes up to her from behind, gently nips her neck, and then picks her up and carries her to the bedroom window, where the two of them watch the evening descend. Although she cries out with surprise at the abduction, she senses that it is a "soft compulsion"; her body surrenders all its tension, as something like a second nature "slackened her limbs with utter tenderness." The movement of the two of them is choreographed as a ballet in words. At the window, they become entrapped in the moonlight and are happy to cancel their social engagement for the evening. What happens to them, their "adventure," is clearly bound up with what Musil calls "lunar nights," *Mondnächte*. In such nights, a richly sentient corporality banishes the bustling vacuity of the day. Yet the way it does so—its particular magic—resists all codifications and all repetitions:

> Thus every inner and outer occurrence of lunar nights possesses the nature of the unrepeatable [*des Unwiederholbaren*]. Every occurrence possesses an enhanced nature. It has the nature of an unselfish liberality and dispensation. Every communication is a sharing without envy. Every giving a receiving. Every reception inextricably interwoven with the excitements of the night. To *be* this way is our only way to *know* what is happening. For the "I" does not retain for itself any elixir of its past possession, scarcely a memory; the enhanced self radiates outward into a boundless selflessness, and these nights are full of the senseless feeling that something will have to come to pass that has never come to pass before, something that the impoverished reasonableness of the day cannot even visualize. And it is

---

8 See 2032–36 for the following. Adolf Frisé is certain that it has to do with Ulrich and Agathe, even though the talk of "a wedding" might well have deterred him. More problematic still is Frisé's remark that the sketch is in any case "remote from the problem of 'love between siblings' " (2129). It is in fact one of Musil's most daring efforts to intensify if not resolve his "problem." An excellent discussion of that "problem" is the section of Wilfried Berghahn's biography titled "The Crisis of the Novel," in *Robert Musil*, 131–47.

> not the mouth that gushes but the entire body from head to foot, the body above the darkness of the earth and beneath the light of the sky, the body yoked to an excitement that oscillates between two stars. And the whispers we share with our companion are pervaded by an utterly unfamiliar sensuality, which is not some person's sensuality but the sensuality of the earth, of all that compels our sensibility, the suddenly unveiled tenderness of the world that touches without cease all our senses and that all our senses touch. (2034–35)

In such a night even the lonely and undistinguished nights of the past are transfigured, "like an endless bramblebush covered in silverplate, moonstains on the grass, drooping apple trees, singeing frost and gilded, opaque waters" (2035). These sheer particularities or pieces of the moonlit empirical have no rhyme or reason to come together; the rhythm they obey flows from a source that is itself unseen, like the dark side of the moon. In *Being and Time* Heidegger reminds us that even when the moon is at the full we do not see it in its entirety (SZ 243). In the end, one can never be sure whether any of this lunar effluence and influence is more than mere moonshine and romanticism, as the young wife in Musil's sketch comes to believe, for she soon sees her husband transformed into a ghostly Pierrot Lunaire; the young man too quietly concedes the likelihood of their mutual lunacy, as the two—inexplicably and disappointingly—go their separate ways. Their "adventure" comes to an abrupt end; too abrupt, one is tempted to say. Musil will later use this sketch for Part Three of his novel, and one has to wonder whether Agathe will be so quick to spurn her fraternal Pierrot.

Part Three opens with the pious Professor Lindner having distracted rather than rescued Agathe from her tailspin. He now proceeds to seek her conversion. She finds that she enjoys parrying his efforts: each time he believes he has found an unshakable truth of moral reason Agathe displays witty insouciance. Only gradually does the professor discover that he is interested in more than her soul, and at that point Agathe does not fail to play cat and mouse with him. Here is a typical exchange, one that comes from a plan of Musil's that is difficult to date with precision, but which I estimate to postdate 1933:

> "Have you no will power?"
> "No."
> "You are full of fantasies and you have no discipline!"
> "Yes."

> After a brief pause, Agathe smiled and added this remark: "My brother says I am a fragment of a human being. That's cute, isn't it? Even if you can't really tell what it means. One might think of an uncompleted volume of incomplete poems." (1463)

Lindner is flummoxed by this last remark; he can say nothing. Perhaps he is forced into silence because Agathe has just delivered a perfect description of *Der Mann ohne Eigenschaften* as a whole, except that each of Musil's "poems" is remarkably polished.

Just as it is easier for Agathe to engage in repartee with Lindner than with her brother, so it seems to be less trying for Musil himself to write these opening chapters of Part Three. That his later return to the siblings is more fraught is shown by the many revisions in the manuscripts. He knows by now, as Agathe does, what brother and sister will say to one another. What they can possibly *do,* what gestures of tenderness they can invent for themselves, remains unclear to him. A plan from the mid-1920s, before Part Three is begun, imagines "a journey to Paradise" for the siblings: "Yet it must also be that they are again and again delighted with one another. The gamut of the sexual, testing all the variations [*Die Skala des Sexuellen mit Variationen durchmessend*]" (1653). The radicality of these plans of the mid-1920s never finds its way into a chapter that Musil feels prepared to send to Rowohlt; yet the search for gestures of tenderness is clearly present in chapters 45–47 (1081–1104), and we ought to take a closer look at them.

Chapter 45, "The Beginning of a Series of Remarkable Experiences," reproduces almost word for word the April 16, 1933 *Mondrausch* sketch, although there are significant alterations to and expansions of the dialogue between the two figures. Ulrich too will appear as Pierrot Lunaire, and Agathe will abruptly close the curtain on the scene. Yet the ballet of tenderness between the two is in every sense decisive, even if once again it leads to the window and not to the bed. When the siblings look into one another's eyes, they see that "the decision has fallen and that every prohibition is now a matter of indifference to them" (1083). The moon discloses to them both "the suddenly revealed tenderness of the world," *die plötzlich enthüllte Zärtlichkeit der Welt,* indeed, "the tenderness of feelings that hollow out the marrow and so create a flute" (1085). As in the 1933 sketch, Agathe wonders aloud whether the ballet is mere romantic moonshine. Suddenly she leaves the room, but as she is closing the door behind her, the two have their final exchange:

> "You will sleep restlessly tonight, as though on the eve of a long journey," he called out to her.
>
> "That is exactly what I will do!" was her reply as she closed the door. (1087).

Chapter 46 has the promising title "Moonbeams by Day." When brother and sister meet in the morning, however, they can see that they are weary on account of their adventure, even if their weariness "shaded them with tender warmth" (1087). They are perhaps happy in the way that lovers "are proud that they almost died of pleasure" (ibid.), and yet it would be an exaggeration to say that Ulrich and Agathe are now *Liebesleute* or that they have exhausted themselves in their pleasure. During the course of their conversations in the garden that day Ulrich is forced to admit, "How wild her nature is compared to mine!" (1091). Yet Agathe's reflections about the night before are not as wild as they are accurate, and they have to do with Ulrich's reluctance and diffidence:

> "He doesn't want it to become a mere love story," she thought. And she added, "That is also to my taste." She then immediately thought, "He will love no other woman after me, for this is no longer a mere love story; it is the final love story of all, the last possible story!" And she added, "We will surely be a kind of Last of the Mohicans of love!" At this moment she was capable of adopting such a tone toward herself, for when she thought it all over quite honestly it was naturally the case that this enchanted garden where she and Ulrich found themselves was more wish than reality. She did not really believe that the Millennial Kingdom could have already begun, in spite of the name that Ulrich had once given it, which sounded so well-grounded. (1094–95)

There is nothing in the following chapter, "Transformation among Human Beings," that could possibly encourage her or the reader, however. The narrator, following Agathe's cue, speaks of their state as one of promise, *Verheissung*, the sort of promise "that a pause during intense intercourse grants to lovers" (1096). The irony of the comparison does not seem to befuddle the narrator, who adds, referring to Ulrich, "The pleasure without issue [*Die Lust ohne Ausweg*] had sunk back into his body and filled him with a tenderness as indeterminate as that of a first day of spring or last day of autumn" (ibid.). Ulrich does begin to have the feeling that as soon as he speaks the words are "coming out of his mouth several days too late" (1097). Even though these garden conversations are "cheerful and tender" (1100), the interlocutors are forced to admit this: "It was so difficult to get these things right, because the language of love is a secret language; in its highest accomplishment it is as silent as an embrace" (1102). Ulrich will find a new name for the two of them. They are "the Inseparable and the Disunited" (1104); yet this rubric can please neither them nor the narrator. Where in all this is the silent, secret language of love?

Chapter 48, "Love Makes Us Blind; or, Difficulties Where They Are Not Sought," comments on that "cheerfulness" of the siblings' conversations mentioned a moment ago: the narrator notices that Ulrich continually flees from the seriousness of their situation to an "unbroken cheerfulness," flees from seriousness like a "wild brook" (1107). Indeed, this *bachartig flüchtende Heiterkeit* is part of the problem, not its solution. With Ulrich taking the lead, as always, the siblings try to render an encyclopedic account of love. Yet, as always, Ulrich's "protracted efforts to get it right sometimes tried her patience" (1110). Agathe's restiveness speaks through her final remark in the chapter, and it is appropriate to their situation in general: "What is to be done when there is no possible way to behave?" "*Und was tut man, wenn es kein Verhalten gibt?*" (1113).

That Musil was not happy with these chapters, especially numbers 47 and 48, is indicated by the fact that he withdrew all twenty of them after they had been set in type. He recomposed and expanded a number of them during the final years and days of his life. The six sketches that he produced in good copy, evidently with the plan to have them set in type, must now receive our attention, especially two of them. The new chapter 49, "Conversations About Love," in spite of the unpromising title, would have been the shortest and one of the most remarkable chapters of the book. The last of the six, "Breaths of a Summer's Day," which Musil completely rewrote five times, does not solve the problem of what the lovers will be able to *do*, but it gives us the finest portrayal of *den anderen Zustand*. Here is the new chapter 49, *in toto*:

> The human being, quite properly the speaking animal, is the only being that needs conversations in order to reproduce. And not merely because he or she will speak in any case, as though by the way, but rather because his or her delight in loving [*seine Liebseligkeit*] is apparently bound up essentially with delight in talking [*Redseligkeit*], so secretly and profoundly that it reminds us of the ancients, according to whose philosophy God, human beings, and the things all came to be out of "Logos," by which they meant either the Holy Ghost,

> reason, or speech. Now, not even psychoanalysis or sociology has taught us anything essential about this connection, although these two newest sciences allow themselves to compete with Catholicism in rummaging through everything that is human. One has to discover for oneself the reason why conversations play a greater role in love than almost anything else. Love is the most loquacious of feelings; for the most part it consists almost entirely of volubility. If the human being is young, these wide-ranging conversations pertain to the phenomena of growth; if he or she is mature, they form the peacock's tail, which, even though it consists of nothing but plumage, unfolds all the more splendidly when it does so quite late in the day. The reason may lie in the awakening of contemplative thinking by feelings of love, and in contemplation's constant connection with such feelings. Of course, that would only postpone the answer to the question, for even if the word *contemplation* is used almost as often as the word *love,* it is not any more transparent in meaning.
>
> Incidentally, whether or not what bound Ulrich and Agathe together can be called *love* cannot be decided by the fact that they spoke inexhaustibly with one another. It is also correct to say that what they spoke about one way or another always involved love. Yet it is as true of love as it is of all feelings that its embers glow more brightly in words the more remote those feelings are from action; and whatever it was that moved the siblings, once their recent intense and vague experiences of the heart [*heftigen und unklaren Gemütserlebnissen*] had passed, to give themselves over to conversations that sometimes seemed to them to be an enchantment, it was surely above all else their ignorance concerning how they might act. The diffidence toward their own feelings that accompanied their ignorance and the curiosity that drove them to penetrate these feelings only at their outer limits sometimes caused their conversations to find words that were more superficial than the genuine depth of the feelings. (1219–20)

Agathe wearies of these longwinded disquisitions and dialogues on feeling, and her suspicion grows that her brother's endless explanations—in a later sketch she refers to his "ideocratic disposition" (1254)—may merely be the sign of "weak feeling," or the sign of some experience in his past that makes him unwilling to entertain any strong feelings at all (1228). If, when Musil was correcting the proofs to those chapters intended for publication in 1938, he complained that their "principal mistake" lay in their "overestimation of theory," he was merely repeating what the *woman* without qualities had been telling him for some time now.[9]

Yet it is also true to say that Ulrich gradually becomes aware of the problem; true to say that from time to time brother and sister "look into one another's eyes, cannot tear themselves away, and dissolve into a feeling of the infinite that stretches like rubber" (1232); true to say that something of the tenderness between them transforms their vision of the entire world; finally, it is true to say that something of this *Zärtlichkeit* permeates Musil's own writing, which at this point becomes more dreamlike than wryly perceptive, more softly contoured than wittily sharp. Agathe has borrowed some tomes of the German mystics from Ulrich's library, and Musil himself, perhaps with the help of an anthology by Martin Buber, seems to have peeked into them as well. There is less science and more *Gelassenheit* in these revised scenes than in the earlier ones, nowhere more so than in the continuously revised "Breaths of a Summer's Day."

Musil sketches the *Atemzüge* scene as though it has been limned by Manet or Monet, Pisarro or Seurat; it could also be a scene in Kurosawa's *Dreams*. The siblings are now lying on the grass in their garden, watching the white petals of the blossoms falling from the trees and drifting on the summer breeze like swirling snow. This hovering *Blütenschnee* persists throughout the scene, "and the breath that bore the snow was so soft that not a leaf stirred" (ibid.). The mood is one of both a feast of nature reborn and a funeral procession, both spring and fall, "the speech and the silence of nature, and also the magic of life and death" (ibid.). The thoughts of Agathe dominate this chapter, at least the initial three-quarters of it, and those thoughts revolve about the lament of the mystic (it could be Meister Eckhart or Richard of St. Victor or yet another, perhaps someone in the Jewish mystical traditions, Musil does not say), who writes that God's love has penetrated his heart like a thorn that lies too deep to be plucked out. "Time stood still, a thousand years had as little weight as the opening and closing of an eye; they had reached the Millennial Kingdom,

---

9 Berghahn, *Robert Musil*, 142. Yet even if Musil faults himself for his book's "excessive theory," it remains true, as Maurice Blanchot observes, that his ideas "are *not yet* thoughts"; it is as though the world of truth will begin for both Musil and his heroes only tomorrow. In the meantime, even for a man and a woman without distinct particularities, there remain only "concrete scenes" and "acting personnages," even if these personnages do not know what to do (LA 183–84).

perhaps even God gave himself to be felt" (1233). Yet this god is not the usual graybeard who slaps the wrists of naughty boys and girls. This is the Kingdom of Love. And Agathe is quietly astonished. Even her hatred of Hagauer, her husband, evanesces; she cannot imagine why she despised him so much. When she finally breaks the silence it is to remark to her brother, "Doesn't it seem to you to as though everything else, compared with this moment, is superfluous?" (1235). Ulrich replies that if feelings can be divided into animal and vegetable kingdoms, the two of them have by now become vegetables.[10]

Their fate, gradually disclosing itself to the two during this idyll, seems to be "an occurrence without something happening," *eines Geschehens, ohne daß etwas geschieht* (1237). For Ulrich, it is not a matter of sheer passivity; it is rather something between nihilism and activism, something, one might say, that is searching for the Greek middle voice. The chapter closes in this way:

> Naturally, it was clear to him that the two kinds of human being that were the stakes in this game could result in nothing other than a man "without qualities" in contrast to one who possesses all the qualities that a human being could possibly possess. You might also call him a nihilist who dreams God's dreams; you might also say that in contrast to the activist, who in his impatient way of behaving is also a kind of godly dreamer and not at all a realist, he is engaged in the world in a clear and active way. "So why can't we call ourselves realists?" Ulrich asked himself. The two of them were not that, neither he nor she; their thoughts and actions had long since left no doubt about that; but they were nihilists and activists, sometimes the one, sometimes the other, depending on how things went. (1239)

Thus ends Musil's version of Monet and Seurat, rather prosaically and whimsically. Of the *Atemzüge* scene, Blanchot writes, in one long breath, "What is unexpected and, I believe, what surprised and disoriented Musil himself is that the extraordinary experiences that he draws [from this scene], the ravishment that draws the two lovers into a luminous garden remote from the world, on the edge of being, the creative generosity that never allowed him to put this episode behind him, obligating him to pursue it over hundreds of pages as though in secret protestation against the final disappointment, all these excessive developments that unbalance the book and yet give it renewed power,

---

10 Once again I refer the reader to the wonderful book by Elaine P. Miller, *The Vegetative Soul*, cited in chapter 4.

far from representing a failure, enable an impossible love to shine—even if it is only a mirage—with a happiness and a truth whose illusory nature Musil, against his expectation [*son attente*] and his plan, could not bring himself to destroy" (LA 178).

Yet why those endless revisions to "Breaths of a Summer's Day"? The final preliminary form of the chapter has Ulrich asking Agathe about the kinds of men she has chosen in her life: "Is it not really remarkable that your feelings have so often chosen men who could not have been dear to you, neither in soul nor in body! Doesn't it look as though right from the start you wanted to weaken the tendency toward reality [*den Zug zum Wirklichen*] in you, to weaken a destiny that had always rebuffed you [*das immer allzu kurz angebundene Schicksal*]?" (1246). It is difficult to know exactly what Ulrich means by this, although it seems likely that he is projecting onto his sister his own involvements with Leona and Bonadea. Another version of "Breaths of a Summer's Day" alters Ulrich's remark, which now says "that right from the start you wanted to weaken the tendency in you to the real, to desire [*Begehren*]" (1328). In any case, Musil deleted all this from the "good" copy. He also deleted Ulrich's reflection on those people (including Ulrich himself) who enjoy building matchbox structures out of their ideas, engaging in a *Bastelei in Gedanken*, or hobby-kit of thought (1249). In several earlier plans for the chapter Musil has Agathe say, in words that Bonadea too could have spoken, "You analyze the possibility of extending your hand according the laws of nature and morality; why don't you simply reach out?" (1274, 1278).

At some point around the year 1938, Musil once again contemplated an explicitly sexual relation between the siblings. Similar plans from the mid-1920s show that he had been contemplating this for some time. The abbreviation *coit.* appears in such plans as the following:

> The other state needs no morality; it is morality itself!
>
> "Attempts at unification" are, theoretically considered, now really unthinkable. Or merely as an attempt: how far does it go? how far does this combination of the other feeling with the compulsion of drives lead? Probably it presupposes coit[us], but, as natural, [one must] remain silent about it; and these are mere sidelines [*Nebenlinien*]. (1282)

I have no idea whether Musil was familiar with the devastating fates of Georg and Gretl Trakl in 1914 and 1917, respectively, although it is certain that he knew the poet's work.[11] Yet he cannot have had an optimistic view of a successful sexual relation between Ulrich and Agathe—whatever that may mean even apart from the question of incest. It is one thing to theorize about the (im)possibility of incest with Rousseau and Morelly, another to recognize the severity with which our civilization enforces the prohibition; one thing to observe that incest *begins* only with the *prohibition* of incest, as though the pillar of exogamous civilization collapses as soon as it is erected, another to see the devastation that comes to individual lives when the pillar falters for them. Even so, Musil attempted to recount the siblings' effort in this regard, although these attempts never wound up in good copy or in print. In one of the many revisions of "Breaths of a Summer's Day," in fact in its longest and most elaborated form, the narrator notes that brother and sister "ultimately ended up on a dizzyingly narrow borderline between the greatest happiness and pathological behavior [*einer schwindelnd schmalen Grenze zwischen größtem Glück und krankhaftem Benehmen endeten*]" (1311). This does not prevent Ulrich from asking himself:

> And so, he desired? Actually, he was astonished that he was admitting this to himself only now; clearly he now stood eye-to-eye with the two possibilities he had to choose from. Either he really had to believe that he was preparing an adventure unlike any that had ever been, and that he only had to hasten, without further thought, to repel it? . . . Or what could hinder him from doing what he wanted to do? A biological superstition, or a moral one? in short, the judgments of others? (1313)

An earlier revision of the same chapter frames Ulrich's interior monolog in the following way:

> He asked himself whether he desired her, and he did this as though the matter pertained to someone else, and at that moment he seemed somewhat ridiculous to himself. Agathe too "desired" him, and the beauty of her body was almost as familiar to him as that of a wife would have been, their lips had already on occasion become friends who are intrigued with one another, their souls went together like echo and loneliness. Without wanting to, he imagined, under a

11 See chapter 7 of Krell, *Phantoms of the Other*, cited in note 5, above, for an account of the poet and his sister, both of them suicides.

> pretext that Agathe would have believed as little as he himself did, proposing that they go back into their room, taking her hand with the dry trembling that was in his own hand, a trembling that would betray his intention to her: these hands in their precious blindness and these eyes in their muteness would then lead them irresistibly along the path from which there is no return. (1333–34)

Plans presumably from the years 1933–34, under the title "Crisis and Decision," take up once again Agathe's suicide attempt, or near-attempt, and her passion for her brother: "Suddenly Agathe kisses him, and the kiss is sensual" (1480). In the mid-1920s, Musil describes the scene as follows: "As his hand brushed hers, seeking pardon, Agathe closed her brother in her arms and kissed him. And without willing to do so, agitated, with sisterly solace, but then losing control of the situation, she opened her lips to his for the first time with that unrestrained womanliness that offers the full fruit of love, down to the innermost" (1648).

However, if Agathe cannot reach the Millennial Kingdom, death is her preferred option (1484). Very often in the earlier plans from the mid-1920s, during the period when Ulrich is given the name Anders, perhaps inasmuch as he is "otherwise," Musil invokes what he calls "the loving anxiety," in which brother and sister are brought to tenderness precisely by their anxiety in the face of death (1639–40). Agathe begins this part of the conversation, and Musil underscores her words:

> *We are the unfortunate ones* [Wir sind Unglückselige] *who bear in ourselves the law of another world*, without being able to carry out its prescriptions! We love what is forbidden, and we won't defend ourselves.
>
> A[nders] sat down beside her and embraced her. *We won't let anything kill us before we have tried it!*
>
> What?—Agathe looked at him tremblingly.
>
> God has. . . . A[nders] smiled . . . The lost Paradise!—We need not ask ourselves whether what we intend to do will withstand every test: *everything is fleeting and fluid. Whoever is unlike us will not understand us. Because one understands nothing of what one sees being done or what one does, but only what one is.* Do you understand me, my soul?
>
> *And if it goes awry, we will kill ourselves?*

> Let us kill ourselves!—There are voices in them that seem to form a choir of heavenly storms, and the voices sang, *Do what you feel . . . !!* (1651)

Musil is occasionally tempted to help his stricken lovers by a ruse. In 1926 he writes a sketch—later struck through—in which Agathe discovers a handwritten note of her father's that refers to her birth. She knows that their father's marriage was an unhappy one, and she believes that she finds grounds in the father's scrawled note to claim that she and Anders are only half-siblings. She is ecstatic about this until her brother, studying the note, shows her how entirely groundless her excitement is (1817). No such ruse will save either her or her brother. Nor will it save their narrator. At about this time, Musil sketches out his most detailed plan for Anders's (or Ulrich's) "Journey with Agathe" (1827; cf. 1835 and 1852). The two will escape to Italy—the Paradise that northern Europeans have always sought out and still seek out today, sometimes for the purposes of what Musil would call "a sensuous adventure." The sketch is highly developed, occupying some twenty-five book pages (1651–75), and there seems to be little doubt that up to the end of his life Musil intended to use it in some fashion or other.

Brother and sister leave Vienna by train for Ancona, on the Adriatic coast. There they take a boat trip—during which they are both wretchedly seasick, so that their romantic adventure begins ignominiously—to a small coastal village, perhaps somewhere in the Marche region of Italy. At their albergo they are taken to be a young married couple and they accept the *letto matrimoniale* that is offered them. It is here that Musil refers to the *Skala des Sexuellen* with all its variations. One note reads, "Exhaustion through excessive enjoyment in the body, the marrow entirely consumed. It shames them and makes them happy [*Es ist beschämend und beglückend*]" (1653). The dominant motif of these remarkable pages, however, is the sea, as in the following note:

> The legends of well-nigh all the ancient peoples report that humankind came from the water and that the soul is a puff of air. Remarkably, science has determined that the human body consists almost entirely of water. One is reduced in size. Having got off the train on which they had crossed through the compact network of European energies, and still jumpy from the motion that had hustled them along, the siblings stood before the tranquillity of sea and sky not otherwise than they would have stood a hundred thousand years ago. Ag[athe's] eyes welled up, and A[nders] bowed his head. (1654)

The tranquillity of the sea holds the moment captive, whether they are bathing in it or looking out over it from the balcony of their room. "The moment held; it did not sink and it did not soar. Ag[athe] and A[nders] felt a happiness that as far as they could tell might also be a mourning, and only the conviction that they were chosen to experience the unusual, which inspired them, prevented them from weeping" (1656; cf. 1665). The narrator calls the sea "that which never responds," *dieses niemals Antwortende,* which is fitting for the siblings, who do not know what they are about. "Their bodies, while the souls in them stood erect, found one another as animals do when they are seeking warmth. And that is when the miracle occurred for these bodies. A. was suddenly in Ag. or she was in him. . . . Wherever they touched one another, whether on the hips or hands or a strand of hair, they penetrated one another" (1656–57). If one tries to describe Musil's writerly achievement in these pages, the term "tender agility," *zärtliche Beweglichkeit* (1659), seems to leap from the page, a *Beweglichkeit* that has not lost the sense of the primacy of *Bewegtheit,* in the passive or middle voice. And the word *tenderness* is often repeated, "a tenderness that was insatiable" (1662). Musil manages to bring the two together as bodies, but as living bodies, bodies after the manner of Merleau-Ponty rather than Descartes. There is no lesson in physiology or anatomy here, nor anything vulgar or crude, but also nothing sentimental or overintellectualized. Which leads us to the strange thought that the issue of incest, in spite of all we have said thus far, is not the primary one: the issue is whether and how sexual intimacy and tenderness can ever be expressed in literature or in thought in a way that is convincing and moving without being spiritualized and sanitized or vulgarized and diminished. That said, it must also be admitted that the "scale" of the sexual, with all its variations, is unsung here. Musil's perhaps most telling note to self is this: "And so give a very light suggestion of repeated coitus [*Ganz leichte Andeutung wiederholten Coit so geben*]" (ibid.).

The great discovery in these pages, at least for Anders (Ulrich), is that the thoughts and deeds of love are not about unification. Rather, he realizes more intensely than ever before that his sister is different from him. "He was struck by the thought that now he could see, with full clarity, that precisely this is the secret of love, that the two do not become one" (1660). Even so, the lovers move in the confidence that nothing has ever really come between them:

> To understand a human being we love, there dare not be any sort of espionage. Rather, it has to be a giving based on a supreme fullness of happy inspirations. One dares to know only what enriches. One

> grants properties [*Eigenschaften*] in the inconcussible certitude of an accord that has been determined ahead of time, such that no separation was ever present.——— (1663)

It is as though what the siblings discover is what lovers always hope to discover, namely, both "sexuality and camaraderie," the one accompanying the other (1667). The camaraderie is determined by humility and the sexuality by the sea: "And on the other side (of this humility) lay the sea. The great beloved, adorned with the peacock's tail. The beloved with the oval mirror. The rising eyelid of the beloved. The beloved become God. The indefatigable demand" (1670).

But can it last, every reader must be asking, and Musil asks the same. For the sketch seems to take a turn (at 1671ff.) in the direction of everydayness, impatience, weariness, and the anxiety surrounding death, especially a self-willed death. The disillusionment emerges much more suddenly than the long journey toward Paradise would have led us to expect. "And what had happened? It had dissolved in a psycho-optical deception and a repeated physiological mechanism. As with every human being!" (1674). That is of course the voice of Ulrich. And Agathe? Once again it seems to Agathe "that U[lrich] does not have enough courage" (ibid.).[12] The end of the "voyage" is devastating, and one has to wonder whether suicide is indeed the only possible solution for a woman and a man without qualities:

> They were quiet for a while. Agathe opened and closed the shutters and she began to pack. The storm rattled the doors. Then Agathe turned around and asked her brother in a way that had changed and that was calm:
>
> —But can you imagine that tomorrow or the day after tomorrow we arrive home, find the rooms just as we left them, begin to pay calls on people? . . .
>
> A[nders] failed to notice how great her resistance was, how she struggled with this notion. He could not think of all that. But he

12 Astonishingly, the text has "U." here and not "A.," even though the sketch, from 1929, everywhere else refers to Ulrich still as Anders. It is as though the name Ulrich is invented for the first time at the very end of "the voyage to Paradise," and invented precisely as the one who will not have sufficient courage. Unless, of course, the editor has made a mistake: a handwritten cursive *a* might be mistaken for a *u*, and I have not seen the manuscript page, so that the matter is uncertain.

> felt a new tension, even if it was an unhappy task. In this moment he did not pay Ag[athe] sufficient heed. (1674–75)

The sketch closes with the laconic remark that the story is to continue with Clarisse arriving the next day, the day following "this baneful conversation," *diesem unseligen Gespräch* (1675). More than unhappy: unblessed, well-nigh accursed, boding ill. One should not really juxtapose the following terrible remark, which, however, does seem to come from the year 1929: "Portray U[lrich] as being just as unsympathetic as I myself am" (1831). Yet that note to self does introduce the final task of my own chapter, which is to ask how the failed or failing story of Ulrich and Agathe fits into the scope and the fate of the unfinished novel as a whole.[13]

•

One of the most intriguing notes from the *Nachlass* bears the heading "AZ. u. Ag/U.," that is, "The other state [or condition] and Agathe/Ulrich," presumably from late in the year 1929, that is, while Part Three is still being planned. Musil begins by saying that the story of the siblings is "well-nigh identical with the portrayal of the other state" (1831). However exceptional their situation may appear to be, Musil sees in it the only possible response to the collective suicide of public and private life in Europe and especially in Kakania. Why is Europe running out of possibilities? There is little evidence that Musil read Heidegger, even though there is often a tantalizing affinity between the vocabularies of *Der Mann ohne Eigenschaften* and *Sein und Zeit*. In the note under discussion the word *Möglichkeitssinn* is one of those instances of linkage: whereas for Heidegger Dasein is possibility-being, Musil defines "the other state" as that which has the power to determine and hold on to the very meaning of

---

13 To repeat, it seems that Musil intended to retain the Italian adventure for the final form of his novel. Against interpreters who believe that Musil abandoned this 1929 sketch of the trip to Italy and the siblings' lovemaking, Wilfried Berghahn musters some telling evidence. See Berghahn, *Robert Musil*, 141–42. The problem, of course, is whether the eventual *failure* of tenderness in the two, especially in Ulrich, can be made convincing without destroying the reader's interest in "the other state." The lovers' initial seasickness, when love's body becomes the wretched dogsbody, hardly seems to explain the failure of their love. I do not doubt that Musil labored over this question—although, as far as we know, there are no later revisions and emendations of the 1929 sketch, at least none that wind up in print or even in good copy, and this itself is quite surprising.

possibilities. Yet Musil immediately observes that such a meaning eludes the man without qualities: "The world has no goal for U[lrich]. Universal disinclination, for which no inclination seems to be given—the missing supplement among such human beings is the other condition" (ibid.). *Der andere Zustand*, in other words, is meant to compensate for the evanescence of possibilities, and yet, as an ersatz, it too is missing. There is considerable evidence, and we see it here, that whether or not Musil has read Heidegger, who in the 1930s was searching for *das andere Denken* and *den anderen Anfang*, the "other thinking" and "another beginning," precisely at the time when Musil was searching for *den anderen Zustand*, he certainly has read Nietzsche, and with enormous penetration. An edition of Nietzsche's complete works, we recall, is Ulrich's gift to Clarisse on her wedding day. Musil clearly has given himself the same gift.

Allow me in what follows to present a smattering of Musil's thoughts in these many pages of notes, interspersing only now and again a brief comment. For they will bring us to a conclusion—not of the novel, but at least of the present chapter. In what follows I will spell out Musil's abbreviations; needless to say, the sense of these fragments is often elliptical, so that my translation of them inevitably involves an excessive degree of speculation. In any case, and especially when it comes to the fates of Ulrich and Agathe, the fragments often contradict one another.

> Love between siblings: Is a hermaphroditic ideal on the rise, through the dismantling of the unnatural tension of the polarity? Psychic unity and sexual camaraderie?
>
> Describe the efforts at unification realistically, that is, with full seriousness [*mit vollem Ernst*].
>
> After their journey, the relationship of Agathe and Ulrich follows the same development in broad strokes[.]
>
> The other state is a feeling, a sake for which one speaks and writes, a component of morality—split off from it.
>
> Agathe has a remarkable memory for the chit-chat of the man's world. But no understanding for it. (1833)[14]

---

14 A later note on Agathe's memory is worth recording here, because it explains part of Ulrich's (and the reader's) delight in her: "Agathe's memory does not tie things together. The things lie there as in the bottomless pocket of a child, altogether without meaning; but when an object pops out of it, it is magically original. Ulrich the Abstract loves this memory" (1840).

> It is the eternal story of loved ones who are far away. [Musil's sentence appears in a "box" on the page: *Es ist die ewige Geschichte von der fernen Geliebten.* This may well be, Don Kelly Coble tells me, an allusion to Ludwig Klages's notion of "remote Eros" (*Eros der Ferne*) in *Vom kosmogonischen Eros.*] (1834)
>
> Every deed is to be outdone. In that lies the entire moral dynamism. (Ibid.)
>
> Their first attempt to undress entirely. They climb over the rocks to a cliff terrace that is almost impossible to reach. Even their undressing has no effect. The stimulating play of clothing when one is indoors has no force here. The naked body as a kind of hiatus [*wie ein Strich*]. If only it were at least sunburned.
>
> Unification. Like two one-celled animals. Conscious—during a pause, when there is no moon—sex. as the summit of a goal and a path. There has to be this penetration [*dieses Eindringen*]. Until they release one another, exhausted and sated. They lie on their beds like sifted flour in human form. Happy, confused; yet all human content was blown away. Can that be repeated? Only if an intelligent system is there, for example, the *unio mystica* or some such. Such a system might really be possible. The tragic: a world that has not been born.
>
> In Ulrich and Agathe we find the normal longings. Yet always suppressed, until they begin to languish on account of the usual obstacles, such as rivals. (1835)

A note that is particularly difficult to decipher has the title *Plot (!).* It consists of five points, the first two bracketed and with this note attached to them: "Real and moral involvements by way of [falsification of the father's] testament. Brotherly-sisterly feelings to the point of love and the other state." The first point says that Part Three of the novel "begins with the 'brother,' " yet a footnote is added to the word *brother,* and the footnote is important because it ventures the thought that Part Three might best unfold as the story of a *woman* without qualities, rather than the story of her brother: "It would be easier and provide greater variety if we took our departure from Agathe. Disappointment with the man's world, not wanting to get mixed up in it; just as little does she want to be like other women with their silly eroticism, and this underlies the asocial disposition which is her brother's"

(1838).[15] Here is the note on *Plot (!)*, whereby the exclamation point perhaps tells the entire story:

I. Begins with "brother," ends with the criminals (begins with the same taste.)

II. Begins as reaction to an anomaly, ends with the Millennial Kingdom; moral motives for their flight. . . . (Primitive demands of reality are not in relation to the vaporous consequences of morality)

III. Begins with the Millennial Kingdom, ends with normal-criminal *sexus*.

IV. Contains Agathe's wicked *sexus*, ends—? Prospect: Enhancement of the criminal.

V. Redemption by way of the War, a kind of end.

The note is horrific for more than one reason, and it is a blessing that Musil did not follow it when actually writing Part Three. As his exposés for the novel clearly show (1844–45, 1850–51), the looming disaster of World War I is the hellish ocean into which all the streams of his novel are destined to flow. One thinks not only of Thomas Mann's fictional Hans Castorp but also of Georg Trakl, who in August 1914 could not resist the feeling that at last something decisive had happened; a kind of wrathful *deus ex machina* had now descended upon an entire civilization. Yet what Musil can possibly mean by Agathe's *bösen Sexus* is entirely unclear, inasmuch as it is Ulrich who has been sexually active in Parts One and Two of the novel, whereas Agathe has been quietly and uneventfully married, and in any case is off-stage. Is "Agathe," named after the feminine form of "the Good" in Greek, merely to become another "reliquary of Eve"? The *Verbrechen*, "crime" or "criminality," that is invoked here generally has to do with her forging their father's will, but in this note it is associated

15 My translation is perforce speculative. Yet Musil seems to be contrasting Agathe to Diotima, Ulrich's beautiful cousin, who has become a "convert" to psychoanalysis, if only to a very intellectualized and sentimentalized version of it. The footnote to the note, particularly difficult because of the lack of punctuation, reads: *Ginge leichter von Ag aus u abwechslungsreicher. Enttäuschung von der Männerwelt, Nichthineinwollen ebensowenig Gleichsein den Frauen mit ihrer blöden Erotik stiftet die asoziale Bruderdisposition.*

with sex. One recalls Agathe's warm garter, placed into the inner pocket of their father's funeral garb. As for "Eve," another note of Musil's suggests that it is precisely Agathe's tendency toward religion, at least of a mystical sort, that underlies her asocial nature: "Ironically, the religious human being as the evil one. The criminals = the women" (1843).

Yet the question that such "criminality" raises is surely the one that Freud—not Diotima's Freud, but Freud's Freud—would have posed: is not the dilemma of the two siblings precisely that of all lovers, and perhaps not only those who live in Vienna at the outset of the twentieth century, the dilemma, namely, that where they love they cannot abide the pulsions of desire. Or, in other words, the dilemma that sensual love requires the most common form of degradation of its "object"? The grand success of Part Three of *Der Mann ohne Eigenschaften* would be that Musil postpones forever the traditional capitulation to this dilemma, the capitulation to which this note would have committed him. The qualities that Agathe most lacks are the ones that would make her either unlovable or undesirable. Yet the demands of tenderness are severe, and certainly Ulrich—though not he alone—is not often up to them.

Let us return to the notes, where Agathe's brother and lover is now the subject under scrutiny:

> Perhaps if he now had done just a little bit more (had he relented), the ties that bind life may have loosened; he would then have glided into something that was neither madness nor reality. He could not muster the courage to let himself entirely go, to let himself into it and out of it. . . . Yet Agathe already feels that he doesn't take it seriously enough. . . . (1839)

The same note continues to comment on Agathe, this time more positively, yet also in a way that causes us worry—worry about her ability to survive:

> Agathe, from the time of her meeting Ulrich up to the end of the journey, finds herself to be in a productive state; she says and does something that makes something, forms something; she does not have the feeling, or soon will not have the feeling, that this is a continuation of her earlier life; rather, she has the impression of a time of blossoming, a time that comes only once. When it has passed, she throws herself away. (Ibid.)

When we read the following note, it is important to remember that the expression "the last of the Mohicans of love" was originally placed in the mouth of Agathe, not Ulrich:

> Ulrich knows himself and Agathe to be in a way the last Romantics of love.
>
> Yet this is also a main theme: The enormous race of dumbheads and mediocre heads, and the tiny race of geniuses. Quite apart from all the political problems of the world. Ulrich's destiny is to be a kind of Last Mohican. . . .
>
> War: Ulrich's system is disavowed in the end, but then so is that of the world. (1844)

Finally, the dream that lovers in general will prove to have been brother and sister, identical and even Siamese twins, goes up in smoke even before Musil begins to compose Part Three: "Thus the idea of twins is an illusion. *The* illusion. The counter-illusion of normal people [that they will find their] completion. Collapses: end of the journey or with debauches" (1851). And then this: "*Danger*: The story of Ulrich and Agathe is, as the acme, too personal and too 'perverse' " (1852). Yet the same is true, one must say, with the nationalist fantasies of the Parallel Campaign, with Clarisse's mad plan to rescue Moosbrugger, and all the rest. The "fundamental idea" of the novel is that "all lines converge in the War" (ibid.).

These notes are terrifying to those of us who live in times when dumbheads rule, times when the only possibility seems to be that once again one must become the Last of the Mohicans. Yet the relevance of Musil's novel to our own times and places compels us to remember that the insight into the failure of all such grand solutions to the riddle of the world and the enigmas of love and destiny is an old insight. It is an insight that defeats all our plans. Maurice Blanchot notes this about Musil's obsessive plans for his novel: "I believe that one cannot neglect the profound trouble that rises to confront him in this book that he cannot altogether master, the book that resists him and that he too resists, insofar as he seeks to impose on it a plan that perhaps no longer suits it" (LA 167).

Is the story of Ulrich and Agathe too "personal," too " 'perverse' "? Or is it not the story of an entire civilization that stumbles into war that is, if impersonal, all too perverse? Perhaps it is the word *too* rather than the words *personal* or "*perverse*" that is important here in both cases. When Friedrich Hölderlin in the late 1790s was trying desperately to complete his play, *The Death of Empedocles*, he noted that Empedocles, the ancient Sicilian sage, embodies the *exceptional* qualities of his people and his times. Empedocles is a man of genius, a polymath, but also a man who loves both men and women with exemplary passion and tenderness. Hölderlin was struck precisely by the *exceptional* and *excessive* nature of these qualities. Empedocles, one might say, is "too much." It was this *excess* that indicated to Hölderlin that his Empedocles play would have to be a tragedy or "mourning-play," inasmuch as his hero was doomed. The following passage, from "The Basis of Empedocles," is obviously quite hastily written, with Hölderlin finding no time for punctuation. For this is Hölderlin's great discovery, the discovery of the "too much," and of the tragic character of excessive "individuality" and "intensity":

> [T]he times demanded a *sacrifice* in which the whole human being becomes actual and visible, a sacrifice in which the destiny of his times appears to dissolve and the extremes appear to unite actually and visibly in one, although precisely on that account they are united too intensely, and in these extremes therefore the individual goes down in an idealized deed and has to do so. . . . [16]

Musil's problem with Ulrich and Agathe, which is the problem of "the other state," is the very intensity and exceptional nature of the relationship between the siblings. And what sort of "idealized deed" would be suitable for these exceptional personages? For Empedocles, it is his suicide, his leap into the crater of Etna. But for Ulrich and Agathe? No matter what the siblings may do, no matter what sort of idealized deed Musil can come up with for them, one does not see how they can survive in the world. And, again, no matter what they do, the collective destiny of Europe in 1914 will overwhelm them.

Let that not be the last word, however. For Ulrich and Agathe, "united too intensely" beneath the moon and in the face of the sea, do offer us a vision of "the suddenly unveiled tenderness of the world." That is why, no matter what their destiny might have been, and no matter how cruelly the world may disclose itself to them and to us, we, like Musil, will never be finished with them. Taking Agathe as our instructor, we tremulous ones will continue to insist on tenderness.

---

16 Friedrich Hölderlin, *The Death of Empedocles: A Mourning-Play* (Albany: State University of New York Press, 2008), 147–48. The German text appears in CHV 1:872–73.

Part Two

Cruelty

(*Grausamkeit*)

Chapter Seven

Caress of Gestation, Cudgel of Birth

> —What are you suffering from, then?
>
> —I have such a hard time breathing; not always, but sometimes I feel so throttled I think I'm going to suffocate.
>
> —Freud/Breuer, "The Case of Katharina"

IT IS NOT AS THOUGH cruelty has not been a theme from the outset. Each chapter of Part One has tried to show that the default of tenderness is enough to induce cruelty—in the families that populate the Greek tragic stage, especially the family of Oedipus and his sister-daughters, on the bloodied plains beneath the walls of Troy, in the degradations to which lovelife in modernity is heir, in our incapacity to guarantee the presence of the persons we love and need, and in the failure of siblings and lovers to find the fitting gestures of tenderness. The chapters of Part Two will examine at least some facets of cruelty, particularly the need and desire to impute guilt and to punish, sometimes to the death, but also, more generally, the drive to mastery and power. Sometimes it seems as though the anxieties provoked by our very birth condemn us to such needs and desires, so that there would be no way of getting beyond cruelty. However, could the power we experience in artistic creativity—not a power we possess but one that possesses us, not a form of mastery but a giving-over to the demands of a creative life—help us to evade cruelty? Could it be art that gives tenderness a chance? These are the themes and questions of the remaining chapters.

•

In October 1799, the very year of Friedrich Schlegel's *Lucinde*, the second volume of Hölderlin's novel *Hyperion* appeared in print. Quite striking is the fact that Hölderlin chose a passage from Sophocles's *Oedipus at Colonos* to serve as the epigraph of this second volume. Six decades later, the epigraph struck the young Nietzsche with particular force, for it contains the kernel of what Nietzsche will call "the wisdom of Silenos," the wisdom that dominates Nietzsche's entire reading of Greek tragedy and perhaps Hölderlin's as well. Hölderlin cites lines 1124–27 of the Greek, signing them simply with the name *Sophocles*. In translation the epigraph reads: "Never to have been born—that is the supreme thought for a human being; yet once one has come to be, to return as quickly as possible whence one has come—that is second best" (CHV 1:696).

Nietzsche, who labored over the formulation of the wisdom of Silenos for many months in 1870, wound up with two versions. One appears in his revised manuscript of "The Dionysian Worldview," originally written in the Maderan Valley of the central Swiss Alps in August and then revised in December 1870; the other, a more succinct version, appears a year or so later in *The Birth of Tragedy from the Spirit of Music* (KSW 1:35, 560, and 588). Otto Rank chose the later, shorter version as the epigraph of his 1924 monograph, *The Trauma of Birth and Its Significance for Psychoanalysis*. The theme of Rank's work invites us to read Sophocles's words in an entirely new way, inasmuch as the expression "never to have been born" assumes a quite literal sense that Sophocles, Hölderlin, and Nietzsche—and perhaps even the daimonic Silenos himself—probably never (consciously) intended. Nietzsche writes, in the more succinct version:

> There is an ancient saga that tells how King Midas for many years tried to hunt down the wise Silenos, the companion of Dionysos, who roamed the forests. Yet he was unable to capture him. When Silenos finally fell into his hands, the king asked him what was best and most advantageous for a human being. The daimon, who would not be moved, was as silent and as hard as stone. Finally, compelled by the king, he laughed his shrill laugh and burst out with these words: "You wretched, ephemeral brood, you children of accident and toil, why do you do me violence so that I will tell you what it is most propitious for you not to know? The most excellent thing for you lies altogether beyond your reach: not to have been born, not to be. To be nothing. The second best for you, however, is—to die soon." (KSW 1:35)

"Never to have been born," for Otto Rank, now means never to have suffered the trauma that haunts mammalian existence from beginning to end. Human mammals in particular will never get over the shock of their birth—the compression of the head and near-suffocation, the brisk handling of midwives and obstetricians, and the sudden chill of air—and they will never liberate themselves entirely from their primordial fantasy of a return to existence in the mother's tender womb.

In a chapter on "Religious Sublimation," Rank cites a wonderful text from the minor *Midraschim*, "The Book of the Creation of the Child." The following extract, on the *birth* of the child, may be taken as a kind of second epigraph for the present chapter:

> And as soon as the time arrives, that it should go out, the angel comes and says to it: "Go out, for the time has come for you to go out into the world." And the spirit of the child answers: "I have already said to the One who when He spoke the Word the world was created that I was perfectly satisfied to remain in the world in which I have been dwelling." And the angel replies: "The world to which I will introduce you is beautiful. Furthermore, you were formed in your mother's body against your will, and against your will you will be born in order to go out into the world." Upon which, the child weeps. And why does it weep? It weeps for the world that was, and that it now must leave. And as it is going out, the angel strikes it under its nose and extinguishes the light above [in] its head. It brings the child out against the child's will, and the child forgets everything that it has seen. And as soon as it comes out, it weeps. (OR 118–19n. 3)

Yet does the child, even after the cruel blow of birth, even after the cruel angelic cudgeling that produces the philtrum, which is that vertical groove between upper lip and nose, actually forget everything? Why, then, does it weep a second time? Is there not a residue of fetal memories, both tender and fatal fetal memories, memories enough to plague a lifetime?

•

Rank begins his book with a "preliminary observation." The claims he makes there are extraordinary, and they must have astonished the man to whom the book is dedicated, Sigmund Freud. The scope of Rank's investigation, he says, will be "the entire development of humankind, indeed, the very becoming of humanity" (OR 1). Human history includes the history of both human biology and the productions of the human spirit. Whereas the tendency of the natural sciences is to reduce the latter to the former, Rank observes that "also a large segment of organic or biological development can be 'understood' only in terms of the psychical," which is to say that biology itself is one of the many cultural endeavors that our cognitive faculty undertakes (OR 2). Inasmuch as psychoanalysis studies the unconscious seedbed of cognition as such, biology can claim no superiority over it. Rank thus believes himself to have stumbled upon "the ultimate origin of the psychic unconscious within the psychophysical realm," *auf den letzten Ursprung des Seelisch-Unbewußten im Psychophysischen* (OR 3). This enables him, in his own view, to reach "the foundation and the core of the unconscious" (ibid.). Indeed, he claims that it has cost him no particular labor to "connect the deepest biological strata of the unconscious with the highest manifest content of humanity's intellectual productions," such that the foundation and the gabled roof of his own theoretical structure are in absolute harmony (OR 3–4). The structure itself will reveal, he suggests, "a universally valid psycho-biological law," one that now becomes manifest for the first time in the history of the psychoanalytic movement (OR 4).

Freud, for whom the Oedipus Complex never lost its status as the most important factor in the etiology of neurosis, must have been not only astonished but also dubious. In his 1914 essay *On the History of the Psychoanalytic Movement*, he tells how Rank first became a participant in that movement:

> From the year 1902 on, a number of younger physicians gathered around me with the express intention of learning, practicing, and expanding the influence of psychoanalysis. A colleague who had himself experienced the effectiveness of analytic therapy was responsible for this. On certain evenings the group came to my apartment in order to discuss in a disciplined way this new area of research, which was strange to them; they also tried to awaken the interest of others. One day a young man who had graduated from a trade school submitted to us a manuscript that showed an extraordinary level of understanding. We convinced him to attend the *Gymnasium,* then to visit the university, in order to devote himself to the nonmedical applications of psychoanalysis. In this way the small organization gained a hard-working and dependable secretary, and in Otto Rank I gained the most loyal helper and colleague. (GW 10:263)

In 1924 he added a footnote on Rank: "Presently the chief editor of the International Psychoanalytic Publishing House and editor of the *International Journal of Psychoanalysis* and *Imago,* both of these from the outset." Yet after the year 1924 and the publication of Rank's masterpiece, the relationship was strained to the breaking point.

Das Trauma der Geburt has eleven chapters. Allow me to offer a detailed account of at least the initial chapters. After that we may feel free to discuss in a more general way the issues the book raises for both psychoanalysis and our own meditation on cruelty and tenderness, the cudgel and the caress.

1. "The Analytical Situation"

Rank's sense of the importance of the birth trauma is such that he equates it with the analytical situation. Just as Fräulein Anna O. gives Freud his notion of "the talking cure" as a kind of "chimney sweeping" of a sooty psyche, so Rank's patients, men and women alike, give him accounts of their experience of psychoanalytic healing as a kind of rebirth—indeed, a rebirth that is preceded by months of transference as a "bonding with the mother" (OR 5–6). Rank, like most men, may make for an odd mother; the patient may therefore wish to offer the father (analyst) a child, as though the patient himself or herself were the analyst's spouse. This fantasy is often associated with the "rescue" fantasies of children, who wish to offer the father another child out of gratitude for the gift of life they have received. Ludwig Janus, in his introduction to Rank's text, notes that the Vienna Psychoanalytic Society, from about 1908 on, often discussed these rescue fantasies, emphasizing that the rescue of the father often involved a response to the danger of the father's suffocating, and that such fantasies became important for Rank's theory (OR i). The fantasy of rescuing the father is not often discussed in the psychoanalytic literature, it seems to me, where the father most often is portrayed as the threatening patriarch, Karamazov senior, as it were. I have remarked on the importance of the rescue fantasy in chapter 1, in the context of the theme of tenderness, yet here I would like to add a note to those earlier remarks, a note that involves sea-rescue.

When my second child, a daughter, was about eight years old, and her younger brother was about six, we were enjoying some months of sabbatical leave in the north of Greece near Mount Pelion. Every day we played a silly game on the beach, one that involved the children's tugging their (relatively) weightless father through the sea. I would dash into the water, which was almost always calm, then pretend to stumble. I'd then splash about and call for help in a melodramatic voice. My two children, laughing gleefully as I remember, rushed to the rescue and dragged me to shore. Twenty-five years later I was recounting this game to a friend in my children's presence. "It was great fun," I remarked. "It may have been fun for you," said my daughter, "but for my brother and me it was all in earnest." One of the most unexpected aspects of old age is seeing one's children—when they are not busy correcting their father's mistakes—still assiduously rescuing him in the most tender and earnest ways.

In a manner that is not completely clear, neither to Rank nor to anyone else, such rescuing of the father may actually be a way of reattaching to the mother. In those cases where the analysand wishes the analysis to continue indefinitely, observes Rank, it is invariably because of a mother-fixation, a fixation on "the earliest purely physiological relation to the maternal body" and on the disastrous interruption of that relation due to birth (OR 8). The analytical situation offers the patient a second opportunity to achieve a less traumatic separation from the mother—again, whether the patient is male or female—in a second parturition. Even if this second birth is merely "*so to speak* biological," Rank denies that birth trauma is a mere "metaphor" for matters purely biological. He sets the following in spaced type for emphasis: "The analytical situation in the end thus proves to be the achievement *après coup* of the incompletely mastered birth trauma" (OR 8–9). He insists that this equation (analytical situation = birth trauma = fixation on interrupted intrauterine existence) is a mere extension of Freudian theory: if psychoanalysis compels the ego of the patient to assume "libido positions" that go ever farther back in time, then it is perfectly logical that one eventually arrive at the intrauterine situation. If the "active therapy" practiced jointly by Rank and Sándor Ferenczi often results in the dissolution of the analysis after a period of somewhere between four and eight months, this too is no mere metaphor (OR 9). Analysis is a pregnancy, and transference-libido is maternal, regardless of the paternal aspect of the analyst. The analytical situation nevertheless approaches only "asymptotically" the "primordial situation," which may be characterized in the following way: "The reposeful position in a semi-dark space, the somnambulant condition [*Hindämmern*] of being in a state of phantasizing (hallucinating) that is well-nigh free of reality's demands, the presence and simultaneous invisibility of the libido object [i.e., the maternal womb], and so on" (OR 10–11).

It is curious to see Rank's description of the "primordial situation," primordial at least in the days immediately following birth, being echoed almost verbatim by Martin Heidegger in his 1928–29 *Introduction to Philosophy*. Heidegger allows himself there to describe human existence, *das Dasein*, in the earliest phase that is available to his observation, as the father of two small children. He describes infantile existence in this way:

> What determines this Dasein at first is quiet, warmth, nourishment, sleep, and a kind of twilight-state [*Schlaf- und Dämmerzustand*]. It has been concluded from this that such Dasein is at first at least to some extent folded in on itself and enclosed within itself, that the subject is still entirely sequestered in itself. This very presupposition is fundamentally skewed, insofar as the reaction of the child—if we may orient ourselves with the help of this word—has the character of shock, of fright [*des Schocks, des Schrecks*]. Perhaps the first cry is a very particular kind of shock. (27:125)[1]

In short, Dasein is from the start *anxious*, so that it will not surprise us when Rank's second chapter takes up the theme of infantile anxiety. Heidegger is not a philosopher of the cognitive faculties, so that he says nothing about the origins of memory or about possible later memories of shock and fright. Yet he does insist that Dasein—even at birth—is a being in the world. He enables us to understand Rank as pushing the origin of such being in the world back beyond birth, back to that still earlier stage of *Hindämmern* in the womb of the mother.

In *The Psychopathology of Everyday Life* and in other texts, Freud is concerned to show that psychoanalysis is in some sense always an investigation into the birth and development of *memory*, inasmuch as the soul would be nothing without some sort of retention and reproduction. Rank expands on Freud's insight by claiming that the birth trauma can account for both the retention and the distortion of infantile memories, indeed that the "primal repression of the birth trauma is the cause of memory in general" (OR 11–12). "In this sense, all infantile memories are in a certain way to be conceived of as 'screen memories,' and the entire reproductive faculty would in general be attributable to the fact that the 'primal scene' can never be remembered as such, because the most painful of all 'memories,' the trauma of birth, is 'associatively' connected with it" (OR 11). To be sure, the "primal scene" referred to here is not that of the Wolfman's parents *a tergo*, nor is it the scene of the infant's search for the nipple of the breast, which Freud recounts so dramatically in his 1895 *Project*. The primal scene, for Rank, is the intrauterine existence that might well have been available to infantile memory were it not for the rude truncation caused by birth. The analytical situation must take the patient back in memory

---

1 See my discussion of "Bébé Dasein" in chapter 3 of *Ecstasy, Catastrophe* (Albany: State University of New York Press, 2015).

to the asymptote of the parabola, which is the Paradise of intrauterine tranquillity that precedes the angel's knockout blow.

2. "Infantile Anxiety"

Rank admits that it would be a difficult task to trace every neurotic form of anxiety back to a single source, and so he decides to theorize about the "normal individual," as though that might be less arduous (OR 14). His initial clue resides in the claim that "every anxious affect at bottom can be traced back to the physiological anxiety of birth," which invariably involves *Atemnot,* "shortness of breath," and he attributes this insight to Freud himself. (Shortness of breath, along with heart palpitations, dizziness, sudden sweats, and a number of other symptoms, is surely an important sign of anxiety for Freud; yet one searches in vain for a claim by Freud that *every* anxious affect may be traced back to *Atemnot.*) Some infantile fears, such as that of the dark, may have to do with separation from the mother, thus pointing back to that first traumatic separation or scission from her. Other fears, such as that of animals, whether large or small, are more difficult to explain. Whether the fear of large animals has to do with their apparent gravidity, and of small animals that they might creep into the child's body precisely in the way that the child would creep back into the mother, is surely controversial. Sándor Ferenczi would have been interested in the claim that toads and frogs—and amphibians in general, which are so important to his theory of bioanalysis—arouse anxiety in the child because, as widespread folk beliefs attest, the frog or toad is taken to be the natural symbol of the maternal womb (OR 19). At all events, Rank does not shy from the claim that every infantile anxiety is an aftereffect of birth and a "partial completion" of the anxiety attending it (OR 20). Most intriguing is the claim that such anxiety actually manifests what Rank calls "the pleasure-unpleasure mechanism," inasmuch as "*every pleasure in the end tends toward the restoration of the primordial intrauterine pleasure,*" even if such pleasure is known to be ephemeral (ibid.).

Perhaps the most common "neurotic" symptom in a child's life, namely, *Enuresis nocturna,* or bedwetting, is also the most "exquisite" indication of this mechanism at work: urination is a "proof of love" of the mother, at least in the mind of any child or Augustinian, inasmuch as it reestablishes him or her *inter faeces et urinas* (OR 21). Bedwetting, as Ferenczi also analyzes it, recreates the intrauterine situation of moisture and warmth, and it is only with the coming of dawn and the sudden chill that the waking child is consumed by paroxysms of guilt and shame—themselves testimony to the repeated failure of the attempted restoration of intrauterine existence and the irreparability of separation from the mother.

What must have caused Freud some teeth-grinding is Rank's claim that castration anxiety—the very core of the Oedipus Complex and of the psychoanalytic account of sexual development in general—pales in comparison with the "primordial castration" of birth (OR 22). Indeed, according to Rank, the ubiquity of the castration complex can be explained only by reverting to the two initial separations from the mother, birth and weaning. Every trauma involving genitality may in fact be traced back to the initial separation of the sexes, and that separation, after the Fall, results from the expulsion of both sexes from Paradise: "[T]he most profound unconscious, which always remains sexually indifferent (bisexual), knows nothing about this [that is, nothing about genital differences and their functioning], and knows only the primary, primordial anxiety of the human act of birth, which is universal" (OR 23–24). The grinding now grows louder, as Freud learns that castration anxiety may even be a form of "consolation," *Trost*:

> In comparison with the truly painfully experienced and real traumas of birth and weaning, even a threat of castration that is actually made seems to make it easier for the child to find a normal release from the primordial anxiety, a release that would come in the form of the consciousness of genital guilt; this occurs at least to the extent that the child soon enough discovers that the castration threat is not serious and is just like all the other untruths that grownups tell. In contrast to primordial anxiety, the castration fantasy, now revealed to be an empty threat, may sooner appear to be a consolation, since the separation cannot really be carried out. (OR 24)

Herewith, in Rank's view, a clue arises to the solution of a puzzle that Aristotle long ago pondered, a clue concerning the compensatory *pleasure* that one takes in Greek tragedy, in which anxiety and terror become sources of satisfaction or ἡδονή (OR 25). Furthermore, the child's sense of death as a mere temporary separation, and not a final one, inasmuch as the expectation of restoration continues unabated, explains why the pleasure-unpleasure mechanism is so powerful: from the beginning, the child's thinking about death "is occupied by a strong unconscious pleasurable affect, that of the return to the mother's womb"; that undiminished affect "extends throughout the entire history of humanity, from the burial rituals of primitive peoples to their recurrence in the astral bodies of the spiritists" (OR 26). Even Freud's interpretation of the work of mourning, says Rank, can be understood in terms of "a repetition of the primordial trauma" (OR 27). The grieving person may in fact envy the departed one's return to the womb of the earth, or may learn to take pleasure and find consolation in it.

After acknowledging sleep as a "temporary return to the womb" (OR 29), an analysis that is reminiscent of the final chapters of Ferenczi's *Thalassa*,[2] Rank concludes with an introductory statement concerning those "socially adapted products of fantasy," namely, art, religion, and mythology, products on which the later chapters of his book will elaborate and which promise some sort of quasi-restoration of intrauterine existence. The more immediate task for Rank is to ascertain why sex, even if its satisfactions involve the most powerful expressions of erotic desire, fails to recapture "the full content" of the infantile wish for restoration (OR 30).

3. "Sexual Satisfaction"

The entire story of sexual satisfaction, as recounted in Rank's third chapter, reverts to the story of Oedipus—though not entirely Freud's Oedipus. The chapter begins by recalling the child's fascination with the question as to where babies come from, a question that has to be translated as the question, "How do I get back in there?!" (OR 31–32). The answer to such a question is frustrated by the child's "denial of the female sex organ," a denial that one way or another is the source of every form of neurosis (OR 33). One recalls the intrepidity of the shrunken scientist in the silent film-within-a-film of Almodóvar's *Habla con ella*, who must summon all his courage in order to enter where angels of both sexes fear to tread. Rank guides the reader through a rapid tour of "perversions," such as fetishism, masochism, sadism (to the point of murder), and homosexuality, in order to display the breadth and depth of human efforts to "come to peace," since that—and not mere "satisfaction"—is the genuine sense of the German word *Befriedigung*. (One must imagine Mick Jagger crooning,

2 Sándor Ferenczi, *Versuch einer Genitaltheorie*, in Sándor Ferenczi, *Schriften zur Psychoanalyse*, 2 vols., ed. Michael Balint (Frankfurt am Main: Fischer, 1972), 2:317–400; cited from hence merely by volume and page in the body of my text. The *Versuch* essay has been translated by Henry Alden Bunker, MD, as *Thalassa: A Theory of Genitality* (New York: W. W. Norton, 1968), reprinted in later years in multiple editions.

"I cannot attain peace," even though he tries and he tries and he tries.) Rank is particularly drawn to male and female homosexuality, in spite of his orthodox inclusion of it among "perversions." For homosexuality may more justly be called the sexuality "of the 'third sex,'" which yearns for and attempts to practice the "bisexuality of the embryonic state that lives on in the unconscious" (OR 36). Most remarkable is the way in which Rank, like Ferenczi, freely admits that psychoanalysis does not do justice to women and to female sexuality generally, whether the cause of such injustice is covert misogyny or overt ignorance:

> Especially in recent times it has been remarked repeatedly that our entire mentality and our attitude toward the world privileges the male standpoint and has practically neglected the female altogether. Perhaps the crassest example of this one-sidedness also in our social and scientific thinking is the fact that very long and quite significant periods of human culture remained under the influence of what Bachofen "discovered" under the term *Mutterrecht*, that is, the dominance of women. Only after great exertion and the overcoming of strong resistances was it possible to rediscover these periods, obviously long repressed by our tradition, and to accept them as fact. How extensively this attitude is still at work in us psychoanalysts is made manifest by the fact that as a rule we tacitly represent sexual relations only for the male—for simplicity's sake, as we say, or, if we are more honest, because we lack all understanding of women's lives. I do not believe, with Alfred Adler, that this results from the social inferiority of women; rather I think that both [social inferiority and the lack of understanding in psychoanalysis] are expressions of that primal repression that seeks to deny and to diminish womankind socially and intellectually because of woman's connection with the birth trauma. By trying to make the repressed primal memory of the birth trauma [*die verdrängte Urerinnerung an das Geburtstrauma*] conscious again, we believe that we can also rehabilitate at the same time a high respect for women, and to do so by liberating the female genital from the curse that has plagued it. (OR 37)

That curse is pronounced (unconsciously) by both men and women, adds Rank, since both suffer the pain and pressure of birth (OR 38–39). It is noteworthy that in his extended version of Silenos's words Nietzsche adds a specific remark concerning those children of accident and toil, "all of you—both men and women alike" (KSW 1:588). Both genders endure the burden of misogyny—ever since the story of an Eve who is confounded by the serpent and the story of Plato's *Timaeus* about when and how women came to exist in an otherwise perfect universe.[3]

Although Rank follows Ferenczi in recognizing the need to pay more attention to the riddles of feminine genitality and sexuality (OR 39), his own lucubrations on female "passivity" do not progress beyond the usual psychoanalytic tale. In this third chapter nothing is said of Antigone, but a great deal about Oedipus. If sexual love is the most ambitious attempt to restore in some symbolic way our existence in the womb, and if the round creatures of Plato's Aristophanes are the avatars of the drive to reunification, it is Oedipus who makes the best effort to take that drive all the way to its primal source. Admittedly, and Rank begins his account of the hero with this, Oedipus's effort ends in tragedy:

> In fact, behind the Oedipus saga stands the obscure and fateful question of the provenance of humankind. Oedipus wishes to resolve the question not in terms of insight but by factically returning to the maternal womb. In symbolic form his effort succeeds perfectly well, for his blinding represents in the deepest sense his return to the darkness of the mother's body; his final disappearance into the underworld when the earth's surface gapes open expresses the same wish, this time in terms of mother earth. (OR 43)

Yet Rank does not end his account with Oedipus's enucleation, death, and transfiguration. Instead, he says a great deal more about Oedipus's effort to get to the heart of the riddle and his "partial" success:

> From the standpoint of birth trauma, we can descry in the Oedipus Complex the first genuine attempt to overcome anxiety in the face of the (maternal) genital by occupying it pleasurably as a libidinal object. In other words, this means that one transpose the original—intrauterine—possibility for pleasure onto the genital *opening*, which is occupied by anxiety; thus it means to reopen a source of pleasure that has been covered over by repression. This first attempt is from

---

3 See Krell, "Female Parts in *Timaeus*," in *Arion: A Journal of Humanities and the Classics*, New Series II, 3 (Fall 1975): 400–21. As for Eve, it is perhaps enough if we recall Augustine's remark on the imperfections of his saintly mother, who, whether "sainted" or not, contained "a reliquary of Eve."

> the start doomed to failure ... principally because the effort takes place on the site of the primordial object [*das Urobjekt*], the site to which all the anxiety and the repression of the primordial trauma [*des Urtraumas*] is still attached. (OR 44)

If the first separation is birth, and the second is weaning, the third is the Oedipus Complex, which takes the primordial repression impacted in the birth trauma all the way down to Orcus or Tartarus, the underworld (ibid.). Admittedly, by this time the story has become entirely the male's story, with little or no relation to the desires and sexual experiences of women.

As for the story of the male, Rank does not cite the extraordinary words of Jocasta to Oedipus—indeed they are rarely cited by anyone—even though a contemporary reader of *Oedipus the King* has the uncanny feeling that Jocasta is addressing Rank and all his fellow analysts. Sophocles sets the scene immediately after Oedipus learns of Polybus's death, that is, the death of Oedipus's adoptive father, at which point Oedipus is overjoyed to find that the oracle is apparently mistaken about his being a parricide. Yet he confesses to Jocasta that he is still terrified by the oracle's second warning—that he will some day sleep with his mother. I cite Hölderlin's eloquently shattering translation of Jocasta's reply:

> Was fürchtet der Mensch, der mit dem Glük
> Es hält? Von nichts giebts eine Ahnung deutlich.
> Dahin zu leben, so wie einer kann,
> Das ist das Beste. Fürchte du die Hochzeit
> Mit deiner Mutter nicht! denn öfters hat
> Ein Sterblicher der eignen Mutter schon
> Im Traume beigewohnt: doch wenn wie nichts
> Diß gilt, er trägt am leichtesten das Leben. (CHV 2:287)

> For what does a human being have to fear if his luck
> Holds? There is no clear presentiment of anything at all.
> To live straight ahead, as well as you can,
> That is best. Do not fear wedding
> Your mother! For oftentimes
> In dreams a mortal has slept with
> His own mother: yet when he takes this as counting for
> Nothing at all, he can most readily bear life.

In his "Notes" on Oedipus, Hölderlin says that in this scene Jocasta is trying to seduce Oedipus "back into life" by insisting that every boy (or, as Rank would insist, every *child*) dreams of sleeping with his (or her) mother, but that this should be taken as really nothing at all. As we know, Jocasta's attempted seduction of her son—even and precisely because she is the *Urobjekt* of his love *and* his terror—does not and cannot succeed.

Yet once again Rank is reluctant to end with the downfall of Oedipus. Oedipus's unwitting achievement can be described as "the greatest possible approximation to that primal pleasure," a pleasure that is barred and blocked by trauma and repression. Even if the pleasures of sex be asymptotic, which is something like Hegel's bad infinity, there is still *einen möglichst innigen Kontakt,* "a most intimate possible contact" between two human beings, symbolized by *l'animal à deux dos,* very much as Plato's Aristophanes portrays it. Even if a ravishing desire seems to imply the incorporation and ingestion of an other, and even if orgasm resembles nothing so much as "a minor hysteric fit," Rank seems reluctant to interpret sexual "coming to peace" as sheer catastrophe, even if all the evidence he can muster points in that direction.

4. "Neurotic [and Psychotic] Reproduction"

More intriguing than neurotic reproduction of the birth trauma is its *psychotic* reproduction. That is to say, as Rank works through the various forms of neurosis it becomes clear that the most convincing examples of the anxiety attendant upon birth and the pleasure surrounding intrauterine existence preceding birth arise in schizophrenia and dementia. Rank clearly states his thesis: the "kernel" of "every neurotic disturbance" is anxiety, and anxiety—according to Freud himself, says Rank—has its provenance in birth trauma (OR 46). After the publication of Rank's *Trauma der Geburt,* Freud will write *Hemmung, Symptom und Angst* partly in order to correct or at least modify Rank's claim, and I will examine briefly Freud's critique at the end of my chapter. For the moment, one will allow Rank to insist that the formation of every neurosis, "in all certainty," involves "reproduced reminiscences of birth, or the pleasureful stage that precedes birth" (ibid.). Birth trauma is "universally human," and it constitutes "the psycho-biological substrate" of human experience in both health and illness (OR 47). More specifically, neurotic and psychotic illness can be distinguished from health in terms of the relative success or failure of the "partial coming to peace in the return to the mother" that occurs in sexuality; if the sexuality of the human being remains "infantile," disturbed or truncated in its development, it is a sign that he or she "is demanding a *total* return to the mother" (ibid.). Such a total return can only be hallucinatory and ultimately tragic.

Rank now reverses Breuer and Freud's etiology of neurosis, which posits a "bodily conversion" of psychic trauma to physical symptoms such as the paralysis of an extremity, facial tic, and so on. Rather, says Rank, it is a question of how a purely corporeal expression, the literal expression of the infant in birth, produces the initial psychic experience of anxiety (OR 50–51). The symptoms of "bodily conversion" are in fact the epiphenomena of birth trauma and the anxiety that birth invariably provokes. Shortness of breath, migraine, and muscle cramp are eminent examples in neurosis. Recalling perhaps Ferenczi's focus on the genitofugal displacement of erotisms toward the head in instances of stuttering, stammering, or even mere blushing, Rank notes that the head of the infant, even if it is the first part of the body to pass successfully through the birth canal, sustains the most intense pressure during birth (OR 52). It is not inconceivable that Rank is thinking of Laurence Sterne's *Tristram Shandy*, the comic masterpiece that attributes Tristram's entire life of *tristesse* to the birth trauma that damaged his head and nose. At all events, in Rank's view it is birth trauma that provides *ein reales Substrat*—always this Scholastic-Aristotelian terminology describing the *Ursituation*—for psychic conversion (OR 53).

The most radical conversions on the common arc of the biological and the psychic are manifested in psychosis, however, and Rank devotes the final pages of his chapter (OR 62–71) to catatonic schizophrenia, dementia, progressive paralysis, and psychosis in general. "It is a fact that the contents of psychosis, sometimes quite obviously, sometimes in the symptoms of degradation in the patient's own thinking and speaking, are thoroughly permeated by the most extensive representations of birth and intrauterine existence" (OR 64). And yet it is the specific differences—and not the universality—that make for the most gripping reading in Rank's text. For example, in psychotic patients who ingest their own excreta, the patients' own explanation is often that they need such nourishment for their own rebirth; just as often, the patient identifies himself or herself as both mother and infant in the process of gestation and birth (OR 67). Rank refers in detail to Alfred Storch and Viktor Tausk's work with psychotic patients, and it is Tausk who describes catatonia as "the *ultimum refugium* of a psyche that surrenders even the most primitive ego-functions and draws back entirely toward the fetal stage or the stage of the suckling babe" (quoted at OR 68). Tausk cites a patient as saying, "I feel that I am constantly growing younger, smaller; now I am four, then I'll be in diapers, and then I'll be in my mother" (ibid.). Such a patient is reenacting the fate of Antigone, living out the myth proposed by Plato in his *Statesman*, according to which, we recall, there was an earlier age ruled by Kronos in which humans were born as senescent creatures from the womb of the earth and grew younger and more beautiful every day. The myth, we recall, does not speak directly of a return to the womb of the mother, since during this age the Earth is our only mother, but merely tells us that the creatures become smaller and smaller until they are hidden to the eye.

In the final pages of the chapter, Rank refers to two well-known authors—Fyodor Dostoevsky and August Strindberg—who describe their illnesses (epilepsy and schizophrenia, respectively) in terms of birth trauma. Most interesting is Dostoevsky's description of the *aura* that precedes *le grand mal,* the feeling of repose, happiness, and even blessedness that precedes the violent cramp, as though gestation and birth were being compressed into a moment. As for Strindberg, he himself traces his mental illness to the devastation wrought on him by a woman who betrays him for another man, a woman against whose menacing "rays" he then has to protect himself, especially at night. His account, cited by Tausk and once again by Rank, has an extraordinary impact on anyone who is familiar with Schelling's account of the divine potencies. For the very first potency of God is what Strindberg appears to be describing.[4] Tausk reports the following account by Strindberg, and he does so in a run-on sentence that reflects Strindberg's anxiety:

> When he is in love, he melts altogether into the woman he loves, but then, when he has lost his "form" and his "self" entirely to her, his self's drive to survival reawakens, and in his anxiety that he will lose his self by virtue of the power of love that makes him her simulacrum [*durch die ähnlich machende Macht der Liebe*], he tries to liberate himself from her, in order that he may find himself once again as *something existing for itself.* After the psychosis he withdraws into solitude, spinning himself into a cocoon fashioned out of the silk of his soul. (OR 71n. 1)

---

4 For an account of this "first potency," in the figures of Poseidon and Kronos as portrayed in F. W. J. Schelling's *Philosophy of Mythology*, see chapter 5 of Krell, *The Sea: A Philosophical Encounter* (London: Bloomsbury Press, 2018).

5. "Symbolic Adaptation"

The scope of Rank's investigation now expands beyond the analytic couch and the psychiatric clinic to all of nature and culture. My account of it here will perforce be selective. "Adaptation," the German *Anpassung*, has to do with all the responses of nature and culture to "the fundamental significance of the birth trauma and of our immortal longing to overcome it" (OR 72). Sleep, the night, the phases of the moon, our nocturnal dreamlife—these are Rank's initial themes. It is not difficult for him to associate anxiety dreams with birth trauma, wish-fulfillment dreams—along with dreams of flying—with intrauterine existence. Rank's own explanation of this ease of interpretation appears now with startling clarity: "For the fetal situation, at least in the final period of pregnancy, along with the situation of birth, is immediately given to the individual as such [*dem Individuum als solchem doch unmittelbar gegeben*], and as such that situation is doubtless capable of reproduction [*und als solche zweifellos reproduktionsfähig*]" (OR 82). "Reproduction" is here meant in terms of reproductive memory, memory perhaps of a preconscious or unconscious sort, even though precisely what consciousness and the unconscious may be is the question here. In any case, the initial claim is that the so-called maternal womb fantasy is no fantasy at all but a genuine reminiscence.

The claim of "immediate givenness" seems to be of the sort made by phenomenology in its most optimistic phase, that of transcendental phenomenology; yet the phenomenologist, unlike Descartes, who could well imagine the necessity of the "I think" of the fetus, surely never dared to trace self-givenness back to the fetal situation. It is as though, for Rank, infantile reminiscences achieve the sort of evidence that Husserl dreamed of for perception—although it is arguable that even for Husserl *memory* possesses evidentiary possibilities that no perception can match.[5] As for infantile memory, Rank, early on in his book, is impressed by the fact that researchers have discovered the suckling reflex in the six- or seven-month-old fetus (OR 21n. 2); they have also found that the fetus is generally sensible of a "tickling" sensation due to the motions of the amniotic fluid (OR 35n. 2). However, the assertion that something like *memories* of the intrauterine situation are capable of reproduction—barring the

5 See my "Phenomenology of Memory from Husserl to Merleau-Ponty," *Philosophy and Phenomenological Research* XLII, no. 4 (June 1982): 492–505.

repression that regularly accompanies birth trauma—is a claim for which the reader is unprepared. It is not that Rank would deny the poet's assertion that our birth is but a sleep and a forgetting; that blow beneath the nose delivered by the canny angel, the blow that produces that slight crevice above our upper lip, is not without effect. The light is put out. It is merely that in Rank's view the oblivion that occurs by virtue of repression is not total, or at least need not be total. The light is not entirely snuffed.

Rank now begins to describe the achievements of culture and civilization in terms of prostheses or extensions of the mother's womb and the remembered intrauterine state (OR 83). If the German can designate a woman simply as a room, *ein Frauenzimmer,* a term that today occurs only in derogatory remarks, Rank feels that he can interpret all of architecture in terms of the intrauterine situation. In an unheard-of sense, architecture becomes *arche-ticture,* since the ancient Greek τίκτω means sexual reproduction. Architecture is primordial, archaic tictology.[6] He cites a cultural historian and linguist for whom the word *Haus* reverts to *Haut*, "skin," and the word *Hütte* to both "hut" and "hat," these in turn being an ersatz *caul,* or placental amnion and chorion. Most interesting for Rank's (and Ferenczi's) bioanalytic theses is the fact that human beings imitate the sun by going to bed when the sun descends into the sea. The original bed is a water bed, and the word for water, *Wat*, produces both *Bett*, the "bed," and the Hebrew *Beth* or house. "When a human being went to bed, he or she entered the water. The covers between which they lay were waves, made from materials that softly flowed."[7]

Intriguing too is Rank's insistence that even in patriarchical societies the protection offered by the king is derived entirely from the king's standing in for his mother. The king is always a child, the Sun King forever a son king. His aegis is the mask of Medusa. Matriarchy, presumed to be *passé,* continues to rule in patriarchy: "The king is thus originally not the father but the son, and indeed a little son, an *infans,* who cannot speak for himself—'his majesty the child' " (OR 88). When the people of France rebel, and the key figures in the popular revolt are women, their principal

6 See chapter 1, "Tic Talk: Space, Time, and Lovemaking in Plato's *Timaeus,*" in Krell, *Archeticture: Ecstasies of Space, Time, and the Human Body* (Albany: State University of New York Press, 1997).

7 Rank (OR 85n. 1) is citing Ernst Fuhrmann, *Der Sinn im Gegenstand* (Munich, 1923), *passim*, and *Der Grabbau* (Munich, 1923), the latter at 43ff.

enemy is not a hapless king but his arrogant queen. All patriarchy is but an expression of the primal repression resulting from birth trauma. Not only that, but every indication of technical progress, whether it is (in Ferenczi's words) autoplastic or alloplastic (OR 97), is but an expression of what Rank calls *Mutterlibido* (OR 92). Every tool and every weapon is fashioned to master *matter,* which is always a matter of *mater,* even if—or precisely because—the mother is never completely reoccupied. Every technological perfection is thus driven unconsciously by "the eternally unsatisfied tendency toward a complete penetration of the mother" (ibid.). Nothing changes when we consider the matter of maritime progress: "According to the (as yet unpublished) bioanalytic researches of Ferenczi, the earth itself appears as an ersatz of the primal mother of all living beings, namely, sea water (the ocean as symbolic of the mother)" (OR 92n. 3). In short, the apparently masculine drive to master nature "in the end has only maternal significance" (OR 93). To designate the drive to such "mastery," Rank uses the term *Bewältigungslibido,* borrowing from Freud the word *Bewältigung,* one of Freud's most important designations of "the reality probe" or the "reality drive," which has an uncertain place in Freud's theory of drives.[8]

As for the "real," which resists our efforts at mastery, Rank writes, "The real world, as fashioned by human beings, proves to be a concatenation of incessantly renewed symbolizations, which, however, do not serve merely to replace the primal reality that has been lost, constructing symbols that are as true to the original as possible; rather, such symbolizations must also reawaken as little as possible memories of the primordial trauma that is bound up with that reality" (OR 96). There is the rub. Memories of Paradise evoke above all the memory of how Paradise was lost. And the loss goes on forever in a world where language itself, which is the public secret of human nonmastery, begins

8 I have already touched on this question in chapter 5, and I will take it up again in chapters 8 and 10, below. One is also invited to read Otto Rank's pages on the *Mutterlibido* as the driving force of technological "progress" against Martin Heidegger's "The Question Concerning Technology" (1953). In such a reading, Aristotle's "four causes" would, *pace* Heidegger, have to bow to a Platonic first principle—that of τίκτειν as such and of a certain Ananke or "choric" principle. There is at least one Heidegger who would not flinch in the face of such a reading, and Derrida above all would be open to it.

with the primal scream of birth and continues—by way of the selfsame syllable, *ma*—as the cry for milk and succor (OR 98).

To be sure, patriarchal culture desperately tries to repress the maternal altogether. Its God will always be a graybeard. Yet in a later chapter Rank cites the seventeenth-century French theologian Denis Pétau (Dionysius Petavius), who in his work on the Trinity feels constrained to supply the Father with a womb, presumably so that he may bear a Son. Obviously, since God is incorporeal, there can be no reproductive organs of any kind; yet Scripture says that the birth of the Son is a true birth, so that the Father willy-nilly gets a womb (OR 118n. 3). Which makes one wonder why Mary was necessary at all for the birth of the Son. But of course it is precisely she who is most necessary, and right from the start, so that the Father, confusing his own thigh with the thigh of Zeus, is confounded.

•

We may take it that by now Rank's "system" is clear to us, or as clear as so daring a thesis can be. Yet to stop short here is doubtless to do Rank an injustice: the strength of his book lies in its ethnographic and cultural—religious, artistic, and philosophical—research and speculation. For the moment, only the chapter on philosophy, "Philosophical Speculation," will claim its right to a close reading.

For Rank, quite oddly, "artistic idealization" means the self-assertion of a Doric, masculine culture over Near Eastern and Egyptian matriarchy; such idealization in sculpture, painting, and poetry recapitulates the painful "strivings" of the fetus and the newborn, again quite oddly, "to achieve release from the mother" (OR 140). A certain reading of Nietzsche's *Birth of Tragedy*, doubtless a one-sided reading, far more Apollonian than Dionysian, underlies Rank's entire interpretation of art. However, like Nietzsche, Rank does see the Olympian panoply of the Homeric gods as the transparent screen that enables the Greeks to gaze into the abyss of a Titanic and monstrous human existence without danger of self-destruction. Unlike Nietzsche, however, Rank has virtually nothing to say about the Dionysian birth of tragedy from "the spirit of music," which, of course, is Nietzsche's principal interest.

Nietzsche's *Philosophy in the Tragic Age of the Greeks*, from the year 1873, nonetheless plays an important role in Rank's chapter on "Philosophical Speculation." Ultimately, for Rank, if not for Freud, philosophical speculation does not approximate paranoid delusion or even Rank's "compulsive neurosis."[9] Rather, philosophy is a success story—the story of the advance from Thales to Socrates and from myth to science. The same story, *mutatis mutandis,* has been told by historians of Greek philosophy for hundreds of years in dozens of languages. Yet it may be worthwhile to examine Rank's reflections on philosophical speculation in some detail. For it is as much a symptom of the birth trauma as an explanation of it.

Rank confronts the development of philosophical and scientific idealization with an ambivalence that more than resembles ambivalence surrounding the mother. On the one hand, he respects the scientific thinking that underlies and culminates in psychoanalysis; that sort of thinking resists the mythical, "Oriental," and matriarchal sorts of thinking that the Greek miracle overcomes. On the other hand, it is precisely the highly intellectualized Western world that is in denial of the mother, and such denial is nothing other than an expression of the unannealed trauma of birth. In other words, Rank *wants* to follow Nietzsche's reading of Western philosophy, and there is no other philosopher, not even Schopenhauer, who has this importance for him. And yet, for all his extensive citations from Nietzsche's works, especially the 1873 *Tragic Age*, Rank arguably misses the radicality of both Nietzsche's reading of the Greeks and his later genealogy of *ressentiment* in the 1887 *Genealogy of Morals.*

The story begins positively enough with Thales. Rank writes:

> As we know, Greek philosophy begins with the statement of Thales that *water* is the origin and the womb of all things. Before we pursue

---

9 Rank is kinder to the philosophers of "system" than Freud is. Freud's preface to Theodor Reik's 1919 *Probleme der Religionspsychologie* (GW 12:325–29), a fascinating text, serves as a brief introduction to the entire history of psychoanalysis. Among its most remarkable features is Freud's concession—one that Otto Rank would affirm—that the emotions that are important to psychoanalysis are precisely those that creative writers and poets, *die Dichter,* have always stressed—above all, the emotions involved in lovelife. Later in the preface the poets return, as Freud approaches the proper subject of Reik's book: "The hysteric is doubtless a poet, even if in what is essential he presents his fantasies mimically and without paying attention to the understanding of others. The ceremonial aspects and the proscriptions of the compulsive neurotic force us to conclude that he has created a private religion for himself. And even the delusions of the paranoid manifest unwittingly an extrinsic similarity and an inner affinity with the systems of our philosophers" (GW 12:327). The philosopher can only cross his or her fingers and hope that the "inner affinity," like the "similarity," is in fact merely "extrinsic."

> the further development of Greek thinking on the basis of this lapidary formulation, let us be clear about the fact that the formulation offers us the first cognitive conception of the origin of individual human beings as a universal law of nature. The mechanism of such an insight, which is doubtless correct in terms of biological occurrence, is that it distinguishes itself from the cosmological and mythical projection of celestial waters (the Milky Way) and underworld streams (the river of the dead) by making an actual dis-covery, by actually drawing back the curtain, or, as we would say, relieving a repression that has heretofore obstructed our seeing in water the origin of all life precisely because one had oneself at one time emerged from amniotic fluid. The presupposition for discovery of truth is thus recognition by the unconscious of something in the outside world [*die Agnoszierung des Unbewußten in der Außenwelt*] by canceling an inner repression [*durch Aufhebung einer inneren Verdrängung*] that immediately proceeds—and this is what the development of philosophy clearly shows—from primal repression. (OR 161)

Thales, then, is above all else a psychologist who makes philosophical discovery possible by releasing the pressure of the birth trauma. Yet how does Thales overcome the obstructions arising from primal repression? Rank can offer no explanation.[10]

Anaximander's formulation, which both Nietzsche and Heidegger ponder, now claims Rank's attention: "The place from which things take their provenance is the place into which they must perish, according to Necessity; for they must pay a penalty and must be judged for their injustices, in accord with the order of time" (OR 161–62). Rank follows Nietzsche in seeing in Anaximander's statement the foundation of pessimistic philosophy up to and including Schopenhauer. According to Nietzsche, "We pay penalty for our birth twice over, first by living, then by dying" (cited at OR 162). Rank comments: "Anaximander's statement thus supplements the insight of Thales

---

10 At the point where he asserts the biological truth of Thales's statement, Rank footnotes a reference to Sándor Ferenczi: "See now Ferenczi's phylogenetic parallel to individual development (*Versuch einer Genitaltheorie*, 1924)" (OR 161n. 3). For a more detailed account of Thales in the context of Ferenczi's bioanalysis, see chapter 4 of *The Sea*.

by emphasizing the return to origins; it has thereby discovered a second natural law by psychological intuition, one that in only slightly altered form has been taken over by our scientific thinking of nature" (ibid.). Rank now footnotes one of Nietzsche's most remarkable unpublished speculations on life and death in nature, one that has captured the imagination of commentators such as Heidegger and Derrida. Nietzsche's note, from the winter of 1872–73, has the Mette-number 23[34]: "*Alle unorganische Materie ist aus organischer entstanden, es ist todte organische Materie. Leichnam und Mensch*" (KSW 7:554). "All inorganic matter originates out of the organic; it is dead organic matter. Corpse and human being." Rank calls the note an "anthropomorphic 'intuition,'" but his remark reveals that the "anthropomorphism" here is no objection: "Who knows," he says, whether or not Nietzsche's intuition "will some day 'revalue' our sciences of nature" (OR 162n. 1).

But we must allow Rank to continue with his mad dash through Western philosophy. For as soon as there is mention of an Anaximandrian "indeterminate," ἄπειρον, and as soon as that "primal essence" has been identified as "the womb of all things," Rank is ready to move on quickly to the idealisms of Plato, Kant, and Schopenhauer. The further development of pre-Platonic thinking, as a proto-scientific thinking, takes Greek philosophy farther and farther away from its original inspiration—the question of the provenance, the *whence?* and *whither?* of human existence. It is Plato's genius, coupled with the genius of Aristophanes, who stops this drift. Freud had already shown how enamored a philosophic psychologist could be of Plato and Plato's comic genius, but Rank outdoes the master in enthusiasm for Plato's doctrine of Eros:

> Here for the first time the philosophical problem is grasped at its root, and therefore we need not be surprised that Plato, in presenting his doctrine, reverts to images that come quite close to the biological facts. He grasps *Eros* as the yearning for a lost condition [*die Sehnsucht nach einem verlorenen Zustand*—shades of Musil's *der andere Zustand*], indeed, more significantly, for a lost unity, and also in his famous metaphor of a primal essence cut into two halves that strive to be reunited. This is the clearest conscious approximation to the child's longing for reunification with the mother that has ever been achieved in the history of the human mind, and Freud was able to be the first to attach to it his theory of libido. [In a footnote Rank makes a general reference to Freud's *Beyond the Pleasure Principle*.] Indeed, taking up the impulse of Orphic-Dionysiac religion, Plato

> comes to the well-nigh ultimate biological insight that *Eros* is *the pain with which the daimon, who through his own mysterious guilt has plunged into birth, longs to be back in the Paradise of his own pure and proper being that has been lost.*
>
> Plato, who by virtue of the unusually intense intuition within him had grasped this yearning and brought it to representation, now—in accord with a relentless primordial repression—projects it onto the collective outer world. In this way he comes to recognize in all things their yearning for the suprasensible, their striving for completeness, their will to dissolve into the primal image of the "idea." (OR 165–66)

The price Plato has to pay for his insight into the human longing for reunification with the mother is his allergy to the sensible world. The allegory of the cave is not simply a womb fantasy, something that psychoanlysts prior to Rank had already noticed, but a depiction of the tendency of the erotic drive to sublimate. The cave allegory itself is "the supreme philosophical sublimation," one that lies behind every later idealism (OR 167). With Aristotle, philosophy begins its long reaction to the Platonic synthesis, a reaction that goes in the direction of "logical-dialectical speculation," along myriad "twisted paths of repression and intellectual displacements" (ibid.). Only with Schopenhauer and the underground tradition of Vedic mysticism is the original Platonic insight regained. The egoism of Descartes and Kant, and especially the "Titanic intellectual achievement" of the latter, as "the most inflexible ethician" in the history of repressive philosophy (OR 128), along with "the hypertrophic ego-system of Fichte" (R 170), receive only brief mention from Rank. By reducing Kant's thing-in-itself to its human form, thus liberating it from "transcendental enchantment" (*Verhexung*), Schopenhauer leads the way to Nietzsche's notion of will to power, which in turn enables the psychoanalytic rediscovery of an "unconsciously efficacious primal libido" (ibid.).

Yet Rank's sprint through the history of Western thought does not end here. Strangely, he now returns to Plato's and Xenophon's Socrates, though not recognizing how indebted every account of Socrates remains to Plato's Dialogues. This is doubtless consistent with his and Freud's conflation of Aristophanes and Plato in the latter's *Symposium*, where, after all, "Aristophanes" is a figure of Plato's imagination. Rank in effect proclaims the Socrates who adopts the Delphic command, "Know thyself," to be the ancient instigator of psychoanalysis. Indeed, the final words of Rank's book invoke Freud's "talking cure" and take Socrates—the midwife's son who only spoke, never wrote—to be Freud's forerunner. What is oddest about his celebration of Socrates is that Rank fully accepts Nietzsche's critique of "Socratism" in *The Birth of Tragedy* and his analysis of the "decadent" Socrates in *Twilight of the Idols*. Equally as odd is the fact that he does not say a word about Nietzsche's positive appreciation of "the erotic Socrates" or "the music-practicing Socrates," an appreciation that would have bolstered Rank's own admiration of Socrates. Rank recognizes that Socrates is Nietzsche's opponent; indeed, he speaks of "Nietzsche's inimitable and sharp-sighted psychoanalysis of his arch-enemy" (OR 171). However, if in Rank's view Socrates is the ancient instigator of psychoanalytic self-knowledge, Nietzsche himself is well-nigh a member of the psychoanalytic *Ring*. Yet Rank seems to have no sense of Nietzsche's suspicions concerning the sort of self-knowledge that Freud himself identified as deriving from "our God, Λόγος" (GW 14:378). He has no sense of what the third treatise of the *Genealogy* calls the genealogist's self-vivisection, his being "a nutcracker of the soul," one who when he exhausts himself by poking and prodding his own life runs the risk of making life *less* worthy of living; he has no sense of the ascetic ideal that in Nietzsche's view underlies all science, including the science of psychology. Finally, unlike Nietzsche, Rank has no sense of the "mixed form" that is Platonic Dialogue, no sense of how demanding and complex the Dialogues are. To say nothing of all the other texts he ignores in his chapter on "philosophical speculation."

Two chapters later, however, in the final pages of his book (on "therapeutic efficacy"), Rank returns to the problem of "Socratism." He now expresses his faith in therapy, but it is the faith that therapy can achieve the normal, shared unhappiness of humankind, the faith that Freud confesses at the end of *Studies on Hysteria* (GW 1:312), "to transform hysteric misery into common unhappiness," *hysterisches Elend in gemeines Unglück zu verwandeln*. Rank writes: "We must be especially on guard not to fall prey to the 'Socratism' that Nietzsche rightly criticizes, a danger that Socrates himself escaped ultimately by violent means" (OR 198). Socrates's death, somewhere between execution by the state and suicide, is presumably what Rank means. The profound unconscious cannot be changed; neither birth trauma nor the longing to return to the mother's womb can be expunged. "The only thing that we psychoanalysts can achieve is an *altered relation of the ego to the unconscious*" (ibid.). This is the true *Hebammekunst*, the proper art of Socratic midwifery.

•

Allow me a brief *coda* on Freud's critique of his erstwhile disciple's daring work. A thorough account would require that we study Freud's critique of Rank's book in both *Inhibition, Symptom, and Anxiety* and *The New Series of Introductory Lectures on Psychoanalysis*, yet that would necessitate an investigation all its own. Allow me to say simply that Freud's critique seems to me to be reasoned and sober, far less strident than the literature on the split between Freud and Rank would lead us to believe. Freud merely observes that Rank fails to notice that whereas only mammals give birth in the manner Rank depicts, anxiety itself is arguably common to many other forms of animal life. In other words, life itself, which constantly confronts dangers, seems to spawn anxiety, and not merely in mammals (GW 14:165). Birth is certainly a dangerous moment for the human fetus, Freud concedes, but in and of itself birth "has no psychic content" (GW 14:166). Tacitly denied here is Rank's claim that birth as such is the origin of memory and that memories of gestation and birth trauma are genuine reminiscences rather than fantasies. Tactile sensations may in some way be retained by the newborn, but we have no direct evidence of this somatic memory—certainly not of the experience that Rank imagines the newborn to be having. And if later the child is afraid of the dark and the stillness and solitude of the night, whereas it ought to be delighted by this presumed return to the conditions prevailing in the mother's womb, no invocation of Paradise, whether lost or regained, can resolve the contradiction. Thus there is much in Rank's thesis that seems forced and far-fetched. In general, Freud concludes, it is not as though life begins with an overwhelming experience of anxiety that later abates; rather, the child's capacity for anxiety seems to develop along with its other aptitudes. Among the instances of anxiety Freud invokes, the most important is the child's anxiety over the mother's disappearance—for example, when a stranger comes to "baby sit" or the child is taken to daycare. In other words, anxiety arises when the mother becomes unavailable, and the child's recognition of her absence (recall the case of little Ernst, pulling strings) takes some time to develop. It is not a mere reinstantiation of birth anxiety (GW 14:168–69). As for Paradise itself, "we should not forget that during intrauterine existence the mother was not an object, and that during this period there were no objects at all" (GW 14:170).

Freud now proceeds to those later phases of child development in which anxiety may arise, the enmity and jealousy felt toward the father, the internalized threats made by the superego, especially the threat that one will lose the love and approval of one's parents, and so on. These phases of development and instances of anxiety are familiar to us by this time, and so there is no particular need to follow Freud there.

One word more, this time from Rank's closest ally, Sándor Ferenczi. Ferenczi objects—mildly—to Rank's theory of the birth trauma in a way that reminds one of Ferenczi's own account of the ambivalence of sexual intercourse, either as a partly successful (albeit merely symbolic) restoration of existence in the womb or as a hallucinatory process driven by the destruction-and-death drives. To Rank's own principal vacillation, namely, that between unpleasureful birth *trauma* and pleasureful *intrauterine existence* in transference, Ferenczi responds, not in *Thalassa* but in a 1925 essay on psychoanalytic technique, with the following:

> In any case it was to his [Rank's] credit that he pointed to the unconscious *birth* fantasy, along with the fantasy of *existence in the womb,* both of which required our attention. Whether it is, as Rank believes, merely a matter of reminiscences of "the trauma of birth," or, as I am inclined to believe, a matter of a phantasmatic *regression from the Oedipus conflict to an experience of birth that has fortunately been overcome and is therefore less likely to provoke unpleasure,* future research will have to say. (2:181, Ferenczi's emphasis)

Here it seems that Ferenczi reverts to a more strictly Freudian approach to birth trauma, which regards the Oedipus Complex as a more compelling form of unpleasure than the trauma of birth. The threatening father, even if only in the form of an archaic avatar, haunts human development more than the mother who ostensibly abandons us over and over again to our solitary life. Even more noteworthy here is Ferenczi's inclination toward the more pleasureful fantasy of having overcome the trauma of birth, the pleasure taken in sexual intercourse, as a "festival of memory," *Erinnerungsfest* (2:352–53). Yet all three, Freud, Ferenczi, and Rank, would agree that if life is in need of *fiesta* that is because it can be and often is cruel. Whether all its cudgelings can be traced back to the ordeal of birth, two of the three are given to doubt.

If all human beings suffer the cruelty of birth, it remains the case that the effects of such generalized cruelty differ widely. Some manage to live a life in which tenderness plays a major role; others find life more difficult to bear, and some of them respond by lashing out. Some of these latter are then brought to justice, as we say. And some of them—even in our own time—find that the cruelty they have unleashed on others will reap for them the reward of an institutionalized and sovereignly sanctioned cruelty, a deadly retribution that staunchly denies its own cruelty. It is to such cruelties, overt and covert, and to the history of the blood flow that such cruelties have founded and sustained up to the present that we must now turn.

Chapter Eight

The Nervous System of a Specter

> It is strange that we, who are capable of so much suffering, should inflict so much suffering.
>
> —Virginia Woolf, *The Waves*

"CRUEL AND UNUSUAL PUNISHMENT." Abjured both in the 1689 English Bill of Rights and the Eighth Amendment to the Constitution of the United States in 1791. Yet tomorrow's unusual is today's usual. The history of cruelty, one can always hope, is one of amelioration. The outermost point of such a history, one can always hope, would take us to the neighborhood of Kant's eternal peace. Or would the history of cruelty be better understood as the transition from bloodshed to a more "psychological" form of cruelty, perhaps best expressed by the German word *Grausamkeit*? Such a history of cruelty is the focus of a two-year seminar conducted by Jacques Derrida in Paris during the years 1999–2001.[1]

•

1 I will organize my discussion of Derrida's seminar by following each numbered session (there are eleven of them during the first year and ten of them in the second). Only after a direct quotation will I refer to the volume and page of the French edition. The English translation of the two volumes, by Peggy Kamuf and Elizabeth Rottenberg, was published by the University of Chicago Press in 2014 and 2017. Because I worked on Derrida's seminars before the English translation appeared, my version sometimes varies from it. Only where matters are controversial will I mention the differences. As always, I am full of admiration and gratitude when it comes to Derrida's translators. So will every other English-language reader of the volumes be—grateful and admiring. I will not cite the pages of the English translation only because, very helpfully, the pages of the French edition are shown in the side margins of the Chicago volumes.

For Derrida, the death penalty is the prime instance of cruelty in our cruel history. He is not unaware of the cruelties of war and crime, and not unsympathetic to the victims of war and crime. Yet the premeditated cruelty of the death penalty is in his view the cruelest of crimes.

1. Is the death penalty what is proper to the human being *as* human? Is it *le propre de l'homme*? (1:23). This question recurs throughout the two volumes.[2] It seems preposterous. Surely some more humane practice or quality would characterize humanity in its own self-estimation? What suggests that the question is not so preposterous is the fact that no philosopher, *as* philosopher, has spoken out against the death penalty. At least, in every case that we can bring to mind, the philosopher has confirmed the death penalty as the essential, exceptional mark of sovereign power, that is, the power exercised by "the alliance of religion and the state" (1:48). Philosophers dependably come down on the side of despotism—if indeed Melville is right to claim "how efficacious, in all despotic governments, it is for the throne and altar to go hand-in-hand."[3] Derrida would amend Melville's claim only by including the governments of every sovereign nation, whether "despotic" or not. The essence of sovereign political power, formulated always in terms of theologico-political principles, as Carl Schmitt insists, expresses itself preeminently in the exclusive right to pronounce and execute the death sentence or to grant pardon. The philosopher who dominates both volumes of Derrida's seminar, Kant, will insist that the very dignity of the human being, that is, what is most proper to the human being and estimable about it, is the right to be punished for wrongdoing. And to be punished, if need be, mortally, at the crack of dawn.

Why at dawn? Derrida stresses throughout the seminar—against Foucault's suggestion that in modernity punishment has become less spectacular and less conspicuous—the theatricality and spectrality of the death penalty. The specular and spectacular character of executions is vital to sovereignty; the ritual is always carefully controlled, as in the case of all sacrificial rites. And there is always an audience for the rite—the rite and the right—of execution. When the rite is botched, when the death machines falter, the state trembles.

Derrida cites four cases at the outset and at the end of his two-year seminar, four cases that demonstrate the theologico-political nature of the

---

2 For example, at 1:33, 149, 268, 315, 322, and 2:202, 283, and elsewhere.

3 Herman Melville, *White-Jacket; or The World in a Man-of-War*, ed. Harrison Hayford et al. (Evanston and Chicago: Northwestern University Press and The Newberry Library, 1970), 156.

death penalty: Socrates, condemned for having subverted the gods of the polis and for having seduced the youth in the direction of such subversion; Jesus, dangerous to both the Roman governor and the local priests; El Hallâj, condemned for his mysticism and for his purported insights into the truth of Islam; and Joan of Arc, executed for her military acumen, her sex, and her visions of God. Each of these victims claims special insight into matters of religion, and each runs afoul of the established political and ecclesiastical orders. Socrates's invocation of his tutelary spirit, his δαίμων, during his defense is enough to transform his punishment from banishment to death. Yet the death penalty is older than Socrates. Soon after the commandment "Thou shalt not kill" is delivered to the Jewish people, the people are informed of an entire list of crimes that are punishable by death. Thou shalt not kill, unless. . . . Derrida cites (in two different translations) the list of sins or crimes punishable by death in Exodus XX, 1–17, as well as the sundry formulations of the law of the talion in Leviticus 24:15–22, Exodus 21:23–25, and Deuteronomy 19:21. No wonder the Israelites are terrified by Yahweh's "sinister message" (1:45). That message is as old as Cain's sacrifice of Abel and the ominous blood requirement that lies behind it.

Whereas philosophers have always rallied to the cause of the death penalty, many figures in the history of literature have spoken out against it. Even a writer such as Jean Genet, who in his novels celebrates the executions of lovers and relates with relish his own desire for funereal pomp, never speaks out on behalf of The Law. Among the writers Derrida mentions, Percy Bysshe Shelley, Victor Hugo, and Albert Camus, the latter two will dominate many sessions of the two-year seminar. Hugo's wit and eloquence and Camus's passionate yet sober portrayal of death by guillotine offer the brightest—or the darkest—lights of the seminar. Literature itself and as such, Derrida dares to say, is written on the winding sheet or shroud that wraps the corpse; in Joyce's memorable phrase, literature is composed upon the cerements of the grave. Sometimes it seems as though literature is called upon to mourn what philosophy has wrought.

This leads Derrida to the odd juxtaposition of two Johns, Jean Genet and John the Evangelist at XX, 10–18, and to the bizarre story of Mary Magdalene at the tomb of the resurrected Christ. *Noli me tangere!* cries the specter, when Mary approaches it. The reason proffered is strange: the resurrected Christ declares that he has not yet ascended to his Father. It is as though, unimaginably, Mary could touch the specter after it has ascended. In what state, then, is the executed Christ's glorified body? Is it corpse or host? Blood or wine? Literature will always be fascinated by such questions, whereas philosophers and theologians will tremble before them and recoil from them.[4] Yet even as they tremble, philosophers and theologians from Aquinas down to the present will speak out in favor of the death penalty, as though taking the part of the Father rather than that of the Son. Although a recent pope will confess publicly the past "faults" of the Church, he will not include the Church's refusal to condemn the death penalty.[5] At all events, among Derrida's questions the following is not a minor one: Why do so many important *writers* dedicate themselves to abolition, whereas the most important *philosophers* up to the present support the death penalty?

Another feature of the seminar, one that remains constant, is the special role of the United States of America in preserving and practicing with vigor the death penalty. In this, to repeat, the USA aligns itself with other nations in the world that it regards as its enemies: China, Iraq, Iran, North Korea, and others. The 1972 declaration by the Supreme Court, in a five to four decision, that the death penalty is "cruel and unusual punishment," is reversed in 1976, again by a five to four decision, because of the innovation of lethal injection preceded by anesthesia. The argument is that if the condemned is sedated to unconsciousness, nothing cruel or unusual can touch him or her. Except death, one might object. The innovation of sedation reverses a long tradition that insists on the clear-mindedness of the condemned at the instant of execution; just as suicide is not permitted, so must, at least traditionally, the condemned die in full lucidity. It is as though the condemned criminal is to be granted the special privilege of carrying over from this world into the next the greatest gift of spirit, namely, full consciousness of self. Or, alternatively, as though the executioners desire that the pain of an ignominious death endure as the criminal crosses the threshold. In the case of lethal injection preceded by sedation, the principle of lucidity is

---

4 Nicholas Royle discusses insightfully the uncanny "spectrality of Christ" in terms of Derrida's analysis in *Specters of Marx*; see Royle, *The Uncanny*, 285–86.

5 In 2015 and 2016 Pope Franciscus published a letter and delivered an address demanding that the death penalty be abolished worldwide, no matter how grave the crime of the offender. He claimed that John Paul II, to whom Derrida is referring, had already demanded such an abolition. Michael Naas, who first informed me of these developments, commented that Franciscus's "is a very strong statement and one that leaves little wiggle room for governments, somewhat unusual for popes." Luckily, the United States is predominantly Protestant in those states that particularly relish the death penalty; similarly, most of the other countries in which the death penalty is actively administered, countries that the USA otherwise takes to be its barbaric enemies, lie outside the reach of Christendom. "Wiggle room," therefore, is unfortunately guaranteed.

revoked or at least revised. Derrida remains fascinated by this "great technological refinement in cruelty or barbarity" (1:73), which seems to conflate execution with euthanasia, and he returns again and again in the seminar to the question of cruelty—and the apparent elimination of cruelty by grace of anesthesia.

2. Does anesthesia successfully counter the charge of cruelty? Does it herald the disappearance of cruelty? Or could it be that the age of cruelty continues—albeit with a very important alteration? The word *cruelty* comes from *cruor*, "I bleed," so that the history of cruelty up to now has been the history of bloodshed. Yet if death is delivered in a way that avoids the horror of bloodshed, does that portend the end of cruelty? Derrida will select another word for cruelty both here and in his July 2000 address to the Estates General of Psychoanalysis in Paris, namely, the German word *Grausamkeit*. One of the historical transformations that Derrida sees in the tide of globalization, better, *mondialisation*, involves the transformation of cruelty as bloodshed to cruelty as *Grausamkeit*. That word occupies many pages of the Grimm Brothers dictionary (my own notes on their entry occupy twenty-five pages of single-space type, and I will comment on Grimm in the following chapter), so that it is not easy to say what lies behind Derrida's choice. It surely has to do with a more "psychological" kind of cruelty, one that has to do with the covert pleasures derived from letting suffering occur or actively causing it—suffering involving an other or oneself. In his characterization of "Goneril" (not Lear's daughter, although clearly a distant relative of hers) in *The Confidence-Man*, Herman Melville remarks: "Those who thought they best knew her, often wondered what happiness such a being could take in life, not considering the happiness which is to be had by some natures in the very easy way of simply causing pain to those around them."[6] That is the sort of *Grausamkeit* that Derrida sees in the apparent amelioration of cruelty in the successive modes of delivery of the death penalty. He discusses at length Robert Badinter's book *Execution*, admiring that jurist's passionate condemnation of the death penalty, yet noting how much of the book's argumentation, centered on the value of the "humane," might well serve the cause of the proponents of the death penalty by lethal injection.[7] What disquiets Derrida above all, to repeat, is the subterfuge by which anesthetization seems to transform the death penalty into euthanasia.

6 Herman Melville, *The Confidence-Man: His Masquerade*, ed. Harrison Hayford et al. (Evanston and Chicago: Northwestern University and The Newberry Library, 1984), 61.

7 Robert Badinter, *Exécution* (Paris: Grasset, 1973; Livre de Poche, 1976).

Cruelty may appear to be in abeyance, and the hangman can now claim to be practicing an altruistic profession: instead of operating "the noose" or "the widow" or "Sparky Charlie" or the gas chamber, the hangman now wields a syringe. He resembles no one so much as Nurse Ratchett.

3. Once again it is a question of anesthesia as a false form of euthanasia, the practice of sedation followed by lethal injection, now sometimes labeled as a "pain killer." Derrida offers a disturbing statistical analysis of executions in the United States after 1976, discussing the background role of the Civil War and its continuing effect, through Reconstruction, on the sentencing of poor black males; he makes special mention of the state of Texas, where during the years 1976 to *circa* 1999 some 198 of the 597 executions in the USA occurred. That state was governed for many years by George W. Bush, who holds the record for refusals to declare an exception—120 death sentences and not a single commutation. Readers may recall that Bush's "favorite philosopher" was Jesus. Such is life and death and religiosity in these United States.

One of the most important recurring themes of Derrida's seminar is the equivocal role of Christianity and the Christian churches with regard to the death penalty. For every Sister Helen Prejean there are legion George W. Bush's. Derrida repeats many times the thesis of Albert Camus, to the effect that only a thoroughly secularized society will ever see the abolition of the death penalty. In this respect it is telling that in his discussions of globalization Derrida refers to the phenomenon as *mondialisation*. The reason, he says, is that one must keep in mind the Christian sense of *le monde*, so that the economic hegemony of the USA is also clearly understood to be a religious hegemony. And in "God's own country," as Freud ironically touted the nation, one finds perhaps the most perfervid proponents of the death penalty. As Derrida later notes, they are almost always—at least when it comes to the topic of abortion—spokespersons for the right to life. Right-to-lifers are almost invariably right-to-executioners. When the Christian points to the cross of Christ on the wall, one is not sure whether the intention is to save a fetus or kill a malefactor.

Another equally disquieting aspect of Derrida's discussion is the relation of *war* to the sovereign exception, that is, the exceptionality of the right to take or grant life. As Freud notes in his two essays on war, the state reserves for itself the right to send its citizens off to perform atrocities that at home would cost them their lives. Given the prevalence of violence in the relations of nation-states, perhaps today more than ever, the (possible) abolition of the death penalty seems to be out of step. Derrida sometimes seems to be comparing—as David Wills and Elisabeth Weber have recently done in very powerful ways[8]—death by drone to death by lethal injection. What sort of exceptionalism does each act claim for itself as its justification?

Finally, returning to the theme of humane behavior, as opposed to cruelty, Derrida notes that Beccaria's motivation in opposing the death penalty and proposing instead life imprisonment is not what the enlightened may imagine: his argument is that death for the condemned comes too quickly, and that life imprisonment is a more grueling—hence more cruel—punishment for malefactors (1:142–43; see also 2:82). This leads Derrida to ask again about the meaning (*sens*) of cruelty whether with or without (*sans*) blood (*sang*). In the homophony of the *sans sang* he hears the refrain of a less apparent yet more profound cruelty, the radical evil of "suffering inflicted in order to make someone suffer" (1:145). To say that evil is radical, however, is also to accept that its roots are hidden.

4. The fourth hour is devoted to the extraordinarily eloquent and powerful abolitionist texts of Victor Hugo.[9] For any reader like me, whose knowledge of Hugo goes as far as the phrase *ceci tuera cela*, Derrida's account of Hugo is truly stirring. Again Derrida notes the role of literature and its winding sheets of text devoted to the abolitionist cause. As for Hugo, he is, says Derrida, a prototype of deconstruction. And yet, because he is profoundly Christian, there is something equivocal about his gesture toward the crucifix. One cannot be sure whether *le for intérieur de l'homme*, when making such a gesture, will decide for mercy or for the law of the talion. Derrida compares and contrasts Hugo with Maurice Blanchot, especially Blanchot's admiration of the absolute sovereignty of Sade, which is a sovereignty of madness and cruelty. If one emphasizes death as the impossibility of dying, death as unending *attente*, what can one say of the death penalty, where the waiting comes to an end, indeed, a predetermined end? And if so many writers *and* thinkers stress the *sacrificial* nature of death—Derrida cites Kant, Hegel, Bataille, and Blanchot—what is the relation of execution to sacrifice? Derrida has no ready answer to the questions he poses to Blanchot, and they return to haunt his seminar.

---

8 For the continuity of the history of bloodshed in our time, see Elisabeth Weber, "Ages of Cruelty," in *Mosaic* 48, no. 2 (2015): 1–27, and David Wills, "Drone Penalty," in *SubStance* 43, no. 2 (2014): 174–92. An expanded version of the latter will appear in Wills's *Killing Times: The Temporal Technology of the Death Penalty* (New York: Fordham University Press, forthcoming).

9 Victor Hugo, *Écrits sur la peine de mort*, ed. Raymond Jean (Arles: Actes Sud, 1992).

5. Kant's *Metaphysics of Morals* is now introduced. It will dominate the entire second year of the seminar. Above all, it is Kant's insistence that the law of the talion, "an eye for an eye, a tooth for a tooth, a life for a life," is nothing less than the categorical imperative itself and as such that strikes Derrida. He is in awe of Kant's transcendental argumentation, his *principled* support of the death penalty. Yet what undercuts the transcendental argumentation, as always in Kant, is the absurdity and often perversity of his empirical examples. Kant's "extraordinary rationality" is counterbalanced by the "uselessness" and "inanity" of his logic when it comes to cases. Kant speaks out for the *homo noumenon*, whose dignity and worth are said to soar far beyond the worth of mere life. For the sake of that transcendent dignity, the creature who oscillates between beast and angel sometimes has to be put to death. Derrida does not cite Robert Musil's *Der Mann ohne Eigenschaften*, as I will once again in the next chapter, but every reader of that novel will recall the way in which all the arguments in favor of the death penalty for the psychopathic killer Moosbrugger conform perfectly to the aberrant reasoning of Moosbrugger's own madness. Although Derrida does not go so far, he comes very close to saying what I take to be clearly the case: *pace* every Kantian who ever wrote, Kant is not interested in the human being as an end in itself; he is interested in the dignity and worth that the human being most often fails to attain, the respect that he most often does not merit. Nor, as we will see, is Kant interested preeminently in freedom; he is interested in freedom as the necessary condition for inflicting punishment. He is therefore interested preeminently in imputability and accountability, that is, the rational basis for declaring culpability. Hence Nietzsche's and Adorno's sense that (in Nietzsche's words) Kantian morality "reeks of cruelty."[10]

One of the most bizarre of Kant's empirical examples or practical applications with regard to the death penalty is his insistence that a mother who has killed her illegitimate infant should *not* be condemned to death. For the

10 For Nietzsche's "reeks of cruelty," see KSW 5:300; on Adorno, see the editorial note at PM 2:277n. 2. As far as I can see, it is not the *Minima moralia* that Derrida is (or ought to be) referring to, but *Negative Dialektik*. In the third part of that work, "Models," in the chapter titled "Freedom: Toward a *Metakritik* of Practical Reason," Adorno criticizes Kant's insistence on "consistency," a tendency that causes him to reduce "the multiplicity of the nonidentical." Kant's moral philosophy remains "antinomial," argues Adorno, and he (Kant) can conceive of *freedom* in no other way than "suppression," *Unterdrückung*. "Every concretization of morality in Kant bears repressive traits," *Sämtliche Konkretisierungen der Moral tragen bei Kant repressive Züge*. See T. W. Adorno, *Negative Dialektik* (Frankfurt: Suhrkamp, 2000), 253. I am grateful to Gerhard Richter of Brown University for the reference.

infant ought not to have existed in the first place: the bastard is not a recognized member of the community and the state, so that the woman is merely correcting her error and erasing the cause of her shame and the community's embarrassment. It is as though, *per impossibile,* Kant has been contemplating the fate of Faust's Gretchen. For in the final scene of *Faust I,* as also in the *Urfaust,* Goethe places Gretchen in a dungeon, imprisoned because (unless her madness deceives her) she has drowned her and Faust's infant in a forest pond. In the *Urfaust* her fate is clear: Mephistopheles declares, "She is judged," *Sie ist gerichtet.* In the later *Faust I,* a "voice from above" reverses Mephisto's claim on her soul: *Sie ist gerettet,* "She is saved," cries the voice. She is saved so that in the famous final scene of *Faust II* she can engineer Faust's salvation. In any case, even if we set the case of Gretchen aside, it remains difficult to know what Kant is thinking about with this example of his, or precisely how his thinking twists and turns when it comes to certain infanticides. To be sure, Derrida's point in reporting this exception to the rule in Kant is not to propose the death penalty for the mother; it is to show how the claims of state sovereignty and a morality backed by the churches are able to concoct the contorted logic of punishment. One can readily imagine a host of right-wing politicians in the United States affirming Kant's logic, at least initially, although in the end they would surely see reason and insist on condemning the mother to death.

Another of Kant's moments of manic or maniac morality comes when he insists that if an island nation were devastated by a tsunami, such that the nation is destroyed and all the surviving inhabitants are forced to abandon it, the final act of the last survivors would have to be that they summarily execute any condemned criminals who are still alive. Only then may the *honnêtes gens* flee to safety.

6. It is difficult to summarize Derrida's reading of Nietzsche's *Genealogy of Morals* (treatises 2 and 3) undertaken during the sixth session. I take that reading to be one of the highlights of the two-year seminar. Derrida begins with the opening of Nietzsche's third treatise, on the relation of Wagner's *Gesamtkunstwerk* to the ascetic ideal; only then does he turn to the second treatise and its treatment of cruelty in relation to the formation of human memory. Derrida's treatment is highly dramatic. He opens the sixth session with a *dedascalie* or stage direction to himself: *"Very slowly."* Why the theatrics? Derrida adduces a new reason to the former one, which is that the death penalty itself is traditionally—and, to repeat, down to the present day—highly theatrical, a spectacle. The new reason is that Derrida fears that a seminar on the death penalty, taught and taken by persons who are quite unlikely ever to

be victims of the death penalty, may not achieve the level of seriousness and intensity it deserves. For most of us, capital punishment is not "cruelly menacing," as it is for someone on Death Row (1:199). It is the cool "disinterestedness" of Kantian pure reason, which insists on the justice of the death penalty, inasmuch as the law of the talion has the force of a categorical imperative, that disquiets Derrida: the one who has killed perhaps in the heat of passion must now be killed coolly, and not because of the call for vengeance, nor for any utility or advantage or "interest" of society, but solely because of the coolly rational imperative of retributive justice.

Nietzsche, however, is the one who sees behind the putative Kantian "disinterestedness" something very much like "interest." Interestingly, it is initially an insight not into the Kantian metaphysics of morals but into Kantian aesthetics that enables Nietzsche to unmask the purported "disinterestedness" of reason. It is ultimately the matter of "life" interest and of the hostility to "life" of the purported disinterestedness of the categorical imperative that send Derrida to the third treatise, as though the death penalty had some connection with ascetic ideals even in art. Derrida cites section 11 of the third treatise, which deals with the implacable "interestedness" of "life." He cites only one part of one sentence, a sentence having to do with the species of life Nietzsche identifies as "the ascetic priest": "It must be a necessity of the first order that causes this species that is *hostile to life* to grow and flourish—[Derrida's quotation begins here:] it must be an *interest of life itself* that such a self-contradictory type not die out" (KSW 5:362–63; PM 1:204).

Derrida elaborates on this "internal contradiction" within life itself, to wit, the fact that life has an "interest" in preserving something that turns against life's own "interest," something that turns against its proper self. I believe it is fair to say that right from the start, and certainly by the mid-1970s, Derrida's primary focus with regard to Nietzsche's philosophy of "life" is this internal, infernal contradiction, namely, that "life," precisely as will to power, enables or allows those who are hostile to life—those whose will to power is impotence to power—to prevail and even to flourish. No doubt, we are here at the core of Derrida's thought of *autoimmunity*. In the death penalty seminar Derrida comments on this familiar yet troubling paradox in the following way: "One cannot allow a type of self-contradiction to die out. Life has an interest in preserving the ascetic precisely there where it, the ascetic type, consists in contradicting itself, that is to say, in leading a life that is hostile to itself" (204n. 3). This is what links *interest* to *cruelty*. It seems as though beauty—for here it is a question of the beautiful, as that which promises "happiness," Stendhal's *promesse de bonheur*—has to do not only with Eros but also with its eternal opponent, which Freud calls "the destruction-and-death drives." The contradiction between sensuality and *pudeur* feeds the ascetic ideal in all its cruel appearances—in religion, science, philosophy, art—and now law as well.

Naturally enough, Derrida's own question is what ascetic ideals mean with regard to the death penalty. For the moment, the only two clues are (1) the claims of "exception" in sovereignty or absolute power, and (2) "a logic of cruelty" that seems to bind capital punishment to the far-flung network of ascetic ideals that may prevail even in artistic practice. Derrida emphasizes, however, that the logic of cruelty may work for either or both sides of the controversy surrounding the death penalty.

In pursuit of the logic of cruelty, Derrida now turns to the *second* treatise of the *Genealogy*, " 'Guilt,' 'Bad Conscience,' and Related Matters." Nietzsche scarcely mentions the death penalty, inasmuch as the genealogy of punishment reveals the fatal outcome of most traditional punishments in any case. Derrida reads a large portion of section 3 of the second treatise, which insists on the need for inflicted *pain* to produce *memory*, which is to say, to produce the human animal. As the passage goes on—and Derrida cites it to the bitter end—we begin to find ourselves in the strange world of trauma as the *basis* of memory, the by now familiar yet utterly uncanny world of Kafka's "Penal Colony," in which the very inscription of the law, law memorialized in the flesh, requires excruciating pain.

Yet another aspect of inflicted pain draws Derrida's attention, an aspect that appears to take us to the heart of the "interest" in and of the death penalty. For pain is also an important part of the equation that seeks an *equivalence* for damages. Nietzsche is able to show how bizarre, how incredible, the confidence in such an equivalence is. It is the entire history of *Vergeltung*, "recompense," "restitution," "retribution," "requital," "indemnification," that captures Nietzsche's imagination and indignation, a history as old as prehistory and as current as the most recent execution. How can there be an equation or an economy of *Schaden und Schmerz*, of defaulted payment and inflicted pain, that is credible or creditable? The creditor, in German, is *ein Gläubiger*, a "believer." The creditor, as "believer," believes in the oldest forms of purchase, sale, exchange, commerce, and trade. And he believes in trading inflicted pain for defaulted payment (ZGM II, 4; KSA 5:298). Like all believers, however, the creditor is credulous, especially when he believes in the absurd equation of damages and degrees of inflicted pain. That is his "interest" in the affair of punishment. "The origin of the belief in equivalence," writes Derrida, "that is to say, in the penal code, the origin of our belief in the right to punish, the origin of the credit that we give or, in truth, that we think we have a right to give, is belief itself" (1:217). Such belief is always dogmatic and always credulous. As for "belief" itself, Derrida offers the following analysis, which might not please all the folks in the Bible Belt: "Belief—that is the strange state or the strange divided movement, somewhat hypnotic, in which I am no longer myself, in which I do not know what I know, do not do what I am doing; it is that divided movement in which I doubt the very thing I believe or that in which I believe. In short, to believe is not to believe; believing is not believing" (1:219).[11]

The result is quite broad in scope and profound in impact: "And the entire origin of religion, like that of society, culture, and of contract in general holds to this disbelief that lies at the heart of belief" (1:219–20). Such internal division or dissociation in all belief, which goes beyond skepticism, is a kind of gap or "schiz" in which belief is haunted by disbelief; its hypnotic state could be described as spectral, hallucinatory, or, in a word, "unconscious" (1:220). Such disbelief reemerges as the central theme of the third session of the seminar's second year. There Derrida cites Montaigne's essay "On Glory": "We are in some way—I know not how—double in ourselves, which causes us not to believe in what we believe." One wonders whether Twain's Pudd'nhead Wilson ("Faith is believing what you know ain't so") had the opportunity to read Montaigne. The merely apparently stable equivalence of damages and inflicted pain is therefore commodious—but utterly fictitious. It belongs to comedy. Recall that Shakespeare's "Merchant of Venice" is a comedy. Of sorts.

Yet the pound of flesh that the "believer" all the more desperately hopes to extract need not come from the body, which, as Portia and Shylock both point out, bleeds. It may come from the twenty-one grams of the unaccountable and incalculable soul. Retribution may be psychical and symbolic. The creditor may take intense pleasure—*Wohlgefühl,* Nietzsche calls it, a feeling of well-being—in causing the other to suffer incalculable psychic pain. This would be the origin of the theme of *Grausamkeit* that haunts Derrida's seminar over both of its two years. It is this psychological or even "spiritual" cruelty to which Nietzsche himself turns in the later sections of the second treatise. In section 22 he analyzes "the Executioner-God" of Christianity, an analysis that is crucial for Derrida's seminar, especially when it takes up Camus's thesis that only a secularized society, a society

---

11 Nicholas Royle points us once again to Derrida's *Specters of Marx* for more extensive remarks on "belief"; for the references, see Royle, *The Uncanny,* 180 and 291–92.

freed from the plague of the churches, will be able to abolish the death penalty. For the death penalty seems to be founded on and grounded in that "willful insanity of psychic cruelty," *Willens-Wahnsinn in der seelischen Grausamkeit*, that invents for its enemies a punishment beyond all hope of pardon (ZGM II, 22; KSA 5:332). At this point Derrida is reminded of Nietzsche's complaint, mentioned earlier, that Kant's categorical imperative "reeks of cruelty." And it is at this point that he recalls the psychoanalytic problem of *Bemächtigung* or *Bewältigung* (1:227), "empowering" and "overpowering," which is the problem taken up in the final chapter of the present book. It is the problem that in Derrida's view must occupy psychoanalysis from now on—if indeed it is to have a future at all.

The shift in Derrida's discussion in the direction of Freud and psychoanalysis will continue during the second year of the seminar, where Theodor Reik's response to questions concerning the death penalty will occupy many sessions. For the death penalty has to do with the *Grausamkeit* of the destruction-and-death drives and the "mixture of drives," *Triebmischung*, that causes the erotic to spin in the maelstrom of sadism-masochism. Particularly interesting in this respect is Derrida's positive use of Lacan's remarkable essay, "Kant with Sade," on the "rectification of ethics."[12] Yet Derrida reverts to Nietzsche once again in order to stress the "festive" nature of punishment: no public or private celebration is complete without some humiliation or annihilation of another—*cruelty* as "the great festival joy of prior humankind," "Grausamkeit *die grosse Festfreude der älteren Menschheit*" (ZGM II, 6; KSA 5:301). And the history of human culture as a history of blood? It is the history of "the waxing spiritualization and 'deification' of cruelty," *Vergeistigung und 'Vergöttlichung' der Grausamkeit* (ibid.). True, the "semiotics" of punishment, as Nietzsche himself calls it (KSA 5:317), will not allow us to reduce that history to some sort of definition or set of principles. Cruelty is inventive. Yet it is here, with the "spiritualization" of cruelty, that Derrida sees the "progress" one has made in the anesthetization of the death penalty, the transition from the bloodshed of the guillotine to the lullaby of lethal injection, a progress affirmed by both the practitioners and the opponents of capital punishment.

7. The question now is whether there can be an "economy" of the death penalty at all, that is, whether the supposed equivalence of debt and inflicted pain enables us to calculate what is at issue in the death penalty. What undercuts such calculation in every case, according to Derrida, is the fact that belief in one's own lack of cruelty, in one's perfect "disinterestedness," is invariably

12 Jacques Lacan, *Écrits* (Paris: Gallimard, 1966), 765.

subverted by an unwitting participation in myriad covert cruelties, exclusions, and persecutions. Derrida mentions, by way of parallel, the AIDS epidemic in Africa and the Far East and the high cost of Western pharmaceuticals. The Westerner conceals from himself the cruelty of which he is nonetheless aware—the unbelief that haunts and taunts belief—and gets on with his life. He sees well enough the cruelty of sweatshops in the production of cheap clothing and of drone strikes designed to protect natural gas pipelines—and he is relieved by his ostensibly rational assertion that it is a hard world out there. And yet concealed cruelty contaminates. It infiltrates all belief and plagues it. Always there is *une croyance sans croyance*, especially when one confronts *une cruauté sans cruauté* (1:238). And denial exacerbates the cruelty.

However, the subversion or contamination of death penalty rationality transpires also more directly. One of the most precarious "calculations" for proponents of the death penalty involves the distinction between condemnation for political as opposed to other sorts of crimes. Both Victor Hugo and Karl Marx, at the time of the Paris Commune and the post-Commune constitutional convention, find themselves caught up in such a calculation. As Marx clearly realizes, the Republic's abolition of the death penalty for political crimes has less to do with "enlightenment" than with the rise to supremacy of the bourgeoisie and of a certain contradictory Christianity. The same equivocal features of such calculation, Derrida argues, can be seen in the nineteenth-century debates in the United States surrounding the death penalty. The reader begins to realize that it is "calculative thinking" as such that runs into a blind alley, and the name of that *impasse* is *la peine de mort*.

8. "The mechanism falls like lightning, the head flies, the blood gushes, the man is no longer." Derrida reads this quotation twice (1:265), waiting a considerable time before he reveals the source—it is Dr. Guillotin himself who speaks so eloquently, even poetically, of his invention (1:304). The eighth session is devoted to the false homophony of *sang* and *sens*, with *sans* as the equivocal pivot. Blood flow with and without meaning, cruelty with and without blood flow. Dr. Guillotin is hailed as a "hero of euthanasia" (1:269). He is not such for Victor Hugo, however, whose texts against the death penalty occupy the remainder of the session, with support from Shelley's "The Triumph of Life," a poem familiar to Derrida since his "Living On: Border Lines."[13] And as though

13 "Living On: Border Lines," trans. James Hulbert, in *Deconstruction and Criticism* (New York: The Seabury Press, 1979); "Survivre," in Derrida, *Parages* (Paris: Galilée, 1986), 117–218.

willing to take a plunge, the seminar once again invokes the American hero of the death penalty, George W. Bush (1:297).

9. In the ninth session, Derrida reaches perhaps the most profound philosophical depth of his meditation on the death penalty, introduced by the disquieting question, "When to die, finally?" (1:299). The session works on the distinction between what it means to be condemned to die and to be condemned to death. All of us must die, each of us is condemned to die. Yet it is one thing for a man (Derrida taking himself as his example) to die in his own bed at age seventy-four (Derrida actually cites that age, as though knowing what he cannot possibly know) of "natural causes." What is intolerable for a human being is always double:

> The alternative is terrible, and it is infinite: I may deem it intolerable—and this is the case with the death penalty—to know that the hour of my death is fixed by others, by a third party, determined as occurring on such and such a day, at such and such an hour, down to the second, whereas if I am not condemned to death but am merely to die, such calculable knowledge is impossible. But, inversely, I may deem it intolerable that I do not know the date, the place, and the hour of my death, so that I may dream of appropriating such knowledge, of having it at my disposal by condemning myself to death, at least phantasmatically. This would grant me some calculable certainty, some sort of mastery, be it quasi-suicidal, over my death. (1:300)

Derrida risks the question as to whether the death penalty is the cruelest of tortures or the conferral of a privilege, to wit, the privilege of knowing, down to the date and the hour, when one will die. He does not mention in this context pseudo-Aeschylus's *Prometheus Bound*, but it seems relevant to his meditation here. For, as we saw back in chapter 3, when the Oceanides ask Prometheus whether he has offended Zeus in some graver way than by the theft of fire, Prometheus admits that he gave human beings the greatest of gifts, namely, the gift of blind hopes. Such is man, cultivating the land, sailing the sea, taming the beasts, subduing all the rest of nature, creating technologies, forging ahead and blind to his limitations. But how did the Titan plant such blind hopes in the human being? Answer: merely by eliminating foreknowledge of the day of one's death. For, prior to this, human beings were of a different sort of essence, knowing as they did the *when* of their demise. Only ignorance of the death-date, only blind hopes, could give them the drive to storm heaven and challenge the reign of Zeus. Yet Derrida's addition to the Prometheus story is that blind hopes also drive the human phantasm of being in control of one's own death, which phantasm is surely bound up with the death penalty. One can imagine Nurse Ratchett comforting her "patient" by saying in a soothing voice, "At least you will know the precise *when* of your dying, and now I will show you the *how*. This may pinch a little."

Or, to shift from Athens to Rome, and from Rome to Texas, one must wonder whether the power to condemn a human being to death derives from the divine burning bush of the biblical desert or from the unflappable, inflammable Bush of the governor's mansion? Violence in any case comes from *le Très Haut*, the infinite *hauteur* of religious-political power. One may joke about the tools wielded by such power, as I noted earlier, calling the guillotine "the Maiden" or "the Widow," and lethal injection "the Pain Killer" (1:305, 308), but such jokes are but droll blasphemy. Derrida recounts his own memories of Camus's "Galoufa," the dogcatcher of the Algerian villages, as the children of the village seek to rescue stray mutts from capture and certain death. Derrida also recounts the reaction of Camus's father, initially a strong supporter of the death penalty, after he witnesses—for the first and only time—an execution: he returns home, says not a word to his wife and family, and vomits away the entire day.

If one takes seriously Descartes's identification of the pineal gland as the seat of the soul, then what is at issue in death by guillotine is the question of the soul's severance from the body, the putative instantaneity of death, the absolute end of sensibility, and the cessation of time. For if the animal spirits cannot return to the pineal gland in order to report what has happened to the body truncated at the nape of the neck, there can ostensibly be no experience of pain. The only sensation of the criminal or victim, whose collar has been carefully tailored away in order to facilitate the work of the Widow, is "a refreshing wind gently blowing on the neck" (1:308). Such is Dr. Guillotin's description, which does invite one to wonder how he knows this. His description is challenged by two more recent pathologists who examine the fresh corpses of the guillotined. Camus cites their report at length in his text, and Derrida does not spare his students. The doctors observe the "stupefying contraction and fibrillation" of the entire musculature of the body, the continuous twisting of the intestines, the erratic (yet "fascinating") beating of the heart, the continued grimaces of the mouth; the eyes immobile, the pupils dilated, the eyes presumably and "happily" seeing nothing, even if they are still clear, not yet opalescent; these phenomena, observable in all the vital systems of the body, continue for many minutes after decapitation, sometimes hours, so that death is by no means immediate; the experience of the victim—insofar as the pathologists can speculate—is "horrific," so that guillotining is in their judgment "a murderous vivisection followed by a premature interment" (1:321).[14]

Leaving his students and now his readers stunned by this account, Derrida takes up Heidegger's treatment of death in *Sein und Zeit*, asking once again what the "proper" of humankind is (1:322). He asks: "Must one think death prior to the death penalty? Or is it rather the case that, paradoxically, one must take the death penalty as one's point of departure, the question of the death penalty being only apparently and indeed falsely circumscribed in order to pose the question of death in general?" (1:323). All the questions of *Aporias* would have to be raised again, says Derrida, including (1) the question as to whether there is an instant that cuts cleanly between life and death, (2) the question of "the calculating mastery" (1:324) that one presupposes to be at work in first-degree (premeditated) murder or suicide, but that in any case is unquestionably at work in capital punishment, and finally (3) the question of the "calculable credit" that we give to the word *death* when we invoke the death penalty—"there where it is indissociable from both murder and suicide" (1:325). One dreams of "deconstructing death" (1:326), Derrida concedes, and yet the vigilance that one exercises in such deconstruction may be no more than "a convulsive movement to have done with death" (1:327). At all events, in its analyses of both "natural death" and "death by execution," deconstruction must do without "the alibi of the Beyond" (1:327, 344). Dream and vigilance—these are two of the multiple "guardian angels" of deconstruction, and yet they are often more like crowing cocks and alarums than angels.

10. Derrida once again cites a homily by Pope John Paul II during the year 2000 confessing the Church's "faults of the past" and praying for forgiveness. Neither the homily nor the commission report that spurred it mentions the

---

14 Derrida cites Albert Camus, "Réflexions sur la guillotine," in Camus, *Essais*, ed. R. Quilliot and L. Faucon (Paris: Gallimard "Pléiade," 1992). Derrida does not cite Michel Tournier's fictional version of the last public guillotining in Paris, that of the German serial murderer Eugen Weidmann. The crowd assembles during the night, enjoying picnic lunches while waiting for the dawn. When day breaks, however, so does "the Grand Widow": its blade fouls, the prisoner squirms, the head remains attached, the blood-drenched assistants pull it by the ears and hair. "It is grotesque; it is intolerable," comments Tournier's narrator, Abel Tiffauges, who then follows the example of Camus's father. Whether in our own day lethal injection avoids or merely alters the horrors cited by Camus's pathologists remains a matter of—horrific—controversy. See Michel Tournier, *Le roi des aulnes* (Paris: Gallimard Folio, 1970), 164. I am grateful to Jonathan F. Krell for the reference.

Church's support of the death penalty from the early Middle Ages to the present, nor does it reflect on the malefic power that created Hell and populates it with the damned. Furthermore, death and the death penalty are at the heart of the story of the father and the father's only begotten son, such that the death penalty as such tolls *un certain glas de Dieu* (1:333).[15]

All too briefly, even tantalizingly, Derrida takes up Hannah Arendt's justification, in *Eichmann in Jerusalem*, of the hanging of Eichmann. Arendt argues that there is need of a judgment if the crime is to be at all acknowledged. Yet that such a judgment needs to terminate in the termination of a life Derrida calls *un réquisitoire fictif pour justifier la pendaison de Eichmann* (1:343). Oddly, even uncannily, those who respond to Arendt's book with the most intense vituperation would probably find their sole comfort in this *réquisitoire fictif*, and one wishes that Derrida had written at greater length about Arendt's effort at justification. Such a discussion would doubtless make Arendt's book more controversial than ever.

Derrida readily accepts Baudelaire's critique of Victor Hugo and of all opponents of the death penalty, his critique being that such opponents are merely trying to save their own necks. Yet why not admit that the desire to live is powerful? At this point, Derrida responds quite lucidly to what I have called the Promethean moment of the human essence—its lack of foreknowledge concerning its death. Derrida's weightiest complaint concerning the death penalty is this: it interrupts "the principle of indetermination" that defines the human being in the face of the to-come, *l'a-venir*; the death penalty imposes an "end to the incalculable *aléa*" of human life and of all life (1:347). The death penalty plays with the phantasm of putting an end to facticity and finitude as such. Here Derrida follows a number of leads suggested by Heidegger: (1) Heidegger's insistence on the *futurity* of existence, the *Zu-kunft* of Dasein, which routs every sort of calculable representation or manipulation of death; (2) Heidegger's reading of Anaximander's τίσις, traditionally understood as

15 For reasons that are unclear, the transcript of the course is oddly disrupted immediately after this moment (1:336–39). Yet these pages are important, for here Derrida cites Norman Mailer's extraordinary fiction/faction, *The Executioner's Song*, and he rehearses what he often called the "impossible sentence," the sentence that cannot be pronounced, namely, "We will see one another die." Not even Romeo and Juliet's *Liebestod* achieves such simultaneity. Pages 337–38 also contain a remarkable note on Camus's text concerning the self-justification of the murderer, a text reinforced by Camus's own classic work *L'Étranger*, which Derrida rereads after decades have passed, finding that the novel has lost none of its uncanny power.

"penalty." With regard to the first, Derrida comments on the phantasm that finitude can be averted or mastered. As paradoxical as it may seem,

> the death penalty, as the only example of a death whose instant is calculable by a machine or by several machines (not by some person, ultimately, as in murder, but by all sorts of machines: the law, the penal code, the anonymous third party, the calendar, the clock, the guillotine or some other apparatus), the machine of the death penalty deprives me of my proper finitude; it even exonerates me of my experience of finitude. The madness of the death penalty purports to put an end to finitude when it puts an end to a life in this calculable fashion. [Derrida adds this extemporaneous remark: "This is the infinite perversity—properly infinite and infinitizing—of the death penalty. This is the madness: putting an end to finitude."] Hence the seduction that it exercises on those who are fascinated by it, both those on the side of the condemning power and sometimes those on the side of the condemned. Fascinated by the power and by the calculation, fascinated by the end of finitude, fascinated, in sum, by this end to our anxiety in the face of the future, the end that is procured for us by the calculating machine. The calculative decision, by putting an end to life, seems paradoxically to put an end to finitude; it affirms its power over time, mastering the future, protecting us from the irruption of the other. It only *seems* to do so, I say, because such calculation, such mastery, such decidability remain phantasms. It would no doubt be possible to show that this is even the origin of phantasm in general.
>
> And perhaps of what is called *religion*. (1:348–49)

Derrida adds the uncanny remark that the phantasm of putting an end to finitude "is at work in us all the time," and that the calculative decision "embraces the dream of an infinitization and thus of an infinite survival assured by the very interruption" (1:349). The terrifying result of this thought is that each of us in some sense *desires* the death penalty for ourselves, dreaming that we can revert to the essence we used to be, the essence that knew the day of its death. And when Derrida says *we*,

> it means that in this dream we occupy, simultaneously or successively, all the positions of the dream, those of the judge or judges, the jury, the executioner or the assistants, and, to be sure, the position of the

> condemned, as well as of the witnesses, whether they are loved or hated. And it is the force of this effect of phantasmatic truth that will probably remain invincible, forever assuring us, alas, of a double survival—the survival of both the death penalty and the abolitionist protest. (1:350)

Such is the price we pay—and this is the second, the Anaximandrian point—for our having been *damned* or con*demn*ed by nature to die, as it were. At this point, Derrida reverts to the credulity of every belief in the equivalence of damages and calculated recompense. He offers a detailed analysis of Émile Benveniste's research into the complex sense of the words *ghilde, Geld,* and *Wergeld* in his *Vocabulary of Indo-European Institutions.*[16] Once again it is the question of *Vergeltung,* retribution, recompense, or ransom, having to do with the fantasy of declaring a value for a human life. The session ends by referring back to John Paul's neglect of the Church's support of the death penalty and its affirmation of eternal damnation. It appears that both the death penalty and eternal damnation will outlast the papacy, however, and Derrida wonders aloud "how one is to measure the time of the Son's agony" (1:363).

11. The first year of the seminar comes to a close by stating a series of paradoxes that will take an entire additional year to unravel. *Comment sur-vivre?* (1:365). How to survive, how to live-on, how to live beyond life—if there is no Beyond and if to live *is* to live-on? The condemned pays with his or her life, but what is the price of a life? What is the value of a life taken? Does the law of the talion define that value? Is there any rational calculus for such value? Does Kant's account of *das Ehrwürdige,* of honor, dignity, and respect, and of the human being as an end rather than a means, define that value? Derrida promises to spend part of the next year trying to show that Kant is an unwitting abolitionist, precisely because his conditions for a justified condemnation to death are virtually impossible. The crime committed against another is always equally a crime against oneself, says Kant, so that every execution, as Kant does not say, is in effect the suicide of the executioner. Montaigne writes of marching ahead toward one's fatal day, going out to meet it rather than waiting passively for it. Hélène Cixous, writing of her father's death in *Or,* eschews the expression "dying a natural death" and speaks instead of "dying of one's living" (1:374).

---

16 Derrida cites the chapter on "Gift and Exchange" in the first volume of Benveniste's *Vocabulaire des institutions indo-européennes* (Paris: Minuit, 1969), 74ff.

Yet the death penalty, even if it obfuscates itself as a pain killer, and even if it purports to eliminate finitude, remains a form of sacrifice, perhaps even a form of cannibalism. Nowhere in the seminar does Derrida invoke the *bouc émissaire,* the scapegoat that is omnipresent in ethnography and in studies of mythology and religion. Yet the shadow of a beaten and eaten daimon haunts the entire seminar. The closest he comes to a response to Réné Girard's *Violence and the Sacred* is a reminder concerning his own detailed discussion of the φαρμακός (note the sigma at the end of the word, replacing the nu) in "Plato's Pharmacy." Nothing is less certain even in our globalized world than that the desire for such sacrificial victims can be abolished. The principle of cannibalism expresses itself in the rhetorical question, "How to love a living being without being tempted to take it in?" He adds a word that his reading of Novalis may have given him: "Love and Eucharist" (1:380).

The first year of the seminar ends by recalling Camus's insistence that to put an end to the death penalty is to *mettre fin à l'Église* (1:381). Derrida's motive for recalling Camus's insistence on such an end is surely his own dream that the call for such violent sacrifices will also come to an end.

•

To analyze the death penalty, says Derrida at the outset of the second year of his seminar, is to examine "the nervous system of a specter" (2:22). The second year is dominated by three apparently very simple questions: (1) What is an act? (2) What is an age? (3) What is a desire? All three questions are directed toward the proponents of the death penalty. The first question takes up the distinction between crimes of premeditation and passion, and considers the nature of premeditated execution; the second poses the problem of maturity and of juvenile crime, but also the question of the execution of the mentally infirm or psychotic; the third asks whether the *desire* for murder can be proscribed or effectively curtailed. Above all, the question of desire wants to know what *presides over* such desire, whether among the condemned or among the presidents who refuse to pardon? The shadow of Prometheus is cast over the second year as well: "If there is one thing that is not given me to know and thus to calculate with absolute precision, it is the given moment of my death" (2:23).

An important source for the seminar is Theodor Reik's *The Need to Confess.*[17] Reik's thesis is that the need to confess will eventually obviate the need

---

17 Theodor Reik, *Le Besoin d'avouer. Psychanalyse du crime et du châtiment*, tr. S. Laroche and M. Giacometti (Paris: Payot, 1973).

for the death penalty. Presumably, if the need to confess becomes sufficiently endemic in the species, capital crimes will diminish and eventually disappear. If that seems phantasmatic, the thesis nonetheless calls for an investigation of "a logic of the unconscious or of the symptom" (2:29); in Derrida's view such an investigation will determine whether or not psychoanalysis has any real future.

With reference to his second question, that of age, Derrida's report concerning the execution of minors sixteen to eighteen years of age, or those with an estimated mental age of nine or ten, is profoundly disturbing, to say the least. Derrida refers to the bizarre arguments of the jurists who defend the death penalty as "kites," which in French are "flying deer," *cerfs volants*; but in the present case the soaring deer are expressions of the torpidity of mind that characterizes the self-proclaimed expert jurists or forensic psychologists, *les cerveaux lents*. However, questions concerning time, age, and maturity are obstreperous even for very agile minds, such as Freud's. It is in fact very difficult either to affirm or to deny Freud's insistence that the unconscious has no sense of time, no identifiable age, and no shared history in any of the usual senses of those words. Operating simultaneously within us at any given moment of our lives, Derrida affirms with Freud, are the infant and the dotard, the citizen of the twenty-first century and the Neanderthal (or at best Cro-Magnon); or, pushing back into deep time, a superior ape, a tiger, and a squirrel. Derrida's claim that all these creatures are alive and well within us at any given moment will seem exaggerated—except to those readers who have recently attended a faculty meeting or seen tweets by certain heads of state. Derrida's discussion turns quite naturally to the practice of the death penalty in a time of undeclared yet pervasive warfare and terrorism, a time of gang wars and death by drones (2:39–40; cf. 70). In such times, the *poena* ("penalty, punishment, pain") of the *peine de mort* is scarcely (*à peine*) thought, seldom a theme for reflection. Again Derrida raises the question of Anaximander's διδόναι . . . δίκην καὶ τίσιν, thought by Heidegger as the way in which beings grant one another order (*Fug*), and this by way of mutual "esteem" and "reck" (*ruoche*), in this way alone overcoming tragic "disorder" (*Unfug*, ἀδικία).[18]

2. Derrida raises the thematic question of the problematic calculus that seems to allow the proponents of the death penalty to weigh the pain of suffering and retribution against the guilt of the criminal. The principal difficulty in the

18 Martin Heidegger, "Der Spruch des Anaximander," in H 296–343; EGT 13–58. From the time of "Différance" onward, this essay of Heidegger's is of enormous importance to Derrida.

calculation is the infinite pain of the loss of life for a finite existence, or, to put it in terms of the dubious calculus, estimation of the punitive value of execution. To traverse all these aporias, says Derrida, is the categorical imperative of deconstruction. In the following pages he discusses Walter Benjamin's thesis on "the monopolization of violence" by the state, a thesis for which Benjamin receives a letter of congratulation from Carl Schmitt, and Kant's distinction between natural punishment (*poena naturalis*) and court-administered punishment (*poena forensis*). Whereas every criminal naturally suffers a loss of worth by committing a crime, damaging himself as much as his victim, it remains the obligation of the state to pronounce and execute juridical or forensic penalty. To repeat, Kant's *Metaphysik der Sitten* considers the penal code as a whole to be an instance of the categorical imperative. The dignity and value of human life lies in its *Strafbarkeit*, its susceptibility to pain and punishment. If one pushes this just a bit, then the end or purpose of a metaphysics of morals is not to demand respect for human beings, who after all are equivocal creatures, but to esteem human life above all other forms of life precisely because of its capacity to suffer and to inflict retributive punishment. Juridical punishment is therefore a supplement to natural punishment, and in both cases what is important is not the often entirely contemptible creature as such but *der Straf*.[19]

Kant's thesis concerning the *poena naturalis*, the self-degradation of the criminal, is challenged by the fact that the "great criminal," from Robin Hood to Bonnie and Clyde, has always been profoundly admired not only by other less renowned criminals but also by the sovereign authorities themselves. The criminal in the grand style, whereby grandeur is flaunted ignominy, is the φαρμακός, both exalted by and excluded from society at once, both admired and condemned, so that the relation of crime and punishment, as of violence and the law—for example, in Benjamin's *Kritik der Gewalt*—is equivocal in the extreme.

Derrida now develops most fully his thesis that the death penalty poses a challenge to Heidegger's existential phenomenology and its analysis of the death of Dasein. To be sure, Heidegger never discusses the death penalty as

19 Derrida's pages on Émile Benveniste's discussion of the relation of the language of *honoring* to that of *punishing* are quite gripping (2:84–85). Unfortunately, neither Benveniste nor Derrida ever mentions Hölderlin's reading of Kant in this respect. For Hölderlin sees quite clearly that punishment is the essence of Kant's understanding of law and even of human worth. Just as human freedom is for the sake of imputability, so human dignity and worth are grounded in the capacity to suffer punishment. I will take up Hölderlin's reading in the following chapter.

such.[20] In Derrida's view, the death penalty is nothing less than a *skandalon* for the existential analysis. For in the executions of the condemned the *when* of death is known precisely—even if there is no being-here, no Da-sein, but only a no-longer-Da-sein, to experience the *when* precisely when it takes place. Which it therefore never does. Thus the death penalty works by way of a kind of prestidigitation, and execution is the act of an illusionist. There *are* executions, of course, but they are *not* executable. It is as though execution were a kind of necrophilia, a manipulation of corpses, a playing with cadavers: *Dead Man Walking*, as it were. Echoing Lacan perhaps, Derrida speaks of "the monstrosity of *the* desire," of *la Chose,* that dominates both judge and hangman. Again he asks, what *is* desire? What is the desire of the death penalty advocate? Appeals to rationality reduce to drivel when such questions are posed seriously.

3. The third session is devoted to theater and presidency, the theater of the presidency, especially when it is a question of "the election of a decider," *élection d'un décideur* (2:88). (In our own time, when the "decider" is a flagrant xenophobe and a transparent narcissistic bully, the issue of the presidency and of the "presiding officer" has become more acute than ever. Ours is also a time when certain presiding officers of particular states are rushing executions because the lethal drugs they use are reaching their expiration date—presumably, beyond that date the drugs might inflict harmful side effects. Such are our times, our places, and our disgrace.) It is the theatricality of inflicted pain that disturbs Derrida, both the pain of the victims of crime and the pain of executed criminals, even if the death penalty itself seems mere shadow play, "a theater of postcards" (2:97). Derrida argues that Kant's thesis on "natural punishment" makes every execution an ignominious suicide of the executing agency, with the shame of execution thus surviving the death of the condemned one; again he refers to belief (as belief in the equivalence of crime and inflicted pain) in terms of a contaminating unbelief, citing once again Montaigne on "our being double within ourselves" (2:102; cf. 1:219). All spectation involves our believing without belief, whether at musical or dramatic performances, and perhaps even in our reading; but can there be a willing suspension of disbelief when we

20 It is not unreasonable to suppose, however, given many of his remarks during the 1930s, for example in the *Schwarze Hefte*, and even in the 1950s, for example his remarks on the "fallen" of World War I as "the accursed race," that Heidegger would be no exception to the general rule that philosophers *as* philosophers favor the death penalty. Yet cannot one dream of a different response if Heidegger is, as he claims, not a philosopher but a *thinker*? It is of course getting more and more difficult to dream the dream.

witness an execution? Not for Camus's father. Nor for Tournier's Abel Tiffauges, who scorns not the criminal but the "abject" Albert Lebrun, President of the Republic at the time of Eugen Weidmann's beheading, the President "who, sitting behind his monumental desk, free from all pressure, refuses to perform that small gesture that would stop the perpetration of legal assassination."[21]

It is true that we owe a debt (a death) to nature, so that the very idea of death includes the notions of debt, guilt, and condemnation within it. Heidegger too uses the notions of debt or guilt in *Being and Time* (sections 48 and 58), although he does not develop the idea of death as the payment of a debt. If George W. Bush, who presided over many deaths, forever incapable of that small gesture, had an idea of any sort, it might have been about the payment of a debt to society. As the "decider," however, he would have been allergic to the tendency in Freud and Reik to think the notion of an *unconscious* act. He would also have been allergic to the thought that the human being, even the murderous human being, is *weltbildend,* "world-shaping," as Heidegger says in his 1929–30 lecture course. By contrast, Derrida is inclined to think of each death, even that of the executed criminal, as "each time unique, the end of the world." Or, as he puts it here: "The end of the world, which sets the seal on death as my death, remains incommensurable" (2:119). "Incommensurable" means "intolerable," and "intolerable" means outside of all calculation and mastery: "The intolerable, the unthinkable, and thus the only thing worthy of being thought, the only thing that remains always to be thought, is not death, murder, or the death penalty; it is the end of the world, and the fact that this end remains always imminent" (2:120).

4. To love life; to love living; but to love a life that is *worth* living. Such loving, which hates the end of the world in each case, now moves to the center of Derrida's reflection. But what sort of life is *worth* living? For Kant, such worth or worthiness, as *Würde* and *Ehrwürdigkeit,* is valued incomparably more highly than life itself. For Kant, the worth and esteem of the moral law—and of the categorical imperative with which he identifies the death penalty—far exceed the worth of life as such, even if one might have thought that an appeal to human dignity might also be used to oppose execution. The point of Derrida's deconstruction of the death penalty, however, is not to redefine oppositional structures but to show how permeable and fluid these structures are. Thus deconstruction demonstrates the way in which Kant's distinction between *poena naturalis* and *poena forensis* begins to tremble: in a sense, every

21 Michel Tournier, *Le roi des aulnes*, 159.

verdict that condemns a rational creature to death amounts to an announcement of self-inflicted punishment by the punishing party. For in his *Metaphysik der Sitten* (at 332 of the *Akademieausgabe*) Kant writes, in the language of the Decalogue, "The unjustified ill that you inflict on another you inflict on yourself" (2:131). Respect for the law is ostensibly a disinterested interest of every rational creature. If reason is absolute, then judicial or forensic condemnation and punishment are but supplements to natural punishment. Respect for persons is therefore indirect, a mere byproduct of respect for the moral law as categorical. To this extent it is no exaggeration to say that *Strafbarkeit*, "punishability," comes first in the Kantian system. And just as there must be a "decider," so must there be a "punisher." That is why, for Kant, regicide is the most terrible of crimes—since the very definition of the sovereign is that his is the prerogative to punish. Hence he himself cannot be punished. The entire structure of forensic punishment, already fragile, crumbles if the king may be killed. For the king, at least in one of his two bodies, embodies the divine law of the talion and of all retaliation. Again Derrida cites Leviticus 24:15–22, Exodus 21:23–25, and Deuteronomy 19:21, along with several passages from the Qur'an. And if Levinas finds the Bible to be "sweet" and "gentle," Derrida confesses that he has seldom found the Book to contain those qualities (2:146–47).

5. In an appendix to his *Metaphysik der Sitten*, Kant discusses the penal code and the proper punishment for various crimes—in the case of pedophilia, for example, the proper punishment is castration. Accepting Kant's cue, Derrida turns the seminar in the direction of psychoanalysis, inasmuch as Freud argues for a kind of unconscious equivalence between death (especially by decapitation) and castration—as though Percy Grimm's mutilation of the mortally wounded Joe Christmas were not a shocking exception but the rule itself. With this theme in mind, Derrida discusses at length Reik's 1926 responses, confirmed by Freud, to questions concerning capital punishment, which are generally questions of fathers and sons.[22]

The principal problem is *le nom du père*, which is always the *non!* that the father addresses to his sons, at least until the murder by the sons of the

---

22 Derrida cites and discusses during his seminar the principal thesis of *Totem und Tabu*, namely, the murder of the father by the sons. Freud, in his preface to Theodor Reik's 1919 *Probleme der Religionspsychologie*, which I cited in the foregoing chapter, compresses or reduces that thesis to a single clause: "that God the Father once walked upon the Earth in flesh and blood and exercised his power to rule as the chief of the primal human horde—until his sons, working together, slew him" (GW 12:328).

father—or, if Kant is right, the implied protracted suicide of all the murderous sons. Here, in the primal horde, the very distinction between God and Man disappears. "The Father is at once God-Man-Beast and none of these" (2:160). By the same stroke, or coinage, one might say, the entire seminar on the death penalty could be a question of the *Schlag* or *coup* of de*cap*itation and *culp*ability, the *cap* and the *culp* that imply one another, at least if *cap* may also refer to the isthmus of the neck: *Du cou coupé, la coulpe n'est jamais très loin* (ibid.). The father is thus both survivor and revenant, as in *Hamlet*. He organizes succession, but because of the regicide he "disorganizes" time in such a way that the times are forever "out of joint." In such times, the death penalty, as Reik's *The Need to Confess* argues, is "murder sanctioned by the law" (2:172). Reik clearly identifies himself and all of psychoanalysis as representing a superior ethics, and yet the very confidence in its moral mastery and ethical superiority are problematic for Derrida. For, as Derrida elsewhere argues, the power of mastery, as a pulsion or drive, is the pulsion that dominates psychoanalysis itself as a form of will to power. That said, its logic of the unconscious is crucial for a deconstruction of the death penalty.

6. Once again it is the *ius talionis,* that is, the problem of the calculation of an equivalence between crime and inflicted pain, that is the issue. And once again the focus falls on Kant's problematic claim that harm to others is harm to oneself (one sees Thrasymachus and Callicles rolling their eyes) and the consequent claim that heteropunition is in reality (or in ideality) autopunition. "All of that," says Derrida, "all these laws of the *autos* (autonomy, autopunition, automatism, automobile) come back to the blinding or blindly calculating pulsion of a calculus that gives itself out as reason itself" (2:191). Derrida notes that the *talion* of the *ius talionis* derives from *talis,* which gives the French its *tel* and *tel quel*, which refer to some state or quality, "such and such" a crime meriting "such and such" a punishment, "such and such" a payment in exchange, "such and such" restitution, justifying "this or that" retaliation. Yet what about this last? Baudelaire, for his part, stresses the theatricality of the mechanisms of execution, making of the human spectator both victim and victimizer, both "assassin and executioner." Derrida is closer to Baudelaire than to Kant: he sees in the death penalty the entire social machine churning away, the machine operated by the wealthy against the poor and fueled by the law of the talion from biblical times to the present:

> In other words, the social machine continues to work not only according to talionic law but also according to the talionic law that works

> as a calculating machine of the marketplace, a marketplace that is properly financial, where the substitute called "money" continues along subtle and shifting paths to assure absolution by saving certain heads, playing a role analogous to the one described in the Bible, even though this marketplace and the stratagems of its mercantilization are deferred, mediatized, and taken over by complex machineries, and even though the apparatus of deceptions is sometimes entirely disguised and always denied. (2:196)

At this point Derrida, as though in shock over "the nudity of an acephalic cadaver" (the sole reference to the *acéphale* in the seminar), begins to take up Heidegger's *Satz vom Grund*, on "the principle of reason," in an effort to challenge the calculating machine. For such calculating reason is itself *la question capitale* (2:197). Whatever reservations Derrida may have about Heidegger, and there are many of them, he follows Heidegger's analysis of *ratio* as *rechnen, richten, Recht, richtig, rechtfertigen* quite closely and in considerable detail (2:199–214). For the accounting that reason renders makes the accountants accountable. At one point in the 1957 *Satz vom Grund*, Heidegger refers scornfully to the Roman merchants who coin the word: "*ratio—ein Wort der römischen Kaufmannssprache*," a word invented by Roman merchants (SG 197; PM 2:200). Again the shadow of Shylock hovers, as it does throughout the seminar, and one recalls with regret and something more than regret that for Heidegger the entire Mediterranean region is dominated and denigrated by what he sees as the Levant. Derrida notes again that in *Sein und Zeit* there is no discussion of crime and punishment, much less of the death penalty; once again he insists that the notion of *ursprüngliche Schuldigsein*, "original indebtedness," requires that Heidegger recognize that the death penalty, however derivative and even "inauthentic" it may seem to be, "remains the proper of human being as Dasein" (2:202–203; 1:23). At the very end of the hour Derrida returns to Kant and the calculating machine of reason. For, surprisingly, in the same appendix in which Kant offers some hair-raising examples of the punishing calculus at work, he presents what may well be the first reference in judicial history of "crimes against humanity."

Derrida follows this new and perhaps more generous possibility of Kantian reason along the path of the *mondialisation* of psychoanalysis. For Freud's "unconscious" is not the avatar of irrationality, as is commonly said, but may be the core of a new concept of rationality—one that does not serve the death penalty machine. And yet the history of reason since Freud may demand a new concept of the unconscious, and Derrida will not shrink from the task. I will take up this question in the final chapter of the present book.

7. Derrida begins the seventh session with assistance from Theodor Reik and Émile Benveniste—in the strange company of Hegel. The key words here are *verdict* and *ordeal, ordalie* and *veridictum,* the latter word meaning to tell the truth *sans alibi. Ordalie* derives from *ordalium, aordela, ordâl, ordäl,* and from it come the German *Urthel, Urtheil, Ur-teilen.* Derrida refers to Hegel's *Enzyklopädie,* §166, on "the unity of the concept . . . *als die ursprüngliche Teilung,* the "primordial separation" or "allotment." Derrida has no trouble committing to Hegel as the thinker of *Differenz.*[23] Yet Hegel's sense of judgment, at least at its most precarious moments, leads Derrida to cite a second passage from Hegel on the possible consequences of such moments for the philosophy of law. In the *Rechtsphilosophie* (§282) Hegel invokes the "supreme acknowledgment of the majesty of spirit," which is its capacity to "forget and forgive," namely, its *Begnädigungsrecht,* the right to grant pardon. Thus spirit, which is otherwise interiorization, memory, and the unrelinquishing *grasp* of the concept as *Besitzergreifung,* achieves its highest goal in "annihilating the crime in forgiveness and forgetting," *im Vergeben und Vergessen das Verbrechen zu vernichten* (HW 7:454; PM 2:223). This is perhaps as close as any great philosopher comes to opposing or at least resisting the logic of the death penalty. As we have seen and will further see, the majesty of *Kant's* spirit is made of sterner and less forgiving stuff.

In Kant's long appendix on the penal code Derrida observes that various sexual crimes are to be punished variously by death, banishment, or castration: without delving into the sexual life of Immanuel Kant, one must affirm that in him too the relation of castigation to purification and of purification to castration continues to dominate. Derrida pursues the captivating chain of words including *castitas* and *castigatio* in their relation to *castratio* and *castus,* yielding the French *le chaste, le pieux, le religieux, le saint.* He does not shrink from avowing that the law of the talion is a law not only of exchange but also of sexual substitution. Furthermore, he agrees with Freud's *Totem und Tabu* that

---

23 This is of course a long and complicated story, unless one is absolutely sure about what Hegel means by *das absolute Wissen.* Yet the recent work of the best Hegelians—I am thinking here of Angelica Nuzzo, Rebecca Comay, and Kristina Mendicino—finds itself, as Nuzzo puts it, in an *interregnum* in which differences proliferate to the point where one can only wait upon (in the sense of Blanchot's *l'attente*) a sense of the absolute.

sexual crime is the primordial crime. He refers to Theodor Reik on the unconscious itself as "unforgiving," that is, as without gratitude or a sense of pardon. He then reminds his students of all the things the unconscious "ignores": time, contradiction, death, prudence—and now extenuating circumstances, gratitude, and pardon! Derrida has to wonder whether the new sense of *reason* in psychoanalysis will compensate. He predicts that because this characteristic oblivion in the unconscious undermines all authority and all sovereignty, the very notion of the "unconscious" will someday disappear from the public domain altogether. One can imagine what sort of notion of the "unconscious" a president might have who does not hesitate to declare who the "bad hombres" are and what is to be done about them.

Derrida pins all his hopes on "another concept of the unconscious" (2:232), one that is not tied to *Bemächtigung* (empowerment or overpowering), self-preservation, or memory operating as calculative repression. This new concept of the unconscious would welcome the im-possible, the un-conditional, the gift, pardon, and hospitality—all the themes of Derrida's seminars for the past decade or two. He realizes that this new concept would have to combat the force of reason in Kant and even in Freud. In such im-possible combat, Derrida appeals to "a certain radical forgetfulness" that would no longer be repression (2:232–33). In all this, he resists Theodor Reik and Freud himself. Nevertheless, he recognizes the value of Reik's genealogy of "vengeful Christianity," especially with regard to the origins of anti-Semitism. He makes yet another reference to Shylock and to "mercy," the quality of which has been "strained" enough in the long histories of Judaism and Christianity alike. He enters into detail concerning Reik's account of "the oral ordeal," in which the suspected criminal is forced to swallow the consecrated host: if he vomits it out, then his nausea has condemned him. This practice, one of the earliest of the trials by ordeal, is a remnant of the "pagan" ordeal of forcing the accused to swallow poison. If he dies, he is guilty. These practices invite a discussion of introjection and cannibalistic incorporation, but also of such sacramental matters as modes of judicial inquiry and condemnation. Once again one feels the force of Freud's speculation on the original crime as the murder and cannibalistic ingestion by the sons of the father, holy communion as both incorporation and oral ordeal. At all events, culpability is linked to the Oedipal situation, and sexual desire to the guilt that lies at the origin of all crimes. For one of Reik's most daring theses is that the death penalty not only does not deter crime but even impels it. In every case, he argues, punishment *precedes* the crime and operates as its libidinal force. What Nietzsche interprets as the interiorization of cruelty (memory as "bad conscience") Reik sees as always already at work before the crime—and as *leading to* the crime. Not crime and punishment but punishment and crime. This would be the secret of our admiration of the "great criminal," and the secret of the libidinal energy that drives all violent crime. The death penalty—and not only for Jean Genet—feeds on and is fueled by that same libidinal flame. Spirit not as the majesty of a forgiving-and-forgetting mercy but as the truculent genie of the flame.

At the end of the hour Derrida returns to Kant, but not as a return to reason. It is here that he recounts the story of Kant's insistence that the island inhabitants whose civilization is destroyed kill the remaining criminals as their last act before abandoning the island. Kant with Tarentino. Kantian formalism is fueled by the pulsion for purification; its libidinal interest is a cleansing action, compulsive pyrification. Hence *cette folie de la raison kantienne* (2:249).

8. It is therefore not completely mad to ask, "Who will have been the more cruel of the two, Kant or Robespierre?" (2:251). As far as we know, Kant beheaded no one, so that the answer seems clear. Yet Derrida warns that apparent abstinence from all overt cruelty covertly produces what one would have to call "a supplement of cruelty" (2:252). In this respect, Kant belongs to the Abrahamic tradition of the law of the talion, and his categorical imperative is linked to the supplement of the Decalogue: Thou shalt not kill—but whoever kills will be killed. *Ne pas tuer mais qui tue sera tué* (2:254). The supplement of cruelty screeches to a halt before regicide: "The condition of the possibility of the death penalty cannot become the object of a condemnation to death" (2:254–55). Regicide would be the suicide of the state. Thus Kant himself performs a kind of proto-psychoanalysis of the phantasms and pulsions of the French revolutionaries, including Robespierre, who is responsible for many of the 17,000 executions by law, not to mention the estimated 35,000 executions without trial. A sordid tale of many more than two cities, to be sure. No such horror can be laid at the feet of Kant.

And yet to teach and write, says Derrida, is also an act. What is an act? What is an age? What is a desire? For example, when it comes to such acts as pederasty, pedophilia, sodomy, or murder by execution? Again Derrida insists that wherever capital is at work, and in the mondialized world it is at work everywhere, the usual distinctions between act and non-act falter. The supplement of cruelty contaminates. Even Kant is vaguely aware of this—hence his ambivalent enthusiasm for and horror in the face of the French Revolution. The one detail on which Derrida focuses is the fact that early on in his career Robespierre was an ardent opponent of the death penalty, whereas Kant, from beginning to end, was "a cruel partisan of the death penalty" (2:274). Derrida's contemporary paper, *States of the Soul*, which I will take up in my final chapter, develops the thesis that a cruelty risks becoming ever more cruel as it persists in believing that it abstains from all cruelty.[24] Such cruelty wears the mask of sovereign authority, from the icy Nurse Ratchett to the smiling behavioral psychologist of *A Clockwork Orange*. Derrida accepts Nietzsche's thesis that idealism, which is sovereign in philosophy, is essentially excessive, hence vengeful and cruel (KSW 5:43, 54–55). Not passion but idealization produces the worst crimes, the cruelest crimes. The "pure idea *a priori*" is the cruelest idea, the elevation of moral sentiments inherently excessive, hence bound to be most cruel. The blade falls from the highest height, the most veridical verticality. In agreement with Reik on this point, Derrida affirms that only an "*assouplissement des exigences idéales*," a softening or easing of ideal exigencies, can lead us beyond the cruelty of moral idealism (2:276–77). In any case, says Derrida, thinking perhaps again of Lacan's "Kant avec Sade," avoidance of "excessive rectitude" is the essential lesson to be drawn. If Kant is more cruel than Robespierre, it is because he is even more idealistic. Be that as it may, Derrida speculates that for both Robespierre and Kant "cruelty would be the proper of man" (2:280). Here, at the point where Derrida summarizes Kant's appendix, it is necessary to quote the seminar at some length:

> The death penalty is a cruel chastisement designed to punish the cruelty of murder. Castration, a cruel chastisement designed to punish sex crimes against nature and against humanity. Yet who will punish the cruelty of the death penalty and the cruelty of all the castrations (literal or figurative), all the circumcisions (literal or figural), all the excisions (literal or figurative), and all the castigations that in the end take aim at life itself? Might cruelty be what is proper to the human being? The animal, or what one blithely calls the animal, as if such a thing existed in general and in the singular—can the animal be cruel? Is the animal capable of cruelty? (2:280–81)

Derrida speculates that cruelty might be defined as "an excess that consists of doing evil for its own sake, taking evil as its own good, at one blow suffering

---

24 Readers interested in Derrida's *États d'âme* for its discussion of both *Grausamkeit* and Freud's *Bemächtigungstrieb*, will find important references in volume 2 of the seminar we are now examining: see especially 2:28, 104, 117, 173, 184, 232, and 274.

in order to cause suffering, and doing so in the name of the law, the law as the evil of the good" (2:280–81). He continues:

> In any case, and let us weigh each word here, the rational and calculated possibility of sovereignly *deciding*, of making the decision *to cause someone to die* (I deliberately say *faire mourir*, by what one calls an *act*, and not *laisser mourir* [merely to *let* someone die]). For it is surely a matter of inducing death through some kind of machination; it is a matter of putting to death and not merely of leaving someone to die. Thus the possibility, the rational and calculated possibility, as the power sovereignly to *decide*, to make the decision to *put to death* an other who is deemed responsible and guilty, and to claim to answer for this decision in a responsible way, to claim to give an account and justify it in terms of reason—all of this would define what is proper to the human being, the essence of humanity. (2:283)

The entire procedure, posing as rational, appears to be an uncanny board game in which one tosses the dice, moves one's token, and falls prey to whatever disaster the board prescribes—*un jeu de l'oie*, the French says, something between *Monopoly* and a wild goose chase. Derrida's question is a simple one, namely, whether we can stop playing the game. *Peut-on sortir de ce jeu?* (2:285).

9. As in Derrida's *Circonfession*, the ninth session of the death penalty seminar proposes to write a history of blood. That proposal comes in the midst of a passage from cruelty-as-bloodshed to cruelty-as-*Grausamkeit*. The last of Freud's three essays on lovelife, "The Taboo of Virginity" (1917–18), plays an important role in the proposal, as does Reik's *The Need to Confess*. According to Reik, the guilt culture in which we live will eventually substitute confession for punishment. To some extent this has already occurred, remarks Derrida ironically, in a time when heads of state hope to restore their virginity by publicly confessing their crimes. The history of blood will eventually embrace the phenomena of blushing and weeping, and embrace them not merely with irony. Derrida alludes to Sándor Ferenczi's phylogenetic psychoanalysis or bioanalysis, asking what happens in the body when we laugh, blush, or weep.[25]

---

25 Allow me to refer the reader to two further chapters of my recent book, *The Sea: A Philosophical Encounter*, which deal with Ferenczi's "bioanalysis," namely, the second and third. The importance of phylogenetic history for psychoanalysis in general is, if I may say so, a fascinating topic—in need of the most serious study. My own book is a very modest first step.

On the basis of Freud's *Totem und Tabu*, along with the "Virginity" essay on the taboo of blood, Derrida affirms that castration (and not decapitation) is the original punishment. According to Freud, who in a strange turn of his essay cites Friedrich Hebbel's 1839 play, *Judith*, castration is a feminine operation, acting out the woman's vengeance on the person who perpetrates her deflowering. Beheading is therefore not a virgin's patriotic act, as in the apocryphal biblical story, but a woman's reaction to penetration. Freud, inspired by conversations and seminars with Ferenczi, comments on virginity—and its deflowering—by way of "a paleobiological speculation" (2:310–11). Freud's thesis is that an entire range of neuroses teach us that women often seek vengeance upon the man who deflowers and appropriates her, and that hers is "a castrating vengeance." Ferenczi suspects that such vengeance is more common than supposed, and that it may go all the way back to the antediluvian scene in which life divides into two separate sexes. Initially indistinguishable at a time when there is but one gender among proto-amphibians, some members of the species prove to be stronger than others, penetrating the weaker in their search for moisture in a world that is struck by the catastrophe of desiccation. The enmity and warfare between the resulting sexes has such dominance, submission, and penetration as its source. Freud is careful to say that such speculations are "permissible" only if one is careful not to "overvalue" them. Derrida reminds his students of Plato's (rather, Aristophanes's) three genders, each divided in twain, and then comments on Ferenczi's speculation concerning that earlier scene of life in which there is only one gender, one *genre*, as such:

> According to Ferenczi's speculation, it is a matter of explaining not love and Eros between men and women but war, hostility, *polemos* or *eris*—not Eros but Eris—the war in fact waged by women against men as a reaction against the man's natural superiority, his greater natural strength; in this case there is only one sex, and copulation first takes place between two individuals of the same gender. One of the two, having become stronger than the other, forced (*zwang*) the weaker one to endure passively, to undergo (*erdulden*), to suffer sexual union (*die geschlechtliche Vereinigung*). (2:311–12)

Derrida then repeats Freud's commentary on Ferenczi's speculation, a speculation that Derrida admits is a "somewhat delirious phantasm," to the effect that the vengeful reaction to the paleobiological situation is still visible "in the disposition of women today" (Freud). Such vengeance would make of "penis envy" a mere epiphenomenon, a sort of skirmish in the otherwise pitched battle between what later become male and female. One is left with the figure of Judith (the heroine of Hebbel's *Judith*) decapitating the Holofernes who has deflowered her. And it would make of the long and bloody history of decapitation in capital punishment a skirmish in that same pitched battle—this, in spite of the fact that when it comes to active abolitionism the number of committed women most likely exceeds that of men.

Setting aside the history of blood as (male) phantasmatic female vengeance, Derrida now relates the "rectitude" of the law, the rigorous law, to the erect stature of the human and to the human being's identification with the vertical axis and with elevation. He emphasizes "the profound pessimism of Freud, his remarkable conservatism" (2:317) when it comes to the possibility of altering or even ameliorating the war of the sexes—or for that matter the violence that plays itself out in the entire history of blood and bloodshed. The history of what Freud calls *organic repression*—of blood, urine, feces, sperm, and tears—would suffer no real alteration. Just as repression may be ineradicably rooted in the erect posture of the human being, so may the history of bloody cruelty and vengeance be bound up with the paleobiology of the species. In all this, Freud refuses to entertain any illusions about the future, even as he does battle against the future of religious illusion. If the efforts of psychoanalysis—here of Freud and Reik—to alter the history of crime and punishment should bear fruit, such fruit would be a mere addendum, a supplement to what has been. "History would be the mere supplement of a *différance*" (2:320).

One of the most surprising moves in the seminar occurs at this point (2:322). Derrida, recalling his earlier reading of Heidegger, contrasts Freud's pessimism with the strategy that Heidegger employs in his *Satz vom Grund*, a strategy that by means of a mere shift of emphasis could, as Heidegger seems to hope, initiate a new history of being, a history that would think the abyss, *der Abgrund*, of reason. Not the confident "*nothing* is without *ground*" of metaphysics, but "(the) nothing *is, without* ground." Derrida is uncertain about the success of Heidegger's strategy. Will a new history for humankind eventuate? Will the human being restore its virginity, regain a status and a stature that would from hence protect it from delusion and destruction? Derrida, it seems, is in the awkward position of wanting something to palliate Freud's pessimism—but also needing something less phantasmatic than Heidegger's "other beginning." Neither of the two grandfathers, neither of the two *pépés*, offers the pleasure he seeks.

10. At the outset of this final session of the seminar, devoted largely to questions posed by the students (the dialogue is not taken up into the transcription

of the course), Derrida promises to offer a glance ahead to the next year's seminar. The promise is not kept, at least not in any detail, even though *The Beast and the Sovereign*, precisely with its focus on sovereign power and violence, is quite continuous with *The Death Penalty* seminar. The only hint of that continuity here is with Derrida's assertion that the death penalty pertains to that as yet unwritten "history of blood," a history of blood flow, a history of *sacrifice*. Even Kant's reflections on the penal code, on morality and the law, are driven by "a sacrificial pulse," precisely the pulse that drives the human being to sacrifice all animal life to human ends (2:326). "Kant's thought is entirely a sacrificial thought; Kantian morality is a sacrificial morality" (2:327).

At this point Derrida turns to an important source for Carl Schmitt, the thinker of the theological underpinnings of sovereignty, namely, Juan Donoso Cortés's *Essay on Catholicism, Liberalism, and Socialism* (1859). It is important here to recall the detailed consideration of Carl Schmitt's *Concept of the Political* (1932) in Derrida's *Politics of Friendship*, or at least to remind oneself of the implications of Schmitt's principal thesis for the question of the death penalty. Schmitt acknowledges the importance of Matthew 5:43–48 and Luke 6:27–31, to the effect that the Christian must "love your enemies and do good to those who hate you." This central commandment or requirement, which is the fulfillment of the Law, is repeated elsewhere in Paul, although the canny Paul, in Romans 12:18, adds, "if it is possible, to the extent that it is up to you." Schmitt, one might say, elaborates on Paul's canny caution: he distinguishes between the "enemy" as *inimicus* and *hostis*, that is, between ἔκθρος and πολήμιος, the first of each pair meaning a private or personal enemy, the second a public and perhaps foreign foe. Whereas Christianity requires us to love the former, the history of Christendom demonstrates beyond all doubt that Christians have never hesitated to urge the killing of the latter, and Schmitt sees this as the saving grace of the command to love. If one can interpret the criminal sociopath as a foe, a common enemy, as it were, then "the real possibility of a physical killing" of the "enemy" would be preserved for the state in the death penalty.

Yet Derrida's turn to Donoso Cortés very near the end of his own seminar on the death penalty remains a strange turn, to say the least, except for the fact that this reactionary theorist is more complex than one might have imagined. In fact, a number of Donoso's doubts and perplexities—for example, concerning the role of Yahweh in the murder by Cain of Abel, Yahweh being the sovereign who insists on blood sacrifice—prove to be Derrida's own.

Derrida now thinks back to his initial four paradigmatic cases of execution by the command of authorities that are both civil and religious (Socrates, Jesus,

El Hallâj, Joan of Arc) and he remarks that "it is evident that the death penalty seals the alliance of the theological and the political" (2:330–31). Thus he accepts the thesis of Schmitt, who avers that "all the pregnant concepts of the modern theory of the state are secularized theological concepts" (*Political Theology*, cited at 2:331). The role that "the exceptional situation" plays in jurisprudence, the "exception" being the sovereign right to execute or to grant pardon quite beyond the strictures of the law, is identical with the role that miracle plays in theology. Neither miracle nor death penalty submit easily to the reasonings of jurists and theologians, and yet they are essential to the numinous reality on which both are founded. Founded on nothing, one may object, but a nothing that spares or kills as it sees fit. A sovereign decision "is also a miracle" (2:332); one is expected to bow before it. Thus, if one is Donoso Cortés, one must react against enlightenment, progressivism, and revolution; one must, in such reaction, become a reactionary. One must put an end to the endless conversation of communicative discourses and come to a decision. Such decision arises ex nihilo, and precisely because it is based on nothing at all, it is utterly godlike. Only an authority that declares what *sin* is can declare what *crime* is, and that would be the authority that gives life and takes it. Such an authority would be absolute hubris if it were not absolute humility, absolute submission to the revealed absolute. Such submission, of course, is unconquerable: Derrida cites Donoso's invocation of *la palabra católica invencible* (2:338).

Derrida, seeing perhaps that his students are squirming in their seats under the glaring gaze of the Inquisitor, mercifully recalls at this point the argument of Camus, who in his "Reflections on the Guillotine" sees that only a thoroughly secularized society can rid itself of the scourge of the death penalty. Derrida's only caution would be, yes, thoroughly secularized, but secularized and "mondialized" otherwise than in the manner of Schmitt. And there is the rub. It is not difficult to discern the "radical pessimism" that underlies Donoso Cortés's invincible faith, his certitude "that the human being is evil" (2:339). The two principles of his faith are *imputation*, namely, the imputation of guilt to all humanity on account of Adam's sin, and *substitution*, by grace of which the Lord substitutes himself (or by which the Father substitutes the Son) as the sacrificial lamb. At all events, faith comes down to "bloody sacrifices" (2:341). Throughout the seminar, Derrida confesses himself to be nonplussed by the implication that lies behind the Cain and Abel story: Yahweh demands blood, and so prefers the bloody sacrifice of the shepherd Abel over the agricultural offerings of Cain, so that when Cain slays Abel he seems to be acting in obedience to, or in emulation of, the Father—or, at best, acting on the basis of a category mistake, taking his brother to be the only sheep available to him. Donoso Cortés expresses similar astonishment. Yet this does not prevent his faith from being invincible, does not deter him from committing himself to the continued shedding of blood.

The substitutional logic of blood sacrifice, according to Derrida, dominates both the Hellenic and the Abrahamic cultures down to the present day. Yet there are signs everywhere that capital punishment is on the wane, and that even the most barbaric cultures are responding to the pressure—but pressure from where? certainly not from reactionary populist politicians—to abolish the death penalty (2:348). It seems that the bloody game is coming to an end. A certain history of blood is thus in transition. For Donoso Cortés, the end of the death penalty would herald political chaos and an even greater flow of blood. For Derrida, it heralds the onset of an age of cruelty that no longer expresses itself as bloodshed but becomes a more psychological or more spiritualized *Grausamkeit*. The transition in the direction of *Grausamkeit* would add a new wrinkle or a new tear (*tear* as both *lacrima* and *laceration*) to our hopes for an increasingly refined civilization and eventual eternal peace.

The reader leaves Derrida's book as his students must have left the seminar room and lecture hall, namely, in a state of intellectual excitement and profound consternation, stepping out into a world that is still committed to violent blood flow but in transition, perhaps, to more subtle yet equally devastating forms of cruelty. In the final chapter of the book I will consider the verticality of power as mastery, which is also the power to impute guilt. My question will be whether this vertical, sovereign power is the sole will to power, or whether will to power can express itself in an altogether different way when it comes to *art* and *creativity* in general. Meanwhile, in the chapter now to come, it will be a question of imputability as cruelty in Kant's philosophy of freedom.

Chapter Nine

Freedom, Imputability, Cruelty

So tadelt man nichtsdestoweniger den Täter. (Nonetheless, one does not shy from blaming the perpetrator.)

—Immanuel Kant, *Kritik der reinen Vernunft* B583

You, Kant, always get what you want.

—Hedwig

KANT'S MORAL PHILOSOPHY, arising from his study of the traditional literature and from his own moral prejudices, is dictated by the need to assert *freedom* in the human order. No freedom, no accountability; no accountability, no imputability; no imputability, no ostensible justification for punishment. The need and the desire to punish are paramount. Yet because Kant knows the complexities surrounding all human action, he also knows that imputability requires a surreptitious exit from this confounding world and an entirely phantasmatic entry into another world, an impossible world. And so he breaks all the self-imposed rules of his own rational critique of metaphysics and postulates a time that is no time and a place that is no place and a human deed that, while indeed a deed, is not merely one deed among others, but *the* deed, *die Tat an sich,* the deed that like a tantalizing *Ding an sich* decides once and for all the intelligible and moral character of each one of the human beings that have populated the world since the emergence of humankind on the planet.

Schelling too is attracted to this idea—of intelligible characters performing intelligible deeds—in his astonishing 1809 *Abhandlung über die menschlichen Freiheit und die damit zusammenhängenden Gegenstände*, attracted to it because he can already see how completely mad it is: the idea of the intelligible deed seeks to connect the two worlds, the *Diesseits* and the *Jenseits*, the

Here-and-Now with the Beyond, by means of an asses' bridge. Better, it is the kind of wonky footbridge depicted in Monty Python's *Holy Grail*, in which a vicious cobold or bridge spirit asks trick questions and poses unsolvable riddles in order to toss perplexed travelers into the abyss. Schelling's analysis begins calmly enough. He writes:

> Free action follows immediately from the intelligible in human beings. Yet it is necessarily a determinate action—for example, to mention the most proximate aspect, a good or an evil action. Yet there is no transition from the absolutely indeterminate to the determinate. The supposition that, as it were, the intelligible essence might determine itself on the basis of pure and pristine indeterminacy, without any grounds, reverts to the system described above, that is, the system of indifferent arbitrariness [*System der Gleichgültigkeit der Willkür*]. (SW I/7:384)

Here the word *Willkür* is spoken or written perhaps for the first time in its modern sense, that of the arbitrary, fortuitous, gratuitous. From here it is only a tiny step to the question Schelling feels compelled to pose over and over again during his long career, namely, that of the *Wesen in dem Wesen*, "the essence in essence," to wit, that which could *freely* determine a determinate action. Such a doubling within *Wesen* indicates a problematic transition, indeed, an impossible *Übergang* into the unknowable Beyond, or *from* the unknowable Beyond *to* the present befuddling world. The intelligible deed must in some rebarbative sense be an *eternal* deed. It will have had to decide, in a future anterior, everything that later occurs in the life of any given human being, determining it *in Einem magischen Schlage*, "in one magical stroke" (SW 7:387). That one stroke will have decided everything in a future anterior tense that seems to imply the vicious circularity of time itself. The "everything" that will have been decided, Schelling remarks in an extraordinary passage that resists all understanding, includes *sogar die Art und Beschaffenheit seiner Korporisation*, "the type and the quality of the being's embodiment" (ibid.). If, as it indeed turns out, Schelling is unable to solve the riddle of evil without implicating "the essence," that is, God and all the anxiety-ridden gods and raging goddesses that ever were, that too will presumably decide the disaster toward which onto-theo-logical metaphysics and morals is heading. For Schelling is clear about what is truly at issue in the matter of intelligible characters doing intelligible deeds: his sole example is Judas Iscariot, who is always painted as the ugly one among the Twelve, the one with the repulsive *Korporisation*, and *the* issue at stake is captured in the crucial word *Zurechnungsfähigkeit*, "imputability" or "accountability" (7:386–87). Moral madness will express itself as the imputation of culpability, which is the consuming need and cruel desire to punish.

Is it not fascinating that the dearest friend of Schelling's youth, Hölderlin, who wrote a two-page essay on "the law of freedom," also composed an essay on punishment, *Über den Begriff der Strafe*?[1] The link that connects all three essays is provided by the following sentences: "The first time that the law of freedom expresses itself to us, it appears by way of punishment. The beginning of all our virtue occurs on the basis of evil." Naturally, all three essays would repay a detailed reading, but here I will restrict myself to the essay on punishment. Hölderlin's is a mere sketch, but its recurrent theme is the circularity—the vicious circularity—of punishment within both the criminal code and the moral law. I suffer punishment, he says, and in my suffering I learn for the first time that I have somehow contravened the law; but if I know the law only after having broken it, I suffer unjustly, or perhaps justly, the circularity making it impossible for anyone to decide. The temporality of punishment, in Hölderlin's view, is the temporality of freedom as Schelling describes it in the tenth of his *Philosophical Letters on Dogmatism and Criticism* (SW 1:336–37): as the tragic hero is free only in the simple past or imperfect tense, proclaiming as he or she goes down, "I *was* free!" so, for Hölderlin, punishment is always a matter of the imperfect. "I *was* at fault, and I *did* deserve the punishment that I, who am innocent, received." Yet whether one can call such punishment "just deserts" is more than dubious, inasmuch as, in Hölderlin's words, "All suffering is punishment" (DKV 2:500). But that seems *cruel*—manifesting a cruelty that is so widespread that we may take it to be of the *essence*. As we recall from Hölderlin's "Fragment of Philosophical Letters," discussed in chapter 1, such cruelty, which is the driving spirit of an "arrogant morality," militates against those "more tender relations" that have to permeate every flourishing community.

The present chapter has three theses. First, philosophy in the form of reflection on practical reason and morality has no genuine interest in the freedom of

1 See Hölderlin's three essays, "Es giebt einen Naturzustand," "Über den Begriff der Strafe" and "Fragmente philosophischer Briefe," CHV 2:46–49 and 2:51–57, and DKV 2:499–501. The sketch on freedom, *Über das Gesetz der Freiheit*, appears at CHV 2:46–47 and DKV 2:496–97.

the self; rather, it has interest only in the freedom of others. Second, interest in the freedom of others has nothing to do with altruism or acknowledgment of the dignity of the human being; rather, it is grounded in the need and desire to assert imputability and accountability, *Zurechnungsfähigkeit*, against the others. Third, the ground of this need and desire—and hence the genuine interest of philosophy in freedom across the board—is not justice; rather, it is cruelty.

My three theses derive from my reading of two philosophical texts, one by Kant, the other by Schelling. After Kant introduces the theme of freedom in the third antinomy of his *Critique of Pure Reason* he takes a hundred pages—rhetorically the most gripping pages of the work, full of the wittiest sophisms, including the sophism he playfully calls "transcendental subreption"—to reclaim for himself all the specious assertions that a critique of pure reason forbids him to think or utter. Under the guise of claims made by "practical reason," itself a sophism of the first order, he turns phrase after phrase in the surreptitious effort (for "subreption" is "surreptition," *Erschleichung*) to transcend all the self-imposed limits of his thought.[2]

Every student of philosophy, I believe, remembers his or her own internal struggles when pondering such phrases in the first Critique as "a *regulative* principle," *ein* regulatives *Prinzip*, that is "appropriate to the object," *dem Gegenstand angemessen*; or "the intelligible cause" as a "causality out of the sequence," *intelligible Ursache [als] Kausalität außer der Reihe*; or "the practical concept," *der praktische Begriff*, that ostensibly makes it possible "to append a causality that is not appearance," *eine Kausalität, die nicht Erscheinung ist, beilegen*. Or finally this: "a way out is still open to us that should not be discredited, should not be declared to be impossible," *noch ein Ausweg [sei] offen, [sei] gar nicht in Abrede zu ziehen, nicht für unmöglich [zu] erklären [sei]*, a way out, an escape hatch that would putatively enable practical reason to identify "the character of the thing in itself," *den Charakter des Dinges an sich selbst*.[3]

---

2 For a detailed and insightful account of subreption in Kant's work, see chapter 3, "Kant and the Error of Subreption," in Zachary Sng, *The Rhetoric of Error from Locke to Kleist* (Stanford: Stanford University Press, 2010). In my own chapter I am pushing beyond the limit of transcendental subreption in *reflective* judgment, whether involving teleological or aesthetic applications, to the question of *moral* or *legal* judgments.

3 Immanuel Kant, *Kritik der reinen Vernunft*, ed. Raymund Schmidt. "Philosophische Bibliothek" (Hamburg: Felix Meiner Verlag, 1956), B472–583.

Why all this suggestive, surreptitious, behind-the-back rhetorical abracadabra? Soon enough, we are given the reason, for Kant introduces the themes of accountability, imputed guilt, and punishment. Freedom is but a corollary of the principal axiom, namely, that the need and the desire to punish are indispensable and inexpugnable, *unentbehrlich.* If κατηγορέω means, "I accuse you," *ratio* is the faculty that means, "I reckon you are indebted and are already guilty, and I am able to calculate the guilt," and *Vernunft* the faculty that declares, "I shall apprehend you."

So it is when Kant, in his apparently harmless "Commentary on the Cosmological Idea of Freedom," gives us an "example" of the intelligible character. Only one example. After assuring us that the human being himself or herself *is* appearance (*Der Mensch ist selbst Erscheinung*, B580), Kant, with no apparent discomfort plants one foot firmly in appearances and the other, with all the grace of a man not well suited for ballet, in the "intelligible realm" of traditional religious and metaphysico-moral discourses. He gives us the "example" of a malicious liar who, no matter how *constitutionally* mendacious he may be, no matter how compelled by his or her very "nature" or "second nature" or "disposition" (*Naturell*) to lie and to lie maliciously, needs to be punished *as though* his lies were freely told. *So tadelt man nichtsdestoweniger den Täter,* says Kant (B583), in one of the most rhetorically powerful, strikingly alliterative, and witty sentences of the Critique—the rhetorical power deriving from the *projective* character of the malicious subreption engaged in by critique itself. And Kant can count on the sympathy of every reader: no one wants to be the victim of a lie, and if the liar is a habitual liar, one who cannot help himself, that only makes matters worse—all the more intense becomes our desire and need to punish him. If the liar were a killer instead of a mere liar, Kant would no doubt announce, with still more glorious alliteration, *so tadelt man mit der Todesstrafe den Täter.* Kant finally reveals what freedom is all about: his is the tale that Hölderlin, when describing the murderous words spoken by a tragic hero or heroine, calls *tödtendfaktisch* (CHV 2:374), killingly factical; it is a tale of *eines tödlichen Tadelns*, deadly blame.

How does the murderous tale unfold? The malicious liar or killer is outfitted—by you and by me, since we are the rational creatures who suffer damages because of the lying and the killing—with his intelligible character (*seinem intelligiblen Charakter beigemessen*), so that we can declare that at the bipolar instant of the crime (*in dem Augenblick*) the liar or killer was both fully free (*völlig frei*) and altogether guilty (*gänzlich Schuld*). And now, because we have slipped one foot gracefully into instantaneous eternity, we may assert that the liar or killer *is*, always *was*, forever *will* be, and eternally *will have been* (and the reduction of time to an eternity of future anterior repetition is essential to the attributives *fully* and *altogether*) both fully free (*völlig frei*) and altogether guilty (*gänzlich Schuld*). As always in the Kantian text, the apparently innocent "example," the sole example, by transcendental surreption, tells the malicious tale. It is the proclamation, spoken from the Beyond, that empowers our desire and fulfills our need to punish.

But now to the second text. When Schelling advances from his astonishing freedom essay to the three grandiose drafts of *The Ages of the World* (*Die Weltalter*), he drops the phrase *in Einem magischen Schlage*, "in one magic stroke" (SW I/7:387). He drops not only the phrase but also the thought, and even the desire for such a thought. One might describe this highpoint in Schelling's thinking, the summit of *Die Weltalter*, as the discovery that where *essence* is concerned the strokes are many, not merely one, and they involve different intensities of languor or longing (*Sehnsucht*), this in turn involving multiple sexual and gender identities for the essence, multiple modes of languishing (*Schmachten*), and hence multiple modes of illness and eventual death—the entire Pandora's box of *finitude*. The magic never ends for the essence, but what comes to an end is the One. What begins is the epoch of Two or More, the δυάς, and in this epoch there can be no proclamation containing the attributives *fully* and *altogether*. Altogether there is always n + 1, which means the end of calculation, the end of calculable blame, and the end of calibrated punishment. Schelling finds his two feet planted firmly in the realm of narrative, the theater of the oldest stories told on Earth, narrative beyond the reaches of dialectic and thus already well beyond good and evil. He finds himself from hence caught up in what, after Nietzsche, we call the philosophy of the future.

•

Allow me to move now from the surreptitious Kant and the infinitely courageous Schelling to Robert Musil and Jacques Derrida. Here I want to focus not on Ulrich and Agathe but on Musil's figure "Moosbrugger." In that context, I will introduce some themes from Derrida's seminar on the death penalty, *la peine de mort*, which we have been studying in some detail. I would like to work through the Moosbrugger chapters of *Der Mann ohne Eigenschaften* because I am convinced by the argument of Don Kelly Coble that there is no more incisive account of accountability and imputability in (the) literature.[4] I then want to add to Musil's account a brief discussion of some aspects of Derrida's death penalty seminar that we have already examined. All this attention to the death penalty may seem odd, inasmuch as civilized nations, Germany and Austria among them, no longer practice it. Nevertheless, as we have seen, at a crucial moment in his seminar Derrida appeals to a German word, one that he says marks the very future of the *question* of the death penalty—the word *Grausamkeit.*

The American word *cruelty* dominates the *first* part of his seminar because of the U.S. Supreme Court's interpretations of the phrase in the Constitution that forbids "cruel and unusual punishment." The death penalty may be justified only if it can be shown that there is nothing unusual about it and if the method of death-delivery can be deemed, if not kind, at least not cruel.

As we have seen, *cruelty* derives from the Latin word *cruor,* "I bleed," as though quoting Shakespeare's Shylock, or "blood flow" in general. Yet Derrida argues in his seminar that *even if* the death penalty were to be outlawed in all the nations and states, including even Texas, a certain form of *cruelty* would continue to flourish unabated and unabashed. And that form, he says, is encapsulated best in the German word *Grausamkeit,* which has no reference to bloodshed, but only to *Grauen,* as in *grauenerregend, grausig, grauslich, gräßlich, Greuel,* and so on. The word is derived, the dictionaries tell us, from "a *specifically German* word," *ein* urdeutsches *Wort,* namely, the Middle High German *grūwen,* which one may translate as *schauderhaft,* something that sends a shiver or a shudder up and down the spine. Our word *gruesome* comes from it.

4 Many years ago now, Professor Coble, working with Professor Lore Hühn of Freiburg University, wrote a dissertation on Kant, Schelling, Robert Musil, and Ernst Mach. His thesis, titled *Inscrutable Intelligibility,* analyzed the philosophical background of both the German criminal code (*Gesetzgebung*) and American criminal law, especially where capital crimes are involved. Coble demonstrated that the philosophical presuppositions of our criminal codes, when it comes to the question of *Zurechnungsfähigkeit* in capital crimes, have not altered in any significant way over the centuries since Kant. He argued further that the most stringent philosophical analysis of accountability and imputability is to be found in an Austrian writer—one who earned a doctorate in philosophy but who never wrote specifically as a philosopher—by the name of Robert Musil. See Don Kelly Coble, "Inscrutable Intelligibility: Intelligible Character and Deed in Kant, Schelling, Mach, and Musil." PhD Dissertation, DePaul University, 1999.

Surely, what intrigues Derrida about *grūwen*, about this shudder, is its undecidable etiology, for it seems to refer to both the destruction-and-death drives and the erotic drive in psychoanalytic thinking. *Grau, Grausamkeit, Greuel,* and *grūwen* have a long and fascinating history in German literature and in folk dialects, and when one thinks of the related words—*gram, grimm, Groll, Griesgram*—the story becomes infinitely complex.

A brief look at the word *grausam* and its general semantic field in the lexicons may be useful. Let me begin with Hermann Paul's etymological dictionary, which is always clear and succinct, and then refer to the massively detailed *Deutsches Wörterbuch* of the Brothers Grimm. *Grauen*, Old High German *(in)grūēn*, Middle High German *grūwen*, is originally related to the Old Slavic *grudu* and is the ancestor of our English word *gruesome*; the verb designates the experience of chills running up and down the spine. Whatever is *grausam, grauenhaft*, or *grauenvoll*, and whatever causes us to utter *mir graut vor*, is *schauderhaft*, that is to say, "bound up with shuddering." The adjective *grausam* therefore originally means *grauenerregend*, that which arouses or excites horror. Later in its history, presumably in the seventeenth century, although already in Luther, the meaning is intensified to mean "frightful," *fürchterlich*—if that *is* an intensification. Yet it is not so much an intensification as a shift in emphasis or even a kind of reversal or inversion: the word now applies to the horrifying *instigator* rather than the horrified and shuddering *recipient*. The shudder that goes up and down the spine of the instigator is one not of horror but of titillation, reflecting a certain twisted Eros in the agent. The current meaning of the word, but, again, already in Luther, is "merciless," *unbarmherzig*. What, then, is this twisted Eros of mercilessness? What is the need or desire to horrify that is impacted in the word *Grausamkeit*? An example of the transition from passive to active *Grausamkeit* is Crusoe's horror of being buried alive or eaten by cannibals, a horror that arguably becomes so obsessive in him that it seems to become a secret desire and even a compulsion—the one who fears being buried alive obsessively seeks out caves and constructs fortresses where he can bury himself and hide.[5]

The mysterious turn in the history of the word *grausam*, which earlier on has to do with the one who *suffers* cruelty but then later applies to the cruel

5 Derrida discusses this aspect of Crusoe's desire for self-castigation and self-destruction in BS 2; see also Krell, *Derrida and Our Animal Others* (Bloomington and London: Indiana University Press, 2005), 43ff. A reading Kafka's *Der Bau* might also take us in this direction.

perpetrator, is the principal subject of the much more detailed story of the word in the Grimm Brothers' dictionary.[6] The word *grausam* goes back at least as far as 1300. The Danish word *grusom* and our *gruesome* are close relatives. The Grimm Brothers find three clusters of meanings for the word.

1. *Grausam* initially refers to the color gray, *grau*, which even in the oldest usages implies those frightful things that make our hair turn gray, but also to the noun *der Grau*, which means "a shudder." *Grausam* thus designates the quality of an object that either in its form or by its behavior is horrifying, savage, or harsh—so much so that it causes the victimized subject to shudder and perhaps feel a rising wave of nausea. A repulsive animal or a cruel tyrant would be likely to evoke the feeling designated in the word; so might the *grausamen* days of the Last Judgment, or a time of plague, or one's own impending death. Hans Sachs has Satan hiss to Eve, *ey meinst, das got so grausam sey, / das er dich umb ein apfel töd?* "You think God would be so *grausam* as to kill you because of an apple?"

2. In the latter half of the seventeenth century, writers begin to use the word as a synonym for the horrifying in the sense of something evil, or of someone maleficent and malicious. Here the original senses of the color gray and even of *der Grau* as "shudder" appear to diminish in importance.

3. Finally, beginning with the 1750s and enduring up to the present, the meaning shifts from the passive *subject* who undergoes a shuddering experience to the active *object* that arouses such negative feelings. (Note, however, that the Satan of Hans Sachs—like the God of Sachs's contemporary, Martin Luther—already uses the word in this new way, as though God himself shows the way to the new *Grausamkeit*.) *Grausam* now designates persons, actions, and comportments that act negatively upon us; more precisely, it names the inner condition—the lack of sensitivity, empathy, or feeling, the coldness or hardness of heart—that lies at the core of such persons, actions, or comportments. *Grausam* now means the dominant proclivity, tendency, or drive to hurt someone. Violence, brutality, and bloodthirsty vengeance are its variegated blooms. For Lessing, Medea personifies *Grausamkeit*; for Carossa, Diocletian; for virtually everyone, the heartless beloved who spurns the honest and dedicated lover. "*Amor* treats me *grausam*!" cries Schiller. Unrelenting *Schadenfreude* seems to

---

6 *Der digitale Grimm*, Zweitausendeins, 2004. *Deutsches Wörterbuch* von Jakob und Wilhelm Grimm, begun in 1834, with the first volume published in 1843; after 1863 linguists continued to work on the dictionary until, in 1960, it appeared in sixteen volumes.

be a constant companion of *Grausamkeit*, even if it is nothing more than fate or destiny that robs us of our future happiness. Illness and accident seem to us undeserved and are therefore *grausam*. Uncertainty is *grausam*, says Lessing, and Hölderlin replies that when the dreams of our youth prove to be bald-faced lies, this above all else is *grausam*. For Goethe, even a kiss is *grausam* sweet—if it is the last one. The most recent uses of the word, concludes the updated Grimm, are increasingly complex, "atmospherically conditioned" by a "hint of pleasureful feeling in the suffering that one undergoes," such that the sadism of the modern uses of the word is matched by the masochism of postmodernity.

Why is Derrida interested in this ambiguous and perhaps even undecidable *Grausamkeit*? Because, he says, of the state of the soul of psychoanalysis as such. And that state—in spite of the immense success of Lacanian analysis in France and in many (though not all) parts of the world—is dire. For if psychoanalysis is to have a future, it must pursue Freud's destruction-and-death drives in the direction of the human (and perhaps also animal) need and desire to practice cruelty and to inflict pain and horror. On whom? On the others, yes, but also, and here once again seemingly undecidably, "atmospherically conditioned," on oneself. This "state of the soul of psychoanalysis" will be the theme of my final chapter.

With regard to pain inflicted on the others, Derrida's principal theme has been, as we have seen, the death penalty. That surely would arouse dismay and indignation among proponents of the death penalty, inasmuch as they see themselves not as cruel but as cool arbiters of retributive justice. Yet with his emphasis on the *desire* of those proponents, a desire that Derrida accepts as being profoundly *unconscious*, he unmasks—must one say *cruelly* unmasks?—their ingratiating self-concept. *Grausamkeit* will be his word for the desires, needs, and deeds that result in the death penalty. Psychoanalysis, more than any other discipline, ought to be expert at plumbing the depths of such *Grausamkeit*.

If psychoanalysis has failed to make much headway beyond the pleasure principle, however, and if it therefore has failed to keep up to date with the world in which you and I live, the philosophers have not done much better. To repeat, not a single philosopher among the greats of our tradition, from Plato through Heidegger, has argued *philosophically* against the death penalty, even if Hegel has put in a word for spirit's magnanimity. All have come down on the side represented by Carl Schmitt, who tells us that fraternity and friendship are grounded in the insight that one always has enemies, or rather *foes*, and that it is essential for the human community that it be "really possible" for these foes to be "physically killed."[7] *Grausam,* we may say, keeping to the older sense of the word. Yet who, Derrida wonders, will be able to take a *principled* stand against the philosophers?

Moosbrugger, for one, agrees with the philosophers. For the "procession of women" who accost him in the dark alleyways of Vienna are *grausam*; they make him shudder; they are his public enemies, his foes. They want something from him, something he is not willing to part with, and his only defense against them is to destroy them, to remove them physically from the scene. From the moment Musil introduces us to Moosbrugger's cheerful face—"*Gutmütige Kraft und der Wille zum Rechten sprachen aus seinem Gesicht*" (67); "His face communicated congenial energy and good will"—we know that Moosbrugger, Kant, Schelling, and the rest of us are in trouble. When it comes to Moosbrugger, Musil's sentences begin very sanely, but by the time they arrive at the final verb they are foundering in madness. These sentences are themselves so cruel that I shall leave most of them to my readers' morose delectation, citing only a few of them here.

Let it be said as straightforwardly as possible: whereas Moosbrugger's behavior is blatantly insane to all who observe it, for Moosbrugger himself that behavior expresses "a stronger and higher feeling of his ego" (71). *Sein ganzes Leben war ein zum Lachen und Entsetzen unbeholfener Kampf, um Geltung dafür zu erzwingen* (ibid.); "His entire life was an awkward struggle on behalf of these higher feelings, a struggle that would make us laugh and cry out in horror." Moosbrugger hates the psychiatrists, who use Latin and French words to debase his character, to turn the mystery of his difficult life into a series of banal and demeaning categories. He works diligently against his own defense attorney and in favor of the presiding judge, precisely because he wants to have his intelligible character, which is the basis of his human dignity, acknowledged by the others. As Musil will later say of him, "Moosbrugger did not believe in God, but rather in his own personal reason" (394). True, his reason fails to

7 Carl Schmitt, *Der Begriff des Politischen* (Berlin: Duncker & Humblot, 1963 [1932], 33. The full sentence reads: "Die Begriffe Freund, Feind und Kampf erhalten ihren realen Sinn dadurch, daß sie insbesondere auf die reale Möglichkeit der physischen Tötung Bezug haben und behalten"; "The concepts friend, foe, and struggle receive their real meaning from the fact that they especially have and retain their relation to the real possibility of physical killing." The real possibility of their killing us calls forth another possibility—that either by way of reaction or preemption we embrace the real possibility of our killing them.

hold things together. Why? Musil explains, *Die Gummibänder waren einfach weg* (395); "The rubber bands had simply gone missing." Earlier on in the novel, Musil tells us about Moosbrugger's trial:

> During the trial Moosbrugger presented his defense attorney with difficulties no one could have predicted. He squatted there like a spectator on the bench, calling out "Bravo!" to the state's attorney whenever he offered evidence that seemed to Moosbrugger worthy of demonstrating his danger to the community, and he sang out the praises of witnesses who declared that they had never noticed anything about him that would point to a lack of accountability [*Unzurechnungsfähigkeit*]. "You are a droll fellow!" said the presiding judge, complimenting him thus from time to time and then drawing tight the snares that the accused had laid for himself.... In the eyes of the judge, Moosbrugger's deeds had their origin in Moosbrugger himself; in Moosbrugger's eyes, his deeds had come to him like birds on the wing. For the judge, Moosbrugger was a special case; for himself, Moosbrugger was a world, and it is difficult to say something convincing about a world. (74–75)

Even the criminal, and perhaps the psychopathic criminal more than anyone else, is *weltbildend* in Heidegger's sense, forming an entire world out of the shards of experience. Moosbrugger's world, no doubt, is rough-edged and difficult to paint.

Recall that for Kant freedom is a causality that falls *aus der Reihe,* outside the chain of causation in the space and time of nature. Moosbrugger is in this respect too a paragon of Kantian freedom, because for him every event in his life, without the rubber bands, falls *aus der Reihe*. Interestingly, Musil invokes not "nature" but the more phenomenological notion of *world,* indeed, a world that resists categorization and objective analysis. In that world, the diachronic form of intuition, the portal that grants entry to an orderly inner experience, is reduced to synchronic anarchy. With Moosbrugger, everything is an indistinguishable *nebeneinander,* even if it ought to have been occurring *nacheinander*. Birds of a feather flock together, and they alight at once on the disordered limbs of Moosbrugger's mind; he examines these birds in the *Perspektiv* of his ever-shifting kaleidoscope in the way that E. T. A. Hoffmann's Nathanael examines Olimpia. The psychiatrists call the results of this disorder of the mind *hallucination*. Moosbrugger knows of course that he hallucinates, but he also knows that the others are not perspicacious enough to see the visions and hear the voices that he sees and hears; he is so much better at hallucinating than normal people are that the psychiatrists have nothing of any value to say to him. Doubtless, Moosbrugger wants to be as intelligible as his worthy judges are, and his judges help him in this endeavor: working together, *Täter und Tadelnder* together elaborate the logic of his death sentence.

Of course, that sentence will be appealed, for everyone can see that even though this socio-psycho-path needs to be locked up or somehow kept at bay he is as mad as a hatter, and whether one lives in Austria or England or America one must never kill a mockingbird—even when his song is wildly and even violently distorted. Moosbrugger's case goes before the forensic psychiatrists, who as usual contradict one another, and ultimately to the forensic lawyers who are the experts on *Zurechnungsfähigkeit*. (Incidentally, among the earliest jurists who had to decide on the accountability of the mad was *Kammergerichtsrat* E. T. A. Hoffmann, the author of *Night Pieces* [1817], which has as its lead story "The Sandman," which features Nathanael and Olimpia along with the Doppelgänger Coppelius/Coppola.) The reader is happy to leave behind Moosbrugger's kaleidoscopic world in the hope that something saner awaits.

Ulrich's father, who has many qualities, is a theoretician of the law and a specialist in the question of the death penalty. As with any university professor, he has enemies in the academy, but even his enemies agree that capital punishment must be carried out from time to time if a society is to defend itself and survive. The logics of justification may vary but the conclusion does not. Every rational creature with qualities seems to agree on this. One of the most unnerving aspects of Musil's unfinished masterpiece, however, is the way in which the minds of Moosbrugger and his judges run along the same lines, so that when we are well into the novel we have a difficult time distinguishing the *non sequiturs* of jurisprudence from the ramblings of a lunatic. Immediately after Musil has given us a splendid show of Moosbrugger's hallucinatory mind, he takes us (in chapter 60) on an "Excursion into the Logico-Ethical Kingdom," *Ausflug ins logisch-sittliche Reich*. Doctors, lawyers, and the rest of us will all agree that Moosbrugger qualifies as someone whose accountability is diminished or reduced: *verminderte Zurechnungsfähigkeit* would be this man's essential quality. Yet can or should "the ethical good of responsibility," *das sittliche Gut der Verantwortung* (243–44), be "diminished"? Concerning the cases of "diminished accountability," *der verminderten Zurechnungsfähigkeit*, and the unfortunate human beings whom we identify as belonging among such "cases," Musil notes the following:

> Characteristic of these unfortunates is that they have not only an inferior state of health but also an inferior illness. Nature has the peculiar proclivity to produce such persons *en masse. Natura non fecit saltus,* nature takes no leaps, it loves transitions, and it largely holds the world suspended in a transitional state between debility and health. But jurisprudence takes no notice of this. Jurisprudence says: *non datur tertium sive medium inter duo contradictoria.* In German: either the human being is able to act contrary to the law or he is not, since between two opposites there is no third thing in the middle. Because of his capacity to act contrary to the law he is punishable, and by virtue of this quality of punishability he becomes a person endowed with rights [*eine Rechtsperson*], and as such he participates in the beneficence that is superior to all persons, the beneficence of right [*überpersönlichen Wohltat des Rechts*]. (242)

Moosbrugger, in short, is no animal; he is by birth a subject of the logico-ethical kingdom; "and thus since punishability is the first of those qualities that raises him to the level of an ethical human being, it is understandable that the man of law must hold on to that quality with iron steadfastness" (ibid.). The psychiatrists, for their part, cannot agree on a diagnosis, whereas the paragons of jurisprudence can. Musil comments:

> For, according to the view of the minion of the law, if one is partly ill, then one is also partly healthy. But if one is partly healthy, then one is also at least partly accountable; for accountability is, as they say, the state of a human being who has the power, independent of all the compelling circumstances that surround him, to determine himself or herself to a particular purpose, and such determination cannot simultaneously be in one's possession and also in default. (243)

The doctors ultimately succumb to the jurists, for no one is willing to deprive Moosbrugger of "the ethical good of responsibility" (243–44), even if the jurists themselves are reminiscent of Senatspräsident Schreber in his least lucid moments. Musil ends his chapter with a devastating understatement: "It is a well-known phenomenon that the angel medicine, after he has listened for some time to the deliberations of the jurists, very often forgets his own mission. He folds back his wings with a noisy flutter and behaves himself in the courtroom like a reserve angel of jurisprudence" (244).

The detailed debate among the jurists is carried out in chapter 111 of *Der Mann ohne Eigenschaften.* Time and space will not permit a discussion of this debate, in which all the arguments go in circles, circles that are entirely reminiscent of Hölderlin's perceptive sketch *Über den Begriff der Strafe*. This is the chapter in which the unfortunate relevance of philosophy and theology for jurisprudence is revealed. The chapter is called, "For a Man of Law There Are No Half-Insane People," *Es gibt für Juristen keine halbverrückten Menschen*. The debate itself is both hilariously comic and, if one may say so, unutterably *grausam*. Let us allow ourselves but two glimpses into this chapter, the first presenting the point of view of those (such as Ulrich's father) who uphold individual responsibility and accountability in terms of universals, the second presenting the view of those (such as Ulrich's father's enemies) who wish to weigh only the *social consequences* of the crime in question. Here, first of all, is the view of the proponents of personal responsibility, who are profoundly affected by the teachings of traditional philosophy and theology. At the heart of the philosophical and theological tendency is the "practical compulsion" to impose a punishment wherever ethically free creatures commit evil deeds, even if no theory can convincingly justify the compulsion:

> Naturally, no technical expert today allows his arguments to depend on the arguments of philosophy and theology; yet as perspectives, that is, something as empty as space and yet effectively jumbling things together, these two rivals in the search for ultimate wisdom get mixed into the expert's optics. And thus in the end the question that everyone had been assiduously avoiding took shape, the question as to whether one is allowed to view every human being as ethically free—in other words, the good old question about freedom of the will, a question that provided a perspectival center for all the various opinions, even though these lay on the outskirts of their discussion. For if the human being is ethically free, one has to exercise a practical constraint on him by way of punishment, a practical constraint that theoretically one does not believe in; but if one regards him as not free, seeing him rather as a pawn of invariable concatenated natural forces, then one can by way of punishment excite an effective deterrent tendency in him, but one dare not in ethical terms hold him accountable for what he does. Because of this question a third party arose, which proposed to divide the perpetrator into two parts, a zoological-psychological part, with which the judge had nothing to do, and a juridical part, which, although merely a construction, was legally free. Luckily, this partitioning remained theoretical. (536–37)

Kant's *Nichtsdestoweniger* subreption would now read: *So tadelt man nichtsdestoweniger den in zwei Teile theoretisch geteilten aber doch ganzen Täter*; "Nevertheless, one does not shy from blaming the entire perpetrator, even if, theoretically, he has been divided into two parts." Because the division into two remains theoretical, and "fortunately" so, it is clear that all of Moosbrugger, his entire zoological-psychological duplex, will be compelled to mount with pride the gallows stairway.

And here is the reply of those who set aside the question of freedom and accountability, considering only the social effects of the crime—a reply, one may predict, that will not increase Moosbrugger's chances to avoid that stairway. Furthermore, the "social" vocabulary employed here, after the horrors of the Third Reich, has to strike us as unutterably *grausam*. Musil writes:

> The social conception tells us that the criminal "degenerate" is to be judged not at all in a moralizing way, but rather only in terms of his being a menace to human society. From this it follows that the more menacing he is the more accountable he must be; from that it follows, in strict logical fashion, that the apparently least guilty of all criminals, namely, the person who is mentally ill and who because of his nature is least able to benefit from the ameliorating influence of punishment, must be threatened with the most severe punishments—in any case, much more severe than the punishments meted out to the healthy, so that the deterrent force will be commensurate. (538)

It is clear to all, however, that Moosbrugger is so seriously ill and so utterly "degenerate" that no threat of punishment, no matter how severe, will deter him. It could only encourage him, as it seems. Logic therefore compels the next step, which is the final step on the stairway.

•

Let us leave the jurists, both the moral universalists and the social consequentialists, but also the theoretical divisionists, to their acrimonious and bootless debate. A few words more, by way of conclusion, on Derrida's seminar on the death penalty. Among the most controversial and least expected arguments Derrida raises in his seminar is one that touches on the *kindness* and *humanity* of certain forms of execution. You will recall that Dr. Guillotin's invention was celebrated for its humaneness, inasmuch as it eliminated the pain associated with more protracted cudgelings, reducing the transition from life to death to a mere fraction of a second. To sever the spinal cord so efficiently—at least when the Widow performed well, which she often did, though not always—was certainly an improvement over the cudgel, the axe, the sword, or the mace, not to mention burning at the stake or a team of disagreeable horses. Who knows but that the victim, at least in the mind of the executioner, might experience a certain thrill at this ultimate instant in the arms of the Widow, something spine-tingling in and as the final sensation of life, the ultimate Eros of Thanatos, as it were?

Derrida sees in this celebration of humaneness and humanity a strange desire at work, to wit, the desire to put an end to the finitude of human existence by manipulating time, that is, by reducing the determination of that finitude to a calculable split second. You will recall that when the chorus of Oceanides asks Prometheus why Zeus is so angry with him, Prometheus concedes that he gave human beings a gift greater than fire, the gift that constituted their humanness as such. He gave them something like an eternal deed or an intelligible character. What did he give us? He gave us the poison or the remedy, the φάρμακον, of "blind hopes," τυφλὰς … ἐλπίδας, hopes that prevent our foreseeing the day of our death (ll. 251–52). The irony is stupendous: Prometheus, he who has and is Titanic "Foresight," gives as his finest gift the *lack* of foresight. And that lack is what enables human beings to learn all the uses of fire, to develop all the cunning and know-how of technology and of culture in general, enabling them even to outsmart the gods themselves with bones wrapped in folds of fat, saving the best of sacrificial flesh for themselves. All that cunning, all that insight, is grounded in lack of foresight, in blindness! Heidegger says it best: the fifth of the existential qualities of our being toward the end is the *certainty* of death combined with the *indeterminacy* as to its *when*.

What has Prometheus to do with the death penalty? The Titanic state, the state of Texas, as it were, grants to the mortal on Death Row the finest of gifts (if you happen to live in Texas), namely, the gift of a determinate *when*, and, even if Heidegger does not mention this, the gift of a determinate *how*. Regardless of the "how," the finitude of a human being is now reduced to the smallest particles of a bifurcated instant, as the bullet penetrates the encircled heart, as the noose snaps the spinal column, as the crystalline liquids flow through the plastic tubing into the vein. It is as though the governor of Texas gives to the inmate the gift that he so desires for himself and for his spouse and children, the gift of knowing precisely when (and how) the transition from the Here-and-Now to the Beyond is to occur—and not by dint of an asses' bridge. Then and precisely then, and at no other time, for the first and last time, once and for all, life is determinate. Perhaps only in its decapitation is Schelling's redoubled "essence," *das Wesen im Wesen,* determinate. The eternal deed, the eternal commencement, the only truly intelligible deed worthy of a truly intelligible character is the gift of such a death. As Silenos urged us all long ago, "Die as soon as ever you may." Quickly. Instantaneously. At that point and in that instant the positions of killer and killed are uncannily reversed: in a logic worthy of Moosbrugger, or of Moosbrugger's judges, sovereignty gives the gift that lasts, the adamantine gift reserved for the very few, the elect, the determinate. Sovereignty gives the gift of the end of finitude, the gift that the German language calls so beautifully *das Gift,* "poison."

Derrida calls this the *phantasm* of the end of finitude, the phantasm of putting an end to, or at least "interrupting," the "principle of indetermination . . . the incalculable chance whereby a living being has a relation to what comes, to the to-come [*à l'à-venir*], and thus to the other as event [*à de l'autre comme événement*]" (1:347). The perversity of the death penalty, its "infinite perversity, properly infinite and infinitizing" (1:349n. 1), its Moosbruggerian madness, is its desire to put an end to finitude, to impose an end in a calculable place at a calculable time by a calculable means. By putting an end to life, the "calculating decision . . . affirms its power over time, it masters the future, it protects against the irruption of the other" (1:349).

Of course, it only *seems* to do all this. For this calculation, this power, this mastery remain phantasmatic. It could even be demonstrated, says Derrida, that such a phantasm lies at the "origin of phantasm in general" (ibid.). In Freudian terms, one might say that the phantasm of the end of finitude is a *primal phantasm.* Derrida's Freudian heritage is unmistakably present in his description of the "dream" that guarantees the survival of the death penalty—even after the death penalty has in many places been abolished. Derrida's sentence, which we have already encountered (at least in part) in the previous chapter, is as complicated as the phantasm itself:

> [S]ince this phantasm [of the end of finitude] is at work in us all the time, even outside of any real scene of verdict and death penalty, since we "recount" this possibility to ourselves all the time, the possibility of a calculating decision with regard to our death embracing as it does the dream of an infinitization and thus of an infinite survival that is assured by the interruption itself, and since we cannot keep ourselves from permanently playing the scene of the condemned one whom we potentially are, the fascination exerted by the real phenomena of death penalty and execution . . . has to do with their effect of

> truth or of acting out: we then see it actually staged, we project it as one projects a film or as one projects a project, we see actually take place in projection what we are dreaming of all the time—what we are dreaming of, that is, what in a certain way we desire, namely, to give ourselves death and to infinitize ourselves by giving ourselves death in a calculable, calculated, decidable fashion; and when I say *we*, it means that in this dream we occupy, simultaneously or successively, all the positions of the dream, those of the judge or judges, the jury, the executioner or the assistants, and, to be sure, the position of the condemned, as well as of the witnesses, whether they are loved or hated. And it is the force of this effect of phantasmatic truth that will probably remain invincible, forever assuring us, alas, of a double survival—the survival of both the death penalty and the abolitionist protest. (1:349–50)

It is purely for the purposes of this fantasy, perhaps, that we are phantasmagorically free. Yet may it not also be the case that we declare ourselves free so that we may find the others accountable and culpable, their guilt imputable, their punishment indisputably merited and to be carried out with iron necessity? If the others are free, it is perhaps so that I, sovereignly human and marvelously humane as you know me to be, may declare them responsible and—at least intelligibly and eternally—reprehensible: that slight tingling sensation they will feel, quite briefly, contrasts in me to a shudder of explosive yet extended ecstasy, an ecstasy of both body and mind. And I will give my ecstasy the highest of names. I shall call it, not *cruelty*, but *justice*. Even if, as Derrida avers, I must occupy *all* the positions in this dream or phantasm of the end of finitude, so that justice will inevitably recoil upon me, *den Tadelnder*, I will cry out that I too—compelled by my cruelty as I am—*was* free!

Many pages ago, I mentioned Nietzsche's name. I have not cited him in this chapter, and yet readers have by now recognized "my" three theses as his work. Allow me to conclude by citing one brief paragraph from *Götzen-Dämmerung*, "The Four Great Errors," section 7:

> [T]he doctrine of the will was essentially discovered for the purpose of punishment, that is, *the desire to find someone guilty*. The entirety of classical psychology, the psychology of the will, has as its presupposition the ones who invented it, namely, the priests who dominated the ancient communities and who wanted to create a *right* to

> inflict punishments. . . . Human beings were thought to be "free" so that they could be judged and punished—so that they could become *guilty*: as a consequence, every action *had to be* willed; the cause of every action *had to be* thought of as having its seat in consciousness (—and with that the *most fundamental* counterfeit in matters psychological was made the very principle of psychology). (KSW 6:95)

Perhaps the transition from ancient communities to civil society may be thought of as the moment when the counterfeiters become executioners. A cruel thought, but not so cruel as the powers that wield the cudgel and the syringe.

However, by reaffirming my Nietzschean theses I am suppressing or averting Derrida's crucial insight. The suggestion seems to be that the origin of cruelty—in capital punishment but perhaps elsewhere as well—resides in the phantasm of attaining absolute power, the power to give myself my own death and thus to survive it. Derrida does not recall here Sartre's "useless passion" to be God, at least not explicitly, but he comes very close to doing so. The phantasm of living on precisely by the projection of my fatal interruption or truncation, Derrida says, "is one and the same as God [*fait un avec Dieu*], or, if you prefer, as belief in God, the experience of God, the relation to God, or as faith or religion" (1:350). The only thing that can save us from such faith is the realization that belief is stubbornly accompanied by unbelief. Such unbelief may offer the only possibility of resisting the cruelest expressions of the omnipotence fantasy, precisely as it may enable our will to power to resist the cruelest exertions of both will and power.

Will to power? What is that? And is it to be found in cruel souls only, or may tender souls apply?

Chapter Ten

Cruelty, Power, Art, Tenderness

Every angel is terrifying.

—Rainer Maria Rilke

UP TO NOW my inquiry has focused on two German words, *Zärtlichkeit*, "tenderness," and *Grausamkeit*, "cruelty" of a "psychological" sort. I hope I will not try my readers' patience by taking up again at the end yet another German word, and a difficult one. Freud used the word *Bemächtigung*, which has the word *Macht* at its center, to talk about a drive to "empower" the struggling psyche to "overpower" something or someone out there in a challenging world. Derrida was fascinated by this word, troubling himself about it over many decades, and in July 2000, in between the first and the second years of his seminar on the death penalty, he presented his "States of the Soul of Psychoanalysis" to the Estates General of Psychoanalysis, convened in Paris, on precisely this concept. The problem, in its simplest terms, is twofold: (1) Is *Bemächtigung*, presumably tied to the "reality probe," in effect the drive that lies behind or within both the erotic and the death drives, serving as something like their transcendental condition of possibility? (2) Does *Bemächtigung*, as "empowerment" or "successful domination," invariably involve violence and cruelty? If we ask these two questions together, we have to wonder whether something like tenderness has a chance whenever power is in play—and that seems to be *always*.

Back in chapter 8 we saw that Nietzsche was able to unmask the ostensible "disinterestedness" of reason in Kant, preeminently in Kant's reflections on art and beauty in the third Critique. In other words, it may be art, both our response to it and our efforts to engage in artistic creativity, that holds the key to the secret chambers of power. That is why Derrida turns initially to the third treatise of Nietzsche's *Genealogy of Morals*, focusing there on Nietzsche's treatment of Wagner, before taking up the questions of "guilt" and "bad conscience" in the second treatise. This surprising decision on Derrida's part will guide my own efforts here at the end.

I will introduce the problem of *Bemächtigung* and of Nietzsche's *Wille zur Macht* as clearly as I can, starting with an attempt at a definition of terms. I will then open a reading of Derrida's *States of the Soul*, but soon digress from that text in order to present some literary figures that seem to embody the problem of empowerment as cruelty. I will then turn to Freud's two texts on war, which are so important for Derrida's effort in *States of the Soul*.

In the second part of the chapter I will continue to read Derrida's text by turning to Nietzsche's *Genealogy of Morals*. Why? Because of the close relation of *States of the Soul* to the death penalty seminar, which provides the context for Derrida's address. Recall that during the first year of the death penalty seminar, in its sixth session, he offers an extraordinary reading of Nietzsche's *Genealogy of Morals*, which in large measure is a genealogy of *Grausamkeit*. Throughout the death penalty seminar, Derrida challenges psychoanalysis to think cruelty *beyond* the history of blood flow toward a more general sense of cruelty—and, surprisingly, he turns to the German word *Grausamkeit* in order to redefine the problem of cruelty.

In the third part of the chapter I will consider what Derrida offers as an admittedly "impossible" solution to the problem of a "beyond" of cruelty. I will then, in the fourth and final part, develop the problem of power in other texts by Nietzsche, especially those on art, the artist, and will to power as art. The question will be whether the "power" of *Wille zur Macht als Kunst* may somehow release us from the usual senses of power as violence and cruelty.

It is clear that the *Bemächtigungstrieb*, the pulsion or drive to empower or overpower, has to do with Nietzsche's will to power: in his 1924 essay, "The Economic Problem of Masochism," surely one of Freud's most understated titles, Freud notes that "moral masochism" can be avoided only if and when the libido makes the destructive tendency harmless for the ego by turning it to objects in the outside world. At this point, he says, "it is then called the *Destruktionstrieb, Bemächtigungstrieb, Wille zur Macht*" (GW 3:376). Will to power seems here to be a synonym for *Bemächtigung* as *Destruktionstrieb*. My question will be: Can will to power be more than that, something perhaps less violent yet no less powerful? An aid or guideline for me will be the two semester-long lecture courses on Nietzsche offered by Heidegger in 1936 and 1939, those on will to power as art and as knowledge. I will treat the second aspect first, will to power as knowledge, closing the chapter and the book with a reflection on will to power as art. Derrida does not take this final step, and he might have been entirely skeptical with regard to it, I do not know. Yet it is he who both in the seminar on the death penalty and in his address to the psychoanalysts takes the questions of *Grausamkeit* and *Bemächtigung* to the very doorstep of Nietzsche's notion of will to power—without entering into the sinuous chambers of Nietzsche's texts on it. As for will to power as *art*, Derrida was not one to discourage efforts in the arts or to underestimate the power of art. I will merely push him—gently, tenderly—in a direction that might well have appealed to him, the direction that as a very young man he called *jeu*, "play."

Let me begin with some notes on the term *Bemächtigung*. Again, the Brothers Grimm will be my mentors. *Bemächtigung* is identified immediately with two words, first, the Latin *occupatio*, presumably in the sense of the "occupation" of a city by an invading power, and second, the German *Gewalt*, which means both a forceful or even violent "overtaking" and a "having dominion over." The verb *sich bemächtigen*, which occurs far more frequently than the noun, is defined by the Latin *potiri aliqua re*, from *potior*, to be lord over, to possess, to enjoy, hence "to have power over something." The *sich*, which is always used with the verb (except in the present and past participial forms), makes it reflexive, so that there is always a reference back to the one having power. Wieland writes the following line, presumably for Amor: " 'Time is precious, dear Psyche,' he said, '*wir müssen uns der Augenblicke bemächtigen*, we must seize the moments for ourselves.' " The objects of such seizure, however, are usually military or political: to capture a kingdom, a city, a fortress, a trench, a ship, or to seize rule for oneself. A less military or political sense of *sich bemächtigen* is one's rising to an occasion or becoming equal to a task, coming to terms with a thing, having disposition, dominion, or mastery over a situation. For Freud, the noun and the verb become technical terms related to both the self-preservation drives and the erotic drive, but also, it seems, to the "reality probe" or "reality principle," which enables the ego to confront and overcome obstacles in its pursuit of pleasure or in the fulfillment of basic needs. Later in Freud's thought the word has to do with an originary sadism and even with a principle *beyond* the pleasure principle, namely, the principle that presumably underlies what he begins to call the destruction-and-death drives. In other words, *Bemächtigung* seems to be in all places at once for Freud. The definition by Laplanche and Pontalis is accurate, but it points only very diffidently toward the problem of Freud's theory of drives in general: "*Bemächtigungstrieb* (English: the instinct to master, French: *pulsion d'emprise*): An expression employed by Freud on several occasions, yet the usage of which cannot be codified. Freud understands by it a drive that is not sexual, one that unites with sexuality only secondarily; its goal is to dominate the object by force" (LP 639–40). At one point in *The Post Card*, as we will see, Derrida speculates that *every* drive or pulsion has to be considered a form of *Bemächtigung.* That would certainly include the destruction-and-death drives, so that a very long and very dark shadow is cast by the *Bemächtigungstrieb* toward the end of Freud's career. Perhaps, to repeat, it involves a double problem: on the one hand, this "empowerment" drive seems to be the strongest evidence for what Freud calls the *Vermengungen* of the *Todes- und Lebenstriebe* (GW 13:376), that is, the "conglomerations" or "intermixtures" of the death and life drives, such that the very notion of a *dualism* of drives seems to be threatened—threatened by what Freud also calls *Triebvermischung,* the "mix" or "mélange" of drives (ibid.); on the other hand, the mix or conglomeration of drives seems to point eminently in the direction of the destruction-and-death drives, that is, in the direction of "will to power" in its Hollywood sense, to wit, pleasure taken in violence, the delectation of cruelty, Spinoza's *sympathia malevolens.*

Nietzsche uses the noun *Bemächtigung* only twice in his work, although the reflexive verb *sich bemächtigen* is quite common in his vocabulary. The English translations of the term are widely and wildly various. Whereas the notions of rising to or becoming equal to a challenge, coming to terms with a thing, being equal to the occasion, having disposition or dominion over the matter at hand are perhaps closest to Freud's sense of the reality probe, the notion of a violent overcoming and seizure, appropriate to the destruction-and-death drives, is perhaps closer to Nietzsche's customary use of the word. The translation of the word as "empowerment" has the advantage of keeping the *Macht* of *Wille zur Macht* at the center of the word but the disadvantage of an apparent self-righteousness—everyone (especially in the USA) regards "empowerment" as a positive achievement. In 1884, Nietzsche jotted down two notes that capture his unswerving belief concerning the drive to knowledge (*Erkenntnis*): (1) "Science: the overcoming of nature for the purposes of the human being [*Wissenschaft: die Bemächtigung der Natur zu Zwecken des Menschen*]" (KSW 11:91); (2) "The entire apparatus of cognition is an apparatus for abstracting and simplifying—aiming not at knowledge but at *attaining power* over the things [Bemächtigung *der Dinge*]" (KSW 11:164). Thus *Bemächtigung* may be seen as lying at the heart of Nietzsche's notion of will to power with reference to what one may call "the knowledge project." A note from 1880 reads: "Will is the representation of a valued object together with the expectation that we will seize it for ourselves [*dass wir uns seiner bemächtigen werden*]" (KSW 9:71).

Let me turn briefly to a second key term, already familiar to us, but now with special reference to psychoanalysis. Freud's uses of *Grausamkeit* are sometimes surprising, as in his assertion that when the infant bites the nipple of the mother or nurse it is a prime instance of cruelty. (But is "cruelty" an adequate translation of *Grausamkeit*? Obviously not—and yet a better translation eludes me, in spite of the many candidates. Shall we say *malice, malevolence,* or *rancor,* or perhaps that lovely word *fell*?) "Cruelty," at least after the *Three Treatises Toward a Theory of Sex*, is closely related to the entire issue of what will become the "destruction-and-death drives" at the center of Freud's 1920 *Beyond the Pleasure Principle*. The cruelties of war, as we know, had an enormous impact on the development of Freud's theories in the direction of these drives.

As for Nietzsche on *Grausamkeit,* there are dozens of references, possibly hundreds. Among them are two in *The Birth of Tragedy from the Spirit of Music*, which refer to the Hellenic insight into "the cruelty of nature [*die Grausamkeit der Natur*]" (§7; KSW 1:56), contrasting that insight with our modern culture's nervousness in the face of "the natural cruelty of things [*der natürlichen Grausamkeit der Dinge*]" (§18; KSW 1:119). Nietzsche's *Genealogy*, which will continue to be a central text for us, emphasizes cruelty as "the great festive joy," *die grosse Festfreude* (ZGM II:6; KSW 5:301), that is, as an essential part of every civic celebration in earlier stages of our own culture. Later and "higher" stages define themselves by *einer Vergeistigung der Grausamkeit* (ibid.), a "spiritualization" or "refinement," even a " 'deification' " (*Vergöttlichung*) of cruelty. *Beyond Good and Evil* (JGB 55; KSW 5:74) speaks of the "very long, many-runged ladder of religious cruelty [*eine sehr grosse Leiter der religiösen Grausamkeit, mit vielen Sprossen*]," arguing that religions are fundamentally systems of cruelty. Recall in this regard Nietzsche's analysis of ascetic ideals as *die Grausamkeit gegen sich*, cruelty turned inward against the self, Joyce's *agenbite of inwit*, Nietzsche's "inventive self-castigation" (ZGM III:10; KSW 5:360). But recall also Derrida's emphasis on the internal, infernal contradiction whereby the ascetic priest—precisely as hostile to life and as apparently impotent, as life in decline—in every age and in every culture attains enormous power. The enigma lies in the fact that life as will to power seems to act against its own interest, which is the flourishing of life. The ultimate passage, the one that best captures this internal, infernal contradiction that seems to lie precisely at the heart of the philosopher's own practice, is Nietzsche's reflection on his activity as a practitioner of genealogy: he calls the genealogists of morals, himself included, "vivisectionists" and "nutcrackers of the soul" (ZGM III:9; KSW 5:358). Can will to power as *art* rescue itself and us from such self-inflicted cruelty?

However, let us now at least begin our reading of Derrida's *États d'âme,* "States of the Soul," which opens with a reflection on "suffering," and "suffering *cruelly.*" *Cruellement* is the adverb that most naturally accompanies *souffrir,* "to suffer," in all its active and passive forms, *souffrir, faire et se faire souffrir, laisser et se laisser souffrir.* One suffers cruelly oneself, or one causes or abandons others to suffer cruelly (EA 9/238). A happy development in the English language allows us to say all this quite economically in the phrase, "to suffer (someone) to suffer," as in Jesus's command, "Suffer the little children to come unto me." Surely, when the good Jesuits cited this passage from the gospels to the young Joyce, that is, to young Stephen Hero and young Dedalus, the schoolboys must have shuddered. *Cruauté* has to do with spilled blood: the words *cruor, crudus, crudelitas* invoke the raw and the bloody (EA 10/238–39). As we have seen, both years of Derrida's seminar on the death penalty, but especially the second, are occupied with "the history of blood," a history that, with lethal injection, seems to be drawing to a close. What is not coming to an end but perhaps only getting under way is the history of *Grausamkeit.* To repeat, this is Freud's word even for the suckling infant who begins to bite—the little sadist, as Freud also says, referring to the adorable darling who wants to cannibalize the mother. And it is also the word for the effects of war in Freud's and our own time.

As we have also seen, the principal problem of the history of the term *Grausamkeit,* even though Derrida does not talk about this directly, is the intensification of the word and the inversion of its sense, that is, the point at which it begins to express not a shudder in the face of the merciless but a certain twisted Eros that is *drawn to* the merciless. Instead of a shudder, a *frisson,* what Derrida calls *le plaisir aigu pris au mal dans l'âme,* the keen pleasure that is taken in the ill or the evil within the soul or psyche (EA 11/239).

Perhaps here we can step for a moment out of Derrida's text. Even though his meaning so far seems clear, it may be useful to think of some exemplars of *Grausamkeit* in literature. Among the exemplars of this inversion of the sense of *Grausamkeit*—in our literatures they are legion, and they exercise the greatest fascination—are the heroes of Sade's fictions and, closer to home, some of the villains in the work of Herman Melville, especially the figures of Claggart in "Billy Budd" and Jackson in *Redburn,* or Faulkner's Percy Grimm in *Light in August.* These characters are spellbinding precisely because they are experts at preying (with an *e*) on their sometimes younger and almost always relatively helpless confreres: their principal drive, one might say, is *Bemächtigung,* and their sovereign pleasure is *Grausamkeit.* The figure of Claggart is well known, that of Jackson in Melville's 1849 *Redburn* less so.

Jackson, who foreshadows the unforgettable Claggart in many respects, is entirely unprepossessing in his person, yet he dominates the ship's crew. Young Redburn is a simple soul, so that Melville has to simplify his vocabulary and crimp his insights. Here is Redburn introducing Jackson:

> In fact he was a great bully, and being the best seaman on board, and very overbearing every way, all the men were afraid of him, and durst not contradict him, or cross his path in any thing. And what made this more wonderful was, that he was the weakest man, bodily, of the whole crew; and I have no doubt that young and small as I was then, compared to what I am now, I could have thrown him down. But he had such an over-awing way with him; such a deal of brass and impudence, such an unflinching face, and withal was such a hideous looking mortal, that Satan himself would have run from him. And besides all this, it was quite plain, that he was by nature a marvelously clever, cunning man, though without education; and understood human nature to a kink, and well knew whom he had to deal with; and then, one glance of his squinting eye, was as good as a knock-down, for it was the most deep, subtle, infernal looking eye, that I ever saw lodged in a human head. I believe, that by good rights it must have belonged to a wolf, or starved tiger; at any rate, I would defy any oculist, to turn out a glass eye, half so cold, and snaky, and deadly. It was a horrible thing; and I would give much to forget that I have ever seen it; for it haunts me to this day.[1]

Jackson's background? He has spent most of his time on ships that worked the west coast of Africa as slavers, "and with a diabolical relish," says Redburn, "he used to tell of the *middle-passage*" (57). Soon Redburn becomes Jackson's Billy Budd, with Jackson eyeing the young man with malevolence and a certain twist of Eros. "For I was young and handsome, at least my mother so thought me," says

---

1 I cite the Newberry/Northwestern Edition of Melville's works, edited by Harrison Hayford et al., here *Redburn: His First Voyage* (Evanson and Chicago: Northwestern University Press and the Newberry Library, 1969), 57. Cited by page number in my text.

Redburn, "whereas *he* was being consumed by an incurable malady, that was eating up his vitals" (58). Jackson's end is bloody and horrific. Yet even before the end, Redburn comes to pity the man he calls "a horrid desperado" (104). Yes, he was a bully, "But there seemed even more woe than wickedness about the man; and his wickedness seemed to spring from his woe; and for all his hideousness, there was that in his eye at times, that was ineffably pitiable and touching; and though there were moments when I almost hated this Jackson, yet I have pitied no man as I have pitied him" (105). If Jackson is Satan, then he is *Milton's* Satan—Milton's *Paradise Lost* being one of Melville's constant literary companions.

The Marquis de Sade's heroes, by contrast, are not fallen angels. Allow me a brief mention of Sade's *120 Days*.[2] The word *cruelty* falls seldom in Sade's text, perhaps because the characters in the book are so busy. If there is a deeper reason for the absence of the word, it would be that the author, who freely admits that there are crimes and vices in the world and in his book, is nevertheless at pains to demonstrate that these atrocious deeds are written in the book of nature. Nature smiles on virtue and vice alike.

The word *cruelty* does fall in Sade's account of *le Président de Curval*, and Derrida's reflections on *presidency* in *La peine de mort* would have benefited from a consideration of President Curval, surely the most dastardly of Sade's four heroes. Sade writes, concerning Curval's taste for the downtrodden poor, "By a refinement of atrocious cruelty, yet one that is easy to understand, the class of unfortunates was the class at which he loved to launch the effects of his perfidious rage" (36–37). "Easy to understand" if Sade means that the poor are without resources, and that the police will never intervene on their behalf; not so easy to understand if the word *raffinement* means that cruelty is a taste or a talent that undergoes development and even subtilization through the fine filters of experience. Yet what else does Nietzsche mean when he describes that advanced stage of culture as the "spiritualization of cruelty"? Such refinement may take the most mysterious and subtilized forms of *ressentiment*, in which will to power is actually *Ohnmacht zur Macht*, "impotence to power," literally "without-power to power." That the effects of Curval's *rage*, his hydrophobia, his moral rabies, can undergo a kind of *éducation sentimentale* is nevertheless not so comprehensible.

And yet. One may readily conjure up the image of the cruelest person one knows in his or her circle of acquaintances—not at the university, of course, since among the learned there are surely none such—perhaps in one's home

---

2 I cite vol. 1 of *Oeuvres complètes du Marquis de Sade*, eds. Annie Le Brun and Jean-Jacques Pauvert (Paris: Pauvert, 1986), by page number in my text.

neighborhood, or perhaps in some high public office. They may simply be louts. Louts can be cruel in some loutish way. Yet is it not more likely that the cruelest are also quite cunning? Perhaps they are even the best-honed of knives, the most refined characters in some Mephistophelean sense, the wittiest and perhaps the best educated? Whence these skills? these refinements? And what complications do they introduce into the theme of cruelty?

Much later in Sade's text (297–98), Curval and his colleague Durcet discuss those cases, those many cases, in which a human being comes to desire his or her own degradation and abasement (*l'avilissement*), finding their *jouissance* in the contempt and contumely showered on them by the others (*de trouver des jouissances dans le mépris*). Certain sick persons, says Durcet, take pleasure in their *cacochysme*. This strange word seems to oscillate between *cacochymy* (the French *cacochyme*), meaning having depraved humors or "bad chemistry," and a perverse response to the word *catechism*. The catechist dins into the ear of the catechumen the questions that have only one answer, dins them into the pupil from a superior position, which is the very meaning of κατηχίζει, until the catechumen below can echo perfectly the perfect truths of faith. If, however, one dins into the ear of the cacochumen all that is evil in him or her, the result of such cacochism will be a very different sort of echo, albeit perfect in its own way. When we read the following passage we are likely to believe that the source must be Rousseau's *Émile*, but no, it is *le Président de Curval* who speaks:

> Once a man is degraded, so that he is debased by excesses, he causes his soul to take a kind of vicious turn, from which it will never be able to escape. In every other case shame would serve as the counterweight to those vices his reason counsels him to abandon. Yet here this is no longer possible: shame is the very first feeling that he has snuffed out, the very first that he banishes to a region remote from himself. And from the state in which one no longer blushes to the state in which one loves everything that incites the blush there is but one small step. Everything that we once took to be disagreeable, finding the soul now differently disposed, undergoes a metamorphosis into pleasure. . . . [Y]et the route taken here is imperceptible, and the path is strewn with flowers. (198)

Tout se métamorphose alors en plaisir. But this would mean that there is no getting beyond the pleasure principle, even when one devotes one's life to death and destruction. It would mean that if there are destruction-and-death drives, these would be fueled by the only libido there is. And that would mean that the exquisite dualism that enables us to reward the good and punish the evil would begin to tremble—or would already have transmogrified into a cruel monotheism or monolith, "slouching," as the poet says, "toward Bethlehem to be born."

But let me slouch back in the direction of *États d'âme*. The challenge, says Derrida, is to discuss the causes of *Grausamkeit* "without alibi, whether theological or otherwise" (EA 12–13/240). Presumably, then, without reference to the eating of forbidden fruit and without reference to the survival of the fittest. Not only that. Derrida's effort will be to think *Grausamkeit* quite *beyond* the principles of pleasure and the death drives, indeed, beyond the *principle* as such, and that would require his going *beyond* in a new way and toward a new goal. Let us read a long and difficult passage that comes up quite early in Derrida's address. He tells the analysts that he will not pose the usual question as to whether there is (or are) a *Todestrieb* or "cruel" destruction-and-death drives; nor will he ask whether there is a trace of cruelty inherent in every instance of the drive to mastery, *der Bemächtigungstrieb,* whether on this or that side of the *principles* of pleasure, reality, or aggression.

> Rather, my question, which I will ask later, will be this: is there for thinking, for the psychoanalytic thinking to come, another beyond, if I can put it that way; another beyond, one that would hold out beyond all these *possibles* that are always *both* the principles of pleasure and reality *and* the pulsions of death or of sovereign mastery, which seem to exert themselves everywhere where cruelty announces itself? In other words, in altogether other words, can one think this thing, apparently impossible, but impossible otherwise, namely, a beyond of the death pulsion or the pulsion to sovereign mastery, hence a beyond of cruelty, a beyond that would have nothing to do with either pulsions or principles? Thus also nothing to do with all the rest of the Freudian discourse, which orders itself on principles in its entire economy, its topology, its metapsychology, and above all in what Freud calls—we will hear him say it—his "mythology" of pulsions? Furthermore, he speaks of his "mythology" of pulsions when he evokes the hypothesis of a nature that is equally "mythological," namely, that of the most solid and most positive scientific knowledge, that of the theoretical physics of Einstein, for example. With regard to this beyond the beyond, is a decidable response possible? What I will call the states of the soul of psychoanalysis today—perhaps this is what finally testifies to some sort of experience of the undecidable. To an ordeal of the undecidable. (EA 14–15/241)

The *ordeal* of undecidability? *Une ordalie,* we recall, is a trial by ordeal, the Medieval *ordalium*. The Old English *ordál* derives from the Teutonic *urteili,* trial by ordeal, which survived in England even after the Norman conquest. As the death penalty seminars demonstrate, "judgment," *das Urteil,* arguably remains embedded in the onto-theo-logical remnants of sheer irrationality and cruelty. Yet Derrida now invokes a different sort of ordeal.

Undecidability would be deconstruction's challenge to psychoanalysis. Yet to undergo such an ordeal, to undergo judgment as a *crisis* in the original sense of the word, crisis as κρίνω and κρίσις, *Urteil* as Hegel's *Ur-teilung,* requires that we try to move beyond at least three atavisms. First, we need to ask whether there can be a future for humankind beyond psychological cruelty, *Grausamkeit*. Second, we have to ask whether there can be a future for humankind beyond the drive to sovereign power, the power of *Bemächtigung*. Third, and most decisive, most decisively undecidable, we have to ask whether we—we psychoanalysts, for example, but also we philosophers—can move beyond *principles* in philosophy and science, that is, beyond the princely principle as ἀρχή and ἄρχων, beyond the *archive* of the *sovereign* as such. If there is any getting beyond, however, it would be only by passage through the monumental archives that record the history of *Grausamkeit*. Passage to what end? To the end of decidability as we know or think we know it, to the event that cannot be calculated and programmed. And if this seems utopian—after all the address's subtitle evokes "the impossible beyond" that would be "beyond sovereign cruelty," *L'impossible au-delà d'une souveraine cruauté*—matters are considerably worse than that, inasmuch as utopias can be programmed, whereas the to-come resists every program. Without knowing what will come of it, Derrida insists that psychoanalysis linger in the archives of *Grausamkeit*. And if the analyst should need a break, a night out after lights out, Derrida recommends that he or she attend whatever is playing in the theater of cruelty (EA 43–44/256).

What troubles Derrida most about contemporary psychoanalysis is not the resistance *to* it, for example in the United States, where no psychologist worth his or her rats and mice would read Freud, although that is disturbing enough to Derrida, but the resistance *within* it, mainly its resistance to the theme of cruelty. Such resistance is reminiscent of the Committee's initial resistance to Freud's *Beyond the Pleasure Principle* and to its theory of the destruction-and-death drives (EA 16–17/242). Such resistance may underlie the inability of psychoanalysis to take up the pressing questions of politics and ethics today—above all, its reluctance to engage in a radical questioning of *sovereignty* and *sovereign cruelty*:

> There is some malady [*un mal*] or in any case an auto-immune function in psychoanalysis, as everywhere, a self-rejection, a resistance to self or to its principate, its own principle of protection. Psychoanalysis, in my view, has not yet undertaken, much less successfully thought, to penetrate and to alter the axioms of ethics, of the juridical, and of the political, notably in these seismic places where the theological phantasm of sovereignty is trembling, where the most traumatic geopolitical events are being produced—let us again say, quite confusedly, the cruelest events of our times. (EA 20–21/244)

Derrida's lecture opens up at this point to the entire *politics* of psychoanalysis, its institutions, its severe fathers, its princes and kings, its Estates General, its stormings, its decapitations, its Terror (EA 49ff./264ff.), all of which have a long and complex history in France. Yet his textual framework for that portentous historical parallel—that of the Estates General—is Freud's response to Albert Einstein on the question, "Why War?"

Again we need to step outside Derrida's text in order to take a preliminary look at these two Freud texts. Allow me to begin with the 1915 "Zeitgemässes über Krieg und Tod" (GW 10:323–55), and a personal remark. What strikes me above all when I read Freud's pages is what an extraordinary *thinker* Freud is. How ironic that Heidegger (to mention another thinker) deprived himself of this eminent exemplar of thinking. For Freud's rich background in neurology, psychology, anthropology, sociology, the fine arts, and modern languages and literatures, to say nothing of his familiarity with the philosophies of Plato, Schopenhauer, and Nietzsche, which of course he was always reluctant to acknowledge, produce not *Subjektität,* as Heidegger complains, but *Denken.* Heidegger, by contrast, is often a victim of knee-jerk reactions, short circuits, and, at least in the *Black Notebooks,* vulgar inherited prejudices and a repetition compulsion that is running amok. That compulsion to repeat, as Freud feared, is most closely bound up with the destruction-and-death drives. What is remarkable about Derrida, who was remarkable in so many different ways, is that he acknowledges, and is devoted to, *both* of his grandfathers, the two pépés, *both* Heidegger and Freud.

But on to Freud's 1915 "timely meditations" on war, the first of his two confrontations with war. One of the reasons for the general discouragement and disappointment we feel over the War, says Freud, is that in spite of all the advancements in culture World War I is as *grausam* as any other (GW 10:329).

Grausamkeit is Freud's first word for the not-yet-formulated destruction-and-death drives. Another early approximation to those drives is the adjective *eigensüchtig*, suggesting a self-aggrandizement that goes beyond the egoistic drive to survival, related perhaps to the *Seuche* or infectious malady that, as Schelling knew, contaminates all *Suchen*, all "searching," all "longing." Already in the 1915 essay it is Eros that promises to ameliorate the destructive narcissism of cruelty.

The problem, to repeat, is to think *grausam* not in terms of *grauenerregend* but as the pulsion of destruction itself. Here libido and Eros seem inevitably to be in the mix. Sade's Curval and Melville's Jackson, along with Faulkner's Grimm, testify to this. The problem with the concept of *Grauen* as originally understood is that it remains extrinsic to the drive—it is a *reactive* concept, expressing horror *in the face of* cruelty. Far more difficult to conceive of is the pulsion *within* that goes *toward* the cruel, the Eros of cruelty, which one might call a *primary sadism*. Already in this essay, and indeed long before it, Freud sees that sadism is a crucial part of early childhood, hence of the unconscious as such, which in this respect too is ageless. At this point (GW 10:332), Freud emphasizes the possible "meldings" (*Verschmelzungen*) of one set of drives with another, for example, the "reactive formations," by which altruism grows out of egoism and compassion grows out of *Grausamkeit*. In any case, the *grausamen* drives surely belong among the "primitive" *Triebregungen*. Here I am tempted to think of *Grausamkeit* as the ancient Γοργώ, but the Gorgo too is a reactive figure. Perhaps the more useful figure of *grauen* would be infatuating doom, Ἄτη—perhaps one must fast-forward to Lacan's treatment of Sophocles's *Antigone* in *The Ethics of Psychoanalysis*. However, instead, and in spite of the many fascinating aspects of Freud's 1915 essay, let us turn to the 1933 "*Warum Krieg?*" which is even more crucial for Derrida's address.[3]

3 One aspect of Freud's 1915 text that I cannot fail to mention, one that must have struck Derrida, is the role played by our denial of death in the genesis of fiction and drama. Freud indicates the key role played by fiction and by the theater in the suppression of our recognition of our inevitable death: we outlive the heroes of our novels and our stage, inasmuch as when they die, we go on to the next hero (GW 10:343–44). Derrida would surely worry about this fickle relation to the heroes and heroines of our literature and our stage; even here he would insist on impossible mourning and a more enduring fidelity, the "each time unique" of "the end of the world" when a hero or heroine—or even a condemned criminal—dies.

Here we find the clearest introduction to the theory of the death drives, along with an important (though not the first) reference to the *Bemächtigungstrieb.*[4] Freud's text, designed for beginners like Albert Einstein, reads as follows:

> We assume that the drives in human beings are of only two kinds: they are either such that want to preserve and unify—we call these *erotic*, altogether in the sense of Eros in Plato's *Symposium*, or sexual, with a conscious expansion of the popular meaning of sexuality—or they are such that want to destroy and kill. These we take together as the drive to aggression or the drive to destruction. You see that this is really only the theoretical clarification of what all the world knows as the opposites of love and hate, an opposition that perhaps sustains a primitive relation to the polarity of attraction and repulsion, a polarity that plays a role in this domain as well. Now, do not too quickly interrupt us to say that these two kinds express the value-judgments of good and evil. Each set of drives is every bit as essential as the other: the phenomena of life emerge from both, as they work together and against one another. Indeed, it seems quite rare that a drive of one kind can ever be activated in isolation from the others; it is always bound up with a certain sum from the other side [*daß kaum jemals ein Trieb der einen Art sich isoliert betätigen kann, er ist immer mit einem gewissen Betrag von der anderen Seite verbunden*]; or, as we say,

---

4 There are, by my count, seventeen appearances of the word *Bemächtigung* in Freud's works. For *Bemächtigungsapparat*, see *Drei Abhandlungen zur Sexualtheorie*, GW 5:58; for *Bemächtigungstrieb*, op. cit., 89, 93, 99; for *Bemächtigung* without further qualification, op. cit., 95. For *Bemächtigungstrieb* once again, see *Der Wahn und die Träume in W. Jensens 'Gradiva,'* GW 7:116, *Die Disposition zur Zwangsneurose*, GW 8:448, 450, *Totem und Tabu*, GW 9:90, *Vorlesungen zur Einführung in die Psychoanalyse*, GW 11:340, *Jenseits des Lustprinzips*, GW 13:14, and *Das Unbehagen in der Kultur*, GW 14:476. For *Bemächtigungsdrang*, see *Triebe und Triebschicksal*, GW 10:231. For *Liebesbemächtigung*, see *Jenseits des Lustprinzips*, GW 13:58. For the reference to *Bemächtigungstrieb* in "*Warum Krieg?*" under consideraton here, see GW 16: 21. *Bemächtigung* is also used in Freud's essay on the human mastery of fire, at GW 16:3. Finally, in *Das ökonomische Problem des Masochismus*, see the remarkable phrase I cited earlier, *Destruktionstrieb, Bemächtigungstrieb, Wille zur Macht*, GW 13:376.

> it is *amalgamated* [*legiert*], so that its goal is modified; or, under certain circumstances, amalgamation first makes possible the achievement of its goal. For example, the drive to self-preservation is certainly of an erotic nature, but precisely that drive needs to have aggression at its disposal if its intention is to prevail. In the same way, the love drive, when directed toward its objects, needs the supplement of the drive to overpower [*Bemächtigungstrieb*] if it is to gain possession of its object at all. The difficulty in isolating the two kinds of drives as they express themselves hindered our knowledge of them, indeed, for quite some time. (GW 16:20–21)

Four remarks:

1. With regard to Plato's *Symposium*, not only Aristophanes's three genders (the solar, male/male), the terrestrial (female/female), and the lunar (or loony, that is, female/male), but also Eryximachus's theory of attraction and repulsion or condensation and rarefaction needs to be remembered in this context, perhaps along with Empedocles's theory of the principles of love and hate in the one sphere of the cosmos. Especially in the Empedoclean sphere, on which Freud himself comments at length in his 1937 "On Finite and Infinite Analysis" (GW 16:91–93), the problem of dualism versus monism is particularly intriguing.

2. Rather obviously, Freud's caution with regard to "good" and "evil" suggests the influence of Nietzsche's *Beyond Good and Evil.* And, speaking of "beyonds":

3. It is difficult to understand how the drives are *legiert,* that is, alloyed or amalgamated, or somehow blended. In cooking, when making a sauce, we would say that the ingredients are blended. In chemistry we would think of a compound, a complex yet relatively stable molecular unit. Is the compound one or two? Table salt is neither volatile sodium nor chlorine gas, but is the salt of the earth or sea. What sort of compound might the erotic and the death drives produce? Would it be stable? Could *Bemächtigung* be a name for such a compound? Would *Bemächtigung* be a stable molecule, or does not the word suggest, as Nietzsche might put it, *immer mehr Bemächtigung,* which is to say, something *incremental,* something that essentially *augments* itself? And is this not the very essence of what Nietzsche calls will to power, especially will to power as *art*? But this is to anticipate.

4. In his earliest writings, Freud contrasts the self-preservation drive with the erotic drive, associating *Bemächtigung* with the first. Now he says that self-preservation is "certainly of an erotic nature," but that "precisely it," *gerade er,* needs the aggressive *Bemächtigungstrieb* as a *Zusatz* or supplement to the erotic. Hence the *supplement* of aggression in matters otherwise tender. Does Derrida's logic of the supplement apply here? In that case, do we not have to doubt whether there can be a *system* of *principles*, an exquisitely *dualistic* system of drives? Would aggression be within or outside such a system? If within, why is it *legiert* to both the erotic and the destructive drives? Why and how? Finally, would such an amalgam be responsible for the malice of cruelty and all things *grausam*? And beyond finally, would there be any chance to move beyond *Grausamkeit*?

Let us return to Freud's question, "Why War?" At least part of the answer is "the pleasure taken in aggression and destruction." There we have it: pleasure in aggression—expressing two drives as one. Concerning this pleasure, *Lust,* Freud says, "numberless horrors [*Grausamkeiten*] in our history and in our everyday lives convince us of its existence and its strength" (GW 16:21). The death drive, *der Todestrieb,* Freud assures us, is a natural extension of the idea of pleasure-in-destruction—granted, says Freud, that it is interpreted "with some exertion of speculation" (GW 16:22). In Derrida's view, that exertion is stupendous. For it is as though the entire construction of the "theory of drives" were mythological, even if in English we hope that biology will save us and rescue scientificity if we translate *Triebe* as "instincts." Perhaps because of the haunting presence of the great physicist to whom he is writing, Freud admits that in fact his is not so much a "theory" as a "mythology" of drives. Yet, he asks, does not every science wind up having to construct such a mythology? (GW 16:23).

How far does such an admission go? How far would such a mythology extend? Would it embrace all of psychoanalysis? All of theoretical physics? And could we understand *myth* as Hölderlin does—thinking now back to the very first chapter of the present book—so that the adjective *mythological,* when applied to both physics and psychoanalysis, would have nothing demeaning or pejorative about it? Whatever the case, Freud now makes an equally remarkable confession. He is aware how difficult it is to find a rational reason for his pacifism, since he knows how cruel the destruction-and-death drives can be and how little humankind has changed since its bloody beginnings. Knowing these things, how can he realistically be a pacifist? He replies, embracing Einstein in the plural "we," "We are pacifists because for organic reasons we have to be," *Wir sind Pazifisten, weil wir es aus organischen Gründen sein müssen* (GW 16:25). Organic grounds? What are they? Will biology save us now?

Derrida does not refer to it here, but there is an extraordinary parallel to this use of the "organic" in Freud's work. Recall the two long footnotes (I referred to them back in chapter 1) that open and close chapter 4 of *Civilization and Its Discontents*, which we might better translate as *What Is Disquieting about Civilization*, *Das Unbehagen in der Kultur*. There Freud lucubrates on the fundamental mystery of psychoanalysis, namely, repression, *Verdrängung*. In these remarkable footnotes Freud floats the idea—the disturbing idea—that repression may be not psychological at all but *organic*. It may be built into the erect and fastidious human animal. Freud's two notes aroused in me the expectation that I would read a paraphrase of Freud's confession in the second volume of Derrida's death penalty seminar: "We are abolitionists because it is in our blood, that is, for organic reasons." No such statement is there, but there are approximations to it, one might argue. In any case, Freud continues in "Why War?" by saying that, *bei uns Pazifisten* war evokes nothing less than *eine konstitutionelle Intoleranz* (GW 16:26). Equal to the moral revulsion aroused by war's *Grausamkeiten* are what Freud calls *die ästhetischen Erniedrigungen des Krieges*, "the aesthetic degradations of war" (ibid.). Aesthetic degradations? He clearly means *aesthetic* in its Greek sense, having to do with the bodily senses, hence with the organism. Yet a host of questions arises. Would the degradations of war parallel those of an unsuccessful lovelife? Would both arise from the failure of tenderness? Could there be an "aesthetic" dimension, perhaps in the more modern sense of the word *aesthetic*, to tenderness in both cases? Perhaps Freud is trying to renew a strong sense of the aesthetic in the direction of Nietzsche. Perhaps this too is pointing us to Nietzsche's will to power as art. Perhaps such a will to power would be constitutional, even organic, physiological. In that case—we can dream it—tenderness might be given a chance, an *organic* chance, as it were. But this, again, is to anticipate.

A wonderful and terrifying book could be written on the possible parallel between organic repression and organic pacifism, or between organic repression and organic abolitionism with regard to the death penalty. Such a work would focus on the phylogenetic or paleoanthropological views of psychoanalysis, such as Sándor Ferenczi's astonishing bioanalytic theory of human genitality in the book we call *Thalassa*. I leave it to my readers to write this new book on organic pacifism and abolitionism. But do hurry. We need it.

By now I have leapt far too far ahead. Allow me to conclude this first portion of the chapter by returning to Derrida's *States of the Soul* precisely at the point where he takes up Freud's "Why War?" (EA 32ff./250ff.). What draws Derrida to Freud's essay is actually Einstein's insight, taken for granted by Freud or at least gently ironized by him, that an effective international organization dedicated to peacekeeping can be founded only with the at least partial reduction of the *sovereignty* of the nation-states. Furthermore, Einstein recognizes what he calls *mächtige psychologische Kräfte*, "powerful psychological forces," that resist such a limitation of sovereignty; he recognizes too the craving for power, *das Machtbedürfnis*, of the governing classes in each state. Derrida of course wants to relate these questions of *Macht* to the equivocal notion of *Bemächtigung* in Freud. Yet he also poses the startling question as to why psychoanalysis has found no firm foothold in the Islamic world, including the world of his own Algeria. The answer to this is not that the Muslim world has experienced no Enlightenment (Avicenna and Averroës, that is, Ibn Sina and Mohammed Ibn Ruschd would dispute such a claim) but that "globalization," which Derrida calls *mondialisation* in order to capture the Christian onto-theological notion of *mundus* that underpins globalization, actually resists genuine engagement with the Muslim world. At all events, Derrida now pursues this notion of the *Bemächtigungstrieb* with which I began. As we know, the theme is not new to him.

•

Let me now retrace Derrida's reference in *States of the Soul* (EA 47/258) to his own prior work on the notion of *Bemächtigung*. The key sources are the *Envois* of *La carte postale* (CP 103) and the *Spéculer* essay later in that same volume (CP 430–32). In the best of all possible worlds, I would work through these dense pages in detail, but let me simply reduce their argument to ten thesis-statements.

1. Derrida confesses his fascination with the "history of principles" in *Beyond the Pleasure Principle*, especially the "political" matter of a drive or pulsion somewhere between the pleasure principle and the reality principle. He does not mention the *Bemächtigungstrieb* by name in the *Envois*, but when he refers to "*Herrschaft*, mastery, authority" there (CP 103), we know what he means.

2. Much later, in *Spéculer sur Freud* (CP 430–32), Derrida refers to Freud's interpretation of the *fort/da* game, discussed in chapter 5, in terms of

a drive to mastery, a drive to gain power over the mother's absences; this time, citing chapter 2 of the *Jenseits* (GW 13:14), the drive is mentioned by name: *Bemächtigungstrieb.*

3. Here, in chapter 2 of *Beyond the Pleasure Principle*, Freud concedes that this drive, which otherwise does not dominate his reflections on the drives, seems to be independent of the pleasure principle, inasmuch as it does not matter that baby Ernst finds the memory of his mother's absences painful rather than pleasurable. The *Bemächtigungstrieb* in baby Ernst grants him the fortitude to deal precisely with these painful episodes of his mother's absences.

4. Yet the *fort/da* game can also be interpreted, says Freud, as the infant's *revenge* on the absent mother, in which case *Bemächtigung* seems to involve "destructive" drives. It seems therefore that *Bemächtigung* cannot be reduced to or subsumed under any particular drive, even as it seems to participate in all of them, the erotic and the destruction-and-death drives along with the reality probe.

5. "One may thus envisage a quasi-transcendental privilege of this drive to mastery, power, or *emprise*"; indeed, power (*Macht*) is the transcendental predicate of the psychoanalytic system of drives.

6. The drive to empowerment thus characterizes the self-relation of every drive, the self-mastery of every drive, so that one may speak of *Bemächtigung* as a transcendental tautology: it is drive *as* drive; it is the *drivenness* of the drive as such; it is the very pulsation of every pulsion.

7. The word *Bemächtigung* has special importance for the theory of sadism, as the pulsion to dominate, control, and consume.

8. Because it has to do with the destruction and consumption of the loved object, hence with the "violent domination of it," *Bemächtigung* also seems to bear a privileged relation to the destruction-and-death drives.

9. The very theory of drives is a theory about which drive it is that has dominion over the others; its dynamic is a "dynasty," such that *Bemächtigung* is the originary principle of drive, and therefore more original than pleasure or the beyond of pleasure.

10. "There is power only if there is a principle or a principle of power." Presumably such a principle might be called, at least in scare-quotes, "will to power."

We would doubtless find hints of Derrida's involvement with this quasi-transcendental drive to empowerment already in the final pages of "Freud and the Scene of Writing," but we may certainly say that from the 1980 *Post Card* to the first year of the seminar *The Beast and the Sovereign*, where *Bemächtigung* plays a role in session 11, Derrida is gripped by the problematic.[5]

In short, *Bemächtigung* plays the role in Derrida's confrontations with Freud that *Walten* plays in his confrontations with Heidegger. And who can doubt that *Bemächtigung* and *Walten* belong to the same querulous family? This might explain Derrida's nervousness with regard to all the power plays in the institutions of psychoanalysis, the absolutely secret Committee of Freud and his closest associates, with its seven cameo rings bearing the head of Jupiter (EA 59–60/264); or Freud's plan in "Why War?" to establish a "dictatorship of reason" in order to quell conflict among the nations, a dictatorship of those who are led by those who lead, the leader in German being called a *Führer* (this in 1933!); or institutional power plays all the way down to Lacan's "symbolic," which rests on the power of the "I can" and is organized by power, the power of the king not as *infans* but as severe father. The future that Derrida envisages for psychoanalysis is notably different: the institution must perdure in undecidability, on the hither side of princely principles and power struggles over sovereignty. There can be no ethics of psychoanalysis—Lacan's seminar of that title notwithstanding—but only acceptance of "a radical discontinuity" within the institution (EA 76–77/273). Undecidability and discontinuity in turn imply something like a positively affirmed im-possibility (the word oddly hyphenated), and this leads Derrida into the strangest and most difficult perorations of his text (EA 82–83/276; 86–87/278). I will begin the third and final portion of my own chapter by reading these pages.

---

5 Freud's attention to the themes of the destruction-and-death drives, the repetition compulsion, the "beyond" of the pleasure principle, originary finitude, and so on, is visible in "Freud and the Scene of Writing," not only in the programmatic notes that open and close the essay, but also in the body of the work itself. See especially ED 294–95, 302, 316, 335–37, and 339. I recall from my visit to the Derrida Archive at Caen that the 1975 seminar on "Life Death" works hard on the concept of *Bemächtigung*. As an example of Derrida's later preoccupation with *Bemächtigung*, one of many possible examples, one can refer to his complaint that Foucault does not seem to have taken the "beyond" of *Beyond the Pleasure Principle* seriously, even though it is an eminent instance of the *pouvoir/plaisir* theme that gripped Foucault himself. On the final page of *Résistances*, Derrida expresses his desire to take the theme of power/pleasure beyond the structures and strictures of *principle*. Such a beyond does not do away with power and mastery, to be sure, for it is death that is the master, *la mort comme le maître*. See Derrida, *Résistances de la psychanalyse* (RP 144–46).

However, let me in the meantime return to Nietzsche's *Genealogy of Morals* and recall the way Derrida reads that text during the first year (1999–2000) of his death penalty seminar. For one of the impasses of *States of the Soul* arises from the apparent fact that Nietzsche and Freud are in agreement that cruelty has no contrary, that in fact *Grausamkeit* "is bound up with the essence of life and will to power" (EA 72/271). That would surely lead to a pessimistic anthropology, one that would please Carl Schmitt but not Derrida. Are there in Nietzsche's philosophy no resources for a "beyond" of cruelty? Is there no possible communication with such a "beyond"?

•

Recall that Derrida opens the sixth session of the first death penalty seminar with a *dedascalie* or stage direction to himself: *"Very slowly."* Why the musical or theatrical direction? Because the death penalty is traditionally—and, *pace* Foucault, down to the present—theatrical, a spectacle that has the telephone as a key prop. *Very slowly* Derrida informs his students that for this session he will speak to them over the telephone. *About* the telephone, *over* the telephone. Why? Because part of the spectacle of executions is the telephone call that may come from the sovereign authority—say, the governor of Texas—in order to declare that the condemned man, on the brink of death, is now permitted to live on. No longer "dead man walking," but a man or woman restored to life by the sovereign power of *exception*, a power beyond every law and all normal judicial process. The paramount exception to the rule of law, albeit sanctioned by the law, is the power to grant *grace* or *pardon*. And, at least in the movies, it arrives as a telephone call to the prison—at the very last minute, as the switch is about to be pulled, the gas released into the chamber, or the poison into the blood of the already anesthetized victim.

Everyone has seen the movie. Yet no one, so far, has seen or heard Nietzsche on the telephone. Surely he comes too early for such technology? At the time Nietzsche is writing his high school encomium to Hölderlin and composing an oratorio for chorus and soloists, "The Annunciation to Maria," inventor Philipp Reis achieves the first successful transmission of the human voice by wire. While Nietzsche is composing the fourth of his *Untimely Meditations*, "Richard Wagner in Bayreuth," Alexander Graham Bell constructs the first successful telephone. Yet by the time the dial is added to the telephone, so that individuals can initiate calls to someone at a remote distance, Nietzsche is staring at his paralyzed hands out on the veranda of his mother's house in Naumburg.

Yet it is not Nietzsche on the phone but Richard Wagner, and he is communicating with the Beyond. Everyone has by now read and studied the third treatise of the *Genealogy*, "What Is the Significance of Ascetic Ideals?" Yet it is safe to say that no one prior to Derrida has eavesdropped on Wagner's communication with the *Jenseits*.

Why the telephone drama? Because, to repeat, Derrida fears that a seminar on the death penalty, taught and taken by persons who are convinced that it is quite unlikely that they will ever be victims of the death penalty, may not achieve the level of seriousness it deserves. This is Derrida's pedagogical way of objecting to the cool "disinterestedness" of Kantian pure practical reason, which insists on the retributive justice of the death penalty inasmuch as the "law of the talion" has the force of a categorical imperative. Nietzsche is the one who sees behind Kantian "disinterestedness" something very much like an "interest," an interest that is quite insistent. As we saw in chapter 8, it is initially an insight not into the Kantian metaphysics of morals but into Kantian *aesthetics* that enables Nietzsche to unmask the purported "disinterestedness" of reason. And yet it is a matter of "life" interest, and of the hostility to "life" of Kant's purported disinterestedness, that sends Derrida to the third treatise of the *Genealogy*. He cites section 11 of the third treatise, which deals with the ineradicable yet enigmatic "interestedness" of life. As we also saw earlier, he cites only one sentence, the final sentence of the passage I will now cite at greater length:

> Read from the vantage point of a distant planet, the capital letters of our earthly existence might seduce us into drawing the conclusion that planet Earth is the *ascetic star* proper, a corner of the cosmos in which we find squatting those bitter, arrogant, and repulsive creatures who could not rid themselves of a profound disgust with themselves, with the Earth, and with everything that lives; as a result, these creatures hurt themselves as much as they can, out of pure enjoyment of the hurt:—it is probably their only form of enjoyment. Let us consider how regularly, how universally, in well-nigh every age the ascetic priest appears on stage; he belongs to no particular race; he flourishes everywhere; he waxes strong among every class of persons. It is not as though his way of evaluating things were bred and passed on through inheritance: the reverse is the case—a profound instinct forbids him, all things considered, to procreate. It must be a necessity of the first order that causes this species that

> is *hostile to life* to grow and flourish—it must be an *interest of life itself* that such a type of self-contradiction not die out. (ZGM III, 11; KSW 5:362–63)

Derrida comments on this "internal contradiction," namely, the fact that life has an "interest" in preserving something that turns against life's own "interest," and hence turns against its proper self. Something in life's own *interest* causes it to practice *cruelty*, even and especially if the cruelty is self-induced and self-directed, as a kind of self-torture and feverishly advancing auto-immune disease. For Schopenhauer, art is what frees one from the torture of the will, *torture* here meaning the cruel rack and wheel of sexuality and the erotic in general. For Wagner, at least prior to *Parsifal*, the art of *music* is to assuage such torture by bathing it in sensuality. With this aim in view, the *Gesamtkunstwerk* places music first among the arts and lets it reign as Schopenhauerian "pure will," *sovereign* will. *Interest, cruelty*, and now *sovereignty*: the key words of Derrida's seminar. Nietzsche now directs Wagner to head toward the telephone:

> He [Wagner] grasped immediately that more was to be done with Schopenhauer's theory and his renovation *in majorem musicae gloriam*—namely, with the *sovereignty* of music as Schopenhauer understood it: music set apart from all the remaining arts, the art independent in itself, not, as with the other arts, offering images of phenomenality, but rather speaking the very language of *the* will itself, speaking directly from the "abyss" as its most proper, most original, most pristine revelation. With this extraordinary enhancement of the value of music, an enhancement that seemed to stem directly from Schopenhauer's philosophy, the market value of *the musician* himself suddenly attained unheard-of heights: from that point on the musician became an oracle, a priest, indeed even more than a priest, a mouthpiece of the "in-itself" of things, a telephone to the Beyond [*ein Telephon des Jenseits*]—from now on he talked not only music, this ventriloquist of God; no, he talked metaphysics. Who can be surprised if one day in the end he talked *ascetic ideals*? (ZGM III, 5; KSW 5:346)

All of this is bizarre, no doubt, and in many different ways. Should not the liberation of music from its theatrical and operatic integument—in other words, should not *absolute* music—engage a form of will to power that is entirely emancipated from ascetic ideals? That would be Nietzsche's question, and it would go to the heart of the Wagner case. For Nietzsche himself feels the power of the *music* even of *Parsifal*—no, *especially* of *Parsifal*—and for the life of him he cannot understand why Wagner needed to yoke such music to the jaded sensuality of the *Graal*, the chalice that Jesus used at the Last Supper and that Joseph of Arimathia then used to capture the last drops of blood and lymph dripping from the side of the crucified Christ. How could such glorious music as that of the Prelude to *Parsifal* get mixed up with Mel Gibson? Far better it had gotten mixed up with Monty Python, since satyr-play at least has nothing of the lugubrious about it. Best of all would have been that there be some truth to the rumor that Wagner in his final days was working on a *symphony* in C major, a symphony without the theatrics of lugubrious cruelty.

Doubtless, Derrida, like Nietzsche, is gripped by tales of blood flow and blood consumption, the cruel, the vampiric, and the sacrificial. Here is the way Derrida introduces the telephone passage:

> Telephone communication is metaphysics; it is the religious, the sacrificial; it is asceticism as such, the priestly as such. Yet, evidently, such ascetic renunciation renounces nothing. It is but another ruse of the ascetic for the ascetic to enjoy; it is the *jouissance* of the priest, who knows what he is talking about, knows how abstinence causes desire to grow and intensify. Such is the pleasure of desire, *jouissance* as the coming of desire itself. (PM 1:210)

Need the telephone connection be to the ascetic Beyond? Need it talk metaphysics and morals? Or is it capable of connecting with tragedy—or at least satyr-play? Naturally enough, Derrida's own question to his seminar students and to the assembled estates general of psychoanalysis is what all this might have to do with the death penalty and a possible "beyond" of cruelty.

In pursuit of the logic of cruelty, Derrida's death penalty seminar, as we saw, turns to the *second* treatise of the *Genealogy*, " 'Guilt,' 'Bad Conscience,' and Related Matters." He reads a large portion of section 3 of the second treatise, which insists on the need for inflicted pain in the production of *memory*, which is to say, in the formation of humankind. Here is a small portion of Derrida's citation of Nietzsche:

> Whenever we become "serious," the past, the longest deepest harshest past, breathes upon us and bubbles up within us. It never went without blood, martyrdom, and sacrifice when the human being found it necessary to form a power of memory for itself; the most

> gruesome sacrifices and pledges (sacrifice of the firstborn belongs here), the most repulsive cripplings (for example, castrations), the cruelest rituals of all religious cults (and all religions in their deepest strata are systems of cruelty)—all this has its origin in that instinct which surmised that pain was the mightiest aid to mnemonic. In a certain sense, the whole of asceticism belongs here: a few ideas are to be made ineradicable, omnipresent, unforgettable, "fixed." The aim is to hypnotize the entire nervous and intellective systems by means of these *idées fixes*—and the ascetic procedures and ascetic modes of life are the means by which to insulate those ideas from every other competing idea, so that they will never be forgotten. (ZGM II, 3; KSW 5:295–96.)

But let us go back to the telephone call, the call that should grant a stay of execution but that talks metaphysics, the ascetic ideal, and the categorical imperative instead. Is it possible to have a different conversation, not with the ventriloquist of sovereign power, but with the exuberant—yet altogether finite—power of art and creativity? That is the question now to be posed. I will focus on what Derrida in his address to the psychoanalysts calls "an unconditional without sovereignty" (EA 82–83/276) and the unlikely possibility of advancing beyond cruelty and the reign of sovereign principles, principles such as those of pleasure and destructive aggression (EA 86–87/278). Such a possibility is so unlikely that Derrida calls it the im-possible, hoping that the hyphen will create a chance where there seems to be none.

•

The unconditional without sovereignty and the im-possibility of our going beyond cruelty: How to approach these unheard-of ideas? Allow me to cite those most difficult pages near the close of the lecture in which Derrida makes his most daring attempt to think *beyond* cruelty, to think with the inflexibility of the unconditional but, uncannily and even disconcertingly, in the direction of undecidability. No wonder he calls the attempt impossible, although spelling it with a hyphen, as though the im-possible might be barely within the range of the possible. What makes such an event unlikely—for it is all about an event possibly to come—is what Derrida develops in the postscript to his lecture (EA 88–90/279–80), his reminder that the drive to mastery seems endemic, organic, "built in," "hard wired," and his concession that it may be "too late" to dream that one can proceed without alibi. His last word will be, *Cruauté il y a*. "There *is* cruelty." There *is* murder; there *is* suicide; and there *are* cruelties that mask themselves with all the disingenuous states of the soul and souls of the state.

Here, then, is Derrida dreaming, albeit trying not to dream all the time; dreaming first of affirming by way of an inflexible unconditional without sovereignty, and then dreaming the im-possible itself. Why such dreaming? In order to oppose Freud's tendency to reduce the psyche—and hence all knowledge, all ethics, and all politics—to an economy of the possible; and likewise to resist Lacan's tendency to reduce the psyche to the order of the "symbolic," both reductions eliminating the radical alterity of the event to come. For the event to come remains for the future to determine. Dreaming, at first in the style of Hegel, of an inflexible unconditional; but then, in the style of a Hegel on involuntary leave of absence, without sovereignty; the combination of the two dreams being precisely im-possible, as dreams always are:

> Thus I will affirm that there is, that there has to be, some reference to the unconditional, an unconditional without sovereignty, hence without cruelty, something doubtless very difficult to think. It is necessary so that this economic and symbolic conditionality be determined. The affirmation that I am advancing advances by itself, ahead of time [*Cette affirmation que j'avance, elle s'avance elle-même, d'avance*], already, without me, without alibi, as the originary affirmation *since which time*—and thus *beyond which time*—the pulsions of death and of power, along with cruelty and sovereignty, are determined as "beyond" principles. The originary affirmation that advances ahead of time in this way takes more than it gives. It is not a principle, a principate, a sovereignty. Thus it comes from beyond the beyond, and is thus beyond the economy of the possible. It has to do with a life, of course, but a life other than that of the economy of the possible, a life that is doubtless im-possible, a hyper-life [*une sur-vie*], one that is not symbolizable, yet the only one that would be worth being lived, without alibi, once and for all, the only one from whose point of departure (I am saying *in departure* from which) a thinking of life is possible. Of a life that still would be worth living, one single time for all times [*une seule fois pour toutes*]. Justifying a pacifism, for example, and the *right* to life, would be possible in a radical way if one were to take one's departure from an *economy of life*, or from what Freud alleges—we have heard him say it—to be under the names of a biological constitution or an

> idiosyncrasy. But that can only be done from a *hyper-life* that owes nothing to the alibi of some mytho-theological beyond.
>
> This originary affirmation of the beyond of beyonds is given in departure from numerous figures of the impossible unconditional. I have studied some of them elsewhere: hospitality, the gift, pardon—and above all imprevidibility, the "per-haps," the "and if" of the event, the advent and the coming of the other in general, its coming to arrive [*arrivance*]. The possibility of these things announces itself always as the experience of an im-possible that is not negative. (EA 82–83/276)

If I dare to comment, it would be merely to enumerate and simplify, to dilute the density of the passage. There is also the risk of taking the thought in a direction Derrida himself would not want to go. Even so, allow me seven remarks:

1. Derrida searches for some "unconditional" affirmation that would define or determine in some way what Freud regards as the idiosyncratic physiological ("organic") development of humankind and what Lacan regards as the "symbolic."

2. The "unconditional" seems to have the value of an "absolute." Yet what remains of the absolute? What remains of absolute knowing? What remains of unconditionals? The Beyond on which our mytho-theologies and politico-theologies have asserted their unconditionals have crumbled. They are now no more than alibis, excuses for not thinking.

3. One is therefore in the parlous condition of responding to a situation that takes from us rather than giving to us whatever securities we thought we had. The search therefore has to be for some "originary affirmation," some "yes-saying," that would come from beyond all the Beyonds.

4. It would be the double "yes, yes" to a life that is worth living. Perhaps closest to this thought of Derrida's, even though Nietzsche's name does not appear in the passage, is Nietzsche's thought of *amor fati,* the tragic affirmation of human existence. Nietzsche's formulation of the thought of the eternal recurrence of the same—of the *une seule fois pour toutes*—in *The Gay Science* (no. 341; KSW 3:570), is perhaps the principal communication of it in his oeuvre:

> *The greatest burden.*—How would it be if some day or night a daimon should steal upon you in your loneliest loneliness and say to you, "This life, as you are living it now and as you have lived it, you will

> have to live once again and countless times more; there will be nothing new about it, but every pain and every pleasure and every thought and sigh and everything unspeakably petty and grand about your life will perforce return to you, everything in the same order and sequence—and precisely this spider and this moonlight between the trees, and precisely this moment and I myself. The eternal hourglass of existence will be inverted again and again—and you with it, you, a speck of dust!" Would you not prostrate yourself and gnash your teeth and curse the daimon who spoke these words? Or have you once experienced a monstrous moment in which you would reply to him, "You are a god, and never have I heard anything more divine!" If that thought came to dominate you, you as you are now, it would transform you and perhaps mangle you; the question to all and sundry, "Will you have this once again and countless times more?" would weigh upon your every deed as the greatest burden. Or how good to yourself and to your life you would have to be in order to *demand nothing more than* this ultimate eternal confirmation and seal?—

5. The hyper-life, over-life, or sur-vival of life implied in the neologism *sur-vie* resist thinking. They cannot be reduced to points. Yet Derrida's seminars during the 1980s and 1990s were all in pursuit of the *sur-vie*, each time approaching it in terms of relentless paradoxes or seeming impossibilities: a decision that can be a genuine decision only if it is unmotivated, a gift that can be truly given only if it is withheld from the economy of returns, a hospitality that risks opening the door to one's own destruction, a pardon that is worthy of the name only if the crime in question is unpardonable.

6. Above all, affirmation says "yes, yes" to the openness and unpredictability of the future. (I have used Joyce's expression from the "Ithaca" section of *Ulysses*, "*imprevidibility* of the future" in order to render Derrida's *l'imprévisibilité* in order to stress *our* inability—*non video*—to see what is *per* happenstance coming.) The arrival that persists in coming: Heidegger no doubt searches for ways to think the *sending* of being as *Ereignis,* whereas Derrida insists always and everywhere on the lack of destination, the per-haps of nonarrival, or the arrival of what no one expected. This is the *fatum* that one would have to learn to love. Schelling says, in his *Philosophy of Mythology* (and it would have to be in the context of mythology, as in the mythology of drives or a mythology of relativity theory, or perhaps the mythology of a community based on the

more tender relations), that Dionysos is the god of arrival, and that the deity is *always* arriving and thus *never* comes. At least not *fully*, not *altogether*, for the reason that Urania remains pregnant with him.

7. Of course, a philosophy of *mythology* is only that, and not a primer of unconditionals. The fact that Freud can concede to Einstein that the theory of drives is more a "mythology" than a respectable scientific theory is already a giant step in the direction of the im-possible. Derrida will simply keep on reminding Freud that he has made this concession, and that *Überdeterminierung*, "overdetermination," guides the entire hermeneutic of psychoanalysis, so that all talk of "principles" will have to stop.

Now for the second passage near the conclusion of *States of the Soul.* It follows Derrida's remarks on the constative mode (theoretical knowledge) and the performative mode (the realm of the promise, of the ethical, of the symbolic), both considered as modes within the practice of psychoanalysis. The preceding remarks are important, but I will once again head straight for the im-possible:

> And here, beyond the most difficult, the im-possible itself. Even there where they register or produce the event, the constative and performative orders remain orders of power and of the possible. Thus they pertain to the economy of the reappropriable. But an event, the coming of an event that is worthy of the name, its unforeseeable alterity, the coming to arrive of what arrives—this is what exceeds even the all-powerful, exceeds every performative, every "I can" and even every "I should," every obligation and every debt within a determinable context. Everywhere where there is law and the performative, even if they should be heteronymous, there certainly can be the event and the other, but they are quickly neutralized in their essential aspect and reappropriated by the performative force or by the symbolic order. The unconditional coming of the other, its event, which cannot be anticipated and which has no horizon, its death, or death itself—these are the irruptions that can and should rout [*mettre en déroute*] the two orders of the constative and the performative, of knowledge and of the symbolic. Perhaps beyond all cruelty. (EA 86–87/278)

Again, only a few remarks:

1. Derrida now focuses on what can be said or written, on speech and expression, on writing, on the expertise—if there should be one—of the scientist, philosopher, and rhetorician.

2. The emphasis falls here on the event that cannot be appropriated or reappropriated, the event whose alterity cannot be neutralized. Of course, our categories, our existentials, our concepts and our calculations all *need to* appropriate and neutralize, so that:

3. What Derrida is talking about is a new mode of *thinking*, which is itself a new mode of *affirmation*. Only such a new mode, unheard-of, may be able to avoid the cruelties—the concealed malice, as it were—of reduction, appropriation, and neutralization.

•

No doubt, cruelty there is and cruelty there will remain. Yet I have a fantasy or a fancy—not a full-fledged dream, but a phantasm—that Nietzsche, the thinker of eternal return, can also help us with this dream of a "beyond" of cruelty. As I mentioned at the outset, my fancy is based on Nietzsche's notion of will to power in relation to *Bemächtigung*, if not *Grausamkeit*; my guideline will be Heidegger's two lecture courses on Nietzsche's notion of will to power. I will consider the third Nietzsche lecture course, on will to power as knowledge, and only then turn to the very first course, on will to power as art, *Der Wille zur Macht als Kunst*. Although I will not discuss it at all, the course that follows the one on art, which takes up Nietzsche's "thought of thoughts," eternal recurrence of the same, *Die ewige Wiederkehr des Gleichen*, is arguably Heidegger's superlative effort with regard to Nietzsche. But one would have to read the entire course, working through it step by step. Let me instead begin with an effort—too condensed, too elliptical—to define in only a few words the themes of the third and the first Nietzsche courses.

Heidegger's understanding of Nietzsche's view of "the knowledge project" or the drive to know the world is that such a project or drive can be defined as *Bestandsicherung durch Befehl*, that is to say, as the securing of a stance in the world by means of command. The knowledge project, as even Kant came close to admitting, puts questions to nature that are framed as commands. *Bemächtigung* here is the securing of an existence in the midst of beings. For whom? For the one Nietzsche in *Beyond Good and Evil* (no. 62) calls *das noch nicht festgestellte Tier*, the animal that is not yet determined or defined, or even the as-yet-undiscovered animal.

By contrast, the creative projects of art—music, dance, theater, performance, painting, sculpture, poetry, fiction, and so on—involve not *Bestandsicherung* but *Machtsteigerung*, the enhancement of the feeling of power. Artistic practice, when viewed extrinsically, seems to be mastery; but when viewed by the practitioner it is something more like a transfiguration of the world, *eine Verklärung der Welt,* and an unaccountable transformation of the artist herself or himself that accords with this transfiguration. As early as *The Birth of Tragedy from the Spirit of Music,* Nietzsche defines the artist not as the sculptor but as "the costliest marble," that is, as the sculpted (KSW 1:30). The artist is that *on which* the enhanced and enhancing power of art works its effects. If there is a command here, then it is the command to love one's fate, *amor fati*—not merely as passive acceptance but as affirmation of existence in the eternal return of the same. The power of such tragic affirmation is experienced preeminently in artistic *Rausch,* which is not "frenzy," even if it is often translated that way, but a focused and sustained *rapture,* a seizure of the artist—objective genitive—by the powers of art and beauty. My question is whether one of the conditions for—but also one of the results of—such a seizure of the artist in artistic rapture is precisely *Zärtlichkeit,* tenderness. As though the artist, when confronting the work of art, is in the position of the Achilles who weeps before his mother or in response to Priam's tears. As though the artist, moonstruck, gently carries his beloved to the window.

Let me see if I can unfold these two aspects of will to power, namely, the knowledge project and artistic creativity, a bit more. Perhaps the best introduction to the knowledge project and to *der Wille zur Macht als Erkenntnis* is found in the opening lines of "Über das Pathos der Wahrheit," repeated as the opening lines of "Über Wahrheit und Lüge im aussermoralischen Sinne" of 1873. It is surely one of the most powerful passages ever composed by a writer of powerful passages, and it is a thought that stops the knowledge-seeker in his or her tracks:

> In irgendeinem Winkel des in zahllosen Sonnensystemen flimmernd ausgegossenen Weltalls gab es einmal ein Gestirn, auf dem kluge Thiere das *Erkennen* erfanden. Es war die hochmüthigste und verlogenste Minute der Weltgeschichte, aber doch nur eine Minute. Nach wenigen Athemzügen der Natur erstarrte das Gestirn, und die klugen Thiere mußten sterben. (KSW 1:759, 875).

> In some remote corner of universal space, glimmering with the numberless solar systems that were spilled out into it, there was once a star on which clever animals invented *knowing.* It was the most arrogant and mendacious minute of universal history, but still only a minute. After nature drew a few breaths, the star congealed, and the clever animals had to die.

These *Atemzüge der Natur* are far more chilling than the siblings' *Atemzüge* of a summer's day. Add to this remarkable passage those two strong statements that I cited at the outset: "*Wissenschaft: die Bemächtigung der Natur zu Zwecken des Menschen*"; and "The entire apparatus of cognition is an apparatus for abstracting and simplifying—aiming not at knowledge but at *die Bemächtigung der Dinge*." *Bemächtigung* may be seen as lying at the heart of Nietzsche's notion of will to power as knowledge.

Far more difficult to access and to assess is *der Wille zur Macht als Kunst*. Perhaps the key is simply this: creativity itself is powerful, and beauty itself is powerful. Recall Plato's definitions of the beautiful in *Symposium* and especially in *Phaedrus*, perhaps the oldest determinations of the beautiful that we have: the beautiful, says Socrates, is ἐκφανέστατον καὶ ἐρασμιώτατον, the most radiant and the superlatively erotic. Schleiermacher translates this as *das hervorleuchtendste*, that which most brightly illumines or itself lights up, and *das liebreizendste*, that which most powerfully stirs us and ignites the spark of love in us (*Phaedrus*, 250d). What is illumination? What is the spark of love?

In Heidegger's view, the Nietzschean artist reaches out toward something that is advancing like a mighty wave from out of the distance, something that he or she will barely survive—for, no doubt, the beautiful *is* powerful. It gives us a taste of hyper-life. Heidegger cites Rilke's first "Duino Elegy," which, he says, is fully in accord with Nietzsche's sense:

> . . . Denn das Schöne ist nichts
> als des Schrecklichen Anfang, den wir noch grade ertragen,
> und wir bewundern es so, weil es gelassen verschmäht,
> uns zu zerstören.[6]

> . . . For the beautiful is nothing
> but the onset of the terrifying, a beginning we but barely endure;
> and it amazes us so, since quite calmly it disdains
> to destroy us.

Heidegger omits the next line, since he despises Rilke's angels. However, if *ein jeder Engel ist schrecklich*, if every angel is horrific, well-nigh *grausam*, that is because the power of beauty and creativity terrify us. The angel of art may appear to be cruel, especially as it chisels its effects into the life and the very

---

6 Rainer Maria Rilke, *Sämtliche Werke*, 3 vols. (Frankfurt am Main: Insel Verlag, 1966), 1:441, ll. 4–7.

body of the artist. Yet art is not Azrael, the truculent Angel of Death. *Gelassen,* the angel lets us be, disdains to destroy us. In any case, the power of art does not reside in the artist. It resides, if one may say so, *beyond.* Will to power permeates the artist, to be sure, but it expresses itself not as mastery, appropriation, and neutralization but as a kind of fascination or delight that calls for the most gentle and most tender responses. At the end of a long note on "the will to truth," written in the spring of 1887, Nietzsche writes:

> For the artist, "beauty" is something outside of all hierarchical order, since in it opposites are conjoined—the supreme sign of power, power over things in opposition; furthermore, without tension:—that there is no further need of force, that everything so readily *follows, obeys,* and brings to its obedience the most amiable demeanor—this delights [*ergötzt*] the will to power of the artist. (KSW 12:258; Ni 1:117)

It is this "most amiable demeanor," *die liebenswürdigste Miene,* of the will to power itself, along with the default of force—"there is no further need of *Gewalt*"—that I see granting possibilities for tenderness. Artistic fascination—*Bemächtigung* as captivation of the artist, the artist's delight—no doubt reaches the fever pitch of *Rausch,* the "rush" and "rapture" of artistic creation; yet the rush waits upon the susceptibility of the artist, better, the *receptivity* of the artist that I believe depends upon and also nurtures a kind of *Zärtlichkeit.* Nietzsche sees it in the possession by the god Dionysos of the tragic chorus. For the devotees of such a god the traditional structures of objectivity and subjectivity, with the one exerting power over the other, collapse. Heidegger writes:

> Rapture as a state of feeling explodes the very subjectivity of the subject. By having a feeling for beauty, the subject has already come out of himself; he is no longer subjective, no longer a subject. On the other side, beauty is not something at hand like an object of sheer representation. As an attuning, it thoroughly determines the state of the human being. Beauty breaks through the confinement of the "object" placed at a distance, standing on its own, and brings it into essential and original correlation with the "subject." Beauty is no longer objective, no longer an object. The aesthetic state is neither subjective nor objective. Both basic words of Nietzsche's aesthetics, rapture and beauty, designate with an identical breadth the entire aesthetic state, what is opened up in it and what pervades it. (Ni 1:123)

What gets detonated in the "explosion" of "the very subjectivity of the subject"? Is it not the will to mastery that at least in the Western world lies at the heart of subjectivity? And would not the aftermath of that explosion leave room for something like receptivity, something like tenderness? Heidegger poses the ultimate paradox of will to power in the following few lines concerning what Nietzsche calls "the grand style": "Will to power [here, will to power *as art*] is properly there where power no longer needs the accoutrements of battle [*das Kämpferische*], in the sense of being merely reactive; its superiority binds all things, in that the will releases all things to their essence and their own bounds" (Ni 1:137).

In artistic creation, power expresses itself as *Gelassenheit*, releasement, or letting-be. In his late work, *Götzen-Dämmerung*, Nietzsche states the paradox whimsically and well, not only for will to power as art but even for will to power as knowledge. We need to learn three things, he says, and they are: to see, to think, and to write. "To learn how to *see*, as I understand it, is well-nigh what the unphilosophical way of speaking would call a strong will: what is essential to a strong will is precisely *not* to 'will,' to be *able* to set judgment aside" (KSW 6:108–109). That would be the *ordeal*: perduring in undecidability—unconditionally. As for thinking, it has to be learned precisely as one learns how to dance, "to dance with the feet, with concepts, with words—and, need I add, with the pen" (KSW 6:110). Earlier on in his career, Nietzsche added *reading* to this list of things we have to learn. Reading is for Nietzsche what the philologist does, at least in the best of all possible worlds, the philologist being a lover of slow and careful gleaning, a lover of discourse, and a teacher of unhurried reading, *ein Lehrer des langsamen Lesens*, "a reading that is deep, retrospective, and forward-looking, a reading with hinterthoughts, with gentle fingers and eyes" (KSW 3:17). Will to power as gentleness? as a will not-to-will? as *Gelassenheit in allen Dingen*? That sounds like what Derrida calls *jeu*, by which he sometimes means not the play between wheel and axle but Nietzsche's—or Zarathustra's—*Spiel* on a newly invented lyre. All of which seem to suggest something like a capacity for tenderness.

Recall Derrida's first lecture in the United States back in 1966, "Structure, Sign, and Play." Is not the *play* of forces in art related to the play of signifiers that captivated Derrida from the beginning? In such play every notion of *maîtrise* fails. Why? Because play involves "infinite substitutions within the closure of a finite ensemble," which is one of Nietzsche's descriptions of eternal recurrence (ED 423). Yet the inability to achieve mastery, the default of *Bemächtigung*, is experienced not as frustration or deprivation but as "the joyous affirmation of the play of the world and the innocence of becoming" (ED 427). Yes, the world plays "without security" (ibid.), and its births may be monstrous (ED 428), as no one recognized more profoundly than Nietzsche. Monstrosity and *Gelassenheit*? Joyous affirmation—without security? That too sounds like tenderness, im-possible tenderness.

In a text produced many years ago now, *The Good European: Nietzsche's Work Sites in Word and Image*, I searched for some examples of this presumably very un-Nietzschean Nietzsche, the Nietzsche of *Gelassenheit*, and I found them.[7] At eighteen years of age Nietzsche completed his "Ermanerich Symphony." Concerning it—and the rapture of its composition—he writes:

> Cosmic pain is introduced by strange harmonies that are quite bitter and dolorous, harmonies that thoroughly displeased me at first. Now they seem to me to be, in the course of the whole, at least milder and pardonable. The compulsion and the wild chase of passion, with all the sudden transitions and stormy outbreaks, are ultimately so full of harmonic monstrosities that I dare not make any decision about them.[8]

"I dare not make any decision about them." Picasso says somewhere, "Never touch a happy accident." Nietzsche would add, "Don't even touch the unhappy accidents, the monstrosities." Even the dissonances have to be received with unremitting tenderness. Hospitality toward every angel.

Twenty-two years after the teenager completed his symphony, Nietzsche wrote to Franz Overbeck about his completion of another sort of "symphony," namely, the third part of *Thus Spoke Zarathustra*. Another explosion:

> Incidentally, the *whole* of *Zarathustra* is an explosion of forces that have been accumulating over decades: with such explosions the detonator can easily blow himself to smithereens. That's the way I feel so often: I won't hide the fact from you. And I know ahead of time that when you see, on the basis of the finale, what the entire symphony properly means to say (and say very artistically, step-by-step, as one constructs a tower), then you too, my dear old faithful friend, will not be able to hold back a terrifying shudder. You have

---

7 Published by the University of Chicago Press in 1997. For the German edition, see *Nietzsche: der gute Europäer* (Munich: Knesebeck Verlag, 2000).

8 Friedrich Nietzsche, *Jugendschriften*, 5 vols., ed. Hans Joachim Mette et al. (Berlin and Munich: Walter de Gruyter and Deutscher Taschenbuch Verlag, 1994), 2:104.

> an *extremely dangerous* friend; and the most foreboding thing about him is his incredible reticence. How happy I'd be if I could *laugh* about all this together with you and your loving and worthy wife (to laugh at myself, laugh myself *to death*!!!). (KSB 6:475)

The explosion of forces in Nietzsche is the work of will to power as art, art setting itself to work in him. Whether at eighteen or forty, Nietzsche himself is astonished by what these forces produce—he does not dare *decide* anything about it. And he is clearly tickled to be such an artist, even if it is Pierrot who is tickling him . . . to death.

There is no beyond of finitude. Perhaps there is no beyond of cruelty. For "there *is* cruelty." Yet, perhaps again, there may be a different relation to the destruction-and-death drives and a new kind of ventriloquism, one that does not dial for metaphysics or succumb to ascetic ideals but that waits upon the call of will to power as art. And that, if anything, might give us a chance to advance beyond cruelty and malice, and beyond the cruelty of principles, perhaps in the direction of a tenderness we could not otherwise have anticipated.

Index

absence, xix–xx, xx–xxiii, 36, 46, 106, 108–18, 121–22, 137–38, 141, 202, 270, 281, 288
accountability. *See* imputability
Achilles, xx, 29–50, 58, 63, 293
activity, xi, 11, 13–14, 17, 20, 77, 88–98, 104, 110–11, 119, 124, 141, 161, 171, 182, 208n5, 209, 239, 250–51, 268, 276
Adler, Alfred, 111, 187
adolescence. *See* latency, puberty
Adorno, T. W., 212
Aeschylus, 8–9, 60, 219, 284
aesthetics, 15, 26, 76, 86, 113, 214, 246n2, 279, 284, 295
affirmation, 13, 101, 102, 197n9, 213, 217, 223–24, 226, 233, 236, 238, 260, 262, 282, 288–93, 297
aggression, xxiii, 16, 25, 28, 152, 272, 276–78, 287
alterity. *See* other
ambiguity, 91, 252
ambivalence, 18, 197, 203, 235
Anaximander, 106, 198–99, 222–24, 226
anesthesia, 208–10, 217, 283
angels, xxiv, 179, 184, 186, 194, 212, 221, 256, 263, 270, 294–95, 297
Antigone, x, xxi, 12, 14, 18, 36, 39, 48, 51–72, 75, 79, 89, 94, 98–99, 121, 188, 192, 275
anxiety, xxiii, 11, 44–45, 52, 75, 86, 103, 107–108, 132, 164, 167, 177, 183–85, 188–93, 202, 223, 244. *See also* fright
ἄπειρον, 199. *See also* Anaximander
Aphrodite, 25, 30–31, 40–42, 47, 49, 66, 68, 75, 86n7, 93–94, 152
appropriateness. See *Eigentlichkeit*
appropriation, 65, 79, 116, 120n10, 219, 238, 291–92, 295
Arendt, Hannah, 6, 222
Aristophanes, 188, 190, 199–201, 238, 277
Aristotle, ix, xix–xx, 7–12, 54, 113, 185, 191, 195n8, 200
artistry, ix, xxiii, xxv, 77, 92, 115, 137, 140, 142, 177, 196, 215, 263–64, 292–98. *See also* creativity, mastery, rapture, will to power
Ἄτη (infatuation, doom), 45, 53, 65–66, 275
Augustine, 3–4, 20, 23–24, 26, 43, 106n3, 184, 188n3
authenticity. See *Eigentlichkeit*
autoimmunity, 214

Bachelard, Gaston, 26–27
beauty, 17–18, 30, 35–36, 41, 49, 57–59, 66–68, 72, 75, 76, 82, 84, 105, 130, 137, 138, 143–48, 163–64,

beauty (*cont'd*)
171n15, 179, 192, 214–15, 260, 263, 293–95
Befindlichkeit ("how one finds oneself to be"), 107, 149
belief, disbelief, x, 6, 13, 26, 65, 72, 73, 81, 82, 83–84, 87, 92, 93, 101, 105, 111, 115, 118, 121, 125, 130, 136, 140, 142–44, 153, 155, 157, 161, 163, 165, 168n13, 173, 180, 184, 187, 202–203, 215–18, 224, 228–29, 236, 253, 257, 262, 266
Bemächtigung (empowering), xxv, 110–11, 119, 122–23, 127, 217, 234, 236n24, 263–66, 269, 272–73, 276–78, 280–82, 292, 294–96. See also *Bewältigung*, mastery, will to power
Benjamin, Walter, 16, 227
Benommenheit ("benumbment"), 142
Bernays, Jacob, 10, 54
Bewältigung ("overpowering, coming to terms with"), 195, 217
Bewegtheit ("movedness"), 148–49, 166
Bible, the, 15, 207, 216, 220, 230–32, 238. *See also* Christianity, churches, religion
biology, xi, 163, 179–80, 182, 190–91, 198–200, 238–39, 278–79, 288
birth, xi, xix, xxiii, 6, 19, 23, 55–6, 61, 69, 70, 72, 112, 127, 165, 177–203, 256, 267, 293, 297. *See also* trauma
blame, 27, 30, 33, 63, 124n13, 127, 243, 247–48, 258. *See also* guilt, imputability
blasphemy, 14, 53, 220
blindness, 16, 35, 60–61, 81, 85, 140, 145, 158, 164, 188, 218, 219–20, 231, 259
blood, xix, xxiii–xxiv, 8–9, 16, 26, 31, 57, 66, 70, 72, 80, 95, 97, 99, 177, 203, 205, 207, 209, 211, 217–18, 221, 230n22, 237–42, 249, 251, 264, 268, 270, 278–79, 283, 286
body, the human, xx, 17, 31, 35, 40, 47, 48, 50, 52, 62–64, 70, 72, 84, 97, 105, 139, 143, 147–48, 151, 155, 157, 162–63, 165, 168n13, 170, 179, 182, 184, 188, 191, 194n6, 207, 216, 220, 237, 261
breast, the, 17, 19, 21, 34, 41, 42, 47, 49, 83–84, 96–97, 99, 119, 138, 142–44, 148, 183. *See also* weaning
Briseïs, xx, 29–33, 35, 37, 40–42, 46–50
brothers, v, xxi, xxii, 4–5, 8, 11n6, 12, 16, 18, 25, 28, 47, 49–50, 53–54, 56–9, 65–66, 68–70, 73–74, 89, 98, 118, 125, 129, 135–36, 145–53, 156–57, 159–67, 170–73, 181–82, 209, 242, 250–51, 265
Bush, George W., 52, 210, 219–20, 229. *See also* president, presiding, sovereignty
Butler, Judith P., 78n4

cadaver, 62, 70, 72, 228, 232. *See also* body, corpse
Calasso, Roberto, 15, 37
calculation, xxiv, 113, 217–18, 221, 223–34, 237, 247–48, 260–61, 273, 292
Camus, Albert, xxiv, 27–28, 207, 210, 216–17, 220–22, 225, 229, 241
castration, 185, 230, 233, 236, 238, 287
categorical imperative, xxiv, 12, 212, 214, 217, 227, 229–30, 235, 284, 287. *See also* talion
catharsis, 6, 10
child, children, xx–xxi, 6, 8, 9–10, 11n6, 14, 17–21, 24, 25, 27n12, 34, 37, 38–39, 48, 51–52, 55, 61–65, 68, 72, 77, 79, 82–83, 91, 95, 98–99, 103–104, 106–12, 116, 118, 121, 123–33, 137, 144, 145–46, 150–51, 169, 178, 179, 181–87, 190, 194, 199, 202, 220, 259, 268, 275. *See also* infancy, latency, puberty

Christianity, 3–4, 11, 54, 58, 70, 81–82, 94, 139, 153, 210–11, 216, 218, 234, 240, 280. *See also* Bible, churches, religion
civil society, xxi, 51–53, 75, 78, 80–81, 89–90, 99, 139, 240, 262. *See also* society, state
civilization, 25–27, 137, 163, 171, 173, 194, 235, 242, 249, 279
Cixous, Hélène, 7, 224
Coble, Don Kelly, 139n4, 170, 248–49
community, xx, 11, 15, 20, 80, 87, 96n11, 213, 245, 252–54, 261–62, 290–91
confession, ix, xi, 23, 33–34, 57–58, 82, 102–103, 114–15, 127, 129, 131, 138, 150, 189, 201, 208, 221–22, 225–26, 230–31, 237, 241, 278, 279, 280
corpse, 8, 14, 35, 37, 48–49, 52, 56–58, 69–72, 199, 207–208, 220, 228. *See also* body
creativity, ix, xxv, 15, 64n9, 127, 152, 161, 177, 197n9, 242, 263, 287, 292–94. *See also* artistry, will to power
crime, criminality, xxii–xxiv, 8–9, 14, 48, 52, 57–59, 71, 74, 89, 115, 136n2, 138–39, 142, 145, 171–72, 206–208, 213, 218, 220, 222, 224–41, 245, 247–48, 249n4, 254, 257–58, 270, 275n3, 290. *See also* murder
culpability. *See* blame, guilt, imputability

Dasein (being-[t]here), xxiv, 107–108, 116, 168, 182–83, 222, 227–28, 232
death penalty, xi, xix, xxiii–xxiv, 139, 206–42, 248–49, 252, 255, 258–61, 263–65, 268, 273, 279, 283–86
deconstruction, 103, 114–17, 211, 218n13, 221, 227, 229–31, 273
degradation, 19–22, 25–26, 88, 172, 177, 191, 227, 271, 279
Derrida, Jacques, xi, xix, xxii–xxv, 26, 64n9, 76, 94–96, 101–33, 144, 145–46, 195n8, 199, 205–42, 248–53, 258–62, 263–98
desire, 3, 8, 18, 20, 24, 26–27, 41, 48, 53, 55, 58–59, 65–66, 78–80, 83, 85, 90–91, 94, 119, 122, 124, 128n22, 140, 143, 145, 149–52, 162–63, 172, 177, 186, 189–90, 207–208, 222–23, 225, 228, 234–35, 243, 245–50, 252, 259–61, 271, 282n5, 286. *See also* needs, pulsions
destruction-and-death drives, xxi, 12, 103, 110–16, 122, 124, 196, 203, 215, 217, 250, 252, 265–67, 271–78, 281–82, 290, 298. *See also* pulsions
dialectic, 26–27, 51–53, 75, 80, 85, 94, 96, 122, 200, 248
difference, 12, 15, 20–22, 28, 36, 62, 64n9, 78, 87, 92–97, 105, 107, 108, 129, 146n6, 149, 152, 166, 185, 191, 219, 226n18, 228n20, 233, 239, 242, 271, 273, 282, 287, 298
dignity (*Würde*), xxiv, 28, 79, 82, 206, 212, 224, 227, 229, 246, 253
Dionysos, 14, 24, 37, 55, 65, 68, 71–72, 178, 196, 199, 291, 295
disinterestedness, 214, 217, 230, 263, 284
doom (ἡ κῆρ), 9, 43–45, 53, 55, 60–61, 65–66, 69, 120–21, 174, 189, 275
dream, 7, 9–10, 19n10, 21, 55, 60, 76, 103, 109, 118, 122, 137, 143–44, 152, 160–61, 173, 189–90, 193, 219, 221, 223, 225, 228n20, 252, 260–61, 279, 287–88, 292
drives. *See* destruction-and-death, Eros, pulsions
Duras, Marguerite, 103

ecstasy, ἔκστασις, 8, 21, 84, 90, 165, 183n1, 194n6, 261. *See also* temporality, time, tragedy
Eigentlichkeit (appropriateness, authenticity), xxiv, 21, 54, 107–108, 232

Einstein, Albert, 123n11, 272, 274, 276, 278, 280, 291
Empedocles, 3, 6, 30, 39, 72, 174, 277
empirical, 140, 155, 212
equity, 12, 215
Eros, erotic drive, xix, xx, xxi, 21–22, 25, 30, 45n6, 58, 66, 68, 70, 88, 96, 115, 122–23, 139n4, 141, 170, 186, 199–201, 215, 238, 250, 259, 263, 265, 268–69, 275–78, 281, 285, 294. *See also* desire, pulsions
eternal recurrence of the same, 110, 289–90, 292–93, 296
eternity, 16, 62, 64, 96n11, 99, 127, 170, 195, 205, 215, 224, 242, 244, 248, 259–61
ethicality, ethics, x, 8, 12, 21, 26, 31, 51, 72, 73, 75, 79–81, 87–90, 98, 200, 217, 231, 255–57, 273–75, 282, 288, 291
Euripides, 54
euthanasia, 209–10, 218
evil, 8–9, 47–48, 56, 66, 71, 78, 80, 90, 172, 211, 236–37, 241, 244–45, 248, 251, 257, 267–68, 271, 276–77, 292

failure, ix, xix, xxii, 3–4, 7, 10, 23, 28, 42, 44, 46, 52, 55, 58, 70, 73, 82, 85–86, 92, 116, 118, 121, 137, 146, 150n7, 151, 155, 162, 167–68, 173, 177, 185–86, 189, 190, 202, 212, 252–53, 279, 296
family, xx, xxi, 7, 8–9, 18, 51–56, 61, 75, 78–80, 83, 87–89, 94, 96, 99, 104, 112, 117, 131, 132, 177, 220, 282
fancy, fantasy, 20, 77, 85, 91, 141, 148, 155, 173, 179, 181, 185–86, 193, 197n9, 200, 202–203, 224, 261–62, 292. *See also* imagination, phantasm
fathers, xx, 3–9, 11, 17, 19–23, 25, 27–28, 29, 33, 40–41, 47, 50, 56, 61, 64n9, 65–66, 68–70, 104, 106–107, 109–12, 117, 119–20, 124–25, 129, 138–39, 145–48, 165, 172, 181–82, 189, 194, 196, 202–203, 207–208, 220–22, 224, 229–31, 234, 241, 255, 257, 274, 282
female, feminine, x, xxii, 3–4, 17–18, 20–21, 24, 25–27, 37, 43–44, 77–8, 83–85, 90–99, 141, 171, 182, 186–8, 238–39, 277. *See also* woman, sisters
Ferenczi, Sándor, xi, 101, 124, 126–27, 129, 182, 184, 186–88, 191, 194–5, 198n10, 202–203, 237–38, 279
festivals, 203, 217
fetus, xxi, 51, 99, 179, 191, 193, 196, 202, 210
fiction, xi, 20, 75–76, 86, 91n9, 102, 117, 119, 150n7, 171, 221n14, 222n15, 268, 275n3, 292. *See also* literature, narrative, stories, writing
finitude, 114, 222–23, 225, 227, 248, 259–61, 277, 282n5, 287, 296, 298
fixation, 19, 138, 182, 219, 287
forgiveness, 16, 127, 143, 221, 233–35. *See also* pardon
fort/da game, 109, 113, 117, 120–23, 280–81. *See also* play
Foucault, Michel, 206, 282n5, 283
fraternity, 69, 74, 155, 252. *See also* brothers
freedom, xxiv, 14, 16, 44, 53, 63, 75, 88, 91, 95, 136, 181–82, 187, 212, 217, 227n19, 229, 242, 243–62, 270, 285
Freud, Sigmund, ix, x, xi, xix–xx, xxii, xxv, 3, 7, 10, 18–22, 23, 25–28, 73, 84, 88, 101–33, 137, 141, 144, 151, 172, 177, 179–86, 190–91, 195–97, 199–203, 210, 215, 217, 226, 229–30, 232–34, 236n24, 237–39, 252, 260, 263–68, 272–83, 288–89, 291
friends, friendship, ix, xx, 5, 8, 12–13, 18, 26, 30, 36, 40, 42, 46, 50, 58, 65,

67, 74, 98, 104, 128, 130, 137, 140, 143, 163, 181, 240, 245, 252, 253n7, 297–98

generosity, x, 12–13, 49, 114, 140, 161, 232
Genet, Jean, 102, 207, 235
gentleness, 17, 25, 29, 36, 47, 50, 83, 140, 143, 230, 295–96
German Idealism, 15, 16n8, 24, 73, 92n10, 199–200, 236. *See also* Hegel, Hölderlin, Novalis, Schelling
Geschlecht, 145–46, 152, 238
gestation, xix, 177–203. *See also* pregnancy, womb
giving-over (*Hingebung*), 81, 91, 96, 144, 177
globalization (*mondialisation*), 209–10, 225, 280
God, gods, goddesses, xxi, 8, 13–15, 24–25, 27, 29, 30, 32–37, 39, 41–42, 44–49, 51, 53, 55, 58, 63, 65–68, 71–72, 75, 79, 83, 88, 93, 98, 99, 115, 132, 136, 138, 140–41, 147, 150, 158, 160–61, 164, 167, 192, 196, 201, 210, 216, 230n22, 231, 241, 244, 251, 253, 259, 262, 285, 290–91, 295. *See also* religion
Goethe, Johann von, 11n6, 18, 34, 36, 52–53, 68, 85–86, 112, 127, 131, 213, 252
Gontard, Susette, 32–34
grausam, *Grausamkeit*, ix, xi, xix, xxiv–xxv, 205, 209, 216–17, 236n24, 237, 242, 249–53, 257–58, 263–69, 272–75, 278–79, 283, 292, 294
Graves, Robert, 32n2, 37, 56
Guillotin, Dr. Joseph Ignace, xix, 218, 220, 258
guilt, xxiv, 25, 71, 86, 91, 177, 185, 200, 215, 226, 229, 234, 237, 241–42, 247–48, 258, 261–62, 264, 286. *See also* blame, imputability
hate (Ἔρις, Νεῖκος), xxi–xxii, 54, 57, 65, 73, 142, 224, 229, 240, 253, 261, 270, 276–77
heart (τὸ κῆρ), 18, 25, 29, 30, 32–33, 39, 41–46, 48–50, 53, 57, 60, 72, 84, 88n8, 92–98, 105, 114, 122, 137–38, 142, 149, 159, 160, 184, 188, 215, 216, 220, 222, 251, 257, 259, 266, 267, 286, 294, 296
Hegel, G. W. F., x, xxi–xxii, 15, 51, 52–53, 73–99, 102, 141, 151, 190, 211, 233, 252, 273, 288
Heidegger, Martin, xxiv, xxv, 3, 6n1, 43, 46, 59, 72, 106–107, 113, 114, 116, 117, 148, 155, 168–69, 182–83, 195n8, 198–99, 221–22, 226–29, 232, 239, 252, 254, 259, 264, 274, 282, 290, 292–96
Helen, 30, 49–50
Hera, 14, 41
Heraclitus, 71
heroes, heroines, xxi, 4, 7–8, 18, 29–32, 34–40, 42, 48–49, 52–54, 61, 63, 67, 72, 74–75, 77, 82, 84, 89, 97, 112, 137, 138, 140, 148, 160n9, 174, 188, 218–19, 239, 245, 247, 268, 270, 275n3
history, xxiii, 15, 20, 64, 68, 70, 83, 85–86, 90, 96, 102–103, 114, 117, 126n17, 139, 179, 180, 185–86, 194, 197, 199–200, 203, 205–11, 215–17, 226, 232, 234, 237–42, 250, 264, 268, 273–74, 278, 280, 293. *See also* blood, civilization, metaphysics
Hoffmann, E. T. A., 88n8, 124, 254–55
Hölderlin, Friedrich, ix, x, xix–xx, 3, 5–6, 10–18, 20–22, 24, 26–28, 29–50, 52–57, 59–60, 63–72, 73, 104, 112, 173–74, 177–78, 189–90, 227n19, 245, 247, 252, 257, 278, 283
Homer, x, xx, 29–50, 55, 196

honor (*Ehre*), xxi, 17, 30–31, 35, 39, 41, 78, 87–89, 91, 93, 97–98, 140, 224, 227n19
hopes, xxv, 6, 15, 17–18, 19, 27–28, 32, 60, 70, 80, 85, 101, 118, 126, 130, 142, 148, 167, 197n9, 205, 216–17, 219–20, 234, 237, 239, 242, 255, 259, 278
house, household (οἶκος), xx, 5, 7–10, 33, 49, 53, 65–66, 74, 87, 110, 115, 139, 141, 152, 180, 194, 283
Hugo, Victor, xxiv, 207, 211, 218, 222
Husserl, Edmund, 109, 114, 193
hysteria, 103, 138, 190, 197n9, 201

imagination, imaginary, xxii, 11, 24, 76, 112, 120n10, 129, 147, 156, 161, 163–64, 167, 186–87, 193, 199, 200, 202, 207, 211, 213, 215, 220, 234, 240. *See also* fancy, fantasy, phantasm
imputability (*Zurechnungsfähigkeit*), xxiv–xxv, 142, 177, 212, 227n19, 241–42, 243–62
incorporation, 73, 130, 190, 234
indifference, 48, 94–95, 97n12, 129, 138, 152, 156, 185, 244
infancy, xxii, 14, 19, 38, 51–52, 55, 61–62, 67, 85, 99, 106–11, 116–17, 120, 129, 182–86, 190–91, 193–94, 212–13, 226, 267–68, 281–82. *See also* child, children, latency
infinite, xxiii, 11–13, 15, 23, 36, 72, 75, 78, 90, 98, 144, 148–49, 151, 160, 190, 219–20, 223, 227, 248, 250, 260–61, 277, 296. *See also* ἄπειρον, unbounded
inhibition, 11, 81, 202
intelligence, intelligible, 79, 139, 170, 243–47, 249n4, 253, 255, 259–61
intimacy, 12, 30, 37, 80, 82, 88n8, 97, 144, 166, 190
intrauterine, xi, xxiii, 21, 182–86, 188, 190–91, 193–94, 202–203. *See also* gestation, Paradise, pregnancy
introjection, 130, 234. *See also* incorporation
Irigaray, Luce, ix, xx, 3, 5, 7, 21, 28, 96n11

Jacobs, Carol, 56
Jocasta, 51, 69, 189–90
Joyce, James, xi, 47–48, 118n9, 136, 207, 267–68, 290
Jung, Carl Gustav, 15, 26, 152
jurisprudence, 241, 255–57
justice, 12–13, 22, 65–66, 114, 125, 138–39, 187, 196, 198, 203, 211, 214, 222, 224, 230–31, 237, 243, 245–46, 249, 252, 255, 257, 261, 284, 288

Kafka, Franz, 20, 215, 250n5
Kant, Immanuel, xxiv–xxv, 12, 79, 113, 139, 199–200, 205–206, 211–14, 217, 224, 227–36, 240, 242, 243–62, 263, 284, 292
knowledge, 62, 83, 201, 211, 219, 222, 264–66, 272, 277, 288, 291–94, 296. *See also* will to power

Lacan, Jacques, ix, x, xix, xxi, 20–21, 24, 27, 37, 48, 53–54, 58–60, 69, 72, 109, 114, 115–16, 120, 217, 228, 236, 252, 275, 282, 288–89
Lacoue-Labarthe, Philippe, 55, 76, 85–86
language, xi, 8n2, 24, 27n12, 56n6, 158, 195–97, 205n1, 227n19, 230, 260, 268, 274, 285. *See also* Logos, narrative, speech, voice, writing
Laplanche, Jean, 19, 123n11, 265
latency, 21, 109. *See also* child, infancy, puberty
law, x, xxi, xxiv, 10, 12, 50, 51–52, 54, 67, 69, 75–76, 86, 89, 94, 98–99, 115, 149, 162, 164, 180, 198–99, 207, 211–12, 214–15, 223–24, 227, 229–31, 233, 235, 237, 239–41, 245, 249, 255–57, 283–84, 291. *See also* jurisprudence, justice, talion

lethal injection, xix, 148, 208–11, 217, 220–21, 228, 268. *See also* death penalty
libido, 22, 115, 127, 182, 188, 195, 199–200, 234–35, 264, 271, 275. *See also* Eros, pulsions
lifedeath, 64n9, 102, 114, 122. *See also* finitude, mortality
literature, x, xi, xx, xxiii, 31, 55, 76, 83, 86, 102, 103–104, 136, 153, 166, 181, 202, 207, 211, 236, 243, 249–50, 264, 268, 270, 274, 275n3. *See also* fiction, narrative, poetry, stories, writing
logic, 12, 68, 74, 81, 86, 92, 94, 120–21, 138–39, 149, 182, 200, 212–13, 215, 226, 231, 233, 242, 244, 255–58, 260, 273, 278, 286
Logos, 158, 201
Lombardo, Stanley, 29, 30n1, 40–42, 46–47
loneliness, 33, 147, 149, 155, 163, 289
love (φιλία), xix, xx–xxii, 3–4, 6–8, 10, 12, 17–19, 21–26, 30, 32–36, 42–43, 46–49, 53–54, 57–58, 65–66, 68, 70, 73, 75, 77–84, 87–88, 91–92, 94, 97–98, 101–103, 106n3, 112, 114–16, 118, 121–23, 125, 130, 132, 138–46, 148–52, 154, 157–62, 164–70, 172–74, 177, 184, 188, 190, 192, 194, 197, 202, 207, 224–25, 229, 237–38, 240, 251, 256, 261, 270–71, 276–77, 279, 281, 290, 293–94, 296, 298. *See also* Eros, lovelife
lovelife (*Liebesleben*), xx, xxii, 18–19, 21, 25–26, 73, 88, 141, 177, 197n9, 237, 279
lunar, 142, 150n7, 151, 153–56, 255, 277. *See also* moon

male, xxi, xxiv, 19–21, 24–25, 27, 37, 77, 79, 83, 85, 91–97, 141, 146, 182, 187, 189, 210, 239, 277
Mann, Thomas, 153, 171
marriage, xxi, 15, 37, 56, 64, 67, 69–70, 74–75, 77–81, 85, 87–90, 98, 125, 137, 141, 146, 154, 165, 171
Marx, Karl, 54, 208n4, 216n11, 218
mastery (*Herrschaft*), xi, xxii, xxv, 96–97, 107, 110, 114, 119, 120n10, 121–22, 123n11, 127, 129, 132, 173, 177, 182, 195–96, 199, 219, 221, 223, 229, 231, 242, 260, 265, 272, 276n4, 280–81, 282n5, 287, 292–93, 295–96
maternity, 21, 23, 34, 84, 140–41, 182, 184, 188, 193, 195–96. *See also* gestation, mothers, pregnancy, womb
meaning, xx, 5, 10, 13, 18, 43–45, 61, 65, 66, 89, 104, 106–107, 109, 146n6, 149, 159, 168–69, 211, 218, 233, 240, 250–51, 253n7, 268, 271, 276, 285
melancholy, 35–36, 127–30
Melville, Herman, 11n6, 59n8, 103, 206, 209, 268–70, 275
memory, 11, 13, 22–23, 25, 27, 45, 66, 79n5, 112, 145, 148, 154, 169, 179, 183, 187, 193, 195, 202–203, 207, 215, 220, 233–35, 281, 286
metaphysics, 63, 70, 86, 107, 212, 214, 227, 239, 243–44, 247, 284–87, 298. *See also* ontology, presence
Miles, Kevin Thomas, 12n7
mirror, mirroring, 12, 15, 94, 108–109, 116, 120–22, 132, 147–49, 167
misogyny, 22–24, 187–88
Montaigne, Michel Eyquem de, 216, 224, 228
moon, the, 18, 21, 36, 59n8, 105, 132, 140, 151, 154–57, 170, 174, 193, 290, 293. *See also* lunar
Moosbrugger, xi, xix, xxv, 138–39, 142–43, 153, 173, 212, 248, 253–58, 260

morality, xxiv, 12–13, 15, 63, 70, 86, 137, 141, 143, 152–53, 155, 162–63, 169–71, 197, 212–14, 227, 229–31, 236, 240, 243–47, 258, 263–64, 268, 270, 279, 283–84, 286, 293
mortality, xxii, xxiii, 6, 27, 31, 39, 41, 44–46, 60, 62, 65, 67–68, 72, 79, 107, 111, 114, 128, 132, 189, 206, 230, 259, 269. *See also* death, finitude, lifedeath
mothers, xxi–xxii, 3–4, 8–9, 14, 19–26, 32–35, 41–42, 47, 49–50, 51, 53, 55–56, 59, 62–63, 68–71, 77, 85, 104–12, 116–22, 124–25, 127, 129, 131–32, 139–40, 142–3, 145–47, 179, 181–85, 188–92, 194–97, 199–203, 212–13, 267–69, 281, 283, 293. *See also* maternity, pregnancy, woman
mourning, xxii, 6, 18, 32–34, 39, 41–42, 46–50, 56, 97, 105, 111–12, 125, 127, 129–30, 132, 166, 174, 186, 207, 275n3
murder, xix, 6, 9–10, 20, 25, 32n2, 44, 46, 112, 131, 138, 186, 221–25, 229–31, 234–36, 240, 247, 288
Murnaghan, Sheila, 29–31, 46, 48
Musil, Robert, xi, xix, xxii–xxiii, xxv, 135–74, 199, 212, 248–49, 253–56, 258
mysteries, 3, 71, 93, 104, 122, 137, 146, 148, 200, 250, 253, 270, 279
myth, mythology, xx, 11, 15–16, 24, 27, 51, 61, 63, 64n9, 102, 117, 123n11, 152, 186, 192, 197–98, 225, 272, 278, 289–91

Naas, Michael, 64n9, 106n3, 133, 208n5
narcissism, 3, 21, 120n10, 125–27, 130, 228, 275
narrative, 15, 104, 108, 119, 135–36, 140–41, 143, 145, 149, 157–58, 163, 165–66, 221n14, 248. *See also* fiction, literature, stories, writing
natural death, 221, 224
needs, xx, xxii, xxiv, 11, 13, 16, 18, 22–24, 55, 58, 72, 81, 104, 110–13, 114, 141–42, 158, 162, 177, 188, 191, 202, 203, 215, 222, 225–26, 231, 237, 239, 243, 245–50, 252, 255, 265, 277–79, 286, 292, 295–96
neurosis, xxiii, 19, 22, 103, 108, 180, 184, 186, 190–91, 197, 238, 276n4
Nietzsche, Friedrich, xix, xxiv, xxv, 16, 27, 86, 90, 106n3, 110, 111n4, 113, 120, 122, 137–38, 144–45, 169, 178, 187, 196–201, 212–17, 234, 236, 248, 261–62, 263–67, 270, 274, 277, 279, 283–86, 289, 292–98
Novalis (Friedrich von Hardenberg), 17, 101, 106n3, 108, 114, 225
nursing, nurture, 7, 19, 21–23, 26, 33, 42–43, 46, 104, 119, 121, 141, 210, 220, 236, 267, 295. *See also* breast, weaning

obsequence, 120–21, 129
Oedipus, 39, 52, 56, 61, 69–70, 79, 111, 177, 186, 188–90
Oedipus Complex, xx, 19–21, 180, 185, 188–90, 203
ontology, xxii, 78n4, 106–107, 117. *See also* metaphysics
ordeal, trial by, 233–34, 272–73, 296
other, the, xxii, 4, 7, 24, 58–59, 83, 91, 96n11, 136, 139n4, 146n5, 149–50, 162, 163n11, 168–70, 174, 216, 238, 246, 252–55, 260–61, 271, 289, 291, 295. *See also* difference
overdetermination (*Überdeterminierung*), 77, 116, 131, 291. *See also* undecidability

pain, xxiv, 33–34, 37, 52, 107, 112–14, 124n13, 125–26, 143, 183, 185,

187, 196, 200, 208–10, 215–17, 220, 225–28, 231, 252, 254, 258, 281, 286–87, 290, 297
Paradise, xxiii, 16, 156, 164–65, 167, 184–85, 195, 200, 202, 270
pardon, xxiv, 164, 206, 217, 225, 233–34, 241, 283, 289–90, 297. *See also* forgiveness
patriarchs, partriarchy, xxi, 4–6, 51, 79, 89, 181, 194–96. *See also* fathers
passivity, 20, 77, 92, 94–96, 111, 161, 166, 188, 224, 238, 250–51, 268, 293
paternity. *See* fathers, patriarchs
peace, 11–12, 32, 34, 36, 148, 186–87, 190, 205, 242, 280
phantasms, xxv, 58, 116, 124, 203, 219–20, 222–24, 226, 235, 238–39, 243, 260–62, 274, 292. *See also* fancy, fantasy
phantoms, 146n5, 163n11. *See also* spectation, specters
physiology, xi, 27, 151, 166–67, 182, 184, 279, 289
Plato, 25, 61, 63–64, 81, 90, 121, 144, 151, 188, 190, 192, 194n6, 195n8, 199–201, 225, 238, 252, 274, 276–77, 294
play, plays, xxi, 6, 17, 37, 39, 51–58, 61–62, 64, 66–69, 71–72, 77, 79, 81, 84, 98, 103, 106–12, 114, 117–22, 126n15, 127, 140, 146–47, 150, 155, 170, 174, 181–82, 222, 228, 237, 238–39, 246, 260, 265, 273, 282, 286, 296–97. *See also fort/da* game
pleasure, unpleasure (*Lust, Unlust*), xxii, 11, 70, 83, 102–103, 106–13, 116–19, 122–24, 127, 143, 157, 184–86, 188, 190, 199, 203, 209, 216, 239, 252, 265–69, 271–73, 278, 280–82, 286–87, 290
poetry, xix, xx, 3, 7, 9–10, 16, 18, 27n12, 32–40, 46, 60, 76, 83, 86, 92–93, 101, 108, 150n7, 163, 194, 196, 197n9, 218, 272, 292. *See also* literature
politics, 52–54, 92, 138, 144, 173, 206–207, 213, 218, 220, 240–42, 265, 273–74, 280, 288–89. *See also* society, sovereignty
Pontalis, J.-B., 19, 265
possibility, im-possibility, xxiii, xxv, 13, 24, 25, 27–28, 37, 40, 56, 63, 98, 116, 122, 137, 145, 162–63, 168–69, 173, 188, 193, 211, 232, 235, 237, 239–40, 253n7, 260, 262, 263, 282, 287, 289–90, 295
power (*Macht*), xx, xxv, 4, 6, 10, 15, 22, 32–33, 35, 40–41, 45, 54, 61, 66, 68, 92–93, 99, 105, 110–11, 115, 122, 123n11, 125, 127, 155, 161, 168, 177, 185–86, 192, 206, 210–11, 215, 217, 220, 222–23, 230n22, 231, 234, 237, 240, 242, 247–48, 256, 260, 262, 263–98. *See also* will to power
pregnancy, 6, 24, 84, 123, 147, 182, 193, 241, 291. *See also* gestation, maternity, mothers, womb
presence, xxii, 5, 23, 34, 46, 80, 86, 87, 106–109, 116, 120–22, 132, 139, 177, 181–82, 278
president, presiding, 20, 30, 52, 225, 228–29, 234, 253–54, 270–71
priests, 8, 13, 15–16, 29, 31, 51, 82, 144, 207, 214, 261, 267, 284–86
Prometheus, 60, 77, 219, 222, 225, 259
psychoanalysis. *See* Ferenczi, Freud, Lacan, Rank, Reik
psychosis, 138, 190–92, 225
psychotherapy. *See* therapy
puberty, xxi, 19, 21, 150. *See also* latency
pulsions (*Triebe*), 55, 67, 72, 113, 116, 172, 231, 235, 264–66, 272, 275, 280–81, 288. *See also*

destruction-and-death drives, Eros
punishment, xxiv, 3, 26, 28, 52, 57, 71, 89, 139, 177, 205–208, 211–17, 221, 226–42, 243, 245, 247–49, 255–58, 261–62, 271

Rank, Otto, xi, xix, xxiii, 6, 178–203
rapture, 150–51, 153–54, 293, 295, 297
reality, reality principle, 90, 107, 110–11, 157, 162, 171–72, 182, 195, 231, 241, 263, 265–66, 272, 280–81
reason, 78n4, 85, 90, 104, 154, 155, 159, 202, 212–14, 230–32, 234–35, 237, 239, 241, 245–46, 253, 263, 271, 278–79, 282, 284
receptivity, xxv, 79, 96, 295–96
regression, 52, 61, 77, 203
Reik, Theodor, xix, 197n9, 217, 225–26, 229–31, 233–37, 239
releasement (*Gelassenheit*), 27–28, 83–84, 296
religion, xxiii, 10, 13–17, 20, 22, 24, 26, 45n6, 73, 77, 82, 84, 98, 172, 179, 186, 196, 197n9, 199, 206–207, 210, 215–16, 220, 223, 225, 230n22, 239–41, 247, 262, 267, 286–87. *See also* churches, God
repetition, 12, 78, 80, 103, 108, 110, 112–13, 118–22, 154, 186, 248, 274, 282n5
repression, 22, 26, 114, 183, 187–90, 194–98, 200, 212n10, 234, 239, 279
rescue, xxi, 14, 20, 27–28, 71, 120n10, 138, 140, 155, 173, 181–82, 220, 268, 278
ressentiment (rancor, revenge), 197, 270
retribution, 203, 214–16, 224, 226–27, 252, 284
rhythm, 68, 155
Rilke, Rainer Maria, 263, 294
romantic, Romanticism, 8n2, 31, 73, 75, 80–82, 86, 89–90, 92n10, 101, 140, 155–56, 165, 173
Rousseau, Jean-Jacques, 106n3, 163, 271
Royle, Nicholas, 103n2, 208n4, 216n11

sacrifice, 20, 22, 29, 31, 37–38, 121, 174, 206–207, 211, 225, 240–42, 259, 286–87
sadism, 58, 186, 211, 217, 236, 252, 265, 268, 270–71, 275, 281
satisfaction, 11–13, 20, 22, 30, 58–59, 106, 108, 111, 141, 148, 149, 153, 179, 185–86, 195
scapegoat (φαρμακός), 225
Schelling, F. W. J., 13, 15, 24, 27, 74, 139, 192, 243–46, 248, 249n4, 253, 259–60, 275, 290
Schiller, Friedrich, 17, 39, 86, 127, 251
Schlegel, Friedrich, x, xxi–xxii, 73–99, 177
Schleiermacher, Friedrich, 64n9, 80, 88n8, 97, 294
Schmitt, Carl, 206, 227, 240–41, 252, 253n7, 283
Schopenhauer, Arthur, 197–98, 199–200, 274, 285
science, 20, 21, 90, 102, 104, 112, 114, 117–18, 122, 126, 129, 131, 137, 141, 159–60, 165, 179, 186–7, 197, 199, 201, 215, 266, 272–73, 278, 289, 291
second death, the, 37, 48, 58–59, 69
seduction, xxi, 37, 41, 49, 63, 65, 74, 80, 83–84, 87–89, 91, 97, 141, 143, 190, 207, 223, 284
Sehnsucht (languor, languishing, longing), 199, 248
senses, the, xx, 11, 63, 74, 81, 118, 126–27, 137, 140, 142, 147, 152, 153–55, 200, 202, 220, 259, 261, 279

sensibility, sensitivity, xix, 11, 16–18, 28, 74, 78–80, 87–89, 91, 93, 155, 193, 220, 251
sensuality, x, xx–xxii, 7, 16, 19, 21–22, 25–28, 41, 74–77, 80–84, 87–93, 96, 98–99, 140–41, 155, 164–65, 172, 215, 285–86
separation, 33, 41, 98, 105, 109, 128n22, 135, 142, 145, 155, 167, 182, 184–85, 189, 233, 238
sex, sexuality, xxiii, 6, 12, 19–22, 27, 41, 62, 64, 82–83, 90, 92, 94, 96, 98, 138, 140–41, 144–46, 151–52, 156, 162–63, 165–67, 169–72, 185–90, 194, 203, 207, 233–39, 248, 266–67, 276, 285
Shakespeare, William, 31, 42, 216, 232, 234, 249
Shelley, Percy Bysshe, xxiv, 207, 218
silence, 39, 56–57, 67, 102–103, 116–18, 121, 123, 131, 142, 148, 152, 156, 158, 160–62, 186
Silenos, 71, 178, 187–88, 260. *See also* Dionysos
sisters, xxii, 18, 49, 56–58, 65–66, 68, 71, 112, 125, 133, 135–37, 140–41, 143, 145–72, 177, 210
sleep, 5, 11, 31, 37, 41, 49, 57, 105, 109, 121, 157, 183, 186, 189–90, 193–94
society, xxi, 3, 6, 30, 51, 53–54, 75, 78, 82, 89–90, 98–99, 114, 126n17, 154, 159, 170, 172, 181, 186–87, 194, 210, 214, 216, 227, 229, 231–32, 240–41, 255, 257–58, 262, 274. *See also* politics
Socrates, 24, 39, 63, 90, 104, 143, 197, 200–201, 207, 240, 294
sophistry, xxi, 73, 82, 84, 87, 89–90, 138
Sophocles, x, xxi, 6, 9, 12, 14, 48, 51–72, 75, 99n13, 107, 111, 177–78, 189, 275
sovereignty, xxiii–xxv, 114, 203, 206, 210–11, 213, 215, 227, 230, 234, 236–37, 240–42, 260–61, 269, 272–74, 280, 282–83, 285, 287–88
spectation, spectators, 10, 113, 228, 231, 254
specters, 123–24, 205, 207, 208n4, 216n11, 225. *See also* phantoms
speculation, 25, 26, 45, 52, 54, 76, 81, 86, 102, 111–14, 116–17, 123, 133, 137, 145, 150, 169, 171n15, 196–97, 199–201, 221, 234, 236, 238, 266, 278
speech, 8, 25, 30, 120, 159–60, 291. *See also* language, Logos, narrative, writing
spirit, x, xxi–xxii, 11–16, 27, 45n6, 61, 71, 73–4, 77–84, 87, 89, 91–99, 101, 131–32, 139, 149, 150–51, 166, 178–79, 186, 196, 207–208, 216–17, 220, 233–35, 242, 244, 245, 252, 267, 270, 293
state, the, xxiv, 52–53, 75–76, 78, 87, 89, 98–99, 142, 201, 206, 208n5, 210, 213, 226–28, 235, 237, 240–41, 249, 254, 259, 280, 288. *See also* civil society
stories, xi, 10, 15, 23, 27, 42–43, 61, 63, 68, 84, 97, 102–106, 108, 110–12, 114, 117, 133, 135–37, 144–45, 151, 157, 168, 170–73, 186, 188–89, 197, 207–208, 219–20, 222, 233n23, 235, 238, 241, 248, 250–51, 255. *See also* fiction, literature, narrative, writing
strife. *See* hate
sublimation, 114, 179, 200
sublime, the, 10, 82, 113–14
subreption, 246–47, 258
suffocation, xxiii, 152, 177–79, 181
suicide, 10, 84, 139, 153, 163n11, 164, 167, 168, 174, 201, 208, 219, 221, 224, 228, 231, 235, 288
supplementarity, 81, 87, 99, 114, 120, 126n17, 130, 169, 198–99, 227, 230, 235, 239, 277–78

Supreme Court, U. S., 208, 249
suffering, 7, 9, 20, 33, 41–44, 57–58, 65, 103, 113, 115, 121, 177–78, 187, 203, 205, 209, 211, 216, 226–27, 236–39, 245, 247, 250–52, 268. *See also* pain, vulnerability

talion, law of the, xxiv, 207, 211–12, 214, 224, 230–31, 233, 235, 284
temporality, 21, 51, 74, 211n8, 245. *See also* time
Thales, 38, 197–98
theater, theatrical, 55, 65, 71, 104, 113, 119, 126n15, 206, 213, 228, 231, 248, 273, 275n3, 283, 285–86, 292
theology, xxiv, 94, 140, 150, 196, 206–208, 240–41, 257, 272, 274, 280, 289
therapy, xi, 118, 180, 182, 201
thinking, xxii–xxiii, xxiv, 12, 16, 18, 20, 39, 43n4, 72, 74, 91, 99, 107, 126, 128n23, 131, 149, 159, 169, 185, 187, 191, 197–99, 213, 218, 236, 248, 250, 272, 274, 288–90, 292, 296
time, times, xix–xxi, xxiv, 5, 8, 22, 26, 35, 38, 41–43, 55, 57, 58, 62–64, 66–68, 73, 77, 98, 107, 119, 125, 130–31, 138–40, 147–48, 150, 155, 160, 172, 173–74, 179, 182, 187, 194n6, 198, 203, 211n8, 220, 223–24, 226, 228–29, 231, 234, 237–38, 243–44, 248, 251, 254, 259–60, 265, 268, 274, 277, 283, 288. *See also* temporality
torture, 58, 219, 285. *See also* pain, punishment, sadism
Tournier, Michel, 221n14, 229
trace, xxiii, xxiv, 3, 4, 7, 21, 23, 65, 111–12, 114–15, 120, 132, 136, 143, 145, 184–85, 192–93, 203, 272
tragedy, the tragic, ix, x, xix–xxi, 3, 6–28, 36, 49, 51–54, 59, 61, 71–72, 90, 107, 112–13, 117, 150n7, 170, 174, 177–78, 185, 188, 191, 196–97, 201, 226, 245, 247, 267, 286, 289, 293, 295
Trakl, Georg and Gretl, 162–63, 171
transcendental, 11, 13, 39, 90, 111n4, 122, 123n11, 193, 200, 212, 246, 248, 263, 281
trauma, xi, xix, xxiii, 103–105, 106n3, 108, 112–13, 178, 181–98, 201–203, 215, 274. *See also* birth
truth (ἀλήθεια), 13, 17, 30, 42, 73, 96, 107, 118, 128, 136, 155, 160n9, 162, 185, 198, 207, 224, 233, 261, 271, 295

uncanny (τὸ δεινόν), 6, 8–9, 53, 58–61, 68, 97, 103n2, 121, 124, 131, 147–48, 189, 208n4, 215, 216n11, 222–23, 237, 260, 287
unconscious, the, xxiv, 15, 122, 180, 185, 187, 193, 195, 198, 200–201, 203, 208, 216, 226, 229–34, 252, 275
undecidability, 113, 131, 250, 252, 272–73, 282, 287, 296. *See also* overdetermination
United States, the, xxiii–xxiv, 28, 205, 208, 210, 213, 218, 273, 296
unpleasure (*Unlust*). *See* pleasure
utopia, xx, 14, 149, 273

victims, 27, 31, 53, 58, 71, 87, 124, 206–207, 214, 220–21, 225, 227–28, 231, 247, 251, 259, 274, 283–84
violence, 9, 16, 28, 36–37, 52, 124n13, 138, 142, 178, 192, 201, 210, 220, 225, 227, 235, 239–40, 242, 251, 255, 263–66, 281
virginity, 19, 23, 26, 70, 84, 237–39
voice, the, 4, 9, 28, 33, 47, 91, 97, 102, 150–51, 161, 165–67, 181, 213, 220, 255, 283
vulnerability, ix, xxi, 41, 51, 141. *See also* pain

weaning, 185, 189. *See also* breast, infant, nursing
Weber, Elisabeth, 210–11
Weber, Samuel, 120n10, 124n13
will to power, xxv, 110, 111n4, 113–14, 122, 200, 214, 231, 242, 262, 264–70, 277, 279, 281, 283, 285, 292–98. See also *Bemächtigung*
Wills, David, 210–11
wisdom (σωφία), xi, xxii, 13, 35, 40, 63, 71, 74, 90, 98, 101, 104, 127–28, 132, 178, 257
woman, x, xxi, xxiii, 4, 6–7, 9–10, 14, 17, 21, 23, 26–27, 30–31, 33, 37, 40–42, 47, 49, 51, 57, 61, 66, 68–72, 74–88, 90–99, 101, 120–21, 127, 135, 137–38, 140, 142, 146, 151, 154, 157, 160, 164, 167, 170, 172, 174, 181, 187–89, 192, 194, 213, 238–39, 253, 283. *See also* female, mothers, sisters
womb, xix, xxiii, 51–52, 55–56, 62–63, 93, 179, 182–86, 188, 192–94, 196–97, 199–203. *See also* gestation, pregnancy
Wordsworth, William, 121
worth (*Würde*), xxiv, 82, 123n11, 126, 139, 143, 169n14, 187, 197, 201, 203, 212, 227, 229, 254–55, 260, 273, 288–91, 298
Woolf, Virginia, 205
writing, ix, x, xx, xxi–xxii, xxiv, 3, 6, 8, 10, 14, 15, 18, 20, 26, 32–33, 36, 38, 47–48, 61, 75, 76, 78, 79n5, 80, 83, 87, 88n8, 89, 92, 96–97, 101–102, 114, 117–23, 125, 126n17, 131–32, 135, 137, 144, 150n7, 156, 160–61, 165–66, 167n12, 169, 171, 174, 178, 197n9, 207–208, 235, 244, 249n4, 251, 270, 278–79, 281–82, 291–93, 296. *See also* narrative

Yeats, W. B., 127

zart, zärtlich, Zärtlichkeit, ix–x, xix–xx, xxii, 1, 3, 5, 10, 11n6, 13–14, 16–21, 25, 35–36, 40, 43, 50, 62, 73, 84, 98, 104, 135, 137, 141, 145, 149, 151, 156, 160, 166, 263, 293, 295
Zeus, 14, 31, 41, 45–7, 51, 56, 60, 62, 64–5, 68, 81, 196, 219, 259
Zimmermann, Bernhard, 9n3, 53

www.ingramcontent.com/pod-product-compliance
Lightning Source LLC
Chambersburg PA
CBHW030128240426
43672CB00005B/59

* 9 7 8 1 4 3 8 4 7 2 9 8 0 *